SOMETHING ABOUT THE AUTHOR®

Something about
the Author *was named
an "Outstanding
Reference Source,"
the highest honor given
by the American
Library Association
Reference and Adult
Services Division.*

ISSN 0276-816X

something ABOUT THE AUTHOR®

Facts and Pictures about Authors
and Illustrators of Books for Young People

EDITED BY
ALAN HEDBLAD

VOLUME 111

GALE GROUP

Detroit
New York
San Francisco
London
Boston
Woodbridge, CT

STAFF

Editor: Alan Hedblad

Associate Editors: Sara L. Constantakis, Melissa Hill, Motoko Fujishiro Huthwaite
Assistant Editors: Kristen A. Dorsch, Tom Schoenberg, Mark Springer, Erin E. White

Managing Editor: Joyce Nakamura
Literature Content Coordinator: Susan M. Trosky

Research Manager: Victoria B. Cariappa
Research Specialists: Gary J. Oudersluys, Cheryl L. Warnock
Project Coordinator: Corrine A. Boland
Research Associates: Patricia Tsune Ballard, Tamara C. Nott, Tracie A. Richardson
Research Assistants: Phyllis J. Blackman, Tim Lehnerer, Patricia L. Love

Permissions Manager: Maria L. Franklin
Permissions Associates: Edna Hedblad, Sarah Tomasek

Composition Manager: Mary Beth Trimper
Manufacturing Manager: Dorothy Maki
Buyer: Stacy Melson

Graphic Artist: Gary Leach
Image Database Supervisor: Randy Bassett
Imaging Specialists: Robert Duncan, Michael Logusz
Imaging Coordinator: Pamela A. Reed

Library of Congress Catalog Card Number 72-27107

ISBN 0-7876-3220-1
ISSN 0276-816X

Printed in the United States of America

10 9 8 7 6 5 4 3 2 1

Contents

Authors in Forthcoming Volumes vii
Introduction ix
Acknowledgments xi
Illustrations Index 229
Author Index 253

Authors in Forthcoming Volumes

Below are some of the authors and illustrators that will be featured in upcoming volumes of *SATA*. These include new entries on the swiftly rising stars of the field, as well as completely revised and updated entries (indicated with *) on some of the most notable and best-loved creators of books for children.

Pam Adams: Now in her eighties, this British author and illustrator of more than one hundred children's books is still busy creating works that contain the bright, clear colors, appealing shapes and fine detail that make them so pleasing to young readers.

Toni Cade Bambara: Bambara was a well known writer, lecturer, and activist dedicated to expanding the profile of African-American culture in literature. Her writings include novels, screenplays, and the children's book *Raymond's Run.*

*Jane Leslie Conly: Conly is best known for *Rasco and the Rats of NIHM* and *R-T, Margaret, and the Rats of NIHM*, both sequels to her father's children's classic *Mrs. Frisby and the Rats of NIHM*. Her recent works include *While No One Was Watching* and *What Happened on Planet Kid.*

Anna Fienberg: Praised for creating whimsical and enchanting tales of fantasy and imagination, Fienberg is the author of many children's picture books, such as *The Magnificent Nose and Other Marvels,* the popular "Tashi" series, and the recent YA novel *Borrowed Light.*

Ian Graham: Specializing in the ever-changing areas of science and technology, Graham is the author of scores of nonfiction books for young people, including the "How It Works" series, "The Science Spotlight" series, and the "Communications" series, which features the titles *Photography and Film* and *Radio and TV.*

Elizabeth Honey: Honey is an Australian author and illustrator of poetry, picture books, and novels for middle-graders. Known for wacky humor and exuberant action, her recent work includes *Mongrel Doggerel,* a collection of poetry for children, and the juvenile novel *Fiddleback.*

*Julius Lester: Lester's award-winning books have helped a generation of African-American youth to approach their culture through their own language and psyche. In his fiction, biographies, and many retellings of black folktales in such collections as *The Tales of Uncle Remus* and *The Knee-High Man and Other Tales,* Lester has worked to preserve an important piece of history.

Anthony Masters: A prolific and eclectic British author, Masters has written biographies, histories, and critically acclaimed fiction for both adults and juveniles. His most recent works for young people include the picture book *Myths and Legends* and *The Curse of the Ghost House,* the latest installment of his popular "Tremors" series.

*Cynthia Rylant: Rylant is the award-winning author of fiction, nonfiction, and poetry for children and young adults as well as an author and illustrator of picture books for children. Her many series books include the popular "Henry and Mudge" and "Poppleton" series. She received the Newbery Medal in 1993 for *Missing May.*

Ted Staunton: Writing both fiction and nonfiction for children from preschool to middle school, Canadian author Staunton delves into the nature of friendship and connects with his young audience through authentic dialogue in such popular books as *Puddleman* and the recent *Hope Springs a Leak.*

*Patricia Wrightson: Best known for her "Song of Wirrun" fantasy trilogy, which blends Aboriginal myth and folklore with the vast Australian landscape, this recipient of the Hans Christian Anderson Medal is considered one of Australia's most distinguished writers for children.

*Jane Yolen: Yolen has written more than three hundred books for readers of all ages. She is best known for her original folk and fairy tales and fables with a strong moral core. Her recent fiction includes *Merlin, Moonball,* and *The Pictish Child.*

Introduction

Something about the Author (*SATA*) is an ongoing reference series that examines the lives and works of authors and illustrators of books for children. *SATA* includes not only well-known writers and artists but also less prominent individuals whose works are just coming to be recognized. This series is often the only readily available information source on emerging authors and illustrators. You'll find *SATA* informative and entertaining, whether you are a student, a librarian, an English teacher, a parent, or simply an adult who enjoys children's literature.

What's Inside SATA

SATA provides detailed information about authors and illustrators who span the full time range of children's literature, from early figures like John Newbery and L. Frank Baum to contemporary figures like Judy Blume and Richard Peck. Authors in the series represent primarily English-speaking countries, particularly the United States, Canada, and the United Kingdom. Also included, however, are authors from around the world whose works are available in English translation. The writings represented in *SATA* include those created intentionally for children and young adults as well as those written for a general audience and known to interest younger readers. These writings cover the entire spectrum of children's literature, including picture books, humor, folk and fairy tales, animal stories, mystery and adventure, science fiction and fantasy, historical fiction, poetry and nonsense verse, drama, biography, and nonfiction.

Obituaries are also included in *SATA* and are intended not only as death notices but also as concise overviews of people's lives and work. Additionally, each edition features newly revised and updated entries for a selection of *SATA* listees who remain of interest to today's readers and who have been active enough to require extensive revisions of their earlier biographies.

New Autobiography Feature

Beginning with Volume 103, *SATA* features three or more specially commissioned autobiographical essays in each volume. These unique essays, averaging about ten thousand words in length and illustrated with an abundance of personal photos, present an entertaining and informative first-person perspective on the lives and careers of prominent authors and illustrators profiled in *SATA*.

Two Convenient Indexes

In response to suggestions from librarians, *SATA* indexes no longer appear in every volume but are included in alternate (odd-numbered) volumes of the series, beginning with Volume 57.

SATA continues to include two indexes that cumulate with each alternate volume: the Illustrations Index, arranged by the name of the illustrator, gives the number of the volume and page where the illustrator's work appears in the current volume as well as all preceding volumes in the series; the Author Index gives the number of the volume in which a person's biographical sketch, autobiographical essay, or obituary appears in the current volume as well as all preceding volumes in the series.

These indexes also include references to authors and illustrators who appear in Gale's *Yesterday's Authors of Books for Children, Children's Literature Review,* and *Something about the Author Autobiography Series.*

Easy-to-Use Entry Format

Whether you're already familiar with the *SATA* series or just getting acquainted, you will want to be aware of the kind of information that an entry provides. In every *SATA* entry the editors attempt to give as complete a picture of the person's life and work as possible. A typical entry in *SATA* includes the following clearly labeled information sections:

- *PERSONAL:* date and place of birth and death, parents' names and occupations, name of spouse, date of marriage, names of children, educational institutions attended, degrees received, religious and political affiliations, hobbies and other interests.

- *ADDRESSES:* complete home, office, electronic mail, and agent addresses, whenever available.

- *CAREER:* name of employer, position, and dates for each career post; art exhibitions; military service; memberships and offices held in professional and civic organizations.

- *AWARDS, HONORS:* literary and professional awards received.

- *WRITINGS:* title-by-title chronological bibliography of books written and/or illustrated, listed by genre when known; lists of other notable publications, such as plays, screenplays, and periodical contributions.

- *ADAPTATIONS:* a list of films, television programs, plays, CD-ROMs, recordings, and other media presentations that have been adapted from the author's work.

- *WORK IN PROGRESS:* description of projects in progress.

- *SIDELIGHTS:* a biographical portrait of the author or illustrator's development, either directly from the biographee—and often written specifically for the *SATA* entry—or gathered from diaries, letters, interviews, or other published sources.

- *FOR MORE INFORMATION SEE:* references for further reading.

- *EXTENSIVE ILLUSTRATIONS:* photographs, movie stills, book illustrations, and other interesting visual materials supplement the text.

How a SATA Entry Is Compiled

A *SATA* entry progresses through a series of steps. If the biographee is living, the *SATA* editors try to secure information directly from him or her through a questionnaire. From the information that the biographee supplies, the editors prepare an entry, filling in any essential missing details with research and/or telephone interviews. If possible, the author or illustrator is sent a copy of the entry to check for accuracy and completeness.

If the biographee is deceased or cannot be reached by questionnaire, the *SATA* editors examine a wide variety of published sources to gather information for an entry. Biographical and bibliographic sources are consulted, as are book reviews, feature articles, published interviews, and material sometimes obtained from the biographee's family, publishers, agent, or other associates.

Entries that have not been verified by the biographees or their representatives are marked with an asterisk (*).

Contact the Editor

We encourage our readers to examine the entire *SATA* series. Please write and tell us if we can make *SATA* even more helpful to you. Give your comments and suggestions to the editor:

BY MAIL: Editor, *Something about the Author,* The Gale Group, 27500 Drake Rd., Farmington Hills, MI 48331-3535.

BY TELEPHONE: (800) 877-GALE

BY FAX: (248) 699-8054

Acknowledgments

ARMSTRONG, JENNIFER. Martindale, Emily, illustrator. From a cover of *Black-Eyed Susan,* by Jennifer Armstrong. Knopf Paperbacks, 1997. Cover art © 1995 by Emily Martindale. Reproduced by permission of Random House, Inc. / Dodge, Bill, illustrator. From a cover of *Patrick Doyle is Full of Blarney,* by Jennifer Armstrong. Stepping Stone Books, 1996. Cover art copyright © 1996 by Bill Dodge. Reproduced by permission of Random House, Inc. / "At the Window," painting by William Merritt Chase. From a cover of *The Dreams of Mairhe Mehan,* by Jennifer Armstrong. Knopf Paperbacks, 1997. Cover art copyright © 1997 by Superstock, Inc. Reproduced by permission of Random House, Inc. / Armstrong, Jennifer, photograph by Phil Haggerty. Reproduced by permission of Jennifer Armstrong.

AYTO, RUSSELL. Ayto, Russell, illustrator. From an illustration in *Mrs. Potter's Pig,* by Phyllis Root. Candlewick Press, 1996. Illustrations copyright © 1996 by Russell Ayto. Reproduced by permission of Walker Books Ltd. Published in the U.S. by Candlewick Press, Inc., Cambridge, MA.

BANG, MOLLY. From an illustration in *Wiley and the Hairy Man,* by Molly Garrett Bang. Aladdin Paperbacks, 1987. Copyright © 1976 by Molly Bang. Reproduced by permission of Aladdin Paperbacks, an imprint of Simon & Schuster Children's Publishing Division. / Bang, Molly. From an illustration in her *The Grey Lady and the Strawberry Snatcher.* Aladdin Paperbacks, 1996. Copyright © 1980 by Molly Bang. Reproduced by permission of Simon & Schuster Books for Young Readers, an imprint of Simon & Schuster Children's Publishing Division. / Bang, Molly, illustrator. From a jacket of her *Common Ground: The Water, Earth and Air We Share.* Blue Sky Press, 1997. Jacket illustrations © 1997 by Molly Bang. Reproduced by permission of The Blue Sky Press, an imprint of Scholastic Inc. / Bang, Molly, illustrator. From an illustration in her *When Sophie Gets Angry—Really, Really Angry.* The Blue Sky Press, 1999. Copyright © 1999 by Molly Bang. Reproduced by permission of The Blue Sky Press, an imprint of Scholastic Inc.

BENSON, KATHLEEN. From a cover of *Count Your Way through Brazil,* by Jim Haskins and Kathleen Benson. Carolrhoda Books, Inc., 1996. Reproduced by permission. / Benson, Kathleen, photograph by Larry Racioppo. Reproduced by permission of Kathleen Benson.

BILBROUGH, NORMAN. Bilbrough, Norman, photograph. Reproduced by permission.

BURNINGHAM, JOHN. From an illustration in *Mr. Gumpy's Outing,* by John Burningham. Henry Holt and Company, 1990. Copyright © 1990 by John Burningham. Reproduced by permission of Henry Holt and Company, LLC. / From an illustration in *Harvey Slumfenburger's Christmas Present,* by John Burningham. Candlewick Press, 1993. Copyright © 1993 by John Burningham. Reproduced by permission of Walker Books Ltd. Published in the U.S. by Candlewick Press, Inc., Cambridge, MA. / From an illustration in *The Shopping Basket,* by John Burningham. Candlewick Press, 1996. Copyright © 1980 by John Burningham. Reproduced by permission of Walker Books Ltd. Published in the U.S. by Candlewick Press, Inc., Cambridge, MA.

CHANG, CHIH-WEI. Chang, Chih-Wei, photograph. Reproduced by permission.

COOLING, WENDY. Moran, Rosslyn, illustrator. From a cover of *Farmyard Tales,* retold by Wendy Cooling. Barefoot Books, 1998. Illustrations copyright © 1998 by Rosslyn Moran. Reproduced by permission of Barefoot Books, Ltd.

COWLEY, MARJORIE. Poole, Colin, illustrator. From a cover of *Dar and the Spear-Thrower,* by Marjorie Cowley. Clarion Books, 1994. Cover illustration © 1994 by Colin Poole. Reproduced by permission of Houghton Mifflin Company.

DAWES, CLAIBORNE. Dawes, Claiborne, photograph. Reproduced by permission of Claiborne Dawes.

DOHERTY, BERLIE. Nolan, Dennis, illustrator. From a jacket of *Street Child,* by Berlie Doherty. Orchard Books, 1994. Jacket painting copyright © 1994 by Dennis Nolan. Reproduced by permission of Orchard Books, New York. / Wijngaard, Juan, illustrator. From a jacket of *Tales of Wonder and Magic,* by Berlie Doherty. Candlewick Press, 1997. Jacket illustrations copyright © 1997 by Juan Wijngaard. Reproduced by permission of Walker Books Ltd. Published in the U.S. by Candlewick Press, Inc., Cambridge, MA. / Andrew, Ian, illustrator. From a jacket of *The Midnight Man,* by Berlie Doherty. Candlewick Press, 1998. Jacket illustration copyright © 1998 by Ian Andrew. Reproduced by permission of Walker Books Ltd. Published in the U.S. by Candlewick Press, Inc., Cambridge, MA. / Doherty, Berlie, photograph. Reproduced by permission of Berlie Doherty.

HOWE, JAMES. Sweet, Melissa, illustrator. From a cover of *Pinky and Rex and the New Baby,* by James Howe. Aladdin Paperbacks, 1993. Illustrations copyright © 1993 by Melissa Sweet. Reproduced by permission of Aladdin Paperbacks, a division of Simon & Schuster Children's Publishing Division. / Howe, James, photograph by Betsy Imershein. Photograph © Betsy Imershein. Reproduced by permission.

HRDLITSCHKA, SHELLEY. Hrdlitschka, Shelley, photograph. Reproduced by permission.

HUBALEK, LINDA. Hubalek, Linda, photograph. Reproduced by permission.

HUTCHINS, PAT. Hutchins, Pat, photograph by Laurence Hutchins. Reproduced by permission.

IVANKO, JOHN D. Warren, Jon, photographer. From a cover of *To Be A Kid,* by John D. Ivanko. Shakti for Children, Charlesbridge Publishing, 1999. Cover photograph © 1998, Jon Warren. Reproduced by permission.

JUKES, MAVIS. Brooker, Kyrsten, illustrator. From a cover of *It's a Girl Thing,* by Mavis Jukes. Alfred A. Knopf, 1996. Cover art copyright © 1996 by Krysten Brooker. Reproduced by permission of Alfred A. Knopf, Inc.

KERR, M. E. Photograph of "M. E. Kerr" (Marijane Meaker) and Mary Margaret McBride on the radio show "The Mary Margaret McBride Show," taken by Ted Kavanaugh; recent head and shoulders photograph of "M. E. Kerr" by Janet Culbertson. All photographs reproduced by permission of the author.

KUSKIN, KARLA. Parker, Robert Andrew, illustrator. From a cover of *A Great Miracle Happened There,* by Karla Kuskin. Willa Perlman Books, 1993. Illustrations copyright © 1993 by Robert Andrew Parker. Reproduced by permission of HarperCollins Publishers. / Kuskin, Karla, illustrator. From a cover of her *City Dog.* Reproduced by permission of Karla Kuskin. / Dervaux, Isabelle, illustrator. From a cover of *The Sky Is Always in the Sky,* by Karla Kuskin. Reproduced by permission of Karla Kuskin. / Kuskin, Karla, photograph by Nick Kuskin. Reproduced by permission of Karla Kuskin.

LEWIS, CYNTHIA COPELAND. Lewis, Cynthia Copeland, photograph. Reproduced by permission.

LIN, GRACE. Lin, Grace, photograph. Reproduced by permission.

LOWRY, LOIS. DeGroat, Diane, illustrator. From a jacket of *Anastasia Krupnik,* by Lois Lowry. Houghton Mifflin Company, 1979. Copyright © 1979 by Lois Lowry. All rights reserved. Reproduced by permission of Houghton Mifflin Company. / From a cover of *Number the Stars,* by Lois Lowry. Laurel-Leaf Books, 1989. Copyright © 1989 by Lois Lowry. Reproduced by permission of Dell Publishing, a division of Random House, Inc. / Lowry, Lois, photograph by Amanda Smith. Reproduced by permission of Lois Lowry.

McKEE, TIM. McKee, Tim, photograph. Reproduced by permission.

O'NEILL, AMANDA. O'Neill, Amanda, photograph. Reproduced by permission.

OLUONYE, MARY N. Oluonye, Mary N., photograph. Reproduced by permission.

PAULSEN, GARY. Waldman, Neil, illustrator. From a cover of *Dogsong,* by Gary Paulsen. Aladdin Paperbacks, 1995. Cover illustration copyright © 1985 by Neil Waldman. Reproduced by permission of Aladdin Paperbacks, an imprint of Simon & Schuster Children's Publishing Division. / McPheeters, Neal, illustrator. From a cover of *Brian's Winter,* by Gary Paulsen. Copyright © 1996 by Gary Paulsen. Reproduced by permission of Dell Publishing, a division of Random House, Inc. / Smith, Jos. A., illustrator. From a cover of *Call Me Francis Tucket,* by Gary Paulsen. Yearling Books, 1996. Reproduced by permission of Bantam Doubleday Dell Books for Young Readers, a division of Random House, Inc. / O'Rourke, Ericka Meltzer, illustrator. From a jacket of *Soldier's Heart,* by Gary Paulsen. Delacorte Press, 1998. Jacket illustration/montage © 1998 by Ericka Meltzer O'Rourke. Photograph of Charles Goddard by Whitney. Reproduced by permission of Dell Books, a division of Random House, Inc. / Paulsen, Gary, photograph. Reproduced by permission.

PECK, ROBERT NEWTON. Robinson, Charles, illustrator. From a cover of *Soup 1776,* by Robert Newton Peck. Alfred A. Knopf, 1995. Illustrations copyright © 1995 by Charles Robinson. Reproduced by permission of Alfred A. Knopf, Inc. / Hess, Mark, illustrator. From a cover of *A Part of the Sky,* by Robert Newton Peck. Random House, Inc., 1997. Cover art copyright © 1994 by Mark Hess. Reproduced by permission. / Waldrep, Richard, illustrator. From a jacket of *Nine Man Tree,* by Robert Newton Peck. Random House, Inc., 1998. Jacket art copyright © 1998 by Richard Waldrep. Reproduced by permission. / Cocozza, Chris, illustrator. From a jacket of *Cowboy Ghost,* by Robert Newton Peck. HarperCollins Publish-

something ABOUT THe AUThOR

ARMSTRONG, Jennifer 1961-
(Julia Winfield)

Personal

Born May 12, 1961, in Waltham, MA; daughter of John (a physicist) and Elizabeth (a master gardener; maiden name, Saunders) Armstrong; married James Howard Kunstler (a writer). *Education:* Smith College, B.A., 1983. *Hobbies and other interests:* Gardening, teaching, music, reading.

Addresses

Agent—Susan Cohen, Writers House, 21 West 26th St., New York, NY 10010.

Career

Cloverdale Press, New York City, assistant editor, 1983-85; freelance writer, 1985—; teacher. Girl Scout leader, 1987-89; Smith College recruiter, 1990-95; leader of writing workshops. Literacy Volunteers of Saratoga, board president, 1991-93; puppy raiser for Guiding Eyes for the Blind. President and cofounder of Children's Literature Connection, Inc., 1997—.

Awards, Honors

Best Book Award, American Library Association (ALA), and Golden Kite Honor Book Award, Society of Children's Book Writers and Illustrators, both 1992, for *Steal Away;* Notable Book Citations, ALA, 1992, for *Steal Away* and *Hugh Can Do;* Teacher's Choice Award, International Reading Association (IRA), 1993, for *Steal Away.* Blue Ribbon Book, *Bulletin of the Center for Children's Books,* 1996, and Children's Books of Distinction, *Hungry Mind Review,* 1997, both for *The Dreams of Mairhe Mehan.* Smithsonian's Notable Books for Children, 1998, for *Pockets.* Children's Books of Distinction Award, *Riverbank Review,* Orbis Pictus Award, National Council of Teachers of English, and *Boston Globe/Horn Book* Honor Award, all 1999, for *Shipwreck at the Bottom of the World: The Extraordinary True Story of Shackleton and the Endurance.*

Writings

Steal Away (novel), Orchard Books, 1992.
Hugh Can Do (picture book), illustrated by Kimberly Root, Crown Books for Young Readers, 1992.
Chin Yu Min and the Ginger Cat (picture book), illustrated by Mary GrandPre, Crown Books for Young Readers, 1993.
That Terrible Baby (picture book), illustrated by Susan Meddaugh, Tambourine Books, 1994.
Little Salt Lick and the Sun King (picture book), illustrated by Jon Goodell, Crown Books for Young Children, 1994.
The Whittler's Tale (picture book), illustrated by Valery Vasiliev, Tambourine Books, 1994.
King Crow (picture book), illustrated by Eric Rohman, Crown, 1995.
Wan Hu Is in the Stars (picture book), illustrated by Barry Root, Tambourine Books, 1995.

Black-Eyed Susan, illustrated by Emily Martindale, Crown, 1995.

The Dreams of Mairhe Mehan (young adult novel), Knopf, 1996.

The Snowball, illustrated by Jean Pidgin, Random House, 1996.

Patrick Doyle Is Full of Blarney, illustrated by Krista Brauckmann-Towns, Random House, 1996.

Mary Mehan Awake (young adult novel), Knopf, 1996.

Sunshine, Moonshine, Random House, 1997.

Foolish Gretel, illustrated by Bill Dodge, Random House, 1997.

Lili the Brave, illustrated by Uldis Klavins, Random House, 1997.

Pockets (picture book), illustrated by Mary GrandPre, Crown, 1998.

Shipwreck at the Bottom of the World: The Extraordinary True Story of Shackleton and the Endurance, Crown, 1998.

Pierre's Dream (picture book), illustrated by Susan Gaber, Dial, 1999.

With Irene Gut Opdyke, *In My Hands: Memories of a Holocaust Rescuer,* Knopf, 1999.

With Peter Jennings and Todd Brewster, *The Century for Young People,* Doubleday, 1999.

MIDDLE GRADE FICTION; "PETS, INC." SERIES

The Puppy Project, Bantam, 1990.

Too Many Pets, Bantam, 1990.

Hillary to the Rescue, Bantam, 1990.

That Champion Chimp, Bantam, 1990.

YOUNG ADULT FICTION; UNDER PSEUDONYM JULIA WINFIELD

Only Make-Believe (part of "Sweet Dreams" series), Bantam, 1987.

Private Eyes (part of "Sweet Dreams" series), Bantam, 1989.

Partners in Crime (part of "Private Eyes" series), Bantam, 1989.

Tug of Hearts (part of "Private Eyes" series), Bantam, 1989.

On Dangerous Ground (part of "Private Eyes" series), Bantam, 1989.

JUVENILE FICTION; "WILD ROSE INN" SERIES

Bridie of the Wild Rose Inn, Bantam, 1994.

Ann of the Wild Rose Inn, Bantam, 1994.

Emily of the Wild Rose Inn, Bantam, 1994.

Laura of the Wild Rose Inn, Bantam, 1994.

Claire of the Wild Rose Inn, Bantam, 1994.

Grace of the Wild Rose Inn, Bantam, 1994.

Sidelights

Jennifer Armstrong is a versatile writer of young adult novels, middle-grade fiction, chapter books, picture books, and series books for both young and older readers. Some of her best writing is in historical fiction, such as the award-winning *Steal Away,* about a runaway slave and a white girl who accompanies her, and *The Dreams of Mairhe Mehan,* a Civil War novel, as well as its sequel, *Mary Mehan Awake.* She asks large questions

in such novels and takes risks as a writer. She has also been lauded for her picture books, such as *Hugh Can Do,* and for such historical series as "Wild Rose Inn," documenting the fictional lives of several generations of young girls whose families all inhabit the same Massachusetts tavern. The number of works credited to her under her real name and under the pseudonym Julia Winfield, some three dozen in all, would be swelled by another fifty-five titles written anonymously in the "Sweet Valley High" series, and its spin-off, "Sweet Valley Kids."

Born in Waltham, Massachusetts, in 1961, Armstrong grew up in South Salem, New York, in a family that prized books and learning. "My childhood was a very happy one," Armstrong recalled in *Something about the Author Autobiography Series* (*SAAS*). There was the stereotypical big sister who bossed her around, but there were also pets, summer camp, trips to nearby New York City for the museums, loving parents, and a physicist father who was fond of reading Shakespeare to his children. There were weekly visits to the local library, play in the open fields surrounding their home, close friendships and crushes. In fact, Armstrong's childhood and adolescence were so happy, that, once she decided to become a writer (in the first grade), she was afraid for her artistic soul because she had suffered so little. "There was even a period in college when I thought that I would not be able to become a writer because I was too happy, too well adjusted, too untouched by tragedy or failure," Armstrong recalled in *SAAS.* Eventually Armstrong came to see that the most important ingredients needed in becoming a writer were "sympathy and an imagination."

Following college at Smith, Armstrong found work as close to books as she could, as an assistant editor at Cloverdale Press in New York. She quickly discovered that such an entry level position was more of a secretarial posting than an editorial one, but after a learning period she began to be entrusted with her own projects. Cloverdale packaged all sorts of adult and juvenile titles, and soon Armstrong came to think she could write books such as the ones she was editing. She began writing for the "Sweet Valley High" series, and then for one of its clones, "Sweet Valley Kids," chapter books for a younger audience, always looking at such work as her apprenticeship. "I learned scene and dialogue," Armstrong explained in *SAAS,* "I learned pacing, I learned plot and chapter structure, and most of all, I learned to write fast. Not infrequently I had to write a one-hundred-and-thirty-page book in four weeks. It was like being trained on a daily newspaper. I also lost all fear of 'writing a book.' I could write books at the drop of a hat."

Writing under the pseudonym of Julia Winfield, Armstrong wrote five series books of her own, two of them for the "Sweet Dreams" series, and three more for "Private Eyes," her tip of the hat to Nancy Drew and the Hardy Boys. Actually, the second title in her "Sweet Dreams" series, *Private Eyes,* inspired the detective series. Of *Partners in Crime,* the first in the "Private

Eyes" series, *Publishers Weekly* noted that it "blends romance with a fairly complicated mystery, providing light entertainment." Such easy reading was exactly Armstrong's intent with these books as well as the middle-grade series she created, "Pets, Inc.," about girls who take care of neighborhood pets.

By the early 1990s, she was ready to go on her own, and her cultivated fearless attitude vis-à-vis book writing came strongly into play with her first novel, *Steal Away.* It is an ambitious amalgam of adventure story, memoir, and coming of age tale which explores friendship, the nature of courage, race relations, and the history of slavery. Taking structural inspiration from Wallace Stegner's *Angle of Repose,* Armstrong moves her story back and forth across time by employing three fictional voices. Two of these voices are the young girls involved in the adventure, the third is that of one of the protagonist's granddaughters, who responds forty years later to the story her grandmother tells her. Young Susannah, abolitionist-minded, is orphaned in Vermont and sent to relatives in Virginia where she is given her own slave, Bethlehem. These two girls become friends and run away together to the North. Well received by critics and readers alike, *Steal Away* ultimately won a Golden Kite Award. Reviewing the novel in *School Library Journal,* Ann Welton noted that "the issues explored in this book run deep . This will go a long way toward explicating the damage done by slavery."

Published the same year, Armstrong's first picture book, *Hugh Can Do,* is an ALA Notable Book which blends a poetic structure with a folktale-like story. "An especially nice balance of dramatic tension, droll humor, and positive philosophy," Kate McClelland concluded in a *School Library Journal* review of Armstrong's debut picture book effort. Several more picture books followed, including the award-winning *Chin Yu Min and the Ginger Cat.*

The critical success of *Steal Away,* however, allowed Armstrong to sell a six-book series of historical romances to Bantam Books, based on the tales of six girls in a single family who live in a family-run tavern in Marblehead, Massachusetts whose lives and stories span three centuries. "Keeping to the same family, the same house, and the same town, while changing historical periods, was an interesting writing job," Armstrong noted in *SAAS.* Throughout the six books in the series, Armstrong was able to trace narrative life spans much larger than the life span of one character or one book. "This is one of the great attraction of writing series books," the author explained in *SAAS.* "[A]lthough the books stand on their own, the whole can be greater than the sum of its parts."

The series starts off in 1695 with *Bridie of the Wild Rose Inn,* in which sixteen-year-old Bridie immigrates to America from Scotland, to be reunited with her family who left a decade earlier. The prospering owners of the Wild Rose Inn, a tavern in Marblehead, Massachusetts, Bridie's family conform to the Puritan ways of the new country and she discovers that she must as well. Trouble

ensues when she is attracted to young Will Handy and is subsequently declared a witch for going to the Indians for an herbal cure for her sick brother. *Booklist's* Sheilamae O'Hara called this a "promising beginning to a series of historical novels that can be read for diversion or as an adjunct to an American history unit." Writing in *Wilson Library Bulletin,* Cathi Dunn MacRae declared that "Armstrong's vivid language paints a striking picture of a harsh land and somber folk." Reviewing the second novel in the series, *Ann of the Wild Rose Inn,* set in 1774, MacRae went on to note that this "dramatic tale of Crown versus Colony telescopes the dawn of the American Revolution into one young girl's view."

A further series approach to history, this time in chapter books, employs a similar unifying technique. Basing stories of immigrants to the United States on a July Fourth motif, Armstrong sets her stories on or around Independence Day. She also allies this unifying principle to folktales, myths, or legends of the country of origin of each protagonist. Thus in *Lili the Brave,* the young Norwegian protagonist must become something of a Viking heroine. In *Patrick Boyle Is Full of Blarney,* a young Irish immigrant growing up in New York's Hell's Kitchen must re-enact St. Patrick's feat of driving the snakes from Ireland. In this tale the legend is replayed as the defeat of a street gang known as the Copperheads. Charlyn Lyons, reviewing *Patrick Boyle Is Full of Blarney* in *School Library Journal,* dubbed it a "beginning chapter book that's sure to be a hit." For *Foolish Gretel,* Armstrong adapted a Grimm's fairy tale and set the ensuing story in Galveston, Texas, in 1854.

"Having designed the series in this way," Armstrong noted in *SAAS,* "I find that there are limitless possibilities for books. World folklore and mythology are full of stories, and reading them in conjunction with the immigration history of different nationalities almost gives me these stories ready-made. It is a delight to write them."

Meanwhile, Armstrong has continued work on both novels and picture books. This latter category includes such popular titles as *That Terrible Baby, Little Salt Lick and the Sun King, The Whittler's Tale, King Crow, and Pockets,* many of them blending magical fairy tale, myth, and history.

In her novels for middle readers and young adults, Armstrong continues to explore the past, as well. Her *Black-Eyed Susan* is about the geography of the prairie and how that bleak environment can either lift or crush the human spirit. A pioneer girl loves her South Dakota home, but for her mother, the prairie is a desert and she longs for the tree-filled landscape of her native Ohio. "Armstrong writes in a simple but quite literary style," a *Kirkus Reviews* contributor observed. Young Susie is finally able to break through her mother's depression with the help of an Icelandic family who are on their way to homestead. Set within a twenty-four-hour span, *Black-Eyed Susan* explores the extent of family relationships and the spirit of the settlers in the American frontier. Margaret B. Rafferty, writing in *School Library*

Journal, felt that "Armstrong's elegant, spare prose is readable and evocatively recreates the time and place."

Armstrong's 1996 novel, *The Dreams of Mairhe Mehan,* "proved to be the most challenging one I have yet written," according to Armstrong in *SAAS.* Young Mairhe Mehan, an Irish barmaid in the Swampoodle district of Washington, D.C., during the Civil War, has a foot in each of two countries. In some ways she is still Irish; in others very much American. Her father is a broken-hearted Irishman and her older brother, Mike, decides to fight for the Union. Mairhe, caught in the middle of the conflict, cannot really decide which side to take. All she wants is that her brother will return safely. Walt Whitman plays a role in this story, as Mairhe's inspiration to work as a nurse in army hospitals. A critic in *Kirkus Reviews* praised Armstrong highly for a "haunting, eloquent story" as well as for her "breathtaking virtuosity" in blending "vision and reality." *Booklist's* Linda Perkins felt that "this grim, gritty, working-class view of the Civil War provides a unique perspective and could be valuable in a curriculum." Armstrong is never one for formulaic happy endings, and with the death of Mike, part of Mairhe's world dies as well.

In the book's sequel, *Mary Mehan Awake,* the young Irish girl is now spelling her name in the American fashion. After the her brother's death, she is persuaded by Walt Whitman to leave Washington for the more therapeutic climes of upstate New York where she is employed as a naturalist's assistant by Jasper and Diana Dorset. Her journey north provides salvation for her, as she begins to recover at the Dorsets', partly as a result of their kindness, partly through interaction with a veteran made deaf by the war who is working as gardener at the Dorsets' home. Anne O'Malley concluded in *Booklist* that although this sequel did not have the "lively action" of the first novel, "the beautiful writing captures personalities deftly, and fully evokes Mary's internal suffering and quietude." Jennifer M. Brabander commented in *Horn Book* that *Mary Mehan Awake* was "*The Secret Garden* for an older audience, with friendship and nature gratifyingly providing healing and wholeness."

Something of a departure for Armstrong was her 1998 nonfiction treatment of the Antarctic journey of the explorer, Shackleton, in *Shipwreck at the Bottom of the World.* This elucidation of the 1914 expedition and the heroic if not crazy efforts to cross Antarctica by foot is crafted into "an unforgettable story of true heroism and the triumph of the human spirit," according to Edward Sullivan writing in *School Library Journal.* Sullivan concluded that this was a book "that will capture the attention and imagination of any reader." Christine Hepperman concluded in *Riverbank Review* that Armstrong's book was one "to finish in one breathless sitting, then dream about all night long."

Armstrong, who looks at herself primarily as an author out to entertain rather than didactically teach, would find such an appreciation of her work spot on. History and dreams—they are sometimes interchangeable in Armstrong's work. "I wanted to write about how we understand history, how we tell it," Armstrong noted in *SAAS,* "how hearing an adventure forty years old can change our lives today, how storytelling is an active, dynamic process rather than a passive, static one." Armstrong wrote these words about her inspiration for her first non-series novel, *Steal Away.* The sentiments could apply to much of the rest of her work also.

Works Cited

Armstrong, Jennifer, essay in *Something about the Author Autobiography Series,* Volume 110, Gale, 1997, pp. 1-15.

Review of *Black-Eyed Susan, Kirkus Reviews,* August 15, 1995, p. 1184.

Brabander, Jennifer M., review of *Mary Mehan Awake, Horn Book,* November-December, 1997, pp. 675-76.

Review of *The Dreams of Mairhe Mehan, Kirkus Reviews,* September 1, 1996, pp. 1318-19.

Hepperman, Christine, review of *Shipwreck at the Bottom of the World, Riverbank Review,* spring, 1999, p. 41.

Lyons, Charlyn, review of *Patrick Doyle Is Full of Blarney, School Library Journal,* August, 1996, p. 115.

MacRae, Cathi Dunn, "The Young Adult Perplex," *Wilson Library Bulletin,* May, 1994, p. 100.

McClelland, Kate, review of *Hugh Can Do, School Library Journal,* October, 1992, p. 78.

O'Hara, Sheilamae, review of *Bridie of the Wild Rose Inn, Booklist,* March 15, 1994, p. 1341.

O'Malley, Anne, review of *Mary Mehan Awake, Booklist,* December 1, 1997, p. 615.

Review of *Partners in Crime, Publishers Weekly,* March 24, 1989, p. 73.

Perkins, Linda, review of *The Dreams of Mairhe Mehan, Booklist,* January 1, 1997, p. 842.

Rafferty, Margaret A., review of *Black-Eyed Susan, School Library Journal,* October, 1995, p. 132.

Sullivan, Edward, review of *Shipwreck at the Bottom of the World, School Library Journal,* April, 1999, p. 144.

Welton, Ann, review of *Steal Away, School Library Journal,* February, 1992, p. 85.

For More Information See

BOOKS

St. James Guide to Young Adult Writers, edited by Tom Pendergast and Sara Pendergast, St. James Press, 1999.

PERIODICALS

Booklist, February 15, 1993, p. 1065; April 1, 1994, p. 1457; June 1, 1994, p. 1801; September 1, 1994, p. 47; June 1, 1995, p. 1781; July, 1995, p. 1882; May 1, 1996, p. 1505; August, 1998, p. 2012.

Bulletin of the Center for Children's Books, May, 1995, p. 299; July-August, 1995, p. 376; October, 1995, p. 45; April, 1996, p. 256; December, 1997, pp. 116-17.

Horn Book, March-April, 1996, p. 193; July-August, 1999, pp. 478-79.

Kirkus Reviews, February 15, 1993; April 15, 1994; October 15, 1994, p. 1404; May 1, 1999, p. 718; June 15, 1999, pp. 968-69.

Publishers Weekly, July 13, 1990, p. 55; March 14, 1994, p. 71; November 7, 1994, p. 78; April 17, 1995, p. 59; October 19, 1998, p. 78; June 14, 1999, pp. 22-23.
School Library Journal, July, 1990, p. 74; July, 1993, p. 84; August, 1997, p. 128; January, 1998, p. 108; October, 1998, p. 86; June, 1999, p. 85.
Voice of Youth Advocates, August, 1992, p. 165; February, 1994, p. 363; August, 1994, pp. 141-42.

—Sketch by J. Sydney Jones

ARMSTRONG, William H(oward) 1914-1999

OBITUARY NOTICE—See index for *SATA* sketch: Born September 14, 1914, in Lexington, VA; died on April 11, 1999, in Kent, CT. Teacher and author. Armstrong was well known for his successful novel *Sounder* (1969), which took place among a group of African American sharecroppers and told the story of a boy, a dog, and the dog's master. According to Kathryn Shattuck writing in the *New York Times,* Armstrong purposefully used no names or locations in the book, saying that "without names, they become universal—representing all people who suffer privation and injustice, but through love, self-respect, devotion and desire for improvement, make it in the world." The book won a Newbery Medal in 1970. Armstrong considered himself primarily a teacher, even though he wrote a number of books which took place in the Shenandoah Valley where he'd grown up. The author taught ninth grade for fifty-three years in Connecticut. Writings by the author include *Tawny and Dingo* (1979), *Study Tips: How to Improve Your Grades* (1981), and *A Pocket Guide to Study Tips,* 4th edition, 1997.

OBITUARIES AND OTHER SOURCES:

BOOKS

Ferrara, Miranda H., *Writers Directory,* 14th edition, St. James Press (Detroit), 1999.

PERIODICALS

New York Times, April 25, 1999, p. A47.

*　　　*　　　*

AYTO, Russell 1960-

Personal

Born July 10, 1960, in Chichester, Sussex, England; son of Glyn Melvyn (a groundskeeper) and Christina Pearl (a postal clerk) Ayto; married Alyx Mary Louise Bennett (a secretary), March 3, 1990; children: Greta Victoria Amy, Emilio George Valentine. *Education:* Attended Oxford Polytechnic; Exeter College of Art and Design, B.A. (with honors). *Hobbies and other interests:* Collecting books on art and illustration, particularly the work of George Grosz, Otto Dix, Gustav Klimt, Thomas Rowlandson, George Cruickshank, Randolph Caldecott, Heath Robinson, Arthur Rackham, and Edmund Dulac.

"Ermajean," complained Mrs. Potter, "you're as dirty as a little pig. Someday, if you're not careful, you'll turn into one."

From **Mrs. Potter's Pig,** *written by Phyllis Root and illustrated by Russell Ayto.*

Addresses

Home-39 Greenhills Park, Bloxham, Banbury, Oxfordshire OX15 4TA, England.

Career

Illustrator. John Radcliffe II Hospital, medical laboratory scientific officer in Department of Histopathology, 1979-80.

ILLUSTRATOR

Ian Whybrow, *Quacky Quack-Quack!,* Four Winds (New York City), 1991.
Vivian French, reteller, *Lazy Jack,* Candlewick Press (Cambridge, MA), 1995.
Anne Cottringer, *Ella and the Naughty Lion,* Houghton (Boston, MA), 1996.
Phyllis Root, *Mrs. Potter's Pig,* Candlewick Press, 1996.
Joyce Dunbar, *The Baby Bird,* Candlewick Press, 1998.
Whybrow, *Whiff,* Barron's (Hauppauge, NY), 1999.
Whybrow, *Where's Tim's Ted?,* Barron's, 2000.

Adaptations

Parts of the book *Quacky Quack-Quack!* have been animated for a videotape featuring various children's books.

Sidelights

Russell Ayto told *SATA:* "I've always liked painting and drawing and have really just ended up illustrating children's books! I never had an idea where or what I might have ended up doing. I just love the process of bringing characters and stories to life visually, adding something extra to the books. The most important thing for me, when illustrating, is to try and bring visual surprises to a book, so that, when you turn a page, you never know quite what is coming."

Critics have praised Ayto's gentle watercolor-and-ink illustrations in books such as *Mrs. Potter's Pig* and *Ella and the Naughty Lion.* The first title concerns a fastidious mother and her extremely messy baby, Ermajean. Mother admonishes the baby that if she isn't careful, one day she will turn into a pig. When Ermajean and a little piglet switch places, surprises abound. *Booklist* reviewer Susan Dove Lempke applauded the "ingenious interplay between text and pictures," calling Ayto "a master of framing and white space." A contributor to *Kirkus Reviews* also noted that the "illustrations are a perfect complement for the rollicking text, imbuing every character with lots of personality."

A jealous sibling protests the arrival of a new baby and welcomes the simultaneous appearance of a troublesome lion in *Ella and the Naughty Lion.* At first Ella doesn't care for her new brother, Jasper, and the lion shows his distaste as well by chewing up Jasper's teddy bear and pulling off his blanket. When Ella eventually warms to Jasper, the lion disappears. A contributor to *Publishers Weekly* observed that Ayto's color-washed "imprecise squiggles of ink" lend a "stuffed-animal softness to the imagery," and *Booklist* critic Ilene Cooper stated that "Ayto's artwork ... raises what eventually becomes a rather pedestrian story to a book with so many amusing visual details that young listeners will take a second look."

Works Cited

Cooper, Ilene, review of *Ella and the Naughty Lion, Booklist,* September 1, 1996, p. 141.

Review of *Ella and the Naughty Lion, Publishers Weekly,* September 2, 1996, p. 130.

Lempke, Susan Dove, review of *Mrs. Potter's Pig, Booklist,* August, 1996, p. 1905.

Review of *Mrs. Potter's Pig, Kirkus Reviews,* July 15, 1996, p. 1046.

For More Information See

PERIODICALS

Booklist, September 1, 1995, p. 73.

Kirkus Reviews, May 15, 1996, p. 749.

Publishers Weekly, July 10, 1995, p. 57.

School Library Journal, October, 1995, p. 125; July, 1998, p. 73.*

B

BANG, Molly 1943-
(Garrett Bang)

Personal

Full name is Molly Garrett Bang; born December 29, 1943, in Princeton, NJ; daughter of Frederik Barry (a research physician) and Betsy (an author, translator, and scientist; maiden name, Garrett) Bang; married Richard H. Campbell (an acoustics engineer), September 27, 1974; children: Monika. *Education:* Wellesley College, B.A., 1965; University of Arizona, M.A., 1969; Harvard University, M.A., 1971.

Addresses

Home—89 Water St., Woods Hole, MA 02543.

Career

Author, illustrator, and translator. Doshisha University, Kyoto, Japan, teacher of English, 1965-67; Asahi Shimbun, New York City, interpreter of Japanese, 1969; Baltimore Sunpapers, Baltimore, MD, reporter, 1970. Illustrator and consultant for UNICEF, Johns Hopkins Center for Medical Research and Training, and Harvard Institute for International Development.

Awards, Honors

Notable book awards, American Library Association, 1977, for *Wiley and the Hairy Man: Adapted from an American Folk Tale,* and 1980, for *The Grey Lady and the Strawberry Snatcher;* illustration honors, *Boston Globe/Horn Book,* 1980, for *The Grey Lady and the Strawberry Snatcher,* 1984, for *Dawn,* and 1986, for *The Paper Crane;* Caldecott Honor Books, 1981, for *The Grey Lady and the Strawberry Snatcher,* and 1983, for *Ten, Nine, Eight;* Kate Greenaway Honor, 1983, for *Ten, Nine, Eight;* illustration honor, *Boston Globe/Horn Book,* 1986, Hans Christian Andersen Award nomination, 1988, and illustration award, International Board on Books for Young People, all for *The Paper Crane;*

Wiley wanted to run away,

but he stayed there.

He said, "Hello, Hairy Man."

And the Hairy Man said, "Hello, Wiley."

"Hairy Man," said Wiley,

"I hear you're the best

conjure man around here."

"I reckon I am," said the Hairy Man.

From Wiley and the Hairy Man, *written and illustrated by Molly Bang.*

Giverny Award for Best Science Picture Book for Children, 1998, for *Common Ground.*

Writings

FOR CHILDREN; AUTHOR AND ILLUSTRATOR

(Compiler) *The Goblins Giggle, and Other Stories* (folktales from France, China, Japan, Ireland, and Germany), Scribner, 1973.

(Under name Garrett Bang; translator and compiler) *Men from the Village Deep in the Mountains, and Other Japanese Folk Tales,* Macmillan, 1973.

(Editor) Betsy Bang, adaptor, *Wiley and the Hairy Man: Adapted from an American Folk Tale,* Macmillan, 1976.

(Compiler) *The Buried Moon and Other Stories* (folktales from China, Japan, England, and India), Scribner, 1977.

The Grey Lady and the Strawberry Snatcher, Four Winds Press, 1980.

(Adaptor) *Tye May and the Magic Brush* (Chinese folktale), Greenwillow, 1981.

Ten, Nine, Eight, Greenwillow, 1983.

(Adaptor) *Dawn* (Japanese folktale), Morrow, 1983.

(Adaptor) *The Paper Crane* (Chinese folktale), Greenwillow, 1985.

Delphine, Morrow, 1988.

Picture This: Perception & Composition (nonfiction for adults), Little, Brown, 1991.

Yellow Ball, Morrow, 1991.

One Fall Day, Greenwillow, 1994.

Chattanooga Sludge, Harcourt, 1996.

Goose, Blue Sky Press, 1996.

Common Ground: The Water, Earth, and Air We Share, Blue Sky Press, 1997.

When Sophie Gets Angry—Really, Really Angry..., Blue Sky Press, 1999.

Line in the Water, Henry Holt, 2000.

ILLUSTRATOR

Betsy Bang, translator and adaptor, *The Old Woman and the Red Pumpkin: A Bengali Folk Tale,* Macmillan, 1975.

B. Bang, adaptor, *The Old Woman and the Rice Thief* (Bengali folktale), Greenwillow, 1978.

B. Bang, adaptor, *Tuntuni, the Tailor Bird* (Bengali folktale), Greenwillow, 1978.

B. Bang, translator and adaptor, *The Demons of Rajpur: Five Tales from Bengal,* Greenwillow, 1980.

Judith Benet Richardson, *David's Landing,* Woods Hole Historical Collection (Woods Hole, MA), 1984.

Sylvia Cassedy and Kunihiro Suetake, translators, *Red Dragonfly on My Shoulder: Haiku,* HarperCollins, 1992.

Bang's illustrations also appear in *From Sea to Shining Sea: A Treasury of American Folklore and Folk Songs,* compiled by Amy L. Cohn, Scholastic, 1993.

Also author and illustrator of numerous health care manuals.

Several of Bang's works have been translated into Spanish.

Adaptations

The Grey Lady and the Strawberry Snatcher, Ten, Nine, Eight, Dawn, and *The Paper Crane* were adapted for filmstrip, Random House.

Sidelights

Molly Bang is a talented, prolific author and illustrator of many popular and award-winning books for children. Well-traveled and worldly wise, Bang weaves her interest in foreign lands, people, and folklore into her many works. While she has published a number of unique adaptations of traditional legends from all over the world, she is perhaps most well known for original tales, steeped in mystery and branded with her unique sense of humor. Among her most famous works are *The Paper Crane,* which won the 1986 *Boston Globe/Horn Book* award for illustration, and 1999's *When Sophie Gets Angry—Really, Really Angry...*

Born in Princeton, New Jersey, in 1943, Bang gained a love for books early in her childhood. Her mother, Betsy Bang—who, like her daughter, is fluent in several languages—is a writer who adapted and translated several folktales, five of which daughter Molly would eventually illustrate. Bang's parents also maintained an extensive library and frequently presented each other with copies of Arthur Rackham's handsomely illustrated books on special occasions, such as birthdays and anniversaries. Rackham's illustrations fascinated Bang and inspired her to think that illustration might someday be her profession.

For years Bang kept her dreams of illustrating books in the back of her mind while she pursued a variety of subjects and interests in high school and college. After graduating from Wellesley College with a degree in French, she went to Japan to teach English at Doshisha University in Kyoto for eighteen months. She returned to the United States to work on master's degrees in Oriental studies at the University of Arizona and Harvard University. Bang then returned to travel, going overseas once more to illustrate health manuals for rural health projects organized by UNICEF, the Johns Hopkins Center for Medical Research and Training, and the Harvard Institute for International Research in such cities as Calcutta, India; Dacca, Bangladesh; and the West-African republic of Mali.

While working with UNICEF, Johns Hopkins, and Harvard, Bang also began her career as an author and illustrator of books for children by gathering and illustrating a group of tales she had read during her travels overseas. Published in 1973, *The Goblins Giggle, and Other Stories* was the first of many books that would successfully incorporate Bang's fascination with international folklore and legends with her love of mystery and suspense. In a *School Library Journal* review of *The Goblins Giggle,* Margaret A. Dorsey commented that these "five spooky folk tales—two Japanese, two European, one Chinese—are smoothly told and greatly enhanced by full- or double-page black-

From When Sophie Gets Angry—Really, Really Angry..., *written and illustrated by Bang.*

and-white illustrations.... This is a charming collection in which humans triumph over supernatural adversaries after a few suitably chilling thrills." And a critic for the *New York Times Book Review* stated that "Molly Bang has a splendid feeling for general chill, and her choices are all scary but end comfortably so as not to keep anyone awake for long. Her illustrations are unique and intriguing."

The Goblins Giggle, and Other Stories was just the first of many books to reveal Bang's talent for interpreting folktales that are rich in mystery and suspense. In such popular and award-winning books as *Wiley and the Hairy Man, The Grey Lady and the Strawberry Snatcher, Dawn,* and *The Paper Crane,* Bang has either breathed new life into original fables or created her own yarns through her skill as a gifted and sensitive writer and a versatile illustrator.

In *Wiley and the Hairy Man,* published in 1976, Bang retells an African-American folktale she discovered in B. A. Botkin's *Treasury of American Folklore.* She illustrated the story after traveling in the southern United States. Set in Alabama, *Wiley and the Hairy Man* tells of a young boy and his mother, who are terrorized by a scary swamp monster. After several frightful encounters, the pair resourcefully fend off the monster. "The tale has all the best elements of entertainment—humor, suspense, action, and ethnic color—with the stylistic simplicity befitting an easy reader," wrote Judith Goldberger in *Booklist.* Goldberger also noted that "flourishes are accomplished via illustrations in moss-grey,

black, and white.... It is hard to imagine a reader unaffected by this book's punch."

Another of Bang's books to capture the attention of readers and critics alike is *The Grey Lady and the Strawberry Snatcher.* The first book by Bang to earn its author a Caldecott Honor Book designation, *The Grey Lady* recounts the tale of an old woman who is relentlessly pursued by a bizarre, strawberry-stealing creature. Patricia Jean Cianciolo remarked in *Picture Books for Children* that, despite the absence of text, *The Grey Lady and the Strawberry Snatcher* "is filled with surprises, lively humor, and suspense. Its unusual colors and its characters are ethnically indeterminate, but the whole is strongly suggestive of a folktale from India. The skillfully executed, impressionistic illustrations, so full of meticulous, often startling details, offer an exciting visual treat to the readers of this wordless book."

Denise M. Wilms commented in a *Booklist* review of *The Grey Lady and the Strawberry Snatcher* that "a wordless picture book depends on eerie art and high drama for holding its scrutinizers, and they will be held.... Bang's art is a sum of disparate colors, patterns, and spreads of gray that unexpectedly blend. None of her figures is conventional: the tropical-type setting is peopled by warm brown faces and hot colors. Backgrounds point to a variety of ethnic motifs—a Persian rug, an Indian woman on a skateboard, a Buddha-like figure smiling out of a shop window, a banjo-picking grandfather at the gray lady's house. It's a visual jigsaw that somehow balances and holds beyond the story line."

In *Dawn* and *The Paper Crane,* Bang retells classic Asian folktales in contemporary settings. Published in 1983, *Dawn* is an updated version of the traditional Japanese tale of "The Crane Wife"—a yarn about a young man who rescues an injured goose—set in nineteenth-century New England. After nursing the bird back to health, he releases the animal. A beautiful young woman suddenly appears and the two fall in love, marry, and have a daughter, Dawn. After the man breaks a promise to his wife, she transforms back into the goose he had saved years ago, rises up into the sky, and disappears amid a passing flock of geese. The father and daughter are left with their grief and sadness, until the daughter decides to set sail to find her mother.

Bulletin of the Center for Children's Books contributor Zena Sutherland wrote in her review of *Dawn* that "Bang's story is a variant of a traditional folk theme, the animal-mate who resumes his or her original shape; the author has made a touching and effective tale of this, and has illustrated it handsomely." Michael Dirda commented in the *Washington Post Book World* that "what makes this version so powerful are, of course, Bang's illustrations. Watercolors alternate with pencil and charcoal drawings ... and the whole book [is] pleasingly designed.... This is a haunting picture book, as affecting to adults as it is entrancing for children."

Based on a classic Chinese legend, 1985's *The Paper Crane* shows an act of kindness being rewarded by a magical gift. In Bang's retelling, a restaurant is losing all of its business because a superhighway bypasses the building. Late one evening a poor stranger enters the restaurant and is treated to a delicious meal by the owner and his son. To thank them for their kindness, the stranger makes a crane out of a paper napkin and presents it to the two with the instructions that the crane will come to life and dance for them when they clap their hands. Word spreads about the dancing crane, and swarms of customers flock to the restaurant, saving the business from closing.

Patricia Dooley stated in *School Library Journal* that "here is that very rare treat, a contemporary folk tale that feels just right. Bang gives a modern setting and details to the consoling story of a good man, deprived by unlucky fate of his livelihood, whose act of kindness and generosity is repaid by the restoration of his fortunes, through the bringing to life of a magical animal—the paper crane." And Hanna B. Zeiger declared in a *Horn Book* review of *The Paper Crane*: "In a world in which we use the word *gentle* to describe everything from laxatives to scouring powder, Molly Bang has restored dignity to the word with her truly gentle tale of *The Paper Crane*.... The book successfully blends Asian folklore themes with contemporary Western characterization."

With her 1994 work, *One Fall Day,* Bang moved into three-dimensional art, as a story about the quiet events of a typical fall day is set forth through the medium of collage. In the story, a group of toys—a doll, a gray stuffed cat, an origami crane, a yellow ball, and others—spend a typical day in the life of a child: they awake to breakfast, play and rake leaves outside until a surprise shower sends them running for cover, then go inside again to read books, draw pictures, and curl up cozily in bed after the sun sets. While noting the sophistication of the photographed collage illustrations—a *Publishers Weekly* contributor likened each one to "a stage set, complete with props"—a critic for *Kirkus Reviews* commented that in *One Fall Day* the "busy, predictable day, crisp images, and primary colors that dominate the art are all perfect for very young children." While maintaining that the absence of any living being imbues the picture book with a "surreal" sense of "isolation and loneliness," Elizabeth Bush added in her appraisal of the work for the *Bulletin of the Center for Children's Books* that Bang's novel approach, and "the varied angles and distances from which her compositions are photographed give the book character and interest."

1999's *When Sophie Gets Angry—Really, Really Angry...* goes to the heart of one of the hardest parts about growing up: learning to control one's temper. In Bang's vividly colored picture book, Sophie reacts poorly when it is her sister's turn to play with a favorite toy—a stuffed gorilla. Kicking, screaming, crying, Sophie finally runs out of the house and into the woods, where quiet time spent in a tree listening to the sounds of nature calms her down. Praising the book for its focus,

New York Times Book Review contributor Jeanne B. Pinder added that *When Sophie Gets Angry* "is perfect for sparking conversations about feelings: what causes anger ... and how different people cope with it." In *Riverbank Review,* Susan Marie Swanson commented positively on Bang's text, "rich in gentle sound-effects," which the reviewer noted contain simple rhythms and alliterations.

Reflecting the author/illustrator's concerns regarding the human environment as a legacy to be handed down to new generations, both *Common Ground: The Water, Earth, and Air We Share* and *Chattanooga Sludge* address ecological matters. In *Common Ground,* Bang uses a picture-book format and clear, brilliant colors to "sound ... a sober warning about increasing demands on earth's dwindling resources," according to a reviewer in *Publishers Weekly.* Framing her lesson within the day-to-day activities of a simple farming village, Bang shows how increased grazing of livestock, overpopulation, and poor land use can cause problems within the village, within society, and, ultimately, upon the earth as a whole if not addressed. Just going somewhere else is

Themes of conservation and shared responsibility for our natural resources underlie this simple parable about sheep and the village common on which they graze. (Cover illustration by Bang.)

From **The Grey Lady and the Strawberry Snatcher,** *illustrated by Bang.*

not a solution; common lands like parks and wildlife reserves are limited resources that should not be recklessly "used up," Bangs argues in her simple text, because once they are gone people won't "have anyplace else to go." With its introduction to basic ecology, *Common Ground* contains "a timely, provocative message, housed in a small, weighty book," maintained a *Kirkus Reviews* commentator.

Written for slightly older readers, 1996's *Chattanooga Sludge* is a true story relating the efforts of scientist John Todd to clean up one of the most polluted waterways in the United States. Using an experimental program

involving "Living Machines"—greenhouse-grown plants and pollution-eating bacteria—Todd attempted to remove industrial toxins from the water, with only partial success. His results "provide . . . readers with a sobering view of the pollution problem and the encouraging but limited ability of science to combat it," according to Elizabeth Bush in her *Bulletin of the Center for Children's Books* review. A discussion of microbiology as it pertains to Todd's experiments is also included, amid brightly colored collages and cartoon frog figures that provide background information on each page. "Bringing this subject to life and making it comprehensible to a lay audience of any age is an impressive feat.

Bang pulls it off nicely," concluded *School Library Journal* contributor Melissa Hudak.

In addition to her many picture books, Bang has also written the adult work *Picture This: Perception & Composition,* which, according to Cathryn M. Mercier in *St. James Guide to Children's Writers* "provides an insightful key to Bang's work in picture books." In *Picture This* she takes artists through the steps of creating an illustration by making them aware of the elements of shape, color, and size, and by showing how different combinations of these elements create differing emotional responses from viewers.

While she is gratified that so many young readers have been delighted and sometimes even inspired by her books, Bang has also expressed concern that many children have minimal access to the enormous variety of books published yearly for young readers. "Ways need to be found to get books to children beyond the privileged class," Bang declared to Robert D. Hale in *Horn Book.* She cited the budget restrictions of both public and school libraries as one of the reasons lower-income children often find reading a difficult skill to master. "[T]oo many children don't know how to use a book, because they aren't given the chance to learn," Bang added. "If they only have flimsy paperbacks, they never experience the feel of a real book. Because they are less available to people who are poor, books become less relevant. In the midst of all this self-congratulation we have to think about that."

Works Cited

Bang, Molly, *Common Ground: The Water, Earth, and Air We Share,* Blue Sky Press, 1997.

Bush, Elizabeth, review of *Chattanooga Sludge, Bulletin of the Center for Children's Books,* April, 1996, pp. 256-57.

Bush, review of *One Fall Day, Bulletin of the Center for Children's Books,* October, 1994, p. 37.

Cianciolo, Patricia Jean, "The Imaginative World: *The Grey Lady and the Strawberry Snatcher,*" *Picture Books for Children,* American Library Association, 1981, p. 151.

Review of *Common Ground: The Water, Earth, and Air We Share, Kirkus Reviews,* August 15, 1997, p. 1302-03.

Review of *Common Ground: The Water, Earth, and Air We Share, Publishers Weekly,* September 22, 1997, p. 81.

Dirda, Michael, review of *Dawn, Washington Post Book World,* October 9, 1983, pp. 10-11.

Dooley, Patricia, review of *The Paper Crane, School Library Journal,* December, 1985, p. 66.

Dorsey, Margaret A., review of *The Goblins Giggle, and Other Stories, School Library Journal,* January, 1974, p. 45.

Review of *The Goblins Giggle, and Other Stories, New York Times Book Review,* January 13, 1974, p. 8.

Goldberger, Judith, review of *Wiley and the Hairy Man: Adapted from an American Folktale, Booklist,* July 15, 1976, p. 1601.

Hale, Robert D., "Musings," *Horn Book,* November-December, 1989, pp. 806-807.

Hudak, Melissa, review of *Chattanooga Sludge, School Library Journal,* August, 1996, p. 148.

Mercier, Cathryn M., entry on Bang in *St. James Guide to Children's Writers,* St. James Press, 1990, pp. 62-63.

Review of *One Fall Day, Kirkus Reviews,* August 15, 1994, p. 1120.

Review of *One Fall Day, Publishers Weekly,* August 8, 1994, p. 428.

Pinder, Jeanne B., "It's a Mad, Mad, Mad, Mad Girl," *New York Times Book Review,* May 16, 1999, p. 27.

Sutherland, Zena, review of *Dawn, Bulletin of the Center for Children's Books,* January, 1984, pp. 82-83.

Swanson, Susan Marie, review of *When Sophie Gets Angry—Really, Really Angry . . . , Riverbank Review,* spring, 1999, pp. 33-34.

Wilms, Denise M., review of *The Grey Lady and the Strawberry Snatcher, Booklist,* July 15, 1980, pp. 1673-1674.

Zeiger, Hanna B., review of *The Paper Crane, Horn Book,* January, 1986, p. 45.

For More Information See

BOOKS

Children's Books and Their Creators, Houghton, 1995, pp. 45-46.

Children's Literature Review, Volume 8, Gale, 1985, pp. 17-24.

PERIODICALS

Booklist, September 1, 1994, pp. 47-48; September 15, 1996, p. 239.

Bulletin of the Center for Children's Books, December, 1997, pp. 117-18.

Five Owls, March-April, 1999, p. 82.

Horn Book, November-December, 1996, pp. 718-19.

Kirkus Reviews, March 15, 1996, p. 444.

*   *   *

BANG, Garrett
See BANG, Molly

*   *   *

BEACH, Lisa 1957-
(Lisa Shook Begaye)

Personal

Born November 27, 2957, in Richmond, IN; daughter of Robert Lewis and Libby (Brim) Shook; married David H. Beach (self-employed), March 7, 1996; children: Jon Tyrone Snowden, Traci Aleen Snowden, Richard L. Berry III; stepchildren: Alaina E. Beach, Blair K. Beach. *Education:* B.A., Indiana University; graduate study at Goddard College. *Politics:* "I've been known to have them." *Religion:* "Yes, I believe." *Hobbies and other interests:* Flowers, Native American history and life, family activities.

Addresses

Home and office—757 Beeson Rd., Richmond, IN 47374.

Career

Writer. Indiana University East, adjunct faculty member. Boston Township Board of Trustees, secretary.

Awards, Honors

Rounce and Coffin Award, for *Building a Bridge.*

Writings

(Under name Lisa Shook Begaye) *Building a Bridge,* illustrated by Libba Tracy, Northland Press (Flagstaff, AZ), 1995.
(Contributor) *Walking the Twilight,* Northland Press, 1996.

Work in Progress

A novel about Aramis Luther Kidd; a collection of short stories; a volume of poetry; research on Native American literature.

Sidelights

Lisa Beach told *SATA:* "When I was in the third grade, I was ill and missed the Valentine's Day party at Hibberd School. My mother knew how disappointed I was, and she began writing me silly Valentine poems and sliding them under my door. I began writing back, and as they say, 'The rest is history.'

"I grew up and lived in the Richmond area off and on for most of my life. I continued to write, but it wasn't until I had the opportunity to love and know the people of the Dineh Reservation that I seriously considered a career in writing. I stopped in Richmond, Indiana, to visit my mother and wrote *Building a Bridge* while sitting at her kitchen table. 'Taking Baby Home' [included in *Walking the Twilight*] was written on the reservation near Bitter Springs.

"My eighth- and ninth-grade English teacher, Stephen J. Martin, told me I was a writer, but it took years for me to really believe it. After I married my husband, David, I decided to finish an English/creative writing degree and go to graduate school. I am working on a novel, collection of short stories, and poetry, but I also wish to teach writing and Native American literature."

*   *   *

BEGAYE, Lisa Shook
See BEACH, Lisa

BENNETT, Rainey 1907-1998

OBITUARY NOTICE—See index for *SATA* sketch: Born July 26, 1907, in Marion, IN; died December 11, 1998, in Lincoln Park, IL. Artist and author. Multi-talented Rainey Bennett spent parts of his life as a jazz musician, and also successfully authored children's books—but he was best known for his talent as a watercolorist. He worked as a musician in the 1920s but his passion for art led him to study it at the college level, earning a Ph.D. from the University of California. After time spent promoting his artwork and painting murals, he was commissioned by Nelson Rockefeller to paint thirty-six South American landscapes. This exhibit later traveled for two years under the auspices of the Museum of Modern Art, and Rockefeller purchased twenty-four of the paintings. Bennett taught at the college level in the 1960s and continued to paint and display his art. He also freelanced as a book and advertising illustrator. In 1960, Bennett successfully combined his writing and artistic talents with the publication of his children's book *The Secret Hiding Place.* Bennett also authored and illustrated *After the Sun Goes Down* (1961).

OBITUARIES AND OTHER SOURCES:

BOOKS

Who's Who in American Art, 1993-1994, Marquis, 1993.

PERIODICALS

Chicago Tribune, December 15, 1998, p. 11.

*   *   *

BENSON, Kathleen 1947-

Personal

Born February 10, 1947, in Keene, New Hampshire; daughter of Roland (a technical representative) and Margaret (a secretary; maiden name, Bliss) Benson; children: Margaret Emily. *Education:* University of Connecticut at Storrs, B.A. (magna cum laude), 1969.

Addresses

Home—325 West End Avenue, No. 7D, New York, NY 10023. *Office*—Museum of the City of New York, 1220 Fifth Avenue, New York, NY 10029.

Career

Writer, 1977—. Education Department, Museum of the City of New York, New York, NY, Chair of Community and Family Programming and Museum Editor, 1969—. Children's Book Review Service, co-founder and member of board of directors, 1971. *Member:* American Association of Museums, New England Museum Association, New York City Museum Educators Roundtable, Phi Beta Kappa, Mortar Board.

Kathleen Benson

Awards, Honors

Deems Taylor Award, American Society of Composers, Authors, and Publishers, 1979, for *Scott Joplin: The Man Who Made Ragtime.*

Writings

WITH JIM HASKINS, EXCEPT AS NOTED

(With Jim Haskins and Ellen Inkelis) *The Great American Crazies,* Condor, 1977.

Scott Joplin: The Man Who Made Ragtime, Doubleday, 1978.

The Stevie Wonder Scrapbook, Grosset & Dunlop, 1978.

Lena: A Personal and Professional Biography of Lena Horne, Stein & Day, 1983, reprinted as *Lena: A Biography of Lena Horne,* Scarborough House (Chelsea, MI), 1991.

Nat King Cole: A Personal and Professional Biography, Stein & Day, 1984.

Space Challenger: The Story of Guion Bluford, Carolrhoda, 1984.

Aretha: A Personal and Professional Biography, Madison, 1987.

The Sixties Reader, Viking, 1988.

African Beginnings, illustrated by Floyd Cooper, Lothrop, 1998.

Bound for America: The Forced Migration of Africans to the New World, illustrated by Floyd Cooper, Lothrop, 1999.

Out of the Darkness: The Story of Blacks Moving North: The Great Migration, Benchmark Books, 1999.

Carter G. Woodson, Millbrook, 2000.

"COUNT YOUR WAY THROUGH" SERIES; WITH JIM HASKINS

Count Your Way Through Brazil, illustrated by Liz Brenner Dodson, Carolrhoda, 1996.

... *France,* illustrated by Andrea Shine, Carolrhoda, 1996.

... *Greece,* illustrated by Janice Lee Porter, Carolrhoda, 1996.

... *Ireland,* illustrated by Beth Wright, Carolrhoda, 1996.

OTHER

A Man Called Martin Luther, Concordia, 1980.

Joseph on the Subway Trains, illustrated by Emily Arnold McCully, Addison-Wesley, 1981.

Contributor to *The Scribner Encyclopedia of American Lives, Curator,* and *Cobblestone* magazine. Creator of numerous curriculum kits, including *The New Metropolis: A Century of Greater New York, 1898-1998,* for the Museum of the City of New York. Compiler of indexes for several adult and children's books for such publishers as Atheneum, William Morrow, and Scarborough House.

Sidelights

Kathleen Benson told *SATA:* "I was born in New Hampshire and spent my first five years in the small town of Winchester. One of my earliest memories is of the two marble busts of great men (I don't remember who they were) that graced the entryway of the town's public library. I am told that I got my first library card when I was three, and that I insisted I could write my own name on the card and did not want my mother to do it.

"My parents divorced when I was very young. When I was five, my mother remarried and we moved to Connecticut. The small house into which we moved had an unfinished upstairs, and my stepfather worked nights after work and on weekends to create bedrooms for my stepbrother, who was two years older, and me. In my bedroom, he built a knotty-pine shelf across the front of the room, and my mother made a pink fabric skirt for it. It was there that I nestled with a flashlight and read after I should have been in bed. As a child, I liked to read books in series—the "Bobbsey Twins" books and a series about a little girl named Mayda come to mind. I also enjoyed biographies. I could not have been more than eight years old when I proudly announced to friends and relatives that I was reading thirty books a month.

"At the University of Connecticut, I became interested in history and enrolled in the first black-history course taught at the school. While I was still in college, I worked two summers at the Museum of the City of New York, which is dedicated to the history of New York City. I then took a full-time job in the museum's education department, and many years later I am still there. My current title is a mouthful: Chair of Community and Family Programming and Museum Editor! I started New York City History Day, which is part of the National History Day program, and enjoy helping students do historical research and use what they have

Count Your Way through Brazil

by Jim Haskins and Kathleen Benson • illustrations by Liz Brenner Dodson

Benson and coauthor Jim Haskins employ the Portuguese words for the numerals from one to ten to teach young readers about the country of Brazil. (Cover illustration by Liz Brenner Dodson.)

learned to create projects for History Day. To me, there is nothing more exciting (and sometimes frustrating) than the "detective work" one has to do to uncover the past through primary documents. I serve on various committees and panels of archivists and historians, whose aim is to bring history to life for young people. In January, 1999, I was named one of one hundred twenty-six Centennial Historians in New York City. I also coordinate the museum's exhibitions with outside community and cultural organizations whose work is making history now.

"I have written one work of fiction, published many years ago and long out of print. *Joseph on the Subway Trains* is about a little boy who got separated from his class while traveling on the subways to visit a museum. Even that book was based on an actual incident involving a class visiting the Museum of the City of New York (the little boy was eventually located at a distant subway station). I prefer nonfiction, because

what actually happens to real people is usually more exciting to me than anything I can make up."

*   *   *

BILBROUGH, Norman 1941-

Personal

Born June 13, 1941, in Feilding, New Zealand; son of William Samuel (a teacher) and Susan (a teacher) Bilbrough; married Jane Westaway (a writer); children: Miro, Paula, Jake Flanigan, Alden Williams. *Politics:* Liberal.

Addresses

Home—191 Wilton Rd., Wilton, Wellington, New Zealand. *Electronic mail*—n.bilbrough@engl.canterbury.

Norman Bilbrough

ac.nz. *Agent*—Total Fiction Services, P.O. Box 29023, Ngaio, Wellington, New Zealand.

Career

Writer. Critiquing fiction for individual writers, teacher of creative writing.

Writings

The Birdman Hunts Alone, Penguin (Auckland, New Zealand), 1994.
The Dump Giants, Cape Catley, 1997.
Dog Breath and Other Stories, Mallinson Rendel (Wellington, New Zealand), 1998.

Work in Progress

Eating Paul Newman (tentative title), a young adult novel about a sixteen-year-old girl becoming a mother.

Sidelights

Norman Bilbrough told *SATA:* "I began my writing career because I read and read and thought and thought, and I felt impatient with study because it had nothing to do with my imagination. My father wanted me to be a lawyer, then an agricultural scientist, then a schoolteacher—but all the time, in my private world I was becoming a writer.

"I hope to reach younger readers with my books and show them the reality of life, the intensity of experiences. I write a story from an emotion, a passing memory, or a fragment of my life. I build this into a whole new story, bringing in other aspects of my experience—using my imagination upon my life, in a sense.

"My advice to writers is to try to have a rich life, externally and internally. Don't try for writing success too young. Read and read some more, and try to keep that boy or girl still alive in yourself."*

*   *   *

BURNINGHAM, John (Mackintosh) 1936-

Personal

Born April 27, 1936, in Farnham, Surrey, England; son of Charles (a salesman) and Jessie (maiden name, Mackintosh) Burningham; married Helen Gillian Oxenbury (a designer, author and illustrator of children's books), August 15, 1964; children: Lucy, William Benedict, Emily. *Education:* Central School of Art, London, national diploma in design, 1959.

Addresses

Home—5 East Heath Rd., Hampstead, London NW3 1BN, England. *Office*—c/o Jonathan Cape Ltd., 30 Bedford Sq., London WC1B 3EL, England.

Career

Author, illustrator and freelance designer. Worked at farming, slum-clearance, forestry, in the Friend's Ambulance Unit, and at school building as an alternative to military service, 1953-55; freelance illustrator traveling through Italy, Yugoslavia, and Israel, 1953-55; worked for a year on set designs, models, and puppets for an animated puppet film in the Middle East, 1959-60; designed posters for London Transport and the British Transport Commission, early 1960s; author and illustrator of children's books, 1963—; freelance designer of murals, exhibitions, three-dimensional models, magazine illustrations and advertisements.

Awards, Honors

Kate Greenaway Medal for Illustration, British Library Association, 1963, for *Borka; The Extraordinary Tug-of-War* was selected one of the American Institute of Graphic Arts Books, 1967-68; Kate Greenaway Medal, 1970, Honorary Award from the Biennale of Illustrations Bratislava, *New York Times* Best Illustrated Children's Books of the Year and Outstanding Book citations, *School Library Journal* Best Book citation, all 1971, *Boston Globe-Horn Book* Award for Illustration, and Children's Book Showcase selection, both 1972, and American Library Association (ALA) Notable Book citation, all for *Mr. Gumpy's Outing;* Children's Book of the Year citations, Child Study Association of America, 1971, for *Seasons* and *Mr. Gumpy's Outing,* and 1976, for *Mr. Gumpy's Motor Car; Mr. Gumpy's Motor Car* was included in the Children's Book Showcase of the Children's Book Council, 1977; *Horn Book* honor list, 1977, for *Come Away from the Water, Shirley,* 1978, for *Time to Get Out of the Bath, Shirley,* and 1988, for *John Patrick Norman McHennessey: The Boy Who Was Always Late; New York Times* Best Illustrated Children's Books of the Year citations, 1977, for *Come Away from the Water, Shirley,* and 1985, for *Granpa;* Deutscher Jugendliteraturpreis (German Youth Literature Prize), Federal Ministry of the Interior, 1980, for *Would You Rather...;* Kurt Maschler/Emil Award runner-up, National Book League (Great Britain), 1983, for *The Wind in the Willows,* and 1986, for *Where's Julius?;* Kurt Maschler/Emil Award, 1984, and *New York Times* Best Illustrated Book Award, 1985, both for *Granpa;* Parents' Choice Picture Book Award, 1988, for *John Patrick Norman McHennessey, The Boy Who Was Always Late;* Parents' Choice Picture Book Award, 1990, and "Book Can Develop Empathy" award, 1991, both for *Hey! Get Off Our Train!*

Writings

SELF-ILLUSTRATED

Borka: The Adventures of a Goose with No Feathers, J. Cape, 1963, Random House, 1964.
(And illustrated with Leigh Taylor) *ABC,* J. Cape, 1964, Bobbs-Merrill, Random House, 1967.
Trubloff: The Mouse Who Wanted to Play the Balalaika, J. Cape, 1964, Random House, 1965.
Humbert, Mister Firkin, and the Lord Mayor of London, J. Cape, 1965, Bobbs-Merrill, 1967.
Cannonball Simp: The Story of a Dog Who Joins a Circus, J. Cape, 1966, Bobbs-Merrill, 1967.
Harquin: The Fox Who Went Down to the Valley, J. Cape, 1967, Bobbs-Merrill, 1968.
Seasons, J. Cape, 1969, Bobbs-Merrill, 1971.
Mr. Gumpy's Outing, Holt, 1970.
(Adapter) *Around the World in Eighty Days,* J. Cape, 1972.
Mr. Gumpy's Motor Car, J. Cape, 1973, Macmillan, 1975.
Come Away from the Water, Shirley, Crowell, 1977.
Time to Get Out of the Bath, Shirley, Crowell, 1978.
Would You Rather..., Crowell, 1978.
The Shopping Basket, Crowell, 1980; Candlewick, 1996.
Avocado Baby, Crowell, 1982.
Granpa, J. Cape, 1984, Crown, 1985.
Where's Julius?, Crown, 1986.
John Patrick Norman McHennessey: The Boy Who Was Always Late, Crown, 1987.
Oi! Get Off Our Train, J. Cape, 1989, published in the United States as *Hey! Get Off Our Train,* Crown, 1990.
Aldo, Crown, 1991.
Harvey Slumfenburger's Christmas Present, Candlewick, 1993.
Courtney, Crown, 1994.
First Steps: Letters, Numbers, Colors, Opposites, Candlewick, 1994.
Cloudland, Cape, 1996.
Whadayamean?, Crown, 1999.

"LITTLE BOOK" SERIES; SELF-ILLUSTRATED

The Rabbit, J. Cape, 1974, Crowell, 1975.
The School, J. Cape, 1974, Crowell, 1975.
The Snow, J. Cape, 1974, Crowell, 1975.
The Baby, J. Cape, 1974, Crowell, 1975.
The Blanket, J. Cape, 1975, Crowell, 1976.
The Cupboard, J. Cape, 1975, Crowell, 1976.
The Dog, J. Cape, 1975, Crowell, 1976.
The Friend, J. Cape, 1975, Crowell, 1976.

"NUMBER PLAY" SERIES; SELF-ILLUSTRATED

Count Up: Learning Sets, Viking, 1983.
Five Down: Numbers as Signs, Viking, 1983.
Just Cats: Learning Groups, Viking, 1983.
Pigs Plus: Learning Addition, Viking, 1983.
Read One: Numbers as Words, Viking, 1983.
Ride Off: Learning Subtraction, Viking, 1983.

"FIRST WORDS" SERIES (ENGLAND); "NOISY WORDS" SERIES (UNITED STATES); SELF-ILLUSTRATED

Sniff Shout, Viking, 1984.
Skip Trip, Viking, 1984.
Wobble Pop, Viking, 1984.
Slam Bang!, Viking, 1985.
Cluck Baa, Viking, 1985.
Jangle Twang, Viking, 1985.

"PLAY AND LEARN" SERIES; SELF-ILLUSTRATED

John Burningham's ABC, Crown, 1985 (published in England as *Alphabet Book,* Walker, 1987).
John Burningham's Colors, Crown, 1985.
John Burningham's 123, Crown, 1985.
John Burningham's Opposites, Crown, 1985.

WALL FRIEZES

Birdland, Braziller, 1966.
Lionland, J. Cape, 1966, Braziller, 1967.
Storyland, J. Cape, 1966, Braziller, 1967.
Jungleland, J. Cape, 1968.
Wonderland, J. Cape, 1968.
Around the World, J. Cape, 1972.

OTHER

(Illustrator) Ian Fleming, *Chitty-Chitty-Bang-Bang: The Magical Car,* Random House, 1964.
(Illustrator) Letta Schatz, editor, *The Extraordinary Tug-of-War,* Follett, 1968.
(Illustrator) Kenneth Grahame, *The Wind in the Willows,* Viking, 1983.
England (adult picture book), Cape, 1993.
John Burningham's France (adult picture book), DK Publications, 1998.

Burningham's books have been published in Afrikaans, Danish, Dutch, Finnish, French, German, Irish, Japanese, Norwegian, Swedish, Spanish, Welsh, and Zulu.

Adaptations

Weston Woods has made filmstrips of *Mr. Gumpy's Outing, Come Away from the Water, Shirley,* and *Mr. Gumpy's Motor Car* (filmstrip with cassette), 1982;

From **Mr. Gumpy's Outing,** *written and illustrated by John Burningham.*

Finehouse/Evergreen has made a filmstrip of *Cannonball.*

Sidelights

Dubbed "one of the most outstanding author-illustrators of children's books writing today," by Fionna Lafferty in *St. James Guide to Children's Writers,* British writer John Burningham has more than fifty books to his credit, including two Kate Greenaway-medal winners. In a career spanning nearly four decades, Burningham has created such memorable picture-book characters as a goose with no feathers in *Borka,* an eccentric rustic in *Mr. Gumpy's Outing* and its sequel, *Mr. Gumpy's Motor Car,* a little girl whose parents desperately want her to stay out of trouble in *Come Away from the Water, Shirley* and *Time to Get Out of the Bath, Shirley,* a little girl and her beloved grandfather in *Granpa,* a balalaika-playing mouse in *Trubloff,* and a nanny-like dog in *Courtney.* Blending wry textual humor with equally humorous line drawings embellished with crayon, wash, and a wide assortment of other media, Burningham has created a signature style to his works. Chris Stephenson, writing in *Carousel,* remarked that Burningham is "one of that small band of innovative, adventurous illustrators who, through a combination of boldness of design and virtuosity of artwork, enhanced by texts which probed, explored, resonated and above all, entertained, completely transformed children's books."

Born on April 27, 1936, in Farnham, Surrey, Burningham was the youngest of three children. His father's work as a salesman took the family all over the country. As a child Burningham attended ten different schools and was forever trying to fit in as the new kid at school or in the neighborhood. Books and being read to, constants amid all the moving about, were an early delight for him. At age twelve, Burningham was sent to the famous Summerhill School, an experiment in liberal teaching methods, run by A. S. Neill. Here lessons were not compulsory and Burningham began drawing and painting, finding his own way rather than having his future dictated to him. Serving alternative service instead of going to the military, he spent two years working at forestry and social work, attending art classes in the evening. From 1956 to 1959 he attended London's Central School of Art and Craft. It was there he met his wife, children's-book illustrator Helen Oxenbury, though the two would not marry for several more years. Out of school, Burningham had a variety of jobs in graphic arts, including designing stage sets, creating magazine cartoons, Christmas cards, cereal boxes, and posters for the London Transport system. He was having no luck with publishers, however, taking his portfolio around London, but winning no commissions. Finally he determined to create his own book.

In 1963, John Burningham published his first book, *Borka: The Adventures of a Goose with No Feathers.* The book tells the tale of a young hatchling who is rejected by other geese because she looks different; eventually Borka finds a home with birds who can accept her as she is. *Borka* earned its author the prestigious Kate Greenaway Medal for illustration, and also launched Burningham's career as an author-illustrator, even though he had not planned on writing for children. "It is difficult to say why things happen," Burningham told Michele Field in *Publishers Weekly.* "If I had written a novel and it had won some kind of award, undoubtedly I'd still be writing novels." *Borka* quickly gained critical approval for its comical style and impressive pictures. "There is humor, boldness and verve in the story," a *Sunday Herald Tribune Book Week* reviewer remarked, "...and in the well-drawn pictures, bright and childlike yet with original and interesting coloring." A reviewer for *Junior Bookshelf* similarly called *Borka* "exceedingly funny in conception," and praised it for its "consistent absurdity." The critic concluded: "So hilarious and lovely a book is a major contribution to the long and glorious history of the English picture book."

Burningham's next four books also feature animal characters behaving in human ways. In *Trubloff,* for instance, the author "gets a great deal of fun and a measure of beauty out of a charmingly absurd story of a mouse with musical aspirations," a *Junior Bookshelf* writer commented. *Cannonball Simp* is about an ugly dog who goes from being unwanted to starring in a circus; its pictures "talk directly to young children," Robert Cohen wrote in *Young Readers Review. Harquin* tells the story of a foxhunt from the fox's point of view, while *Humbert, Mr. Firkin, and the Lord Mayor of London* shows a cart-horse saving the parade on the Lord Mayor's Show Day.

Some critics believe that the storylines of these books are overshadowed by Burningham's illustrations. Richard Kluger of *Sunday Herald Tribune Book Week* remarked that *Trubloff* "is strong as art, a bit flat as story," and Nancy Young Orr wrote in *School Library Journal* that the rich illustrations give *Harquin* "a verve and humor which the text alone fails to supply." But others find Burningham's stories skillfully written. In *Trubloff,* for instance, the author's pictures "are as fascinating as his story," Patience M. Daltry commented in the *Christian Science Monitor.* And a *Publishers Weekly* writer stated in a review of *Cannonball Simp* that "after looking at his wild and glorious creatures and reading the wild and glorious stories he writes about them ... John Burningham is now my favorite Englishman." As a *Junior Bookshelf* critic concluded in a review of *Humbert,* Burningham has "a remarkable gift for inventing very funny stories and putting them into brief, unobtrusively perfect words."

Seven years after his first book, Burningham produced another Greenaway winner in *Mr. Gumpy's Outing.* Mr. Gumpy travels along in his boat and picks up animals and children who promise not to cause trouble. But the creatures cannot avoid breaking their promises, and the whole crew ends up in the water. Nevertheless, the tale ends happily with Mr. Gumpy serving tea to his riders. Dorothy Butler found the book a "classic example" of a story for young children; it is "beautifully paced, each character coming alive through his action and speech, with no need for description," the critic commented in *Signal. Mr. Gumpy's Outing* is "a blessing of a book," Joan Bodger Mercer likewise concluded in the *New York Times Book Review.* "Pored over, read aloud or acted out it should bring joy to the nursery." A sequel about an ill-fated car trip, *Mr. Gumpy's Motor Car,* has also been successful; Virginia Haviland observed in *Horn Book* that Burningham "is blessed with a gift for both verbal and visual storytelling; his flow of words describing the muddy crisis matches the charm of his watercolor scenes."

From **The Shopping Basket,** *written and illustrated by* **Burningham.**

Although his work involving animals has been very successful, "now I am more interested in the relationships between adults and children," the author told Field of *Publishers Weekly.* His new books, Burningham continued, "are exploring that theme, rather than the adventures of some animal." In the books *Come Away from the Water, Shirley* and *Time to Get Out of the Bath, Shirley,* Burningham contrasts the imaginative adventures of a little girl with her parents' warnings to stay out of trouble. Both books feature brightly colored illustrations of Shirley's exploits paired with subdued portraits of her dreary parents. The result is "all too brief a masterpiece of humor and affection, with ... unforgettable illustrations," according to David Anable of the *Christian Science Monitor.* As Margery Fisher concluded in *Growing Point,* Burningham's "Shirley" books provide readers with "a marvelously comical and inventive juxtaposition of everyday taps, toothpaste and domestic admonition with storybook cliches and uninhibited fun."

The tale of a boy who must outwit a series of animals on his way home from the store, *The Shopping Basket* "is the latest in a long line of marvelously humourous, idiosyncratic tales told by John Burningham," Jean Russell remarked in *Books for Your Children.* Lafferty similarly praised *The Shopping Basket* as "one of the best children's books ever conceived. Not only is it a nicely moralistic tale," the critic explained, but its use of vocabulary and repetition make it "a near perfect book for children beginning to read." "Sound psychology, beautifully exact and humorous drawing, a restrained and rhythmic text, it is all here, adding up to a picture book which falls only a little short of perfection," a *Junior Bookshelf* writer commented.

In *Granpa,* Burningham turns away from comic situations to portray a little girl's relationship with her grandfather that is ended by his passing. With just a brief story, the author "suggests a whole life story for Granpa and shows a small girl reacting to death," Pat Triggs wrote in *Books for Keeps.* While death is a difficult subject to introduce to children, Burningham treats it "gently [and] poetically," Andrew Clements commented in the *New Statesman,* using "spare, immensely evocative" illustrations. Despite its sober ending, the book has humor in its "funny drawings"; Burningham "has not been more amusing, more wise," Marcus Crouch remarked in *Junior Bookshelf.* As a result, William Feaver stated in the *Observer,* "Burningham has succeeded in dealing with what, since Victorian times, has been the impossible in picture-book terms: real-life death."

Although both his "Mr. Gumpy" and "Shirley" books have been popular enough to warrant further episodes, Burningham has deliberately avoided creating a long-running series. "I am very fond of Mr. Gumpy, but it would be awful to spend my life doing *just* Mr. Gumpy—or anything else," the author explained to Field. "The problem is that it is easier once you've established a character to keep it going. But I am always more interested in doing something I haven't done before."

True to his word, Burningham has continued to assay new territory with his work. Commissioned to write and illustrate a book for Japan's Expo '90, he created the classic, *Hey! Get Off Our Train* (British title, *Oi! Get Off Our Train!*) about a little boy told by his parents to go to sleep and stop playing with his train. In his dreams he is on his toy train and at every stop a new animal boards the train, ignoring the pleas to "get off our train," because each animal represents an endangered species. In his 1992 *Aldo,* and the 1994 *Courtney,* Burningham "is once again the champion of the child," according to Lafferty. In the former title, a large imaginary rabbit named Aldo is the only friend of a lonely little girl, protecting her from bullies at school and reading to her by night. Another caretaker animal is presented in *Courtney,* the story of children who badly want a dog, but the one they pick out from the pound is not quite the purebred animal their snobbish parents were hoping for. But Courtney turns out to be a Mary Poppins in dog clothing, cooking, juggling, and rescuing all in turn. Deborah Stevenson commented in *Bulletin of the Center for Children's Books* that such a talented dog "will charm quite a few viewers ... as Burningham, with his usual ability to make silent animals personable and friendly, depicts Courtney as a walrus-ish yet debonair individual who never loses his air of mystery." Kate McClelland noted in a *School Library Journal* review of

Courtney that this "is all typically assured Burningham at his ironic best." A contributor to *Kirkus Reviews* commented on Burningham's "familiar cartoon mode" which is "poignantly expressive," and concluded that the book was "[w]itty, well told, and superbly illustrated."

Father Christmas gets the Burningham treatment in *Harvey Slumfenburger's Christmas Present,* in which Santa, exhausted after delivering presents all night, discovers one he has overlooked. Poor little Harvey Slumfenburger is unlikely to get any other gifts this Christmas, Santa knows, so he sets out on foot to deliver it, having already tucked his reindeer into bed. Along the way, Santa finds a variety of transportation and meets other travelers in a book that could become "a classic," according to Keith Barker in *School Librarian.* Sheila Moxley called the book "poignant" and "lightly funny" in *School Library Journal;* "a fully realized story about the true spirit of Christmas." *Booklist's* Carolyn Phelan drew special attention to Burningham's "signature ink drawings with watercolor washes" which "will keep children rapt."

In the 1996 *Cloudland* and the 1999 *Whadayamean?,* Burningham experimented with a wide array of mixed media in his illustrations, particularly in the blending of photographic images with his own artwork. The former title tells the story of young Albert who, out hiking in the mountains with his parents, falls off a cliff. Happily he lands on a cloud, caught by cloud children who introduce him to all manner of lovely pastimes including swimming, painting, dancing, and making music. Seeing the lights of the city below, Albert finally remembers his family and desires to go home. Without question or approbation, his parents welcome the missing child home and tuck him into bed, as much a part of the fantasy as Albert himself. *Booklist's* Julie Corsaro commented that "Burningham explores a common childhood fantasy in an impressively illustrated picture book," employing photographic images of clouds with his sketchy figures overlaid onto them in a three-dimensional effect. Corsaro concluded that *Cloudland* "is likely to be a favorite." A reviewer for *Junior Bookshelf* concluded that *Cloudland* "is a sumptuous example of John Burningham's skill in marrying the magic of the simple story with the splendid page after page of illustrations which will appeal to both reader and listener." George Hunt, reviewing the title in *Books for Keeps,* found it to be a "visually striking and entertaining book."

Even more stylistically innovative is Burningham's environmental story, *Whadayamean?,* in which he mixes satellite photography, paintings, soft focus photos over-painted, pastels, pen and ink, and various other collage features. In the story, God wakes up one day and decides to visit earth, the paradise he/she once created. But now, accompanied by two earthling children found picnicking under a tree, God discovers things have gone terribly wrong on the planet, with pollution, killing, and starvation to be found in abundance. God entrusts the children the task of talking to benighted adults and getting them on the right path, which they do in this eco-

Then Santa Claus set off on the long journey home.

From **Harvey Slumfenburger's Christmas Present,** *written and illustrated by Burningham.*

fantasy. Rosemary Stones called the book a "fable for our times" in *Books for Keeps,* and noted that the "impact is wrenching as the small figures are dwarfed by the scale of our planet's destruction." Joan Zahnleiter remarked in *Magpies* that Burningham "has given the creation story an ecological turn in this spectacular picture book." Zahnleiter went on to note that though there is a mixed bag of media in the artwork, "Burningham's consummate skill as an illustrator has brought them all into an harmonious whole which flows through the book along with the text."

Burningham believes that maintaining his interest in his work contributes to its quality and broad appeal. Really great children's books, he wrote in *Junior Bookshelf,* "contain as much for adults as for children because the person who made them was concerned to satisfy himself as well as his readers. This is an attitude which anyone who embarks on creative work must have if he is to achieve anything."

"I enjoy making children's books—and I use the word 'making' rather than writing because I think of my books as a series of drawings held together by a thread of text," Burningham explained in *Junior Bookshelf.* "I enjoy it because it allows me to work with the maximum freedom and to carry out my own ideas." The author wants his readers to have freedom as well, he continued: "I try not to make my own drawings too formal and finished so that the child who is reading or looking can have the maximum freedom to imagine for himself. The

sense of finding something out is as important in pictures as it is in words."

Burningham has succeeded in using his "tremendous craft" to give his books this open, imaginative feeling, according to *New York Times Book Review* contributor Vicki Weissman. The critic remarked: "Burningham has long since grasped that all children need is a trigger and their imaginations will do the rest. What is more, he is content to leave it to them." In addition, his books excel because "he has the ability to capture in his simple drawings the essence and spirit of his characters— whether animals or people and portray them in a way that little children respond to," Russell wrote. "John Burningham," concluded Stephenson in the *Carousel* profile, "is a quiet man who has a deep respect for the value of words and chooses them carefully; who thinks deeply and cares passionately about the planet; and who, like many serious people, maintains a constant, warm under-glow of humour."

Works Cited

Anable, David, "Shirley Battles Pirates in Deep-Sea Daydreams," *Christian Science Monitor,* November 2, 1977, p. B2.

Barker, Keith, review of *Harvey Slumfenburger's Christmas Present, School Librarian,* November, 1993, p. 147.

Review of *Borka, Junior Bookshelf,* December, 1963, p. 335.

Review of *Borka, Sunday Herald Tribune Book Week,* May 10, 1964, pp. 34-35.

Burningham, John, "Drawing for Children," *Junior Bookshelf,* July, 1964, pp. 139-41.

Butler, Dorothy, "Cushla and Her Books," *Signal,* January, 1977, pp. 3-37.

Review of *Cannonball Simp, Publishers Weekly,* August 7, 1967, p. 54.

Clements, Andrew, "A Serious Business," *New Statesman,* December 7, 1984, p. 30.

Review of *Cloudland, Junior Bookshelf,* October, 1996, p. 182.

Cohen, Robert, review of *Cannonball Simp, Young Readers Review,* December, 1967, p. 16.

Corsaro, Julie, review of *Cloudland, Booklist,* December 15, 1996, p. 731.

Review of *Courtney, Kirkus Reviews,* July 15, 1994, p. 979.

Crouch, Marcus, review of *Granpa, Junior Bookshelf,* February, 1985, p. 12.

Daltry, Patience M., "Imagination Needs No Visa," *Christian Science Monitor,* November 4, 1965, p. B1.

Feaver, William, "Bumps in the Night," *Observer,* November 25, 1984, p. 27.

Field, Michele, "PW Interviews: John Burningham and Helen Oxenbury," *Publishers Weekly,* July 24, 1987, pp. 168-69.

Fisher, Margery, review of *Time to Get out of the Bath, Shirley, Growing Point,* July, 1978, p. 3369.

Haviland, Virginia, review of *Mr. Gumpy's Motor Car, Horn Book,* August, 1976, p. 385.

Review of *Humbert, Mr. Firkin and the Lord Mayor of London, Junior Bookshelf,* February, 1966, pp. 27-28.

Hunt, George, review of *Cloudland, Books for Keeps,* March, 1997, p. 20.

Kluger, Richard, "The Glottis Got Us," *Sunday Herald Tribune Book Week,* September 12, 1965, p. 28.

Lafferty, Fiona, "Burningham, John (Mackintosh)," *St. James Guide to Children's Writers,* , edited by Sara Pendergast and Tom Pendergast, St. James Press, 1999, pp. 196-98.

McClelland, Kate, review of *Courtney, School Library Journal,* September, 1994, p. 180.

Mercer, Joan Bodger, review of *Mr. Gumpy's Outing, New York Times Book Review,* November 7, 1971, p. 46.

Moxley, Sheila, review of *Harvey Slumfenburger's Christmas Present, School Library Journal,* October, 1993, p. 42.

Orr, Nancy Young, review of *Harquin, School Library Journal,* November, 1968, p. 75.

Phelan, Carolyn, review of *Harvey Slumfenburger's Christmas Present, Booklist,* October 15, 1993, p. 450.

Russell, Jean, "Cover Artist: John Burningham," *Books for Your Children,* spring, 1981, pp. 6-7.

Review of *The Shopping Basket, Junior Bookshelf,* February, 1981, p. 11.

Stephenson, Chris, "Out of This World: John Burningham," *Carousel,* spring, 1999, pp. 20-21.

Stevenson, Deborah, review of *Courtney, Bulletin of the Center for Children's Books,* December, 1994, p. 123.

Stones, Rosemary, review of *Whadayamean?, Books for Keeps,* May, 1999, p. 23.

Triggs, Pat, review of *Granpa, Books for Keeps,* November, 1984, p. 4.

Review of *Trubloff, Junior Bookshelf,* November, 1964, p. 288.

Weissman, Vicki, "The Gorilla Was on His Side," *New York Times Book Review,* May 8, 1988, p. 32.

Zahnleiter, Joan, review of *Whadayamean?, Magpies,* May, 1999, p. 22.

For More Information See

BOOKS

Children's Books and Their Creators, edited by Anita Silvey, Houghton, 1995.

Children's Literature Review, Volume 9, Gale, 1985.

Egoff, Sheila A., "Picture Books," *Thursday's Child: Trends and Patterns in Contemporary Children's Literature,* American Library Association, 1981, p. 268.

PERIODICALS

Booklist, March 1, 1994, p. 1264.

Books for Keeps, January, 1996, p. 6; July, 1999, pp. 19-20.

Horn Book, November-December, 1993, p. 729; March-April, 1994, pp. 188-89; January-February, 1995, p. 78.

Junior Bookshelf, August, 1994, p. 127.

Kirkus Reviews, June 15, 1999, p. 961.

New York Times Book Review, May 20, 1990; November 14, 1993, p. 36; October 9, 1994, p. 26; March 16, 1997, p. 26.

School Librarian, autumn, 1999, p. 135.

School Library Journal, October, 1996, p. 7; July, 1999, p. 67.

Times Educational Supplement, December 10, 1993, p. 29; September 6, 1996, p. 7; October 18, 1996, p. 12; November 14, 1997, p. 11.*

—Sketch by J. Sydney Jones

C

CARRINGTON, Marsha Gray 1954-

Personal

Born November 17, 1954, in Richmond, VA; daughter of Cary Ambler (in sales) and Louise Hobson (a fine artist; maiden name, Hall) Carrington. *Education:* James Madison University, B.F.A., 1977; California Institute of the Arts, M.F.A., 1981. *Religion:* "Science of Mind."

Addresses

Home—1601 Maltman Ave., Los Angeles, CA 90026. *Office*—107 South Fair Oaks, Suite 325, Pasadena, CA 91105. *Agent*—Jane Feder, 305 East 24th St., New York, NY 10010. *Electronic mail*—marsgc@mindspring.com.

Career

Visual effects animator in the film industry, c. 1983-96; illustrator of children's books, 1997—. mjZoom (greeting card and gift manufacturer), co-owner. Creator of greeting card and T-shirt designs. *Member:* Society of Children's Book Writers and Illustrators.

Illustrator

Tres Seymour, *Jake Johnson: The Story of a Mule,* DK Ink (New York City), 1999.
Lezlie Evans, *Sometimes I Feel like a Storm Cloud,* Mondo Publishing (Greenvale, NY), 1999.

Work in Progress

Writing and illustrating the picture book *Winney and June.*

Sidelights

Marsha Gray Carrington told *SATA:* "What is important to me is merely that I continue to 'make things.' My creative self has always been the core of my being, and I cannot remember a time when I was not painting, drawing, or assembling something. My interest gravitates toward imagery that is whimsical, playful, and childlike as well as having a bit of a dark side, which I feel we all have. I am drawn towards children's art, and enjoy creating art for children. I think children are much more in touch with not only their bright side, but also their dark side. Being more pure and innocent, not intellectualized, children's expression is raw, more encompassing.

"I began to be inspired by children's books during my graduate studies in fine-art photography. After leaving school, I became involved in the visual effects animation field of the film industry, but my desire to illustrate children's books lingered. I worked for thirteen years on films but never felt fulfilled creatively in a way that nurtured and developed my own ideas. Finally, that creative voice inside me was not just speaking any more. It was screaming, and I joined the ranks of the struggling artists to follow my heart. I have never been happier.

"My pocketbook is substantially lighter, but I believe that it all will work to my greater good in the big picture. Finally I am doing some things that I love, one of which is creating images that speak to children, as well as to the child in me, which is still very much alive—simultaneously curious and enchanted with the world, while still fearing what's under the bed."*

*   *   *

CHANG, Chih-Wei 1966-

Personal

Born August 25, 1966, in Taipei, Taiwan; son of A-Chuan (an engineer) and Chu-Chu (Tsai) Chang. *Education:* Tatung Institute of Technology, B.S., 1988; Fashion Institute of Technology, B.F.A. (summa cum laude), 1996.

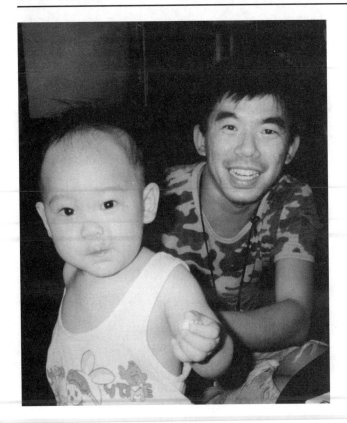

Chih-Wei Chang

Addresses

Home and office—F6, No35, Ln58, Secl, Shih-Pai Rd., Taipei, Taiwan. *Electronic mail*—unohuim@tpts5.seed. net.tw.

Career

Taipei Fine Arts Museum, Taipei, Taiwan, assistant in curatorial department, 1992; freelance illustrator, 1996—. Taipei Fine Arts Museum, assistant in curatorial department, 1998, assistant in education department, 1998—. *Military service:* Served as military police officer, 1989-91.

Awards, Honors

Awards from Educational Foundation for the Fashion Industries, 1994.

Illustrator

Anastasia Suen, *Baby Born,* Lee & Low Books (New York City), 1998.

Work in Progress

Writing and illustrating a story about a little girl who doesn't like the way she looks and stares at herself in a mirror until she is drawn into the reflection.

Sidelights

Chih-Wei Chang told *SATA:* "I get my greatest joy from expressing myself, and illustration is probably one of the best ways for me, so far. It is a quiet performance. It's funny that I did not think of it that way while I was still an electrical engineering major who decided not to stay there, back when I just wanted to do something that appeared to me to be more fun. I went to New York and pursued another bachelor's degree in illustration, especially fashion illustration.

"At the Fashion Institute of Technology, I often struggled between drawing the way I like and drawing the way other people like. One day I was browsing in the Barnes and Noble book store, and I saw *The Three Golden Keys* by Peter Sis. I was intrigued by the pictures and encouraged by the illustrator's freedom to be personal. So I approached Mr. Sis with a letter, asking if he could be my mentor. To my surprise, he answered me with a postcard, saying yes. Peter Sis is the one who introduced me to the field of children's books, and I thank him for that.

"*Baby Born* is my first picture book. After graduation, I sent out my samples with query letters to the publishers that interested me. A couple of weeks later, Lee and Low responded to me with a drop-off interview, then with a manuscript. The words were so beautiful that, the minute I read it, I knew I wanted to do it. Luckily, my nephew was born right at the same time I received this project. It was a happy coincidence.

"I am working part-time at the museum now, and I have been enjoying the balance between being part-time staffer and full-time freelancer. I need to be alone with my thoughts, but I also need to be among the crowd, sharing the energy. I wish I could take on different projects with different people from all over the world. That would make my work so interesting. I love colors and lines, patterns and textures, images and text, feelings and memories, jokes and stories. And I am attached to my dream. I guess that's why I am a children's book illustrator."

*   *   *

CHARLES, Nicholas J.
See KUSKIN, Karla

*   *   *

CHESTER, Kate
See GUCCIONE, Leslie Davis

*   *   *

COFFIN, M. T.
See STANLEY, George Edward

COOLING, Wendy

Personal

Born in England. *Education:* London University, M.A. (education).

Addresses

Home—11 Kingsmead, Barnet, Hertsfordshire, EN5 5AX England. *E-mail*—WendyCooling@Bookconsult. freeserve.co.uk.

Career

United Kingdom Year of Literature festival, Swansea, Wales, coordinator, 1995; WORDPLAY children's festival, organizer, 1995—; Book House Training Centre, director of course on children's publishing, 1995—; Disney Consumer Products, director of course on children's publishing, 1997; National Literacy Strategy and National Year of Reading, contact person, 1999. Former member of the civil service; English teacher, London, England; book consultant and advisor to schools, libraries, and parents; library director; bookstore manager; book promoter; advisory teacher with the ILEA Resources Support Group; head of the Children's Book Foundation; judge of children's literature awards, including the March Award, the Mother Goose Award, and the National Association for Special Education Needs Book Award; researcher for literary organizations; freelance book consultant and reviewer; appeared on the radio program *Treasure Islands,* BBC Radio 4. *Member:* National Literacy Association (executive member), Children's Literature Research Centre (member of advisory panel), Poetry Society (member of advisory panel), Farms for City Children (director), Polka Children's Theatre (member of the board), International Board on Books for Young People (chair of the British section for three years), LISC (member of the working party).

Writings

Finding Out ... How to Find Out, Penguin (Harmondsworth, England), 1989.
Fame!: Who's Who in History at Madame Tussaud's, illustrated by Nick Duffy, Puffin Books, 1992.
Sandy the Seal, Trafalgar Square (North Pomfret, VT), 1994.
(With Paul Kropp) *The Reading Solution,* Penguin, 1995.
Books to Enjoy, 12-16 (guide), School Library Association, 1996.
(Reteller) *Farmyard Tales from Far and Wide* (companion to *Forest Tales from Far and Wide,* edited by Marleen Vermeulen), illustrated by Rosslyn Moran, Barefoot Books (Brooklyn, NY), 1998.

Also author of children's guides for the National Trust. Contributor to periodicals, including *Books for Keeps, Junior Education, Guardian,* and *Times Educational Supplement.*

EDITOR

Paul Jennings, *Thirteen! Unpredictable Tales from Paul Jennings,* Viking, 1995.
Roald Dahl, *The Great Automatic Grammatizator and Other Stories by Roald Dahl,* Viking, 1996.
The Puffin Book of Stories for Five-Year-Olds, Puffin, 1996.
The Puffin Book of Stories for Six-Year-Olds, Puffin, 1996.
The Puffin Book of Stories for Seven-Year-Olds, Puffin, 1996.
The Puffin Book of Stories for Eight-Year-Olds, Puffin, 1996.
Read Me a Story Please, Orion (London, England), 1998.
Centuries of Stories, HarperCollins (London, England), 1999.
Roald Dahl, *Skin and Other Stories,* Puffin, 1999.

EDITOR; "QUIDS FOR KIDS" SERIES

Aliens to Earth, Orion, 1997.
Animal Stories, Orion, 1997.
Bad Dreams, Orion, 1997.
Ghost Stories, Orion, 1997.
Go for Goal, Orion, 1997.
Horror Stories, Orion, 1997.
On the Run, Orion, 1997.
Soccer Stories, Orion, 1997.
Spine Chillers, Orion, 1997.
Stars in Your Eyes, Orion, 1997.
Stories of Growing Up, Orion, 1997.
Stories of Hopes and Dreams, Orion, 1997.
Stories of Past and Future, Orion, 1997.
Stories of Strange Visitors, Orion, 1997.
Stories of the Unexpected, Orion, 1997.
Stories to Keep You Guessing, Orion, 1997.
Time Watch, Orion, 1997.
Top Secret, Orion, 1997.
Weird and Wonderful, Orion, 1997.
Wild and Free, Orion, 1997.

Also editor of *It's Christmas, Simply Spooky,* and *Surprise Surprise,* all for Dolphin.

Work in Progress

A book celebrating the millennium.

Sidelights

Wendy Cooling is a children's book author, editor, and reviewer. Her book *Fame!: Who's Who in History at Madame Tussaud's* offers sketches about thirty-nine of the famous people who have been reproduced for the wax museum in London. Alasdair Campbell wrote in *School Librarian* that about half of Cooling's choices were politically influential in their time and that the rest "are a mixed bag indeed," and include American actress Marilyn Monroe, American singer and actor Elvis Presley, and the murderer Jack the Ripper. Campbell noted that "there is certainly food for some thought in these chapters" about the nature of fame.

Cooling has also edited several collections of stories for young readers, including the anthologies *The Puffin*

Book of Stories for Five-Year-Olds, The Puffin Book of Stories for Six-Year-Olds, The Puffin Book of Stories for Seven-Year-Olds, and *The Puffin Book of Stories for Eight-Year-Olds.* Ann G. Hay, another *School Librarian* contributor, called *The Puffin Book of Stories for Five-Year-Olds* "a delightful collection of old favorites and new." Reviewing the same work, Marcus Crouch of the *Junior Bookshelf* observed that the anthology contains "very fine things" that "have the merit of brevity." Another *Junior Bookshelf* contributor wrote that "the range of subjects" in *The Puffin Book of Stories for Seven-Year-Olds* "is likely to appeal to young juniors," and that *The Puffin Book of Stories for Eight-Year-Olds* depicts "an interesting range of people, places, and magical possibilities."

Cooling edited a number of entries in the "Quids for Kids" collection of books for children. The series takes its name from "quid," the British slang term for the currency measure of one pound. Each of the low-priced books—which cost one pound, or a quid—contains five or six stories centering on a single theme. *School Librarian* contributor Ruth France applauded the objective of making affordable books available to children, and commented that the books' brevity could introduce children "to the world of reading."

Cooling told *SATA:* "After a varied early career and two years drifting around the world, I settled down to teaching. I worked in Inner London secondary schools as an English teacher, deputy- and acting-headteacher for many years, running libraries, bookshops and help sessions for parents in any spare time. In one of the more

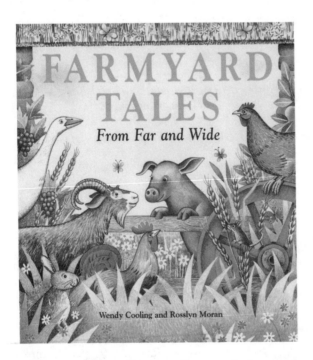

Wendy Cooling's collection offers standard storytale fare, such as the saga of the three little pigs, as well as lesser-known stories, such as the tale of a magical ox who is able to provide food for a hungry farmer and his wife. (Cover illustration by Rossyln Moran.)

exciting times, I worked with a librarian and a media-resources officer to run a library resource center in a secondary school, where the development of autonomous learning was seen as a priority—this at a time when money was not in short supply. I worked for two years as an advisory teacher with the ILEA Resources Support Group, advising schools—infant to F.E.—on the setting-up of libraries, the development of independent reading, and resource-based learning.

"I studied part-time at London University's Institute of Education for an M.A. and wrote a dissertation on the role of the school library in curriculum development.

"At the end of 1990, I left teaching to run the Children's Book Foundation—talking and writing about children's books and reading, organizing National Children's Book Week, overseeing the annual production of *Children's Books of the Year* and working on a range of projects to promote reading.

"One of my most interesting projects was *Bookstart,* which aims to encourage parents to read with their children from a very early age. It is run in cooperation with local health centers and public libraries and involves the gift of a book and a pack about reading to families taking their babies to the clinic for the nine-month health check. I still act as a consultant to *Bookstart,* and the project, now operating in 60 areas and about to go nationwide, has brought many opportunities to speak on radio and at conferences about the importance of pre-school book-related experiences and choosing books. At the other end of the age range, I have discussed teenage reading on BBC Radio 4's *Treasure Islands* with Michael Rosen, spoken at numerous conferences, run courses on Boys and Reading and worked with librarians on the selection of teenage fiction.

"I'm now working as a consultant with a range of children's publishers; reviewing books; running in-service training sessions for infant, primary and secondary school teachers and librarians; making presentations at conferences and to parent groups; working with children on special projects having to do with books; writing children's guides for the National Trust and acting as their Literary Advisor, and editing story collections for Collins, Puffin and Orion. In 1995 I was the coordinator of the children's festival for the UK Year of Literature and Writing, held in Swansea—the children's festival WORDPLAY has now become an annual event which I continue to organize.

"For three years I was chair of the U.K. Section of the International Board on Books for Young People (IBBY) and I served as a member of the LISC working party (set up by the Department of National Heritage to look at school and public library services for young people). I am currently a member of the National Literacy Association executive, on the board of the Polka Children's Theatre, on the advisory panels of the Children's Literature Research Centre and the Poetry Society, and a director of Farms for City Children. I have been involved in judging for children's book awards—currently the Mother Goose Award (for the most promising new children's picture-book illustrator), the NASEN Special Education Needs Book Award and the Marsh Award for a book in translation.

"I worked in 1995 on research for SCAA, published as *One Week in March: A Survey of the Literature Pupils Read,* and have since worked on a range of projects with what is now QCA and with NFER.

"For the last years, I have been Course Director of Book House Training Centre's course on children's publishing; this covers all aspects of children's publishing: editorial, rights, design, production, marketing, and bookselling. In 1997 I ran a similar course for Disney Consumer Products—delegates were from all European countries.

"Currently I am working with publishers, booksellers and library suppliers on the resource implications of the National Literacy Strategy, and on a range of events planned for the National Year of Reading. I am also working on a book to celebrate the millennium—an anthology of 20 stories, one set in each of the last twenty centuries, offering a rich collection of stories and a sense of history.

"I am, as will be clear from the above, immersed in children's books—producing, reviewing, and promoting them. I am really committed to getting more books and more stories to more children."

Works Cited

Campbell, Alasdair, review of *Fame!: Who's Who in History at Madame Tussaud's, School Librarian,* August, 1992, p. 105.
Crouch, Marcus, review of *The Puffin Book of Stories for Five-Year-Olds, Junior Bookshelf,* June, 1996, p. 106.
France, Ruth, review of *Top Secret* and others ("Quids for Kids"), *School Librarian,* August, 1997, p. 136.
Hay, Ann G., review of *The Puffin Book of Stories for Five-Year-Olds, School Librarian,* August, 1996, p. 98.
Review of *The Puffin Book of Stories for Eight-Year-Olds, Junior Bookshelf,* December, 1996, p. 248.
Review of *The Puffin Book of Stories for Seven-Year-Olds, Junior Bookshelf,* December, 1996, p. 248-49.

For More Information See

PERIODICALS

Books, April, 1997, p. 24.
Library Association Record, February, 1997, p. 101.
School Librarian, summer, 1998, pp. 99-100; autumn, 1998, pp. 129-30.

COWLEY, Marjorie 1925-

Personal

Born July 8, 1925, in Dallas, TX; daughter of Jules Hexter and Beatrice Jacobs Hexter Stein; married Charles S. Stein, Jr. (a physician), 1947 (deceased); married William M. Cowley (a writer), 1971 (divorced 1994); children: Allison, Ross, Loren. *Education:* Stanford University, B.A. (cum laude), 1947. *Hobbies and other interests:* Ancient art, archaeology, travel, reading.

Addresses

Home and Office—2544 Hutton Drive, Beverly Hills, CA 90210-1212. *Electronic mail*—MHCowley@aol. com. *Agent*—Tracy Adams, McIntosh/Otis, 353 Lexington Ave., New York, NY 10016.

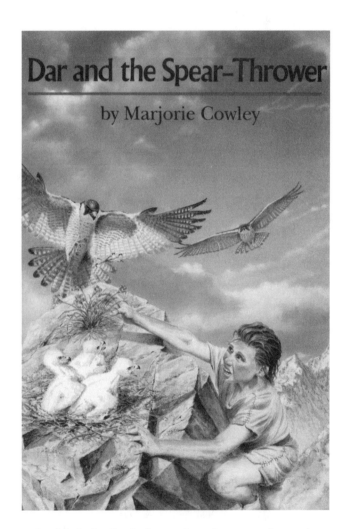

In Marjorie Cowley's coming-of-age novel, set in southern France fifteen thousand years ago, a young man's desire to possess a spear-thrower and prove himself as a great hunter sends him on a dangerous quest. (Cover illustration by Colin Poole.)

Career

UCLA Fowler Museum of Cultural History, Los Angeles, CA, lecturer in prehistoric archaeology, 1973-87; designed and taught prehistoric unit as a professional expert in public and private schools, 1975-88. Graphic designer and calligrapher, 1973-93. Also worked at the UCLA International Service Center, 1961-68; staff member at Venice Morning School, 1970-72. *Member:* Society of Children's Book Writers and Illustrators, Authors Guild, Archaeological Institute of America, UCLA Friends of Archaeology, California Readers.

Writings

Dar and the Spear Thrower, Clarion, 1994.
Anooka's Answer, Clarion, 1998.

Work in Progress

The Golden Bull, a book for children, ages eight to thirteen, concerning ancient Mesopotamia; research on the city of Ur and ancient gold-working techniques.

Sidelights

Marjorie Cowley told *SATA:* "Writing became a part of my life only after the birth of my first grandchild. While putting together a book for his birthday, I fell into a trance of both focus and freedom. Shortly after this experience, I took the first of a handful of courses at UCLA on writing for children.

"I chose as a background for both of my books the rich period of prehistory known as the Upper Paleolithic. This time was full of invention and art and has fascinated me for many years. Writing *Dar and the Spear Thrower* and *Anooka's Answer* allowed me to spend time joining story to background, a pleasure that never flagged for me.

"My new book, *The Golden Bull,* has meant starting with little prior knowledge of ancient Mesopotamia, but the subject has proven to be equally fascinating. My protagonist is a young boy who is an apprentice to a master goldsmith who works for the Temple of Ur. Together they embellish the famous golden bull lyre found in the Royal Tombs of Ur by Sir Leonard Woolley."*

*   *   *

CROWE, Andrew

Addresses

Home—Waitakere Coastline, New Zealand.

Career

Writer, designer, illustrator, and nature photographer. Creator of the poster series "Which Plant?" Also worked as a bookseller, specializing in natural history books.

Awards, Honors

Short-listed for AIM Children's book Award, 1993, for *Earthkids;* AIM Children's Book Award, nonfiction category, 1995, for *Which Native Forest Plant?;* short-listed for AIM Children's Book Award, nonfiction category, 1995, for *Which Native Fern?;* short-listed for Children's Book Award, *New Zealand Post,* winner, nonfiction category, New Zealand Library Association Book Award, both 1998, both for *The Life-Size Guide to Native Trees and Other Common Plants of New Zealand's Native Forest.* Short-listed for Children's Book Award, *New Zealand Post,* 1999, for *Nature's Alphabet.*

Writings

A Field Guide to the Native Edible Plants of New Zealand: Including Those Plants Eaten by the Maori, Collins (Auckland, New Zealand), 1981.
A Guide to the Parks, Woodlands, and Commons of Greater London, Fourth Estate, 1987.
Native Edible Plants of New Zealand, self-illustrated, Hodder & Stoughton (Auckland, New Zealand), 1990.
Which Native Tree?, Viking, 1992.
Which Native Fern? A Simple Guide to the Identification of New Zealand Native Ferns, Viking (Auckland), 1994.
Which Native Forest Plant? A Simple Guide to the Identification of New Zealand Native Forest Shrubs, Climbers, and Flowers, Viking, 1994.
Which Coastal Plant? A Simple Guide to the Identification of New Zealand's Common Coastal Plants, Viking, 1995.
A Field Guide to the Native Edible Plants of New Zealand, Godwit (Auckland), 1997.
The Life-Size Guide to Native Trees and Other Common Plants of New Zealand's Native Forest, Viking, 1997.
The QuickFind Guide to Growing Native Plants, Viking, 1997.
Nature's Alphabet: A New Zealand Nature Trail, illustrated by Dave Gunson, Penguin, 1998.
The Life-size Guide to Insects and Other Land Invertebrates, Penguin, 1999.
Which Seashell?, Penguin, 1999.

Author of more than a dozen other books, including *A Rainbow in the Forest, Earthkids,* and *Which Native Tree?* Contributor to periodicals, including *New Zealand School Journal* and *Geo.*

Sidelights

Andrew Crowe attributes his writing career to being lost in the New Zealand bush. The award-winning creator of more than thirty nature books had an inauspicious beginning to a career that resulted in one of the best-selling books in New Zealand—*A Field Guide to Native Edible Plants of New Zealand.* In an interview with *Magpies'* Vicky White, Crowe said that after his experience in the bush, he realized that there was very little written about edible native plants and he began gathering material. Crowe forged ahead, without a camera, without a car, house-sitting for people and even living in a cave for six months. He ate wild plants and grew his own food. Crowe told White: "I've done many jobs but there are few I found really satisfying. I got into writing with everyone telling me I couldn't make a living at it . . . . However I was happy to live in a simple way. When I ran out of money I would get a job for a few days, or a month, and then get back to what I really wanted to do."

What resulted was *A Field Guide to the Native Edible Plants of New Zealand.* It is a practical handbook that covers more than one-hundred-and-ninety trees, shrubs, herbs, ferns, mushrooms, lichens and seaweeds. Separate sections in the book describe where the plants can be found, how they are utilized, particularly by the Maori people, and poisonous plants that may be confused with edible ones. When he began writing, Crowe thought that the subject matter would fill a niche in the field guide market. "When I was working on the book I had a lot of comments about it being an odd subject to be writing about and no one would want to read it. The book has sold more than fifteen-thousand copies and had five reprints in a country whose population is three million."

Other books followed, including the best-selling *Which Native Tree?* (more than thirty-thousand copies sold), the award-winning *Which Native Forest Plant?, The Life-Size Guide to Native Trees,* and *A Rainbow in the Forest.* Crowe said he usually has children in mind while writing, even if the books are not specifically at children. In the "Which Native Plant" series, children eight years old and up can utilize the images to identify plants and where to find them even if the text is challenging. Taking a series of books called "Patterns in Nature" that he created for preschool-to-early-primary-

grades a step further, Crowe's *The Life-Size Guide to Native Trees* encourages children to use sorting and comparing berries and leaves by color, shape, size, and so forth to aid in identification. "A lot of children want to know about nature. Sometimes they are frustrated by their teachers' and caregivers' lack of knowledge. They enjoy the empowerment that comes from discovering things on their own. My books help them do this." Asked by White if he has a favorite among his books, Crowe cited *A Rainbow in the Forest,* which explains how all the colors in a rainbow are found in New Zealand's native forest. He explained that it is the simplicity of the concept that appeals to him. "I wouldn't change a word," Crowe said.

According to Crowe, the major part of each day is spent writing, brainstorming, sketching, and planning his books. He also spends time talking to children, teachers, and librarians about science topics they are interested in. "I read my own work from a lot of different points of view—as a scientist looking for possible inaccuracies and from the eyes of a child. I continually ask myself: will they see that scientific word and be put off, or will they see it as a challenge?" Crowe maintains that while his main reason for continuing to write is because he enjoys it, he also feels it is worthwhile: "I have absolutely no regrets about choosing what appeared to be a difficult course, so that I can wake up in the morning, excited to start work."

Works Cited

White, Vicky, interview with Andrew Crowe, *Magpies,* July, 1998, pp. 4-6.

D

DAVID, Lawrence 1963-

Personal

Born January 20, 1963, in Boston, MA; son of Barry S. (in business) and Elizabeth (a social worker) David. *Education:* Bennington College, B.A., 1985; New York University, M.F.A., 1987.

Addresses

Home—New York City. *Agent*—Cynthia Cannell, Janklow & Nesbit, 598 Madison Ave., New York, NY 10022.

Career

Teacher's assistant at a school in New York City, 1991-92; Bantam, Doubleday, Dell Books for Young Readers, New York City, assistant to the publisher, 1992-93; freelance writer, 1993—.

Writings

FOR CHILDREN

The Good Little Girl, illustrated by Clement Oubrerie, Doubleday, 1998.
Beetle Boy, illustrated by Delphine Durand, Doubleday, 1999.
Peter Claus and the Naughty List, Doubleday, 1999.

FICTION; FOR ADULTS

Family Values, Simon & Schuster, 1993.
Need, Random House, 1994.

Sidelights

After penning two novels for adults, *Family Values* and *Need,* both exploring the intricacies of human relationships, Lawrence David turned his attention to books for children with much success. The first two titles, *The Good Little Girl* and *Beetle Boy,* are both tales of metamorphosis wherein children adapt to their distracted parents.

Miranda, the young protagonist of *The Good Little Girl,* cheerfully puts up with the strain induced by having two working parents. She dutifully listens to her parents continually make promises of "tomorrow," but when they fail to produce the "Saturday Family Waffle Breakfast," enough is enough for Miranda and she turns into her nasty alter ego, mean-and-green Lucretia. At first, Lucretia wangles Miranda everything she wants, but then Lucretia gets out of hand, demanding that Miranda's mother stick pencils up her nose and sing "Polly Wolly Doodle." Good-natured Miranda is able to take charge again and all is well, but Lucretia rears her head to remind the parents not to ignore Miranda. A critic writing in *Kirkus Reviews* opined that "Lucretia will appeal to every child who has ever succumbed to vague parental procrastinations," and a *Publishers Weekly* reviewer stated: "David, who chose a challenging theme for a first picture book, effectively depicts how disappointment upsets even the best-natured child."

David readily admits that his second book for children, *Beetle Boy,* was inspired by Franz Kafka's *Metamorphosis,* which a *Kirkus Reviews* critic said "translates splendidly into a story for younger audiences." Second-grader Gregory Sampson wakes up one morning and realizes he has become an insect. According to Jean Lenihan in her review on Amazon.com, "David's deft and buoyant comprehension of family life enables him to relate this tale with both pathos and humor." Distressed that no one but his best friend, Michael, sees his hard exoskeleton and six legs, Gregory finally shouts out, "Look at me. I'm a giant beetle." After his exclamation, his father replies: "And I'm a hippo." Finally after finding him on the ceiling of his room, crying, the family has to admit that Gregory is indeed a beetle, but no matter, they love him just the same. Their affirmations help return him to human form and in Lenihan's view: "It's moving, beautifully rendered moment—and most certainly powerful enough to turn a six-legged bug back into a little boy."

Works Cited

Review of *Beetle Boy, Kirkus Reviews,* January 15, 1999, p. 172.

Review of *The Good Little Girl, Kirkus Reviews,* September 15, 1998, p. 1382.

Review of *The Good Little Girl, Publishers Weekly,* November 2, 1998, p. 82.

Lenihan, Jean, review of *Beetle Boy,* Amazon.com, February, 1999.

For More Information See

PERIODICALS

Booklist, August, 1994, p. 2021.

Kirkus Reviews, May 1, 1993, pp. 545-46; June 15, 1994, p. 790.

School Library Journal, December, 1998, p. 82; March, 1999, p. 173.

Publishers Weekly, April 26, 1993, p. 55; June 4, 1994, p. 53.*

*   *   *

DAVIS, Leslie
See GUCCIONE, Leslie Davis

*   *   *

DAWES, Claiborne 1935-

Personal

Born July 6, 1935, in Lake Forest, IL; daughter of William A. P. (a realtor) and Virginia (a homemaker; maiden name, Orr) Watkins; married William N. Dawes (a sporting goods retailer), August 11, 1965 (deceased); children: William B., Elizabeth Dawes Nunes. *Education:* Smith College, B.A., English. *Religion:* Unitarian-Universalist.

Addresses

Home—Concord, MA.

Career

Barrow Bookstore, Concord, MA, owner, 1971-88. Active in community theater.

Writings

A Different Drummer: Thoreau and Will's Independence Day, illustrated by J. Stephen Moyle, Discovery Enterprises (Carlisle, MA), 1998.

Work in Progress

Historical fiction about Concord, Massachusetts, and the Underground Railroad.

Claiborne Dawes

Sidelights

Claiborne Dawes told *SATA:* "*A Different Drummer* is one result of living in Concord for thirty-five years—walking through Walden Woods and around the pond, hearing Thoreau referred to as 'Henry' by people who, while not disrespectful, would be able to strike up a conversation if they met him strolling along Main Street. The Alcotts, Nathaniel Hawthorne, and Ralph Waldo Emerson (always Waldo, never Ralph) are real here, so real that we can speculate about them. That is how *Drummer* began, when I started to wonder what else was going on in Concord on July 4, 1845, the day that Thoreau made his modest move to a small pond a mile or so away.

"The same 'what if' question has prompted my current project, historical fiction for children about Concord and the Underground Railroad and a young slave, given the name of Daniel by one of the 'conductors' who help with his deliverance. The poetry I write is also inquiring: what would Herod have felt as the Wise Men departed? Could Persephone have fallen in love with her dark abductor?

"For seventeen years I owned the Barrow Bookstore in Concord Center. Selling used and rare books is a great preparation for the writing life, fueling speculation about the lives of our thousands of strange and wonderful book collectors. Had I stayed in Illinois, or New Orleans, what would have been different? Now there's a 'what if' . . . ."

*   *   *

DEVORAH-LEAH
(Devorah Leah; Devorah-Leah Garren)

Personal

Born in Portland, ME; daughter of Robert A. (a cantor, director, and manager) and Thelma "Tedde" (a copywriter and choreographer; maiden name, Shain) Wisefield; married Scott L. Garren (divorced); children: Joshua David. *Education:* Brandeis University, B.A., M.F.A., 1975; attended Universite de Paris IV, 1975-76, and Ohr Somayach College for Women, 1978-82. *Religion:* Jewish. *Hobbies and other interests:* Painting, folksinging, guitar, international travel, bluegrass festivals.

Addresses

Home—58 Lancaster Terr., Brookline, MA 02446. *Office*—Curry College, 1071 Blue Hill Ave., Milton, MA 02186. *Electronic mail*—Dvorah-Leah@aol.com.

Career

J.R. Video, Jerusalem, Israel, producer and director, 1982-84; ComTel Television Productions, Derry, NH, producer and writer, 1984-86; Curry College, Milton, MA, associate professor of communication, director of Drama Center, and chaplain, 1986—. *Member:* International Michael Chelenov Association.

Writings

Lost in the Zoo, Judaica Press (Brooklyn, NY), 1983, revised edition published as *Lost Erev Shabbos in the Zoo,* illustrated by Siegmund Forst, 1986.
Shabbos Is Coming! We're Lost in the Zoo, illustrated by Maya S. Katz, Judaica Press, 1998.
Witness for the Prosecution: An American Adaptation for Stage and Video, produced in Milton, MA, at Curry College, 1998.

Some sources cite the author's name as Devorah Leah or Devorah-Leah Garren.

Work in Progress

Mad Michael, a children's book about anger; *Mitzvahs for Free,* a Jewish children's book.

Sidelights

Devorah-Leah told *SATA:* "I'm like the little cartoon character that goes running off the cliff. No one points out that there's no ground beneath, so I keep skipping merrily along. I survived Lebanon during the first few weeks of the war . . . went into Jordan leading a thinly disguised Israeli television crew, long before the peace. I hitchhiked through my baby's childhood, always depending on the 'kindness of strangers,' or, as my then-five-year-old observed, 'The world is just full of friends waiting to meet us.'

"The joys of my life are the moments when the world of 'I and it' dissolves, and the 'I and thou' relationship is restored between people. As a writer and a human being, I say: Let's get rid of the word 'they.'

"I played backup guitar for the Master of the Art of I and Thou, Shlomo Carlebach, on his concert tour of Poland. He breathed life into those downtrodden people until no one was left in the audience. All of them were on stage as we played, guitar to guitar, fingers bleeding, eyes burning into each other's souls, and a halo of angels danced around us—swirling, laughing, crying, and embracing in the glow of the stage lights.

"My writing? I recall the very day in childhood when my teacher, Miss Elizabeth Perry, introduced us to the world of language, the delight of rhyme and meter, the transformational power of adjectives and adverbs. So I've written for children. I've read to children. I've produced children's television. With each opportunity, I delight again in the joy of the child's fresh discoveries of this colorful world of words and images.

"My literary heroes are Shel Silverstein for *Where the Sidewalk Ends,* Dr. Seuss for *Did I Ever Tell You How Lucky You Are?,* Salman Rushdie for *Haroun and the Sea of Stories,* and Sendak for his endless creativity. My real life heroes are Shlomo Carlebach, my dad, my boy, my sweet students, all the friends we have, and all we've yet to meet!"

*   *   *

DOHERTY, Berlie 1943-

Personal

Surname is pronounced "*Doh*-er-ty"; born November 6, 1943, in Liverpool, England; daughter of Walter Alfred (a railway clerk) and Peggy (maiden name, Brunton) Hollingsworth; married Gerard Adrian Doherty, 1966; children: Janna, Tim, Sally. *Education:* University of Durham, B.A. (with honors), 1964; University of Liverpool, postgraduate certificate in social science, 1965; University of Sheffield, postgraduate certificate in education, 1978. *Hobbies and other interests:* Opera, ballet, music of all kinds, singing, theatre, walking in the countryside.

Addresses

Home—38 Banner Cross Road, Sheffield, York S11 9HR, England. *Agent*-David Higham Associates, 5-8 Lower John Street, Golden Square, London W1R 4HA, England.

Berlie Doherty

Career

Leicestershire Child Care Services, Leicester, England, social worker, 1966-67; homemaker, 1967-78; English teacher in Sheffield, England, 1978-80; schools broadcaster for British Broadcasting Corporation (BBC)-Radio Sheffield, 1980-82; full-time writer, 1983—. Writer-in-residence at various schools and libraries. Chair of Arvon Foundation at Lumb Bank, 1989—; member of Yorkshire Arts Literature Panel, 1988-90. *Member:* Writers Guild of Great Britain, Northern Association of Writers in Education (deputy chair, 1988-89), Arvon Foundation.

Awards, Honors

Carnegie Medal, British Library Association, 1986, Burnley/National Provincial Children's Book of the Year Award, 1987, and *Boston Globe-Horn Book* Honor Award, 1988, all for *Granny Was a Buffer Girl;* award from Television and Film Awards, New York, 1988, for "White Peak Farm"; Carnegie Medal, 1991, and Best Children's Play award, Writer's Guild of Great Britain, both for *Dear Nobody;* runner-up, British Book Award, 1992; Nasen Award, 1995, for *The Golden Bird;* Carnegie commendation, 1995, for *Willa and Old Miss Annie.*

Writings

FOR CHILDREN

Tilly Mint Tales, illustrated by Thelma Lambert, Methuen, 1984.

Paddiwak and Cosy, illustrated by Teresa O'Brien, Methuen, 1988, Dial, 1989, illustrated by Alison Bartlett, Orchard, 1999.

Tilly Mint and the Dodo (also see below), illustrated by Janna Doherty, Methuen, 1989.

Snowy, illustrated by Keith Bowen, HarperCollins, 1992.

(Reteller) *Old Father Christmas; Based on a Story by Juliana Horatia Ewing,* illustrated by Maria Teresa Meloni, Barron's, 1993.

Walking on Air (poetry), illustrated by J. Doherty, HarperCollins, 1993.

Willa and Old Miss Annie, illustrated by Kim Lewis, Candlewick Press, 1994.

The Magical Bicycle, illustrated by Christian Birmingham, HarperCollins, 1995, published as *The Magic Bicycle,* Crown, 1995.

The Golden Bird, illustrated by John Lawrence, Heinemann, 1995.

Our Field, adapted from a story by Juliana Horatia Ewing, illustrated by Robin Bell Corfield, HarperCollins, 1996.

Tales of Wonder and Magic, illustrated by Juan Wijngaard, Walker, 1997.

Bella's Den, illustrated by Peter Melnyzcuk, Heinemann, 1997.

The Midnight Man, illustrated by Ian Andrew, Candlewick Press, 1998.

(Editor) *The Forgotten Merman and Other Story Poems,* illustrated by Nick Maland, Hodder, 1998.

FOR YOUNG ADULTS

How Green You Are! (short stories; also see below), illustrated by Elaine McGregor Turney, Methuen, 1982.

The Making of Fingers Finnigan (short stories), illustrated by John Haysom, Methuen, 1983.

White Peak Farm (also see below), Methuen, 1984, Orchard, 1990.

Children of Winter (also see below), illustrated by Ian Newsham, Methuen, 1985.

Granny Was a Buffer Girl (also see below), Methuen, 1986, Orchard, 1988.

Tough Luck, Hamish Hamilton, 1988.

Spellhorn, Hamish Hamilton, 1989.

Dear Nobody, Hamish Hamilton, 1991.

Big Ugly Fat Black Slugs (poetry), Nelson, 1993.

Street Child, Orchard, 1994.

The Snake-Stone, Orchard, 1996.

Daughter of the Sea, illustrated by Sian Bailey, Hamish Hamilton, 1996, Dorling Kindersley, 1998.

Running on Ice (short stories), Reed, 1997.

The Sailing Ship Tree, Hamish Hamilton, 1998.

FOR ADULTS

Requiem (adult novel; also see below), M. Joseph, 1991.

The Vinegar Jar, St. Martin's, 1996.

TELEVISION AND RADIO PLAYS

The Drowned Village, BBC-Radio 4, 1980.

Requiem, BBC-Radio 4, 1982.

The White Bird of Peace, BBC-Radio 4, 1983.

A Case for Probation (also see below), BBC-Radio 4, 1983.

Miss Elizabeth, BBC-Radio 4, 1984.

Fuzzball, BBC-TV, 1985.

Sacrifice, BBC-Radio 4, 1985.

The Mouse and His Child (adapted from Russell Hoban's work of the same title), BBC-Radio 4, 1986.

White Peak Farm (serial), BBC-TV, 1988.

Dream of Unicorns, BBC-Radio 4, 1988.

Children of Winter, BBC-TV and BBC-Radio 4, 1988.

Granny Was a Buffer Girl, BBC-Radio 4, 1990.

There's a Valley in Spain, BBC-Radio 4, 1990.

Dear Nobody, BBC-Radio 4, 1993.

(Adaptor) *The Snow Queen,* by Hans Christian Andersen, BBC-Radio 4, 1994.

(Adapter) *Heidi,* by Johanna Spyri, BBC-Radio 4, 1996.

STAGE PLAYS

Smells and Spells (two-act), produced in Sheffield, England, 1978.

Howard's Field (one-act), produced in Sheffield, 1979.

A Growing Girl's Story (one-act), produced in Hartlepool, England, 1980.

The Amazing Journey of Jazz O'Neil, produced in Hull, England, 1984.

Rock 'n' Roll Is Here to Stay (one-act), produced in Sheffield, 1984.

Return to the Ebro (one-act), produced in Manchester, England, 1986.

Tilly Mint and the Dodo, produced in Doncaster, England, 1986.

A Case for Probation, published in *Studio Scripts,* edited by David Self, Hutchinson, 1986.

How Green You Are!, published in *Drama I,* edited by John Foster, Macmillan, 1987.

Matthew, Come Home, published in *Drama 2,* edited by Foster, Macmillan, 1987.

Tribute to Tom, published in *Drama 3,* edited by Foster, Macmillan, 1988.

Home, published in *Stage Write,* edited by Gervase Phinn, Unwin Hyman, 1988.

Memories (one-act), produced in Halifax, England, 1992.

Who Wants Gold (two-act), produced in Newcastle-under-Lyme, England, c. 1993.

The Sleeping Beauty, produced in Stoke-on-Trent, England, 1993.

Work represented in anthologies, including *School Poems,* Oxford University Press, 1986, and *Best Short Stories, 1989.* Contributor to magazines and newspapers, including *Arts Yorkshire, Times Educational Supplement, Stand,* and *Critical Quarterly.* Author of numerous series for local radio.

Adaptations

Several of Doherty's works have been adapted onto audiocassette by Chivers Press, including *Granny Was a Buffer Girl,* 1988, and *Tilly Mint Tales,* 1991.

Sidelights

Two-time winner of the Carnegie Medal, British author Berlie Doherty has written books for children of all ages, from fantasies and picture books such as *The Tilly Mint* *Tales, Snowy, Willa and Old Miss Annie, Bella's Den,* and *Paddiwak and Cosy,* to short-story collections for older readers. Best known for the novels she writes for young adults, Doherty has been consistently praised by critics for her realistic characters and the vivid settings in which she places them, and for the genuine portrayal of family ties and life which are at the heart of many of her novels. *Granny Was a Buffer Girl,* a generational tale of an English family, and *Dear Nobody,* the story of an unwanted pregnancy, were honored as outstanding works for children by receiving the British Library Association's prestigious Carnegie Medal. Doherty has also written rural tales in *White Peak Farm,* historical fiction in *Street Child,* a haunting mythic tale for older readers in *Daughter of the Sea,* and contemporary novels with hard-hitting themes such as coming to terms with adoption in *Snake-Stone,* and racism and school life in *Tough Luck.* Doherty is also the author of numerous plays for radio, stage, and television that have been performed by theater groups in her native England and produced by the British Broadcasting Corporation (BBC).

Born on November 6, 1943, in Liverpool, England, Doherty moved with her family to a small seaside village when she was four years old. Her family's strong Irish-Catholic background led to her enrollment at a secondary-level convent school. While there, she developed a great enthusiasm for the study of English, inspired in part by her father's example. "When I was a child I remember my father writing," Doherty once told *SATA.* "He loved writing poetry and short stories so it was always a very familiar and comforting thing to see him typing away on the typewriter in the corner of the room." Soon Doherty was following her father's example. Even as a child of five Doherty had known she wanted to be a writer. "I don't know what I thought a writer was or did, but Dad used to tell me bedtime stories every night, and I can remember thinking at a very early age that that's what I'd like to do; I'd like to make up stories for people to read at bedtime. It seemed then a very simple thing to do. It doesn't seem so simple now."

The stories she wrote eventually came to the notice of an exceptional English teacher during one of her last years at school. This teacher introduced the young student to drama and literature and further inspired Doherty to consider writing professionally. Once she was introduced to literature, Doherty never stopped reading. Among her favorite books as an older child were *Heidi* by Johanna Spyri, *Little Women* by Louisa May Alcott, *Swallows and Amazons* by Arthur Ransome, Frances Hodgson Burnett's *The Secret Garden,* and *Nicholas Nickleby* and *David Copperfield,* two novels by Charles Dickens.

After graduating from convent school, Doherty enrolled at the University of Durham and received a degree in English in 1964. She continued on with her studies, obtaining a post-graduate certificate in social science from the University of Liverpool a year later. After marrying Gerard Doherty in 1966, she worked for a year

Doherty's novel is based on the true story of Jim Jarvis, a homeless orphan whose plight inspired a doctor to set up Britain's first children's refuge in the 1860s. (Cover illustration by Dennis Nolan.)

with Leicester Child Care Services as a child care officer before leaving to start a family in 1967. During the years that followed, while she was at home raising her three children, Janna, Tim, and Sally, Doherty found time to obtain an additional post-graduate certificate, this time in education, from the University of Sheffield. In 1978, when her children were old enough to allow her to return to work, Doherty got a job teaching school in Sheffield. It was during the time she spent in the classroom that she was inspired to write for young children. In 1980, Doherty left the classroom to take a position with BBC-Radio Sheffield as a schools radio broadcaster. She was delighted when one of her radio plays, *The Drowned Village*, was produced by BBC-Radio 4 in 1980. She was also pleased to find that several of her stage plays were being produced in the Sheffield area.

In 1982, Doherty published her first children's novel, *How Green You Are!*, a collection of short-story episodes originally broadcast on radio. Characteristic of all her writing, Doherty weaves elements of her own childhood into the background of many of her stories. Taking as its setting the same small town on Britain's

west coast where Doherty lived as a small girl, this collection of short-story episodes is based on recollections from her past. This initial collection of stories features Bee, Julie, Kevin, and Marie, four average teenagers who live near each other in a small seaside town. Their friends, relatives, acquaintances, and the events surrounding them at home and at school provide the subjects for stories that range from funny to sad. Bee entertains a Russian violinist who is defecting to the West; Marie receives a pet monkey for her birthday but then loses it after the animal develops rabies and is shot by the police; and Kevin and a friend are caught in the tide while boating and must be rescued. A. Thatcher noted in a review for *Junior Bookshelf* that the stories contain "all the sadness, stress and problems of real life—strikes, death, illness, as well as the happier events." *The Making of Fingers Finnigan* continues the adventures of these young people. They become civic-minded and attempt to save the old community swimming pool; meanwhile, Julie's mischievous younger brother, Robert, becomes locked in a movie theater only to be rescued by Fingers Finnigan, a small-time crook.

As the mother of three small children, finding enough time to both work full-time and write two novels was difficult. When her first two books had been accepted for publication, she decided to leave her job as a teacher and embark upon a career as a full-time author. In 1984, her first year spent writing full-time, Doherty published both *White Peak Farm*, a young adult novel, and *Tilly Mint Tales*, a fantasy book for younger children. Similar in format to her two previous novels, *White Peak Farm* is a collection of ten interwoven stories about events in rural Derbyshire. Again a young narrator, Jeanie, describes the events that happen with friends, family, and neighbors in episodic format. Critic Maggie Freeman described the novel in *Twentieth-Century Children's Writers*: "The first two stories are gentle, with the dying grandmother setting the underlying theme . . . . Then the father begins to dominate. His hatred, loneliness and bad temper 'divided him from the rest of us and from each other.' Theirs is a 'house of secrets,' of strong suppressed emotions, each person living in their own world." Freeman goes on to praise *White Peak Farm*, calling it "Doherty's greatest commitment to her characters and their setting."

Originally broadcast as a series of radio stories for younger children, *Tilly Mint Tales* is a group of stories about a little girl who is carried off on a series of magical, dreamlike adventures whenever her babysitter, old Mrs. Hardcastle, falls asleep. *Junior Bookshelf* critic E. Colwell praised the book as "an encouragement to children to use their imagination and so make their own magic, a timely stimulus in these days when children rely so much on passive viewing of television." In the book's sequel, *Tilly Mint and the Dodo*, Doherty brings issues such as animal extinction and conservation into her story. Tilly Mint obtains a very large, old egg from the loveable Mrs. Hardcastle. Out is hatched a wise dodo-bird who transports the young girl to the land of yesterday. Tilly Mint comes face to face with the process of animal extinction through her friendship with

This elegant anthology contains nine traditional fairy stories, including a Scottish romance, a British folk tale, and an East-African wonder tale. (Cover illustration by Juan Wijngaard.)

Dodo, and although the book contains an important lesson about the importance of conservation, Doherty imparts her message to her young audience with humor and a delicate touch. Reviewer John Mole commented in the *Times Literary Supplement* that Doherty "instructs by pleasing, and knows that the wisdom lies in the delight." *Tilly Mint and the Dodo* is also unique in that it was a collaboration between Doherty and her daughter Janna, who provided the illustrations. Janna went on to illustrate her mother's first poetry collection, *Walking on Air*.

Because her early writing was originally commissioned for radio, much of Doherty's works take the form of episodes. In her books, each of these episodes serves as chapters linked together through shared characters and settings. *Granny Was a Buffer Girl,* one of Doherty's most popular books, follows this same formula. The novel focuses on Jess, a young woman preparing to leave her hometown of Sheffield, England, to go abroad for a year of study in Paris, France. When three generations of family members gather together to wish Jess well before her departure, her relative's reminis-

cences recall those sometimes bittersweet events that will always unite these people together in a common heritage. Helen Pain, in *Books for Keeps,* asserted that "the reader cannot help but be drawn into these vital and homely stories, with their mix of humor and heartfelt sadness.... Here is a highly memorable insight into family life."

With more recent novels such as *Tough Luck* and the Carnegie Medal-winning *Dear Nobody,* Doherty has adopted a more traditional novel format. In *Dear Nobody* in particular, the structure serves a very specific purpose—it is divided into nine chapters, one for each month of the young woman's pregnancy. Dealing with the sensitive subject of teenage pregnancy, Doherty wanted to structure the book to reflect not only the point of view of Helen, the unborn child's mother, but of Chris, the father, as well. "I didn't want it to be a piece of romantic fiction," Doherty told *SATA.* "I wanted to look seriously and genuinely at love because that's a major part of what being a teenager is about." In a series of letters to her child—the "Dear Nobody" of the title—Helen expresses the feelings of fear, astonishment, and bewilderment of a young mother-to-be. Both Chris's narrative and Helen's letters also explore the feelings of their parents and grandparents—all those who contributed to the support of Helen and Chris throughout the nine months leading up to the birth of their baby. Although Helen and Chris end up parting company during the story, as Doherty notes: "They never totally separate ... it's a journey towards their own parents. It's a way for them to find out as much as they can about their own parents—to come to an understanding about what *parenthood* means."

Reviewing the novel in *Bulletin of the Center for Children's Books,* Deborah Stevenson remarked that "Doherty's excellent writing, combined with the unusual dual point of view from the narration and the letters, makes this a richly nuanced examination of a familiar situation." In a starred *Booklist* review, Stephanie Zvirin declared that Doherty's rendering of the bittersweet tale "will move you to tears," while Alice Casey noted in *School Library Journal* that Doherty's writing presented "some of the loveliest, most lyrical prose to be found in YA fiction."

Much different fare is served up in Doherty's 1994 *Street Child,* a piece of historical fiction with echoes of *Oliver Twist.* Set in Victorian London, the book tells the story of young Jim Jarvis whose mother has died leaving him with the workhouse as his only alternative. But the horrors he finds there force him to flee back to the streets only to be sold off to work for the owner of a coal boat. Finally Jim meets up with Dr. Barnardo, a real historical figure who set up refuges for runaway children. A story of homelessness, *Street Child* would draw readers "as much by the social conditions as by Jim's picaresque adventures," noted *Booklist's* Hazel Rochman. Deborah Stevenson, reviewing the novel in *Bulletin of the Center for Children's Books,* felt that "Jim remains plucky and sincere, a protagonist to root for."

The Snake-Stone brings readers back to the late twentieth century and to the issue of adoption. A young diver whose rigorous training schedule sets him apart from the other kids, James has a nagging question that shakes his focus from competition. An adopted child, James obsesses about who his biological mother was. *Booklist's* Zvirin remarked in a review of the book that it "is Doherty's credible characterizations and her strong, clear prose that keep the pages turning; they beckon readers who appreciate a solid story." A *Kirkus Reviews* critic dubbed *The Snake-Stone* a "poignant and well-crafted story."

From Victorian London and contemporary England, the versatile Doherty moved to the world of myth in *Daughter of the Sea.* In this retelling of the selkie myth, Doherty blends tales from Iceland, Ireland, and Scotland to tell a tale of a childless couple on a bleak northern island who one day fish a baby daughter from the sea and name her Gioga. They mean to hide the real identity of the selkie, but a local woman, Eilean, discovers the shimmery skin the baby has shed when it came on land. When Gioga's seal-father comes to take her back to the water, the mother sends the child to the mainland, and vengeance is set upon the island by wild waters and angry seals. Finally Eilean tells the mother that the only thing that can save the island is that Gioga be sent home to the sea. "In eloquent, descriptive prose, Doherty beautifully re-creates the traditional tales of the selkies," commented Hilary Crew in *Voice of Youth Advocates.* Reviewing the same title for *Booklist,* Grace Anne A. DeCandido called the book a "gorgeous, romantic retelling."

Doherty has also penned a number of picture books and chapter books for younger readers. Popular examples of the former include *Snowy, The Magic Bicycle,* and *The Midnight Man.* The first is a story of a barge horse named Snowy and the little girl who loves him. "A gently exotic adventure with a barge like a swan and a loyal four-footed friend—this will seem like a dream-come-true to many young listeners," noted Stevenson in *Bulletin of the Center for Children's Books.* Doherty relates the story of the difficulties of first learning to ride a bicycle in *The Magic Bicycle,* an "energetic, well-executed picture book," according to Shelley Townsend-Hudson in *Booklist.* Doherty's 1999 *The Midnight Man,* a fantasy in which a pair of dreamers follow the Midnight Man on his nocturnal journey, is "a magical tale," according to *Booklist's* DeCandido, and an "enigmatic bedtime fantasy," according to a reviewer in *Publishers Weekly.*

Chapter books from Doherty include two adaptations of tales by the writer Juliana Horatia Ewing, *Old Father Christmas* and *Our Field,* as well as *Willa and Old Miss Annie* and *Tales of Wonder and Magic.* In these stories, Doherty neatly adapts her episodic style to a format easily accessible to young readers graduating from longer picture books. Chris Brown, reviewing *Tales of Wonder and Magic* in *School Librarian,* called the collection of nine fairy tales from around the world "a beautiful book." Friendship is at the heart of *Willa and*

In Doherty's 1998 picture book, a young boy and his dog follow the midnight man, a fantastical figure who flings sacks of stars into the sky, through a sleeping town. (Cover illustration by Ian Andrew.)

Old Miss Annie, the story of a girl who is heartbroken at moving and having to leave friends behind. But Willa soon finds solace in the companionship of an elderly neighbor who leads the girl on adventures with animals. Elizabeth S. Watson concluded in *Horn Book* that Doherty's "use of language is unusually beautiful and intricate in a book written for and accessible to younger middle-grade readers."

In all of her varied work—picture books, chapter books, YA novels, radio and television plays, and adult novels, Berlie Doherty maintains a clear and deceptively simple prose line. She tells gentle stories of friendship and family relations, but does not shy away from the crises that face adolescents as they begin to make the difficult transition into adulthood.

Works Cited

Brown, Chris, review of *Tales of Wonder and Magic,* *School Librarian,* spring, 1998, p. 24.

Casey, Alice, review of *Dear Nobody, School Library Journal,* October, 1992, p. 140.

Colwell, E., review of *Tilly Mint Tales, Junior Bookshelf,* December, 1984, p. 254.

Crew, Hilary, review of *Daughter of the Sea, Voice of Youth Advocates,* April, 1998, p. 54.

DeCandido, Grace Anne A., review of *Daughter of the Sea, Booklist,* October 1, 1997, p. 319.

DeCandido, Grace Anne A., review of *The Midnight Man, Booklist,* February 15, 1999. P. 1074.

Freeman, Maggie, "Berlie Doherty," *Twentieth-Century Children's Writers,* 3rd edition, St. James Press, 1989, pp. 292-93.

Review of *The Midnight Man, Publishers Weekly,* December 14, 1998, p. 75.

Mole, John, "A Friend Lost, a Lesson Learnt," *Times Literary Supplement,* December 16, 1988, p. 1406.

Pain, Helen, "Carnegie and Greenaway: The 1986 Winners," *Books for Keeps,* July, 1987, p. 11.

Rochman, Hazel, review of *Street Child, Booklist,* September 1, 1994, p. 40.

Review of *The Snake-Stone, Kirkus Reviews,* January 1, 1996, p. 67.

Stevenson, Deborah, review of *Dear Nobody, Bulletin of the Center for Children's Books,* January, 1993, p. 143.

Stevenson, Deborah, review of *Snowy, Bulletin of the Center for Children's Books,* March, 1993, p. 209.

Stevenson, Deborah, review of *Street Child, Bulletin of the Center for Children's Books,* November, 1994, p. 86.

Thatcher, A., review of *How Green You Are!, Junior Bookshelf,* August, 1982, pp. 150-51.

Townsend-Hudson, Shelley, review of *The Magic Bicycle, Booklist,* October 15, 1995, p. 410.

Watson, Elizabeth S., review of *Willa and Old Miss Annie, Horn Book,* September-October, 1994, p. 586.

Zvirin, Stephanie, review of *Dear Nobody, Booklist,* October 1, 1992, p. 329.

Zvirin, Stephanie, review of *The Snake-Stone, Booklist,* February 15, 1996, p. 1004.

For More Information See

BOOKS

Children's Books and Their Creators, edited by Anita Silvey, Houghton, 1995, p. 206.

Children's Literature Review, Volume 21, Gale, 1990.

St. James Guide to Young Adult Writers, edited by Tom Pendergast and Sara Pendergast, St. James Press, 1999, pp. 233-35.

PERIODICALS

Booklist, December 15, 1992, p. 745; December 15, 1993, p. 754; July, 1994, p. 1947; May 15, 1998, p. 1625.

Bulletin of the Center for Children's Books, March, 1996, p. 224; December, 1997, p. 122.

Growing Point, May, 1985.

Horn Book, May-June, 1988; November-December, 1992, pp. 726-27.

Junior Bookshelf, August, 1982; December, 1983; October, 1995, p. 168.

Kirkus Reviews, January 1, 1993, p. 59; October 15, 1994, p. 1406; July 1, 1996, p. 916; January 1, 1996, p. 67; September 1, 1997, pp. 1386-87.

Publishers Weekly, October 25, 1993, p. 30; June 24, 1996, p. 46.

Reading Time, May, 1999, p. 5.

School Librarian, May, 1993, p. 54; August, 1996, p. 97; February, 1997, p. 18; summer, 1999, p. 74.

School Library Journal, October, 1993, p. 43; July, 1994, p. 76; December, 1995, p. 79.

Voice of Youth Advocates, June, 1996, pp. 94-95.*

DRUCKER, Malka 1945-

Personal

Born March 14, 1945, in Tucson, AZ; daughter of William Treiber (a clothing manufacturer) and Francine (a writer; maiden name, Epstein) Chermak; married Steven Drucker (a certified public accountant), August 20, 1966 (divorced, 1987); children: Ivan, Max. *Education:* University of California, Los Angeles, B.A., 1967; University of Southern California, teaching credential, 1968.

Addresses

Home—1726 Kelton Ave., Los Angeles, CA 90024. *Agent*—Andrea Brown, 301 West 53rd, New York, NY 10019.

Career

Writer, 1975—. Teacher at University of Judaism, University of Southern California, and Idyllwild School of Music and Art. Member of board, Idyllwild School of Music and Art. *Member:* Society of Children's Book Writers and Illustrators, Association of Jewish Librarians, California Council on Literature for Children and Young People, P.E.N., Beyond Baroque (member of board), Southern California Children's Bookseller's Association.

Awards, Honors

Jewish Book Award nominations, 1982, for *Passover: A Season of Freedom,* and 1984, for *Shabbat: A Peaceful Island;* Award for excellence in a series, Southern California Council on Literature for Children and Young People, 1982, for "Jewish Holidays" series; Janusz Korczak Prize in Children's Literature, Anti-Defamation League, 1988, for *Eliezer Ben-Yehuda, the Father of Modern Hebrew;* Hungry Mind award, 1991, for *Frida Kahlo: Torment and Triumph in Her Life and Art.*

Writings

FOR CHILDREN

(With Tom Seaver) *Tom Seaver: Portrait of a Pitcher,* Holiday House, 1978.

(With George Foster) *The George Foster Story,* Holiday House, 1979, revised edition, 1980.

(With Elizabeth James) *Series TV: How a Television Show Is Made,* Clarion, 1983.

Eliezer Ben-Yehuda: The Father of Modern Hebrew, Lodestar, 1987.

Grandma's Latkes, illustrated by Eve Chwast, Harcourt, 1992.

(With Michael Halperin) *Jacob's Rescue: A Holocaust Story,* Bantam, 1993.

The Family Treasury of Jewish Holidays, illustrated by Nancy Patz, Little, Brown, 1994.

The Sea Monster's Secret, illustrated by Christopher Aja, Harcourt, 1999.

FOR CHILDREN; "JEWISH HOLIDAYS" SERIES

Hanukkah: Eight Nights, Eight Lights, illustrated by Brom Hoban, Holiday House, 1980.

Passover: A Season of Freedom, illustrated by Hoban, Holiday House, 1981.

Rosh Hashanah and Yom Kippur: Sweet Beginnings, illustrated by Hoban, Holiday House, 1981.

Sukkot: A Time to Rejoice, illustrated by Hoban, Holiday House, 1982.

Shabbat: A Peaceful Island, illustrated by Hoban, Holiday House, 1983.

Celebrating Life: Jewish Rites of Passage, Holiday House, 1984.

Frida Kahlo: Torment and Triumph in Her Life and Art, Bantam, 1991.

A Jewish Holiday ABC, illustrated by Rita Pocock, Harcourt, 1992.

FOR ADULTS

(With Gay Block) *Rescuers: Portraits of Moral Courage in the Holocaust,* Holmes & Meier (New York), 1992.

Adaptations

Rescuers: Portraits of Moral Courage in the Holocaust was adapted as a three-part television series, Viacom, 1997.

Sidelights

The author of numerous works of nonfiction for children, Malka Drucker has expanded the knowledge of young readers through her biographies and books describing traditional holidays and ceremonies honored by people of the Jewish faith. Praised for her writing skill and her objectivity in her works for children, Drucker has also collaborated with fellow author Gay Block on an adult title, *Rescuers: Portraits of Moral Courage in the Holocaust.* Similar in focus to her children's work *Jacob's Rescue,* which recounts a young boy's years spent in hiding while Hitler implemented plans to eradicate the Jewish people in Europe, *Rescuers* profiles the men and women of all faiths who risked their lives to save the lives of Jews during this terrible chapter of human history.

Born in 1945 in Tucson, Arizona, Drucker was raised by parents who placed a high value on reading, and who both wrote. Although she was inspired by their example, she didn't begin to view writing as a serious occupation until her teen years. "When I was fourteen, my pet parakeet died and I was miserable," she once told *SATA.* "I picked up my old diary, long abandoned, and wrote of my grief. The words healed me, and I developed a new respect for the power I possessed with words."

A woman of varied interests, Drucker is inspired to write about those things that have captured her imagination since childhood and continue to spark her curiosity. "Going to baseball games and celebrating Jewish holidays are both vivid, sweet memories for me," she explained. "When you're a Jewish kid in New York,

baseball and religious ceremonies are the most important things in your life, so why not write about them?"

In fact, it was Drucker's interest in baseball that prompted her biographies of baseball greats Tom Seaver and George Foster. Published in 1978, her *Tom Seaver: Portrait of a Pitcher* introduces readers to the man who pitched for both the New York Mets and the Cincinnati Reds before retiring from major-league baseball in the 1980s. Writing the book with Seaver's help—he also contributed the book's introduction—Drucker begins her story with young Seaver's Little-League and high-school career, when his short stature made it questionable whether he would ever get to play in the majors. Calling *Tom Seaver* "an exciting sports biography," *Booklist* contributor Ellen Mandel praised the work for introducing young readers to "the man behind the famous right arm—his tastes, his respect for the arts, his drive for perfection, his family life, and his feelings." A critic for *Kirkus Reviews* expressed relief that Drucker "eschews the usual breezy sports-bio slang and comes through with a rounder-than-usual career rundown." *The George Foster Story* received similar praise from critics; a *School Library Journal* reviewer noted that in her description of the 1977 National Baseball League MVP, "Drucker provides a perceptive biography of the man inside the uniform—his perseverance and commitment."

Other biographies by Drucker include *Eliezer Ben-Yehuda: The Father of Modern Hebrew,* which was published in 1987, and *Frida Kahlo: Torment and Triumph in Her Life and Art.* In chronicling the life of Kahlo, a Jewish artist of the early twentieth century, Drucker captured a colorful and enigmatic subject. Born and raised in Mexico and the daughter of an European Jew, Kahlo rejected traditions in favor of the movements toward political and social independence that were growing during her lifetime. Known for her marriage to famous Mexican muralist Diego Rivera, her adoption of communism, and her outlandish lifestyle, Kahlo became a noted artist in her own right, despite a childhood accident that left her crippled for life. "Drucker candidly and compassionately relates Kahlo's total absorption with work and debunks the myths surrounding the strong, sensual woman and artist," maintained *Booklist* contributor Mary Romano Marks. A *Publishers Weekly* contributor had equal praise for the volume, noting that in dealing with such a controversial subject, Drucker approaches Kahlo's life "with a fearlessness to match Kahlo's own."

Drucker's *Jacob's Rescue: A Holocaust Story* is another factual personal history, although it is presented to young readers in fictionalized form. Published in 1993 and co-authored with Michael Halperin, *Jacob's Rescue* is the story of an eight-year-old boy and his younger brother, whose lives were saved when they were offered a way out of the Warsaw Ghetto in 1941. Hidden by the members of the non-Jewish Roslan family even though it would mean certain death for all if the boys were discovered by the ever-vigilant Gestapo, Jacob and his brother move from hiding place to hiding place, and even receive medical care through the brave family's ingenuity. Praising *Jacob's Rescue* in *Booklist,* reviewer

Drucker's 1994 collection of facts, activities, and stories about Jewish holidays draws from both old and new traditions and features selections from such writers as Barbara Cohen and Isaac Bashevis Singer. (Cover illustration by Nancy Patz.)

Hazel Rochman noted: "What gives the story authenticity is not only the harsh physical danger, but also the candid characterization, the honesty about how fear made people act." Equally impressed by the book, a *Kirkus Reviews* critic hailed *Jacob's Rescue* as "a fine, authentic account of quietly sustained heroism of the highest order."

Jewish holidays have always been a central part of Drucker's life, and she shares her knowledge and enthusiasm for these special times in a number of books for young readers. In titles like *Hanukkah: Eight Nights, Eight Lights, Passover: A Season of Freedom,* and *Sukkot: A Time to Rejoice,* Drucker describes each holiday's ceremonies and Orthodox traditions in detail, and provides the historic backdrop and significance for each season. In *Hanukkah,* for example, Drucker includes sections on crafts, foods, and games. *Booklist* contributor Judith Goldberger called the first section of the book, which describes the origins of the holiday, "a reasoned history that takes speculative matters such as miracles respectfully into account while distinguishing them from documental evidence." Reviewing Drucker's *Passover: A Season of Freedom,* a critic for *Bulletin of the Center for Children's Books* called the text "reverent, lucid, and comprehensive." And in one of the

chapters in *Sukkot: A Time to Rejoice,* Drucker "provides simple, imaginative instructions—a high point of each of her books—for building a sukkah [traditional hut]" as a setting for the harvest holiday celebrations, according to a *Kirkus Reviews* commentator.

In addition to publishing separate books on each of the Jewish holidays celebrated worldwide, Drucker has also compiled several holiday guidebooks that encompass all of the traditions in a more general fashion. In *A Jewish Holiday ABC,* she entertains the picture-book set with descriptions of each holiday's components, from candles to rabbi, all of which center around pictures of a family celebrating the special days together. A more detailed work, *The Family Treasury of Jewish Holidays,* provides both a description of the ten major Jewish holidays as well as poems, songs, and portions of the Old Testament and other writings that reflect the traditions involved. "These holidays are deeply meaningful but can be difficult to explain," noted *Bulletin of the Center for Children's Books* reviewer Susan Dove Lempke, "yet Drucker does so simply, clearly, and tenderly" in a work that the author designed for family members to use together.

Drucker continues to devote her writing talents to children, both in her nonfiction works and in picture books, such as *Grandma's Latkes* and *The Sea Monster's Secret.* Her motivation? "I sympathize with the struggle every child has in making sense of the world," she told *SATA.* "I remember my own struggle clearly and it serves as my creative 'mine.'"

Works Cited

Review of *Frida Kahlo: Torment and Triumph in Her Life and Art, Publishers Weekly,* September 20, 1991, p. 136.

Review of *The George Foster Story, School Library Journal,* May, 1979, p. 83.

Goldberger, Judith, review of *Hanukkah: Eight Nights, Eight Lights, Booklist,* October 1, 1980, p. 208.

Review of *Jacob's Rescue: A Holocaust Story, Kirkus Reviews,* June 1, 1993, p. 719.

Lempke, Susan Dove, review of *The Family Treasury of Jewish Holidays, Bulletin of the Center for Children's Books,* November, 1994, pp. 86-87.

Mandel, Ellen, review of *Tom Seaver: Portrait of a Pitcher, Booklist,* July 1, 1978, p. 1683.

Marks, Mary Romano, review of *Frida Kahlo: Torment and Triumph in Her Life and Art, Booklist,* October 1, 1991, pp. 313-14.

Review of *Passover: A Season of Freedom, Bulletin of the Center for Children's Books,* July-August, 1981, p. 211.

Rochman, Hazel, review of *Jacob's Rescue: A Holocaust Story, Booklist,* February 15, 1993, pp. 1051-52.

Review of *Sukkot: A Time to Rejoice, Kirkus Reviews,* October 1, 1982, p. 1108.

Review of *Tom Seaver: Portrait of a Pitcher, Kirkus Reviews,* June 1, 1978, p. 601.

For More Information See

PERIODICALS

Booklist, February 15, 1992, p. 1108.
Bulletin of the Center for Children's Books, February, 1992, pp. 152-53; May, 1992, p. 235.

Horn Book, March-April, 1995, pp. 204-05.
Kirkus Reviews, November 15, 1994, p. 1547.
Publishers Weekly, February 6, 1978, p. 102.
School Library Journal, May, 1993, p. 104; November, 1994, p. 96-97; June, 1999, p. 113.
Voice of Youth Advocates, June, 1993, p. 88.

E

ELLIOTT, Louise

Personal

Born in England; emigrated to Australia, 1983; married Geoffrey Elliott; children: Lucinda, Rebecca, Ben. *Education:* Brighton College of Art, National Diploma in design, 1961; Birmingham University, Art Teachers Diploma, 1964; Queensland University, B.A., 1990.

Addresses

Home—15 Charlane Ave., Indooroopilly, Queensland 4068, Australia. *Electronic mail*—g.l.elliott@uq.net.au.

Louise Elliott

Career

Writer, designer and illustrator. Has conducted creative-writing workshops at Brisbane TAFE, Wordfest, BCC Writers in Library Project, and Western Writers' Week-end; guest speaker at Somerset College Festival of Literature, Warana Writers' Week, "Out of the Box," and FAW Queensland. Literary competition judge for Suncorp, Society of Women Writers, and others; manuscript assessor for Queensland Writers' Centre. *Member:* Queensland Writers' Centre (member of management committee, 1992-94, secretary, 1993-94).

Awards, Honors

Shortlist, Romantic Novel of the Year Award, 1985, for *This Side of Christmas;* Project Grant, Australia Council, 1994; Notable Books, Children's Book Council (Australia), 1994, for *Dangerous Redheads,* and 1998, for *Summer Ghosts.*

Writings

AUTHOR AND ILLUSTRATOR; FOR CHILDREN

Holly, Jam Roll Press, 1992.
Mr. Hornbeam's Treasure Hunt, University of Queensland Press, 1994.

FICTION; FOR YOUNG ADULTS

Dangerous Redheads, University of Queensland Press, 1994.
Lone Bandits, University of Queensland Press, 1995.
Summer Ghosts, Margaret Hamilton Books, 1998.

OTHER

This Side of Christmas, W. H. Allen, 1985.
The Apple Tree, W. H. Allen, 1986.
(Contributor) *Original Sin,* University of Queensland Press, 1996.

Also contributor of essays on arts and crafts to various periodicals.

Work in Progress

Noah's Boat, a picture book.

Sidelights

Louise Elliott told *SATA:* "At sixteen I went to college to learn to be an illustrator because art was the only thing I had ever wanted to do—or been any good at. But instead I became a designer, which at the time seemed close enough.

"Book writing came later, adult novels first, then young adults, younger readers and now, finally, the picture book.

"I have done illustration, for my own books and other people's, in the traditional way—drawing, painting. But now I use the computer as well, which gives another dimension, photography and effects blending with the good old hand-done stuff. Kind of fun.

"I work at home, I always have done. My husband, the artist, paints downstairs, and I write, illustrate, design, and surf the net upstairs. It's a good combination.

"The nice thing about being a writer, or artist, is that you never have to retire, you can just fade into the sunset while still at work."

*   *   *

EMERSON, Sally 1952-

Personal

Born in 1952, in England.

Career

Journalist, author and novelist.

Awards, Honors

Winner, *Vogue* magazine writers' competition, 1972; winner of awards for journalistic excellence.

Writings

NOVELS

Second Sight, Michael Joseph (London), 1980, published as *The Second Sight of Jennifer Hamilton,* Doubleday (Garden City, NY), 1981.
Listeners, Michael Joseph (London), 1983.
Fire Child, Michael Joseph (London), 1987.
Separation, Scribners (London), 1992.
Hush Little Baby, Signet (New York City), 1993.
Heat, Little, Brown (Boston, MA), 1998.

COMPILER

The Kingfisher Nursery Treasury: A Collection of Baby Games, Rhymes, and Lullabies, illustrated by Colin and Moira Maclean, Kingfisher Books (London), 1988, published as *The Nursery Treasury: A Collection of Baby Games, Rhymes, and Lullabies,* Doubleday (Garden City, NY), 1988.
ABCs and Other Learning Rhymes, illustrated by Colin and Moira Maclean, Kingfisher Books, 1992.
(With Pie Corbett) *Action Rhymes,* illustrated by Colin and Moira Maclean, Kingfisher Books, 1992.
Baby Games and Lullabies, illustrated by Colin and Moira Maclean, Kingfisher Books, 1992.
(With Corbett) *Dancing and Singing Games,* illustrated by Colin and Moira Maclean, Kingfisher Books, 1992.
The Kingfisher Nursery Rhyme Songbook: With Easy Music to Play for Piano and Guitar, music arranged by Mary Frank, illustrated by Colin and Moira Maclean, Kingfisher Books, 1992.
Nursery Rhymes, illustrated by Colin and Moira Maclean, Kingfisher Books, 1992.
The Kingfisher Nursery Collection, stories retold by Susan Price, illustrated by Colin and Moira Maclean, Kingfisher Books, 1993.

OTHER

(Editor) *A Celebration of Babies: An Anthology of Poetry and Prose,* Blackie (London), 1986, Dutton/Dial Books (New York City), 1987.
The Orchard Christmas Treasury, Orchard Books (London), 1994.

Sidelights

Sally Emerson, a native of England, is a novelist, anthologist, and editor who has compiled several anthologies for and about children. She made her debut as novelist with *Second Sight,* a coming-of-age tale set in London during the months leading up to the sixteenth birthday of its main character, Jennifer Hamilton. As Jennifer approaches adulthood, she must cope not only with the usual problems of growing up but also with her adulterous mother and the death of her friend. Jennifer, moreover, is not a typical adolescent, for she has psychic powers ("second sight") that allow her to communicate with the ghost of her hero, the nineteenth-century poet Percy Bysshe Shelley. L. D. Burnard, writing in the *Times Literary Supplement,* declared that *Second Sight* does not have "anything new to tell us about youth and age, love and selfishness, dreams and reality," but praised its "calm authority and delicate wit." He also remarked that the portions of the novel seen through Jennifer's eyes are "unusually rich in observations of colour and costume ... and of nuances of mood and emotion, particularly those of adolescence." A reviewer in *Publishers Weekly* lauded *Second Sight* for its "linguistic virtuosity and well-drawn characters," calling it "a remarkable feat in spite of needless complexities."

Jennifer Hamilton appears again in *Listeners,* this time as a married woman who writes biographies for children. When her husband leaves her for a less introverted and more stylish companion, a lonely and despairing Jennifer falls into the clutches of Mrs. Maugham, the leader of an evil spiritualist group. As the suspense builds, the reader begins to wonder whether the malignant influence of Maugham and her followers will drive Jennifer to suicide. In *Books and Bookmen,* Geoffrey Elborn asserted that "the complex situation of the novel in an almost gothic setting could have seemed merely ridiculous and unconvincing had it been clumsily written. Instead Sally Emerson has created a most memorable novel, out of commonplace circumstances which assume a sinister reality."

In the words of Christina Patterson of the *Times Literary Supplement,* Emerson's fourth novel, *Separation* (1992), is a book "about passion, the passion between mothers and children." It opens with Amanda Richardson, a London management consultant, looking for a nanny for her infant daughter. The job is taken by Sarah Adams, who is living in a rundown hotel after separating from George, her lawyer husband. Sarah and George have a six-year-old daughter, Alice, whom Sarah is being prevented from seeing. Like Jennifer Hamilton in Emerson's first two novels, Sarah has supernatural powers, which allow her to establish a psychic link with Alice. Ultimately, Alice wreaks revenge on George. Patterson wrote that "Emerson conveys the magical, indefinable attraction of babies in descriptions calculated to unleash strong feelings in the least maternal of readers. Her social observation is as good as ever."

Emerson's interest in the world of the very young is reflected not only in *Separation* but also in her work as an anthologist. Her earliest anthology, *A Celebration of Babies,* is a small collection of poetry and prose offering perspectives on infants from a wide variety of authors. Mollie Hardwick remarked in *Books and Bookmen* that the volume "is enriched by beautiful and unusual Victorian paintings, and enchanting woodcuts by Arthur Hughes." *The Kingfisher Nursery Treasury,* aimed at preschoolers, offers games, rhymes, and lullabies from traditional and modern sources. Constance A. Mellon,

reviewing the U.S. edition of the work in *School Library Journal,* praised the book's "design, arrangement, and thoughtful illustrations." *The Kingfisher Nursery Treasury* was followed by several other anthologies in the same vein, including *Baby Games and Lullabies* and *Dancing and Singing Games. The Kingfisher Nursery Rhyme Songbook,* also intended for preschoolers, presents forty-seven songs and includes music for piano and guitar. It also offers suggestions for crafts and other entertainments suitable for a young audience.

Works Cited

Burnard, L. D., review of *Second Sight, Times Literary Supplement,* September 12, 1980, p. 984.

Elborn, Geoffrey, review of *Listeners, Books and Bookmen,* August, 1983, p. 34.

Hardwick, Mollie, "Thou, Lovely Thing," *Books and Bookmen,* May, 1986, p. 22.

Mellon, Constance A., review of *The Nursery Treasury, School Library Journal,* January, 1989, p. 70.

Patterson, Christina, review of *Separation, Times Literary Supplement,* February 28, 1992, p. 24.

Review of *Second Sight, Publishers Weekly,* January 2, 1981, p. 44.

For More Information See

PERIODICALS

New York Times Book Review, February 25, 1990, pp. 24-25.

Publishers Weekly, October 5, 1992, p. 72.

School Librarian, February, 1994, p. 16.

School Library Journal, March, 1993, pp. 189-90; March, 1994, p. 214.

Times Literary Supplement, February 28, 1992, p. 24.*

F

FEIFFER, Jules 1929-

Personal

Born January 26, 1929, in the Bronx, NY; son of David (held a variety of jobs from dental technician to salesman) and Rhoda (a fashion designer; maiden name, Davis) Feiffer; married Judith Sheftel (a production executive with Warner Bros.), September 17, 1961 (divorced, 1983); married Jennifer Allen (a journalist), September 11, 1983; children: (first marriage) Kate; (second marriage) Halley. *Education:* Attended Art Students' League, 1946, and Pratt Institute, 1947-48, 1949-51.

Addresses

Office—c/o Publishers-Hall Syndicate, 30 East 42nd St., New York, NY 10017. *Agent*—Robert Lantz, 888 Seventh Ave., New York, NY 10106.

Career

Playwright, cartoonist, and satirist. Assistant to Will Eisner (cartoonist), 1946-51; ghost-scripted *The Spirit,* 1949-51; drew syndicated cartoon, *Clifford,* 1949-51; held various art jobs, 1953-56, including making slide films, as writer for Terrytoons, and as designer of booklets for an art film; cartoons published in *Village Voice,* New York City, 1956—, in *Observer,* London, 1958-66, 1972—, and in *Playboy,* 1959—; cartoons syndicated by Publishers-Hall Syndicate and distributed to more than one hundred newspapers in the United States and abroad. Member of faculty, Yale University Drama School, New Haven, CT, 1972-73. *Military service:* U.S. Army, Signal Corps, 1951-53; worked in a cartoon animation unit. *Member:* Authors League of America, Dramatists Guild (member of council), PEN, Writers Guild of America, East.

Jules Feiffer

Awards, Honors

Academy Award (Oscar) for Best Short-Subject Cartoon, Academy of Motion Picture Arts and Sciences, 1961, for *Munro;* Special George Polk Memorial Award, 1961; most promising playwright, New York Drama Critics, 1966-67, Best Foreign Play of the Year, London

Theatre Critics, 1967, and Outer Critics Circle Award, and Obie Award, *Village Voice,* both 1969, all for *Little Murders;* Outer Critics Circle Award, 1970, for *The White House Murder Case;* Pulitzer Prize, 1986, for editorial cartooning; Children's Book of Distinction designation, *Riverbank Review,* 1999, for *I Lost My Bear.*

Writings

FOR CHILDREN

(Illustrator) Norton Juster, *The Phantom Tollbooth,* Random House, 1961.
The Man in the Ceiling, HarperCollins, 1993.
A Barrel of Laughs, a Vale of Tears, HarperCollins, 1995.
Meanwhile . . . . , HarperCollins, 1997.
I Lost My Bear, Morrow, 1998.
Bark, George, HarperCollins, 1999.

FOR ADULTS; CARTOONS, UNLESS OTHERWISE NOTED

Sick, Sick, Sick: A Guide to Non-Confident Living, McGraw, 1958, with introduction by Kenneth Tynan, Collins (London), 1959.
Passionella and Other Stories, McGraw, 1959.
(Illustrator) Robert Mines, *My Mind Went All to Pieces,* Dial, 1959.
The Explainers, McGraw, 1960.
Boy, Girl, Boy, Girl, Random House, 1961.
Feiffer's Album, Random House, 1963.
Hold Me!, Random House, 1963.
Harry, the Rat with Women (novel), McGraw, 1963.
(Compiler and annotator) *The Great Comic Book Heroes,* Dial, 1965.
The Unexpurgated Memories of Bernard Mergendeiler, Random House, 1965, Collins, 1966.
The Penguin Feiffer, Penguin (London), 1966.
Feiffer on Civil Rights, Anti-Defamation League, 1966.
Feiffer's Marriage Manual, Random House, 1967.
Pictures at a Prosecution: Drawings & Text from the Chicago Conspiracy Trial, Grove, 1971.
Feiffer on Nixon: The Cartoon Presidency, Random House, 1974.
Ackroyd (novel), Simon and Schuster, 1977, Hutchinson (London), 1978.
Tantrum: A Novel-in-Cartoons, Knopf, 1979.
Feiffery: Jules Feiffer's America from Eisenhower to Reagan, Knopf, 1982.
Marriage Is an Invasion of Privacy, and Other Dangerous Views, Andrews, McMeel, 1984.
Feiffer's Children: Including Munro, Andrews, McMeel, 1986.
Ronald Reagan in Movie America: A Jules Feiffer Production, Andrews & McMeel, 1988.
Feiffer: The Collected Works, Volume 1, Fantagraphics Books, 1989.

PLAYS

The Explainers (satirical review), first produced in Chicago, 1961.
The World of Jules Feiffer, first produced in New Jersey, 1962.
Crawling Arnold (one-act; first produced in Spoleto, Italy, 1961), Dramatists Play Service, 1963.

The Unexpurgated Memoirs of Bernard Mergendeiler (first produced in Los Angeles, 1967, produced with other plays as *Collision Course,* Off-Broadway, 1968), in *Collision Course,* edited by Edward Parone, Random House, 1968.
Little Murders (two-act comedy; first produced on Broadway, 1967 [closed after seven performances]; first American play produced by Royal Shakespeare Company in London, 1967; revived Off-Broadway, 1969), Random House, 1968.
God Bless, first produced by Yale School of Drama, 1968; produced by Royal Shakespeare Co., 1968.
Feiffer's People: Sketches and Observations (first produced in Edinburgh, Scotland, 1968; produced in Los Angeles, 1971), Dramatists Play Service, 1969.
Dick and Jane: A One-Act Play (first produced in New York City as part of *Oh! Calcutta!,* revised by Kenneth Tynan, 1969), in *Oh! Calcutta!,* edited by K. Tynan, Grove, 1969.
The White House Murder Case: A Play in Two Acts [and] *Dick and Jane: A One-Act Play* (*The White House Murder Case* first produced in New York City, 1970), Grove, 1970.
(With others) *The Watergate Classics,* first produced at Yale Repertory Theatre, 1973.
Knock-Knock (first produced in New York City, 1974), Hill & Wang, 1976.
Hold Me! (first produced in New York City, 1977), Dramatists Play Service, 1977.
Grown-ups (first produced in New York City, 1981), Samuel French, 1982.
A Think Piece, first produced in Chicago, 1982.
Feiffer's America, first produced in Evanston, IL, 1988.
Carnal Knowledge, first produced in Houston, TX, 1988.
Elliot Loves (first produced in Chicago, 1988), Grove, 1990.

SCREENPLAYS

Little Murders, Twentieth Century-Fox, 1971.
(With Israel Horovitz) *VD Blues,* PBS-TV, 1972, Avon, 1974.
Popeye, Paramount, 1980, as *Popeye, the Movie Novel,* edited and adapted by Richard J. Anobile, Avon, 1980.
(Adapter) *Puss in Boots,* CBS/Fox Video, 1984.
I Want to Go Home, Marvin Karmitz Productions, 1989.

Contributor of sketches to productions of DMZ Cabaret, New York; writer for *Steve Allen Show,* 1964; author of episode "Kidnapped" for *Happy Endings* (series), ABC-TV, 1975; contributor to periodicals, including *Ramparts.*

Feiffer's books have been translated into German, Swedish, Italian, Dutch, French, and Japanese.

Adaptations

Munro (animated cartoon; based on author's story) was produced by Rembrandt Films, 1961; *Crawling Arnold* was produced by WEAV-TV, 1963; *The Apple Tree* (musical by Jerry Bock and Sheldon Harnick; consists of three playlets, one based on Feiffer's "Passionella") was produced at Schubert Theatre, 1966; *Harry, the Rat with*

From **The Phantom Tollbooth,** *written by Norman Juster and illustrated by Feiffer.*

Women (play) was first produced at Detroit Institute of Arts, 1966; *Carnal Knowledge* was produced as a motion picture, Avco Embassy, 1971), Farrar, Straus, 1971, Cape (London), 1971; *Munro* was adapted for videocassette and included on *Academy Award Winners: Animated Short Films,* Vestron Video, 1985; *Grown-Ups* was adapted for film and produced by PBS-TV, 1986, Warner Home Video, 1987.

Sidelights

Before he published his first self-illustrated children's book in 1993, Pulitzer Prize-winning cartoonist Jules Feiffer was probably more well known to young readers as the illustrator of Norman Juster's classic *The Phantom Tollbooth,* which Feiffer illustrated for its 1961 publication. In the years since, Feiffer's satiric cartoons for adults have become a familiar sight in hundreds of newspapers both in the United States and internationally—writing in the *New York Times Book Review,* Daniel Pinkwater described Feiffer's cartoons as "distinctive loose-limbed drawings"—and Feiffer's plays have appeared on numerous stages. It has been only recently that Feiffer has become reacquainted with a young audience through the publication of several entertaining picture books.

Born in the Bronx, New York, in 1929, Feiffer grew up in a household dominated by his parents' strained relationship. His mother, a Polish immigrant of an independent spirit, was not happy as a housewife and mother. While his father, an immigrant and a gentle man, did not have the business instincts required for success in the competitive markets of the United States. The trials of the Great Depression did not help matters in the Feiffer home. Reacting to his parents' stress over money and other matters, and sensing that he was different from other children, Feiffer spent a lot of time holed up in his room, drawing.

When Feiffer was approximately seven years of age, he won a gold medal in an art contest sponsored by a New York department store. A memorable occasion in his childhood which led him to the decision that the following year would be different. World War II was rumbling in Europe, the Depression was leaving more and more grownups he knew out of work, and money was very tight at home. But it was also the golden age of comic books, and *Detective Comics* had appeared on the newsstands. Discontented with his lot as a child, Feiffer knew the only way to change things was to grow up quick and find a good job doing something at which he could excel. He decided to become a cartoonist.

As Feiffer would recall in *The Great Comic Book Heroes:* "I swiped [ideas] diligently from the swipers, drew sixty-four pages in two days, sometimes one day, stapled the product together, and took it out on the street where kids my age sat behind orange crates selling and trading comic books. Mine went for less because they weren't real." He studied the comic strips in the pages of the *New York Times* and the *World-Telegram,* which his father brought home with him after work. He even salvaged newspapers from garbage cans, or got friends to bring him papers after their parents were through with them. "To see 'Terry and the Pirates,'" Feiffer explained, "we'd have to get the *Daily News,* which my family wouldn't allow in the house." The reason: his parents—both Jewish and both Democrats—believed that the publisher of the *Daily News* was anti-Semitic.

Feiffer's high school years were not ones he would ever care to relive. "My idea of going to school was to mark time until I got into the comic-strip business," he once explained in the *New York Times Magazine.* "But I was never rebellious as a kid. It never occurred to me that I could be. I saw who had the guns. I assumed I was outnumbered from the start, so I went underground for the first twenty years of my life. I observed, registered things, but commented as little as possible."

At the age of fifteen Feiffer enrolled at the Art Students' League. "My mother dragged me," the cartoonist recalled to Gary Groth in *Comics Journal.* "I was a very shy kid, and very nervous, truly nervous about putting this talent that I fantasized a lot about on the line . . . . [So] when she . . . took me by the hand and took me to the Art Students' League, I remember screaming bloody murder, I didn't want to go. But she thought I should study anatomy, and it was wonderful."

A few credits short to enroll in college, Feiffer enrolled at the Pratt Institute for a year, but found that the school's preoccupation with European abstract art was little to his liking and switched to night courses. Meanwhile, in 1946, through a stroke of luck, Feiffer became an assistant to cartoonist Will Eisner, one of his childhood idols. "He said I was worth absolutely nothing, but if I wanted to hang out there, and erase pages or do gofer work, that was fine," Feiffer recalled to Groth. Eisner soon had Feiffer writing and doing the layout for "The Spirit." In lieu of what Feiffer felt should be a well-earned pay raise, Eisner let the apprentice cartoonist have the space on the last page of his current strip, and the "Clifford" comic was born.

"Clifford" came to a close in 1951, when Feiffer was drafted into the Army during the Korean War. His experiences as part of the U.S. military would help to focus Feiffer on the subject he would satirize for most of his remaining career—the workings of the U.S. government. "It was the first time I was truly away from home for a long period of time," Feiffer explained to Groth, "and thrown into a world that was antagonistic to

Jimmy, a young cartoonist who does poorly in school, aspires to be the next Walt Disney in Feiffer's 1993 self-illustrated children's book. (Cover illustration by Feiffer.)

everything I believed in, on every conceivable level. In a war that I was out of sympathy with, and in an army that I despised; [an army that] displayed every rule of illogic and contempt for the individual and mindless exercise of power. [That] became my material."

Released from duty in 1953, and having failed to find a publisher for his comic drawings, Feiffer was at work drawing a weekly comic strip for the *Village Voice* by 1956. "We cut a stiff deal," the cartoonist recalled to *Dramatists Guild Quarterly* of his early attempt to get published. "They would publish anything I wrote and drew as long as I didn't ask to be paid." While the agreement might not sound too financially sound, it had the desired result. Soon, Feiffer got a call from an editor at a different publication, who, as Feiffer recalled, "said, 'oh boy, this guy is good, he's in the *Voice*,' and accepted the same stuff his company had turned down when I had come to their offices as an unpublished cartoonist."

Now that Feiffer had paying cartoon jobs, plus his weekly strip at the *Village Voice,* he began to work on honing his style. Heavily influenced by the work of illustrator William Steig, he worried about finding a medium that would give him the line quality he desired, but that he could also work with. In dealing with reproduction, he tended to stiffen up; he couldn't handle a brush well, he couldn't handle a pen. He could handle a pencil, but pencil lines don't reproduce well. Finally, after almost six months, he stumbled on a technique of using wooden dowels to create a dry line approximating that of pencil, which he would draw using poster and diluted black ink.

While continuing his strip at the *Voice,* Feiffer accepted a paying job at Terrytoons to develop an animated morning series. When that didn't pan out, he went to work for *Playboy,* doing a monthly cartoon. Meanwhile, Feiffer had become interested in transferring his ideas to live action. His first play, *Little Murders,* was produced on Broadway in 1967. Working in the dramatic form was a natural fit for Feiffer, who had originally begun *Little Murders* as a novel before switching to all dialogue. He would go on to write a number of other plays, as well as several screenplays that were produced as major motion pictures. His film *Popeye,* starring Robin Williams, was released in 1980, and his stage works, which include the autobiographical *Grown-ups, The White House Murder Case,* and *God Bless,* have been produced both in the United States and in Europe.

In the early 1990s Feiffer transferred his secondary interest from the stage to the world of children's literature. While his work as illustrator of *The Phantom Tollbooth* was still in print, he had done nothing else in the children's book field for almost thirty years. But 1993 would mark his official debut as a children's author with *The Man in the Ceiling,* a story about ten-year-old Jimmy Jibbett and his efforts to win the friendship of the popular Charlie Beemer by expressing a willingness to translate Charlie's stories into cartoons. The only problem? Jimmy can't draw hands, and besides, Charlie's stories are all about violence and blood and guts, which is a far cry from Jimmy's favorite subject matter. Praising Feiffer's "rough-drawn, signature cartoon illustrations," *Booklist* contributor Elizabeth Bush noted "sharp, brash observations of the rocky road to artistic success form a strong secondary theme that extends the novel's audience well beyond the middle grades." Cathryn M. Camper added in *The Five Owls* that *The Man in the Ceiling* "recognizes that a large part of the formation of an artist takes place in his or her youth.... Feiffer conveys ... this with a sense of humor, combining samples of Jimmy's comics to help tell the tale." "Conveyed with ... verve, Feiffer's age-old message about following one's own vision seems almost brand-new," echoed a *Publishers Weekly* contributor.

Feiffer followed *The Man in the Ceiling* with *A Barrel of Laughs, a Vale of Tears,* which a *Publishers Weekly* contributor described as "a sophisticatedly silly fairy tale that relaxes storytelling conventions." In true fairy-tale form, the story focuses on royalty in the person of Prince Roger, who is so upbeat that everyone he meets dissolves into laughter. Intervention in the form of a quest planned out by a local wizard doesn't exactly go according to plan, but all is right in the end in a story that takes a number of unexpected turns, according to critics. Feiffer's next work, *Meanwhile....,* draws on a fantasy tradition of a more modern sort, as comic-book fan Raymond, pursued by his angry mother, decides to pull the "Meanwhile..." dialogue balloon out of his comic book to see if it will transport him somewhere else in a hurry. It works, drawing him into a host of adventures, including time aboard a pirate ship, where the "Meanwhile...." device still proves useful. "Frantic action and the clever theme make this a great read-aloud," concluded *School Library Journal* contributor Lisa S. Murphy, while Stephanie Zvirin stated in *Booklist* that "Feiffer's funny, freewheeling, action-packed artwork" will be appreciated by even the read-to-me set.

Continuing his work for children, Feiffer has also published *I Lost My Bear,* a more traditional picture-book effort. In this 1998 work, a young girl carelessly tosses aside her favorite stuffed toy, and then cannot find it a short while later. Following the advice of several family members, the little girl turns detective and hunts for the bear in a crazy quilt of rectangular panels outfitted in what *School Library Journal* contributor Julie Cummins described as "hand-lettered text, dialogue balloons, and the breezy line" characteristic of Feiffer's energetic style. A host of lost articles are found, but no bear. Bedtime approaches, which means going to sleep without Teddy, until the mystery is solved by Mom. "The girl's palpable concern for her bear, with all the urgency of an adult's distress over missing car keys, will evoke both amusement and empathy among readers of all ages," in the opinion of a *Publishers Weekly* contributor.

On the heels of the successful *I Lost My Bear* came *Bark, George,* a reversal of the old-lady-who-swal-

Roger, a prince with a gift for making people laugh, is sent on a quest by his father, the purpose of which is to turn him into a sober young man worthy of kingship. (Cover illustration by Feiffer.)

lowed-a-fly story. George-the-puppy's mother wants George to bark, but he can only meow, oink, moo, and make various other barnyard sounds. A trip to the vet produces a whole stable of beasts pulled out of George's mouth, and leads to a surprise ending. Critics commented on the spareness of this title, in text and illustration, but stated in no way did it detract from the book's charm. Stephanie Zvirin of *Booklist* observed that stacked against some of the glitzier picture books, *Bark, George* looked plain. "But oh, the expression Feiffer manages to coax out of a few keen strokes," she said. A *Publishers Weekly* reviewer referred to the pen-an-ink drawings as "studies in minimalism and eloquence," with the characters' body language registering "intense effort and amazement." Karin Snelson, in an online review on Amazon.com, also commented on the simplicity of the offering, but enthused: "In a world of often overdone or underdone picture books, this fine Feiffer creation is just right," and called his illustrations "intensely expressive, alive, and hilarious."

Since the late 1950s, Feiffer's cartoons have appeared regularly in numerous newspapers across the United States, as well as in the *Village Voice, Playboy,* and the London *Observer,* which began including a weekly Feiffer cartoon in 1958. Many of his strips have been

Until it was almost too late. He reached for his gun.

He didn't have a gun.

How could he be a cowboy out West and not have a gun?

The only thing he found in his holster was a rusty bullet.

From* Meanwhile, *written and illustrated by Feiffer.

published in collections, including *Feiffer's Album, Feiffer on Nixon,* and *Feiffer's Children.* In 1986 he was honored with a Pulitzer Prize for editorial cartooning. "[Just] as wonderful as winning the award was the response from friends and strangers," the satirist told David Astor in *Editor and Publisher.* "It reaffirmed the reason I've been doing the cartoons all these years ... and gave me a sense of rejuvenation. One assumes there's an audience out there, but it's not always evident."

Works Cited

Astor, David, "An Unexpected Pulitzer for Jules Feiffer," *Editor and Publisher,* May 31, 1986.

Review of *Bark, George, Publishers Weekly,* June 21, 1999, p. 66.

Review of *A Barrel of Laughs, a Vale of Tears, Publishers Weekly,* November 27, 1995, p. 70.

Brantley, Robin, "'Knock Knock' 'Who's There?' 'Feiffer'", *New York Times Magazine,* May 16, 1976.

Bush, Elizabeth, review of *The Man in the Ceiling, Booklist,* November 15, 1993, p. 620.

Camper, Cathryn M., review of *The Man in the Ceiling, The Five Owls,* January-February, 1994, pp. 66-67.

Cummins, Julie, review of *I Lost My Bear, School Library Journal,* March, 1998, p. 179.

Duran, Christopher, "Jules Feiffer, Cartoonist—Playwright," *Dramatists Guild Quarterly,* winter, 1987.

Feiffer, Jules, *The Great Comic Book Heroes,* Dial, 1965.

Groth, Gary, "Memories of a Pro Bono Cartoonist," *Comics Journal,* August, 1988.

Review of *I Lost My Bear, Publishers Weekly,* January 26, 1998, p. 91.

Review of *The Man in the Ceiling, Publishers Weekly,* October 25, 1993, p. 62.

Murphy, Lisa S., review of *Meanwhile....,* School Library Journal, September, 1997, p. 180.

Pinkwater, Daniel, review of *A Barrel of Laughs, a Vale of Tears, New York Times Book Review,* December 31, 1995.

Snelson, Karin, review of *Bark, George,* Amazon.com, October 20, 1999.

Zvirin, Stephanie, review of *Bark, George, Booklist,* August 19, 1999, p. 2052.

Zvirin, Stephanie, review of *Meanwhile....,* Booklist, December 1, 1997, p. 636.

For More Information See

BOOKS

Contemporary Literary Criticism, edited by Carolyn Riley, Gale, Volume 64, 1991, pp. 147-64.

Dictionary of Literary Biography, Gale, Volume 7: *Twentieth-Century American Dramatists,* 1981, pp. 172-78, Volume 44: *American Screenwriters,* 1986, pp. 132-37.

PERIODICALS

Bulletin of the Center for Children's Books, December, 1993, pp. 120-21; February, 1996, p. 189.

Horn Book, September-October, 1997, p. 557.

Quill & Quire, November, 1993, p. 40.

Kirkus Reviews, July 15, 1997, p. 1110; March 15, 1998, p. 402.

Riverbank Review, spring, 1999, p. 22.

School Library Journal, January, 1996, p. 108; September, 1999, p. 182.*

*   *   *

FINE, Anne 1947-

Personal

Born December 7, 1947, in Leicester, England; daughter of Brian (a chief scientific experimental officer) and Mary Laker; married Kit Fine (a university professor), 1968 (divorced); children: two daughters. *Education:* University of Warwick, B.A. (with honors), 1968.

Addresses

Home—County Durham, England. *Agent*—David Higham Associates, Limited, 5-8 Lower John St., Golden Square, London W1R 4HA, England.

Career

Cardinal Wiseman Girls' Secondary School, Coventry, England, English teacher, 1968-70; Oxford Committee for Famine Relief (OXFAM), Oxford, England, assistant

Anne Fine

information officer, 1970-71; Saughton Jail, Edinburgh, Scotland, teacher, 1971-72; freelance writer, 1973—. Volunteer for Amnesty International.

Awards, Honors

Guardian/Kestrel Award nominations, 1978, for *The Summer-House Loon,* 1983, for *The Granny Project,* and 1987, for *Madame Doubtfire;* Book Award, Scottish Arts Council, 1986, for *The Killjoy; Observer* Prize for Teenage Fiction nomination, 1987, for *Madame Doubtfire;* Parents' Choice award, 1988, for *Alias Madame Doubtfire;* Smarties (6-8) Award, and Carnegie Highly Commended designation, both 1990, both for *Bill's New Frock;* Carnegie Medal, 1989, and *Guardian* Award for Children's Fiction, 1990, both for *Goggle-Eyes; Publishing News's* Children's Author of the Year, British Book Awards, 1990, runner-up, 1991; Notable Book, American Library Association (ALA), Best Books, *School Library Journal,* and International Reading Association Young Adult Choice citations, all 1991, all for *My War with Goggle-Eyes;* Carnegie Medal, 1992, and Whitbread Children's Novel award, 1993, both for *Flour Babies;* Whitbread Children's Book of the Year, 1996, and Notable Book, ALA, and *Booklist* Award for Youth Fiction, both 1997, all for *The Tulip Touch;* Hans Christian Andersen Award nomination (British), 1998. Shortlisted for Children's Laureate, 1999.

Writings

FICTION; FOR CHILDREN

Scaredy-Cat, illustrated by Vanessa Julian-Ottie, Heinemann, 1985.

Anneli the Art Hater, Methuen Children's, 1986.

Crummy Mummy and Me, illustrated by David Higham, Malin/Deutsch, 1988.

A Pack of Liars, Hamish Hamilton, 1988.

Stranger Danger?, illustrated by Jean Baylis, Hamilton Children's, 1989.

Bill's New Frock, illustrated by Philippe Dupasquier, Methuen, 1989.

A Sudden Puff of Glittering Smoke (also see below), illustrated by Adriano Gon, Picadilly Press, 1989.

Only a Show, illustrated by Valerie Littlewood, Hamish Hamilton, 1990.

A Sudden Swirl of Icy Wind (also see below), illustrated by David Higham, Picadilly Press, 1990.

The Country Pancake, illustrated by Philippe Dupasquier, Methuen Children's, 1990.

Poor Monty (picture book), illustrated by Clara Vulliamy, Clarion, 1991, Methuen Children's, 1992.

The Worst Child I Ever Had, illustrated by Vulliamy, Hamish Hamilton, 1991.

A Sudden Glow of Gold (also see below), Picadilly Press, 1991.

Design-a-Pram, Heinemann, 1991.

The Same Old Story Every Year, Hamish Hamilton, 1992.

The Genie Trilogy (contains *A Sudden Puff of Glittering Smoke, A Sudden Swirl of Icy Wind,* and *A Sudden Glow of Gold*), Mammoth, 1992.

The Angel of Nitshill Road, illustrated by K. Aldous, Methuen Children's, 1992.

The Haunting of Pip Parker, Walker, 1992.

Chicken Gave It to Me, illustrated by Philippe Dupasquier, Methuen Children's, 1992, published in the U.S. as *The Chicken Gave It to Me,* illustrated by Cynthia Fisher, Joy Street (Boston, MA), 1993.

The Diary of a Killer Cat, illustrated by Steve Cox, Hamilton, 1994.

Press Play, Picadilly Press, 1994.

Celebrity Chicken, illustrated by Tim Archbold, Longman, 1995.

Keep It in the Family, Penguin, 1996.

Countdown, illustrated by David Higham, Heinemann, 1996.

How to Write Really Badly, illustrated by Philippe Dupasquier, Methuen, 1996.

Care of Henry, illustrated by Paul Howard, Walker, 1997.

Loudmouth Louis, illustrated by Kate Aldous, Puffin, 1998.

(Reteller) *The Twelve Dancing Princesses,* illustrated by Debi Gliori, Scholastic (London), 1998.

Ruggles, Mammoth, 1998.

Charm School, illustrated by Ros Asquith, Doubleday, 1999.

Roll Over, Roly, illustrated by Phillipe Dupasquier, Puffin, 1999.

Bad Dreams, illustrated by Susan Winter, Doubleday, 2000.

FICTION; FOR YOUNG ADULTS

The Summer-House Loon, Methuen, 1978, Crowell, 1979.

The Other, Darker Ned, Methuen, 1979.

The Stone Menagerie, Methuen, 1980.

Round behind the Ice-House, Methuen, 1981.

The Granny Project, Methuen, 1983, Farrar, Straus, 1983.

Madame Doubtfire, Hamilton Children's, 1987, published as *Alias Madame Doubtfire,* Joy Street, 1988.

Goggle-Eyes, Hamish Hamilton, 1989, published in the U.S. as *My War with Goggle-Eyes,* Little, Brown, 1989.

The Book of the Banshee, Hamish Hamilton, 1991, Joy Street, 1992.

Flour Babies, Hamish Hamilton, 1992, Little, Brown, 1994.

Step by Wicked Step, Hamish Hamilton, 1995, Little, Brown, 1996.

The Tulip Touch, Hamish Hamilton, 1996, Little, Brown, 1997.

OTHER

The Granny Project (play; adaptation of author's novel of the same title), Collins, 1986.

The Killjoy (adult novel), Mysterious Press, 1986, Black Swan (London), 1987.

Taking the Devil's Advice (adult novel), Viking, 1990.

Facing Three Ways: Woodfield Lectures VXI, Woodfield, 1993.

In Cold Domain (adult novel), Viking, 1994.

The Family Tree: The Ronald M. Hubbs and Margaret S. Hubbs Lectures, University of St. Thomas, 1995.

Telling Liddy: A Sour Comedy (adult novel), Bantam, 1998.

Telling Tales: An Interview with Anne Fine, Mammoth, 1999.

Also author of radio play *The Captain's Court Case,* 1987. Contributor of short stories to periodicals.

Anne Fine's books have been translated into twenty-six languages and most are available on cassette.

Adaptations

Goggle-Eyes was produced on cassette by Chivers Sound & Vision, 1992, and adapted as a British television series; *Alias Madame Doubtfire* was made into a motion picture starring Robin Williams, Sally Field, and Pierce Brosnan, Twentieth Century-Fox, 1993.

Sidelights

In such children's books as *Alias Madame Doubtfire, The Tulip Touch,* and *My War with Goggle-Eyes,* novelist Anne Fine brings her keen comic insight to bear on family problems, particularly those caused by divorce. "I was brought up in the country, in a family of five girls, including one set of triplets," Fine once told *SATA.* "Family relationships have always interested me and it is with the close members of their families that the characters in my books are either getting, or not getting, along." *St. James Guide to Children's Writers* essayist Anthea Bell characterized Fine's style as "trenchantly witty," and called her books "20th-century comedies of manners, offering stylish entertainment to older children

with a certain amount of sophistication." In addition to books for both children and young adults, Fine is the author of several adult novels, including *Taking the Devil's Advice,* and *In Cold Domain.*

Born in 1947 in Leicester, England, Fine possessed a love of books and reading from an early age. "As the story was always told, the local education authority took pity on my mother and let her pack me off to Highlands Road Infant School two years earlier than usual," the author related in her *Something about the Author Autobiography Series* (*SAAS*) essay. "I was three. And so it is that I can truthfully claim that, apart from stepping off that log into the duckweed, I have no memory at all of a time when I couldn't read." As a result of entering school early, Fine was ahead of her class and was allowed to spend time reading. "I'd read everything in all the classrooms," she recalled. "There was no school library. And so I was allowed to scour the shelves in the headmistress's office for things to read.... And nobody ever came to hurry me or fetch me back. Yes, it was my first library."

Writing became a favorite activity as well. "What I loved writing were stories," the author continued in her *SAAS* essay, "and I was lucky here.... When I was young, we were allowed to fly in English. 'Write an essay,' they'd tell us. 'At least three sides—and I *mean* that, Shirley. No talking. You've got till break. Now just shut up and get on with it.' They'd chalk some titles— any old titles—up on the board.... Oh, bliss! You'd have to be halfway to being an idiot, frankly, not to be able to twist at least one of the titles into something you could write about."

But while the young Fine found writing an enjoyable activity that came easily to her, she didn't harbor ambitions to be an author. "Did I know I was going to be a writer?" Fine related in *SAAS.* "Not at the start.... The earliest I know the idea must have surfaced was when, in secondary school, when I was about twelve, a strange thing happened. Miss Sinton was teaching us English. I think she was probably fed up with us already. Certainly she'd made us pull our desks apart from one another, dished out some written work, and was pacing up and down between the desks, hushing and scolding, and pointing out mistakes. It was no time to start causing trouble.... I must really have wanted to know, to pick that time to stick my arm out like a traffic cop, stopping her in her tracks, and ask her outright: 'Could *I* be a writer?' She looked down her nose at the arm that prevented her from sweeping past. Hastily I drew it back. Then she looked down her nose at me. But I persisted. 'Could I?' And, cross as she was with the whole pack of us, she gave me an answer, and I'll always be grateful for that. She wasn't too friendly about it. But she was straight. 'Oh, yes,' she said. '*You* could.'"

Nevertheless, Fine didn't begin writing until after she had graduated from college, married, and begun to raise a family. At home with her first child, Fine found herself increasingly isolated. "Clinically depressed, and kept from the library by a snowstorm, I waited till the baby fell asleep, then snatched up a pencil and began to write," she recalled in *SAAS.* "It came out fast and easily, far more so than anything I've written since. And it was a sunny book. A lot of what I've written since is comedy, but usually it has a black edge. That first book was truly light in spirit. When I look back at the bleak, miserable creature who sat down to write it, I can hardly believe that she was me, and that she wrote a book like that."

In what would become her first published book, *The Summer-House Loon,* Fine presents Ione Muffet, the teenage daughter of a blind college professor who is sometimes oblivious to her. The novel portrays a single, farcical day in Ione's life as she attempts to match her father's secretary with an intelligent yet fumbling graduate student. Calling the novel "original and engaging ... mischievous, inventive and very funny," *Times Literary Supplement* writer Peter Hollindale praised Fine for "a fine emotional delicacy which sensitively captures, among all the comic upheaval, the passionate solitude of adolescence." *The Summer-House Loon* is "not just a funny book, although it is certainly that," Marcus Crouch of *Junior Bookshelf* likewise commented. "Here is a book with deep understanding, wisdom and compassion. It tosses the reader between laughter and tears with expert dexterity."

Fine's sequel, *The Other, Darker Ned,* finds Ione organizing a charity benefit for famine victims. "Through [Ione's] observations of other people" in both these works, Margery Fisher noted in *Growing Point,* "we have that delighted sense of recognition which comes in reading novels whose characters burst noisily and eccentrically out of the pages." While these books "are not for everyone, requiring a certain amount of sophistication," Anthea Bell remarked in *Twentieth-Century Children's Writers,* for readers "in command of that sophistication they are stylishly lighthearted entertainment."

Reflecting their author's personal dedication to social concerns, several of Fine's novels directly examine such issues as homelessness and care of the elderly. *The Stone Menagerie,* in which a boy discovers that a couple is living on the grounds of a mental hospital, is "devised with a strict economy of words, an acute sense of personality and a shrewd, ironic humour that once more shows Anne Fine to be one of the sharpest and humorous observers of the human condition writing today for the young," Fisher wrote in *Growing Point.* And using humor while "tackling the aged and infirm," Fine's *The Granny Project* "against all the odds contrives to be both audacious and heart-warming," Charles Fox remarked in *New Statesman.* The story of how four siblings conspire to keep their grandmother out of a nursing home by making her care a school assignment, *The Granny Project* is "mordantly funny, ruthlessly honest, yet compassionate in its concern," Nancy C. Hammond noted in *Horn Book.*

Kitty's troublesome relationship with her mother's new boyfriend forms the backdrop of Fine's 1989 novel. (Cover illustration by Rick Mujica.)

Alias Madame Doubtfire brings a more farcical approach to a serious theme, this time the breaking up of a family. "Novels about divorce for children are rarely funny," Roger Sutton observed in the *Bulletin of the Center for Children's Books,* but Fine's work "will have readers laughing from the first page." To gain more time with his children, out-of-work actor Daniel poses as Madame Doubtfire, a supremely capable housekeeper, and gets a job in his ex-wife Miranda's household. Miranda remains blind to her housekeeper's identity while the children quickly catch on, leading to several amusing incidents. But "beneath the farce, the story deals with a serious subject," Mark Geller stated in *New York Times Book Review:* "the pain children experience when their parents divorce and then keep on battling." "The comedy of disguise allows the author to skate over the sexual hates and impulses inherent in the situation without lessening the candour of her insights into the irreconcilable feelings of both adults and children," Margery Fisher concluded in her *Growing Point* review. "Readers of the teenage novel, weary of perfunctory blue-prints of reality, should be thankful to Anne Fine for giving them such nourishing food for thought within an entertaining piece of fiction."

Crummy Mummy and Me and *A Pack of Liars* "are two more books whose prime intent is to make young people laugh," Chris Powling of the *Times Educational Supplement* observed. "Both exploit the standard comic techniques of taking a familiar situation, turning it on its head, and shaking it vigorously to see what giggles and insights fall into the reader's lap." *A Pack of Liars* recounts how a school assignment to write to a pen pal turns into a mystery of sorts, while *Crummy Mummy and Me* presents a role-reversal in the relationship between an irresponsible mother and her capable daughter. "Details of the plots, though neatly worked out, may sometimes seem a little farfetched in the abstract," Anthea Bell noted in her *Twentieth-Century Children's Writers* essay; "in practice, however, the sheer comic verve of the writing carries them off." Powling agreed, commenting that "once again the narrative shamelessly favours ingenuity over plausibility on the pretty safe assumption that a reader can't complain effectively while grinning broadly." Both books, the critic concluded, "offer welcome confirmation that humour is closer to humanity than apostles of high seriousness care to admit."

In *My War with Goggle-Eyes,* Fine offers yet another "comic yet perceptive look at life after marriage," Ilene Cooper stated in *Booklist.* From the opening, in which young Kitty relates to a schoolmate how her mother's boyfriend "Goggle-Eyes" came into her life, "to the happy-ever-after-maybe ending, Fine conveys a story about relationships filled with humor that does not ridicule and sensitivity that is not cloying," Susan Schuller commented in *School Library Journal.* In showing how Kitty gradually learns to accept her mother's new relationship, "Anne Fine writes some of the funniest—and truest—family fight scenes to be found," Roger Sutton observed in *Bulletin of the Center for Children's Books.* The result is "a book that is thoroughly delightful to read," Schuller concluded.

The Book of the Banshee makes fun reading for anyone who has had to share living space with an adolescent female. Estelle Flowers has become a teenager, and the Flowers home has become a war zone, in the opinion of brother Will, who narrates the novel. With his parents distraught over Estelle's constant histrionics, Will fends for himself, in a novel that *Horn Book* contributor Hanna B. Zeiger maintained "will bring many a laugh to the reader." In the opinion of *School Library Journal* contributor Connie Tyrrell Burns, *The Book of the Banshee* "has some of the funniest fight scenes in YA literature," while also operating as "a well-crafted work with layers of meaning and serious themes richly interwoven with the more comic ones." "Estelle's adolescent angst and injuries" are handled capably, according to *Bulletin of the Center for Children's Books* contributor Roger Strong, who added that, "when it comes to family fights," Fine always provides her readers with "the best seat in the house."

Winner of the Carnegie Medal, considered one of England's most prestigious literary awards, Fine's 1992 novel *Flour Babies* looks at the flip-side of the parent-

A NOVEL BY ANNE FINE
AUTHOR OF *ALIAS MADAME DOUBTFIRE*

Flour Babies

★"A poignant, gloriously funny book." —*Booklist*, Starred

Fine was awarded a Carnegie Medal for this 1992 novel about a class of underachieving students who are assigned to take care of "babies," which are actually six-pound bags of flour.

child relationship. Inspired by a magazine article that described a class project to make teens appreciate the hard work involved in parenthood, *Flour Babies* finds underachieving teen Simon Martin and the rest of his class of troublemakers each assigned to care for a six-pound sack of flour as if it was an infant. Along with the rest of his class, Simon ridicules the idea at first, but gradually begins to transfer the caring behavior he was never given as a child to his flour baby. As an essayist noted in *Children's Books and Their Creators,* Fine's "hulking teenage protagonist, Simon Martin, reaches new levels of self-awareness and is perhaps the most appealing character to be found in any of the author's books." While imbuing *Flour Babies* with her characteristic humor, Fine "takes a down-to-earth scenario and, like her protagonist, turns it into an extraordinary adventure in living and learning," in the opinion of a *Publishers Weekly* contributor.

Step by Wicked Step would find its author in a slightly more serious frame of mind than she had been while writing the comical *Flour Babies,* as she tackles her characteristic subject of divorce and shifting family relationships in a serious vein. The novel is narrated by a succession of high school-age classmates, each beginning his or her portion of the story where another has left off. Claudia, Pixie, Colin, Ralph, and Bob are on an overnight field trip and spend a stormy night in a creaky, nineteenth-century house. While exploring the house, the students find a diary written by a previous resident more than a hundred years ago, and a reading of the diarist's entries describing the gradual destruction of his family due to the controlling personality of a strict stepfather sparks a discussion of interactions with stepparents and other aspects of modern family life. Each of the teens tells his or her story of life after divorce, tales imbued with their frustrations, fears, and sadness. "Each storyteller has learned that those who shatter families are sometimes not good at fixing them, and that someone has to try to get along, 'step by wicked step,'" according to Jamie S. Hansen in her summary of the novel for *Voice of Youth Advocates.* Praising the novel as a "surefire success," *School Library Journal* contributor Julie Cummins noted that Fine's protagonists "are genuine, their stories are poignant, and the book as a whole is affecting without being maudlin, didactic, or biblio therapeutic."

The Tulip Touch "takes Anne Fine into new territory," according to Anthea Bell in her *St. James Guide to Children's Writers* essay; "Gone is the wry humour, although the sharp detailed observation of human behavior remains." In this highly praised work, published in 1997, Fine tells the story of Natalie, who lives in rural England where her family manages a grand hotel called the Palace which caters to well-heeled out-of-towners. With children her age at a premium, Natalie is eager to become friends with Tulip, a local farm girl whose eccentric behavior eventually reveals a bitter, dark side to her personality. Only gradually does self-effacing Natalie realize she has lost confidence in herself, as a result of her participation in the increasingly dangerous games initiated by her unusual and strong-willed new friend. "This complex and compelling book hits hard at a society which is aware of child abuse that is just within the limits of the law and so, feeling powerless to act, does nothing about it," explained *Magpies* reviewer Joan Zahnleiter, describing Tulip as a victim of a "sadistic father," "neglected and deeply disturbed with a need to possess and humiliate." Noting that Fine only hints at the state of affairs that brought Tulip to her current emotional state, *Booklist* reviewer Hazel Rochman wrote that, "with thrilling intensity, she dramatizes the attraction the good girl feels for the dangerous outsider.... [Fine's] message grows right out of an action-packed story that not only humanizes the bully but also reveals the ugly secrets of the respectable." Concluding her laudatory review of *The Tulip Touch* in *Bulletin of the Center for Children's Books,* Deborah Stevenson noted that "while many children's books underestimate the intensity of youthful

Natalie is intrigued by the sinister games that her friend Tulip invents until Tulip's "pranks" turn evil and Natalie cannot extricate herself from their destructive relationship. (Cover illustration by Joe Baker.)

friendship and the seriousness of its repercussions, this one goes right to the heart of the matter."

The Tulip Touch was written during a particularly bleak year; as Fine commented in an interview with *Booklist's* Hazel Rochman: The novel was sparked by an incident where two young adolescents kidnaped a toddler from a English shopping mall and killed him. While, like her fellow Brits, Fine was horrified at the murder itself, it was the reaction by the population at large that upset her even more. "Everybody had this sense that our culture— what was left of it—was absolutely in free fall.... There were some horrible, horrible, horrible cases, probably as psychologically damaging to the British as that 'wilding' in Central Park [where a gang of boys murdered another teen] was in the U.S. People were saying, 'We can't have a society like this anymore.'" While Fine usually injects a healthy dose of humor into her children's books, writing about violence perpetrated by young people was a subject where comedy seemed inappropriate; she admitted that *The Tulip Touch* was likely her darkest novel. But she also maintains that it successfully makes the point that, although things are bad, each individual is free to make the personal choice whether to go along with evil or act according to his or her own conscience, and each of us also has the ability to "hold sympathy and responsibility for the ones that fall."

Throughout her many books for children, Fine focuses primarily on "that period during which the stability of childhood, when almost all decisions are made by others, is giving way to a wider world," as she once explained to *SATA*. "A sense of the need for a sort of personal elbow-room is developing, and people outside the family seem to be showing other ways to go. Growing through to a full autonomy is, for anyone, a long and doggy business, and for some more sabotaged than others by their nature or upbringing, it can seem impossible. I try to show that the battle through the chaos and confusions is worthwhile and can, at times, be seen as very funny." And in *SAAS*, Fine summarized her feelings about the power of fiction: "It changes people, and it changes lives. When we are young, we read about the miller's daughter spinning her straw to gold. And that, I believe, is the writer's great privilege. We only gain from letting our childhoods echo down the years, and we're allowed to spend our lifetimes spinning straw."

Works Cited

Bell, Anthea, essay on Fine in *St. James Guide to Children's Writers*, St. James Press, 1999, pp. 367-70.

Bell, essay on Fine in *Twentieth-Century Children's Writers*, St. James Press, 1989, pp. 336-37.

Burns, Connie Tyrrell, review of *The Book of the Banshee*, *School Library Journal*, December, 1991, pp. 135-36.

Essay on Fine in *Children's Books and Their Creators*, Houghton, 1995, p. 239-40.

Cooper, Ilene, review of *My War with Goggle-Eyes*, *Booklist*, April 15, 1989, p. 1465.

Crouch, Marcus, review of *The Summer-House Loon*, *Junior Bookshelf*, August, 1978, pp. 202-203.

Cummins, Julie, review of *Step by Wicked Step*, *School Library Journal*, June, 1996, pp. 121-22.

Fine, Anne, essay in *Something about the Author Autobiography Series*, Volume 15, Gale, 1993, p. 141-55.

Fisher, Margery, review of *Madame Doubtfire*, *Growing Point*, September, 1987, p. 4858.

Fisher, review of *The Stone Menagerie*, *Growing Point*, September, 1980, p. 3756.

Fisher, review of *The Summer-House Loon* and *The Other, Darker Ned*, *Growing Point*, May, 1990, pp. 5343-44.

Review of *Flour Babies*, *Publishers Weekly*, March 21, 1994, p. 73.

Fox, Charles, "Beyond Tact," *New Statesman*, December 2, 1983, p. 26.

Geller, Mark, review of *Alias Madame Doubtfire*, *New York Times Book Review*, May 1, 1988, p. 34.

Hammond, Nancy C., review of *The Granny Project*, *Horn Book*, October, 1983, p. 573.

Hansen, Jamie S., review of *Step by Wicked Step*, *Voice of Youth Advocates*, August, 1996, p. 156.

Hollindale, Peter, "Teenage Tensions," *Times Literary Supplement*, July 7, 1978, p. 767.

Powling, Chris, "Relative Values," *Times Educational Supplement*, June 3, 1988, p. 49.

Rochman, Hazel, "British Author Wins *Booklist* Award for Youth Fiction" (interview), *Booklist*, January 1, 1998, p. 810-11.

Rochman, review of *The Tulip Touch*, *Booklist*, September 15, 1997, p. 230.

Schuller, Susan, review of *My War with Goggle-Eyes*, *School Library Journal*, May, 1989, p. 104.

Stevenson, Deborah, review of *The Tulip Touch*, *Bulletin of the Center for Children's Books*, September, 1997, pp. 3-4.

Strong, Roger, review of *The Book of the Banshee*, *Bulletin of the Center for Children's Books*, February, 1992, p. 154.

Sutton, Roger, review of *Alias Madame Doubtfire*, *Bulletin of the Center for Children's Books*, April, 1988, p. 155.

Sutton, review of *My War with Goggle-Eyes*, *Bulletin of the Center for Children's Books*, May, 1989, p. 222.

Zahnleiter, Joan, review of *The Tulip Touch*, *Magpies*, March, 1997, p. 36.

Zeiger, Hanna B., review of *The Book of the Banshee*, *Horn Book*, March-April, 1992, p. 209.

For More Information See

BOOKS

Children's Literature Review, Volume 25, Gale, 1991, pp. 27-36.

PERIODICALS

Booklist, January 1 & 15, 1998, p. 734.

Bulletin of the Center for Children's Books, May, 1996, pp. 299-300.

Horn Book, September-October, 1997, p. 568-69.

Junior Bookshelf, October, 1996, p. 200.

Kliatt, September, 1999, p. 16.

Quill & Quire, June, 1995, pp. 60-61.

*   *   *

FRANSON, Leanne R. 1963-

Personal

Born August 7, 1963, in Regina, Saskatchewan, Canada; daughter of Hilding Otto (an urban planner) and Elaine Helene (a nurse; maiden name, Schatz) Franson. *Education:* Attended University of Saskatchewan, 1981-82; Concordia University, Montreal, Quebec, B.F.A. (with distinction), 1985, additional study, 1986-88; also attended Banff School of Fine Arts, 1988-89. *Politics:* "Leftist/socialist." *Religion:* "Questioning agnostic." *Hobbies and other interests:* Cartooning, ceramics, literature, weightlifting.

Addresses

Home and office—4323 Parthenais, Montreal, Quebec, Canada H2H 2G2. *Electronic mail*—inkspots@ videotron.ca.

Career

Freelance illustrator, 1991—. Work represented in exhibitions at Flemington Gallery in Australia, Gabrielle Roy Library in Quebec City, Quebec, and Galerie 303 in Montreal, Quebec. *Member:* Association des Illustrateurs et Illustratrices du Quebec (member of board of directors, 1992-93), Regroupment des Artistes en Arts Visuels du Quebec (RAAV).

Awards, Honors

Governor General's Award nomination, illustration of French children's literature, Canada Council, 1997, Prix Saint-Exupery, Paris, France, 1997, and Prix Alvine-Belisle, best children's book of 1997, Quebec Librarians' Association, 1998, all for *L'Ourson qui Voulait une Juliette.*

Illustrator

Linda Brousseau, *Marelie de la Mer,* Editions Pierre Tisseyre (Montreal, Quebec), 1993, translation by David Homel published as *Marina's Star,* J. Lorimer (Toronto), 1997.

Brousseau, *Le Vrai Pere de Marelie,* Editions Pierre Tisseyre, 1995.

Eleanor Allen, *Ghost from the Sea,* A. and C. Black (London, England), 1995.

Daniel Defoe, *Robinson Crusoe* (condensed version by Carmen Marois), Graficor (Boucherville, Quebec), 1996.

The Little Red Hen, Ginn (Aylesbury, England), 1996.

Mark Twain, *Tom Sawyer* (condensed version by Michele Marineau), Graficor, 1996.

Twain, *Huckleberry Finn* (condensed version by Marois), Graficor, 1997.

Double Take Listening and Speaking 3 (textbook), Oxford University Press (Oxford, England), 1996.

Louisa May Alcott, *Les Quatres Filles du Docteur March* (condensed version of *Little Women* by Marineau), Graficor, 1997.

Team Up 6 Manual (textbook), Editions du Renouveau Pedagogique (Montreal), 1997.

Cass Hollander, *On a Hot Day,* Rigby Educational Publishing (New York City), 1997.

Anne Legault, *Une Fille Pas Comme les Autres,* Editions la Courte Echelle (Montreal), 1997.

Jasmine Dube, *L'Ourson qui Voulait une Juliette,* Editions la Courte Echelle, 1997.

Jack London, *Croc-Blanc* (condensed version by Marineau), Graficor, 1997.

Manjusha Pawagi, *The Girl Who Hated Books,* Second Story Press (Toronto, Ontario), 1998, Beyond Words Publishing (Hillsboro, OR), 1999.

Ulana Snihura, *I Miss Franklin P. Shuckles,* Annick Press (Willowdale, Ontario), 1998.

Leslie Ellen, *Quackers, the Troublesome Duck,* Simon and Schuster, 1998.

Judy Nayer, *Best Wishes for Eddie,* Simon & Schuster, 1998.

Nayer, *The Lost and Found Game,* Simon & Schuster, 1998.

James R. MacClean, *The Great Riddle Mystery,* Simon & Schuster, 1998.

Linda LaRose, *Jessica Takes Charge,* Annick Press, 1998.

Agathe Genois, *Adieu Vieux Lezard!,* Editions Heritage (Saint-Lambert, Quebec), 1998.

Legault, *Une Premiere pour Etamine Leger,* Editions la Courte Echelle, 1998.

Stuart Hample and Eric Marshall, compilers, *Calendar 2000: Children's Letters to God,* Workman Publishing, 1999.

Rhea Tregebov, *What-If Sara,* Second Story Press, 1999.

Contributor of editorial illustrations to periodicals, including *Zellers Magalog* and *Today's Parent.*

Sidelights

Leanne R. Franson told *SATA:* "As an illustrator of children's books, I am inspired by the vision of small children cuddled next to Mommy or Big Brother, at bedtime, sharing a cozy story session, or pulling out a new book from the library shelf with excitement, or carrying a favorite book around under the arm, sticky with peanut butter. I have extremely fond memories of all the above moments in my young life, and I am fueled by the possibility of playing such a role in the memories of future readers.

"I think my favorite part of illustrating books is when I take a new script to the corner café and sit down with a

From **The Girl Who Hated Books,** *written by Manjusha Pawagi and illustrated by Franson.*

At lunchtime Franklin P. Shuckles always asks if I would like to share his lunch. Maybe if I chew very loud he'll get grossed out and move. So I did. But he didn't.

From **I Miss Franklin P. Shuckles,** *written by Ulana Snihura and illustrated by Franson.*

café au lait to read it for the first time. The thrill of a new story is compounded by the thrill of being one of the first to get a chance to see it and imagine the scenes and characters brought to life by the author. At that point, all is possible. Often my imagination is fired up so that the sketch process occurs almost automatically in my head.

"Then comes the work part: getting the characters down on paper. Sometimes the expressions and mannerisms are the easiest part, as I imagine them in their world, and more down-to-earth things such as hair color and clothing styles seem quite arbitrary and difficult to pin down. After that is the whole collaborative process with the author and art director, where all our imaginations collide. The author imagined her kid sister who has freckles and is a bit plumper; the art director needs the color red to stand out on the page. Finally it is all worked through, and the final characters emerge. At that point they take on their own lives and must stay in character and 'look' for the entire book. This is less fun for me, but it is exciting to see the original formless sketches become fleshed out.

"When I send off the final artwork, it is like the book disappears from my life and control, and it is sometimes hard for me to disengage. For instance, with *Jessica Takes Charge* the main subject for me was the shadows. For weeks and even months after the book was out of my hands, I was still hooked on studying shadows, coming up with shadow monster ideas.

"The second most exciting part of doing a book is receiving the finished book from a courier at my front door, especially if it has a shiny, glossy, hard cover. It's like fresh candy. It's amazing that my lowly drawings come back as a *real* book! Also, there is some of the excitement of opening that new book package that I experienced when I was four or five, and we received 'Cat in the Hat' books from a book club.

"As I've only had trade books coming out now for several years, it still amazes me to think that anyone can go down to the library or bookstore and pick up my drawings. It's also a huge thrill to see foreign issues released. For now, I love my job and cannot see how it can get any better.

"I am particularly drawn to books where the child protagonists are real. They have full ranges of emotions, are often troubled but strong, vulnerable but proactive. As a child, I was crazy about black-and-white drawings, often of alternative and magical worlds closed to adults; for example, Pauline Baynes in the *Chronicles of Narnia,* Beth and Joe Krush in the 'Gone-Away Lake' books, and Marguerite de Angeli's *The Door in the Wall.* I also loved Maurice Sendak, Beatrix Potter (such child-friendly sizes!), and Ernest H. Shepard's Pooh. As for characters, I was also inspired by Laura Ingalls Wilder, Pippi Longstocking, and the Borrowers. More recently I admire Stephane Jorish, Marie-Louis Gay, Raymond Briggs, and Ralph Steadman. I only wish I had as much time now to revel in the wonders of the children's section of the library as I did when I was five or ten."

G

GARREN, Devorah-Leah
See DEVORAH-LEAH

* * *

GEIS, Darlene (Stern) 1918(?)-1999 (Ralph Kelly, Jane London, pseudonyms; Peter Stevens, a joint pseudonym)

OBITUARY NOTICE—See index for *SATA* sketch: Born April 8, c. 1918, in Chicago, IL; died in a fire in her home, March 25, 1999, in Manhattan, NY. Editor and author. Geis wrote and edited a number of books, including many books for children. One of her earlier books, *The Little Train that Won a Medal* (1947), sold more than three million copies. She also authored and edited a "Let's Travel..." series, which described various locales around the world. Geis worked for the publisher Harry M. Abrams, beginning in 1969, where she served as an editor and author. The author's works include *The Gourmet Cooking School Cookbook* (1964), which she wrote with Dione Lucas, *A Treasury of Great Recipes* (1965), and *The Joys of Wine* (1977).

OBITUARIES AND OTHER SOURCES:

BOOKS

Authors of Books for Young People, 3rd edition, Scarecrow Press, 1990.

PERIODICALS

Los Angeles Times, April 2, 1999, p. B4.
New York Times, April 9, 1999, p. A21.

GLEITER, Jan 1947-

Personal

Born in 1947.

Addresses

Agent—c/o St. Martin's Press, 175 Fifth Ave., Rm. 1715, New York, NY 10010.

Career

Writer.

Writings

FOR YOUNG PEOPLE

Color Rhymes: Teddies (poems), illustrated by Chrissie Wells, Raintree (Milwaukee, WI), 1985.
Seaside Adventure, illustrated by Chrissie Wells, Raintree, 1987.
Tell the Time, illustrated by Chrissie Wells, Raintree, 1987.

BIOGRAPHIES FOR CHILDREN; WITH KATHLEEN THOMPSON

Daniel Boone, illustrated by Leslie Tryon, 1985.
Paul Bunyan and Babe the Blue Ox, illustrated by Yoshi Miyake, Raintree, 1985.
Pocahontas, illustrated by Deborah L. Chabrian, Raintree, 1985.
Annie Oakley, illustrated by Yoshi Miyake, Raintree, 1987.
Casey Jones, illustrated by Francis Balistreri, Raintree, 1987.
Christopher Columbus, illustrated by Rick Whipple, Raintree, 1987.
Johnny Appleseed, illustrated by Harry Quinn, Raintree, 1987.
Kit Carson, illustrated by Rick Whipple, Raintree, 1987.
Molly Pitcher, illustrated by Charles Shaw, Raintree, 1987.
Paul Revere, illustrated by Francis Balistreri, Raintree, 1987.
Sacagawea, illustrated by Yoshi Miyake, Raintree, 1987.

Booker T. Washington, illustrated by Rick Whipple, Raintree, 1988.
David Farragut, illustrated by Francis Balistreri, Raintree, 1988.
Elizabeth Cady Stanton, illustrated by Rick Whipple, Raintree, 1988.
Jack London, illustrated by Francis Balistreri, Raintree, 1988.
Jane Addams, illustrated by Diane Barton, Raintree, 1988.
John James Audobon, illustrated by Yoshi Miyake, Raintree, 1988.
Matthew Henson, illustrated by Francis Balistreri, Raintree, 1988.
Sam Houston, illustrated by Joel F. Naprstek, Raintree, 1988.
Sequoya, illustrated by Tom Redman, Raintree, 1988.
Diego Rivera, illustrated by Yoshi Miyake, Raintree, 1989.
Hernando de Soto, illustrated by Rick Whipple, Raintree, 1989.
Jose Marti, illustrated by Les Didier, Raintree, 1989.
Juniper Serra, illustrated by Charles Shaw, Raintree, 1989.
Luis Munoz Marin, illustrated by Dennis Matz, Raintree, 1989.
Miguel Hidalgo y Costilla, illustrated by Rick Karpinski, Raintree, 1989.
Simon Bolivar, illustrated by Tom Redman, Raintree, 1989.
Benito Juarez, illustrated by Francis Balistreri, Raintree, 1990.

NOVELS

Lie Down with Dogs, St. Martin's Press, 1996.
A House by the Side of the Road, St. Martin's Press, 1998.

Adaptations

Washington Irving, *The Legend of Sleepy Hollow,* illustrated by Dennis Hockerman, Raintree, 1985.
Charles Dickens, *Great Expectations,* illustrated by Charles Shaw, Raintree, 1989.
Sir Walter Scott, *Ivanhoe,* illustrated by Rick Whipple, Raintree, 1989.

Sidelights

Novelist Jan Gleiter has written many books of fiction and nonfiction for children. With Kathleen Thompson, Gleiter penned more than two dozen biographies of American historical figures, including Sacagawea, the Native American who guided Lewis and Clark during the latter part of their celebrated cross-continental expedition, American Revolutionary figures Paul Revere and Molly Pitcher, frontiersman Daniel Boone, sharpshooter Annie Oakley, African American educator and civil rights leader Booker T. Washington, and suffragist Elizabeth Cady Stanton. Gleiter and Thompson also wrote biographies with English and Spanish text of notable Hispanic figures, including the Spanish explorer Hernando de Soto, South American revolutionary leader Simon Bolivar, Mexican painter Diego Rivera, and Puerto Rican governor Luis Munoz Marin. In addition, Gleiter has created adaptations of classic literary works for children: *The Legend of Sleepy Hollow, Great Expectations,* and *Ivanhoe.*

Gleiter made her debut as a novelist in 1996 with *Lie Down with Dogs,* a story that takes its title from a quotation by English poet George Herbert: "He that lies with the dogs, riseth with fleas." In *Lie Down with Dogs,* Carl, an actor, agrees to keep a package for his friend Gerry, a police officer. Someone threatens Carl's four-year-old son, Luke, so Carl takes Luke to their friend Lisa's house to hide. Carl then disappears, so Lisa and acquaintance Robert join forces to find Carl and protect Luke. A *Kirkus Reviews* contributor deemed *Lie Down with Dogs* a "gripping debut," that is "literate" and "straightforward," noting that the plot contains "menacing tension every step of the way."

Gleiter's second novel, *A House by the Side of the Road,* features freelance writer Meg Kessinger, who moves from Chicago to rural Pennsylvania when she inherits a house from her aunt. Meg is content with her new life until she learns some disturbing things. "Gleiter has crafted a novel in which the main character is ultimately the reader," maintained David Pitt in *Booklist.* Pitt, who concluded the novel "a fresh, engaging mystery," continued: "By making us participants in the action, Gleiter allows us to care about the goings-on more, perhaps, than we would be if we'd simply been watching Meg solve the case." A *Kirkus Reviews* contributor deemed the book "an appealingly low-key idyll, even if the menace, like Meg, takes its time settling in."

Works Cited

Review of *House by the Side of the Road, Kirkus Reviews,* May 15, 1998.
Review of *Lie Down with Dogs, Kirkus Reviews,* March 1, 1996, p. 336.
Pitt, David, review of *A House by the Side of the Road, Booklist,* June 1, 1998, p. 1732.

For More Information See

PERIODICALS

Booklist, Feb. 1, 1990, p. 1088; Oct. 1, 1990, p. 349.
Bulletin of the Center for Children's Books, April, 1985, pp. 149-50; June, 1988, p. 204; November, 1989, pp. 56-57.
Publishers Weekly, April 6, 1998, p. 62.
School Library Journal, June, 1995, p. 100.*

*   *   *

GOOD, Clare
See ROSS, Clare

GOODALL, Jane 1934-
(Jane van Lawick-Goodall)

Personal

Born April 3, 1934, in London, England; daughter of Mortimer Herbert (a businessman and motorcar racer) and Myfanwe (an author under name Vanne Goodall; maiden name Joseph) Goodall; married Hugo van Lawick (a nature photographer), March 28, 1964 (divorced); married Derek Bryceson (a member of Parliament and director of Tanzania National Parks), 1973 (deceased); children: (first marriage) Hugo Eric Louis. *Education:* Attended Uplands School, England; Cambridge University, Ph.D., 1965. *Religion:* Church of England. *Hobbies and other interests:* Riding, photography, reading, classical music.

Addresses

Home and office—Gombe Stream Research Centre, P.O. Box 185, Kigoma, Tanzania, East Africa.

Career

Gombe Stream Research Centre, Tanzania, East Africa, ethologist, 1960—; writer, 1965—. Assistant secretary to Dr. Louis S. B. Leakey, 1960; assistant curator of National Museum of Natural History, Nairobi, Kenya, 1960. Visiting professor of psychiatry and human biology, Stanford University, 1970-75; honorary visiting professor of zoology, University of Dar Es Salaam, Tanzania, 1972—. *Member:* American Academy of Arts and Sciences (honorary foreign member, 1972—).

Awards, Honors

Wilkie Brothers Foundation grant, 1960; two Franklin Burr prizes from National Geographic Society; gold medal for conservation, San Diego Zoological Society; conservation award, New York Zoological Society; J. Paul Getty Wildlife Conservation Prize, 1984; R. R. Hawkins Award, Association of American Publishers, 1987, for *The Chimpanzees of Gombe: Patterns of Behaviors;* Centennial Award, 1988; Hubbard Medal, 1995.

Writings

AS JANE VAN LAWICK-GOODALL

(Contributor) Irven De Vore, editor, *Primate Behavior,* Holt, 1965.

My Friends, the Wild Chimpanzees, photographs by Hugo van Lawick, National Geographic Society, 1967.

(Contributor) Desmond Morris, editor, *Primate Ethology,* Aldine, 1967.

The Behaviour of Free-Living Chimpanzees in the Gombe Stream Reserve (monograph), Tindall & Cassell, 1968.

(With husband, Hugo van Lawick) *Innocent Killers,* Collins, 1970, Houghton, 1971.

Grub the Bush Baby, with photographs by the author, Collins, 1970, revised edition published with van Lawick, Houghton, 1972.

In the Shadow of Man, photographs by Hugo van Lawick, Collins, 1971, Houghton, 1971, revised edition published under name Jane Goodall, 1988, abbreviated edition published as *Selected from In the Shadow of Man,* Literacy Volunteers of New York City, 1992.

AS JANE GOODALL

The Chimpanzees of Gombe: Patterns of Behavior, Harvard University Press, 1986.

My Life with the Chimpanzees, Simon & Schuster, 1988.

The Chimpanzee Family Book (for children), photographs by Michael Neugebauer, Picture Book Studio (Saxonville, MA), 1989.

Chimps, Atheneum, 1989, Collier, 1990.

Through a Window: My Thirty Years with the Chimpanzees of Gombe, Houghton, 1990, published in England as *Through the Window: Thirty Years with the Chimpanzees of Gombe,* Phoenix (London), 1998.

The Chimpanzee: The Living Link between 'Man' and 'Beast,' Edinburgh University Press, 1992.

(With Dale Peterson) *Visions of Caliban: On Chimpanzees and People,* Houghton, 1993.

(With others) *The Great Apes,* National Geographic, 1994.

Artaud and the Gnostic Drama, Oxford University Press, 1994.

With Love: Ten Heartwarming Stories of Chimpanzees in the Wild (for children), illustrated by Allan Marks, Jane Goodall Institute, 1994.

Dr. White (for children), illustrated by Julie Litty, North-South Books, 1999.

(With Phillip Berman) *Reason for Hope: A Spiritual Journey,* Warner, 1999.

(With Michael Nichols) *Brutal Kinship,* Aperture (New York City), 1999.

EDITOR; "JANE GOODALL'S ANIMAL WORLD" SERIES; FOR CHILDREN

Chimpanzees, Macmillan, 1989.

Lions, Macmillan, 1989.

Jane Goodall

Hippos, Macmillan, 1989.
Pandas, Macmillan, 1989.
Elephants, Macmillan, 1990.
Gorillas, Macmillan, 1990.
Sea Otters, Macmillan, 1990.
Tigers, Macmillan, 1990.

Contributor to journals, including *National Geographic, Nature,* and *Annals of the New York Academy of Science.*

Adaptations

Several television specials have featured Goodall and her work, including *Miss Goodall and the Wild Chimpanzees,* Columbia Broadcasting System, 1965; *Through a Window* has been adapted for an audiocassette.

Work in Progress

Continued research and teaching on chimpanzee behavior.

Sidelights

Noted naturalist Jane Goodall has spent most of her adult life living in the jungles of Tanzania studying the behavior of wild chimpanzees. Captivated by animals since a young child, she has dedicated herself to enlarging human understanding of the rich social, biological, and cultural interactions among the species most closely related to man. *New York Times* contributor John Noble Wilford described Goodall as "something of a celebrity" in the early stages of her career, when she first caught the world's attention as "the young Englishwoman who plunges into Africa, spends the days and years in communion with chimpanzees, . . . dispatches occasional learned reports and keeps right on studying the animals she finds so fascinating." Through her constant dedication to study, as well as her efforts to share her growing knowledge through books for both adults and children, Goodall has become a respected authority on animal behavior and has been lauded as a role model for young women contemplating a career in the sciences. As Denise R. Majkut noted in *Best Sellers,* in her books Goodall "comes across as a great lover of nature—loving the beauty of the wild jungles of Africa, the continuing struggle for survival there of the chimps, and man's typical behavior."

Goodall was born in England in 1934. Like many children, she had dreams of traveling to the mysterious African wilderness to study the elusive animals that lived there. Growing up in London, she spent hours observing family pets and other animals she discovered near her home; one of her favorite playthings was a toy chimpanzee someone had given her. Deciding to do her research the proper way, she used her allowance to buy books about animals, and took copious notes about her observations of the wildlife she discovered. Shortly after graduating from school, Goodall traveled to Kenya in East Africa, where she met noted anthropologist and paleontologist Dr. Louis S. B. Leakey, and took a job as

Goodall offers an intimate portrait of the chimpanzees she has studied for many years in the jungles of Africa. (Cover photo by Michael Neugebauer.)

the doctor's assistant secretary. This job allowed Goodall to remain in Africa, and she accompanied Leakey and his family on fossil-hunting trips to the remote Olduvai Gorge region, and aided their improvements to the National Museum of Natural History in Nairobi. In 1960, Leakey proposed a new project to his young assistant: a six-month field study of the wild chimpanzees on the Gombe Stream Chimpanzee Reserve in Tanzania, which she eagerly accepted.

When she first arrived in Tanzania, Goodall lacked any formal training in ethology—the study of animal behavior. But her curiosity about chimpanzees, her determination to be a success at the task given her by Dr. Leakey, and her tolerance for the primitive living conditions required of field researchers more than made up for her academic shortcomings. (Interestingly, Goodall would become the eighth person in the history of Cambridge University to receive a Ph.D. without first earning a baccalaureate, the result of a thesis she produced after her first five years in the Gombe Stream Reserve.) Amid outbreaks of malaria and the constant threats posed by cobras, centipedes, and aggressive baboons, Goodall tracked a band of chimps living in the Gombe area. For months she observed the shy animals through binoculars, gradually moving closer as they became used to her presence. Among other things, Goodall observed wild chimps making and using simple tools, stalking and killing small animals for food, battling rival troops of chimps for terrain, and cooperating in such group activities as hunting and defending territory.

After six months on the job, Goodall realized that her task would require years, rather than months, to be done properly. With long-term funding located with the Leakeys' help, Goodall settled in to continue the project that would occupy many years to come, never realizing

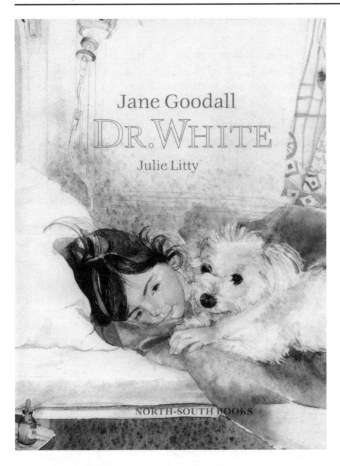

Goodall based this story of a beloved doctor who used pet-assisted therapy to treat the critically ill on actual events that occurred at a London children's hospital. (Cover illustration by Julie Litty.)

that she would eventually become a celebrity. Her earliest work—and much of her subsequent writing—has been scholarly, aimed at the university-trained specialist or the sophisticated general reader. Among her most widely read books are *In the Shadow of Man* and *The Chimpanzees of Gombe: Patterns of Behavior.* She has also been quick to realize that children are particularly fascinated by primates, and many of her books have been directed particularly at young readers.

Among Goodall's books aimed at children is her "Animal World" series, featuring generously-illustrated volumes on a variety of wild creatures. Beginning, appropriately, with the volume *Chimpanzees* in 1989, the series also includes *Lions, Hippos, Pandas,* and *Sea Otters* among its menagerie of titles. Another title for children, *The Chimpanzee Family Book,* contains a variety of "family photographs" of chimpanzee parents and their rambunctious offspring, and features an informative text by Goodall. And in *With Love: Ten Heartwarming Stories of Chimpanzees in the Wild,* Goodall culls particularly meaningful events from her four decades spent in Tanzania, and introduces young readers to a variety of chimpanzees. "Spindle" adopts a young orphaned chimp, "Porn" saves her young brother from a poisonous snake, and "Flint" tragically pines

away after the death of his doting mother. Describing the stories as, by turns, "touching, funny and emotional," *Booklist* contributor GraceAnne A. DeCandido maintained that Goodall's tales would prove popular with children "because they are sometimes silly or gross and because ... young humans will recognize aspects of themselves in these young chimps."

Moving her setting to London, Goodall also composed the picture book *Dr. White,* which finds the tail-wagging "doctor" always on call, ready and eager to administer a healthy dose of cuddles and happy barks to patients at a children's hospital. A surprise visit from a city health inspector threatens to cut short the doctor's rounds, until the inspector's daughter becomes ill and he sees that the feel-good medicine of Dr. White helps put his daughter on the road to recovery. Commenting on the story's sentimentality, *School Library Journal* contributor Arwen Marshall noted that "ardent animal lovers might find some appeal here." However, a *Publishers Weekly* reviewer found much to like in the story, which is based on actual events, and observed that "Goodall's matter-of-fact text serves as the perfect foil for the dog's seemingly magical ability to heal, and her subject is timely." And in *Books for Keeps,* contributor Roy Blatchford concluded of *Dr. White:* "Here is a children's picture book of real compassion and joy, and one that repays many readings."

In line with the mission she undertook decades ago, Goodall continues to work tirelessly to impart her understanding of chimps and other animals to children. "I feel it's something I want to spend more time telling children: that animals are like us," she told *Publishers Weekly.* "They feel pain like we do. We want to make people understand that every chimp is an individual, with the same kinds of intellectual abilities." Bettyann Kevles noted in the *Los Angeles Times Book Review* that Goodall has done more than any other scientist to enlighten humankind about the rich life of chimpanzees. "Thanks to the painstaking efforts of Goodall and her colleagues," Kevles wrote, "we admire the chimpanzees of Gombe because we understand the complexity of their lives." An international traveler who lectures around the world in addition to continuing her field work, Goodall hopes her efforts will help win new respect for members of the animal kingdom. "I want to make [people] aware that animals have their own needs, emotions, and feelings—they matter," she told *Publishers Weekly.* "I want to give kids a passion, an understanding and awareness of the wonder of animals."

Works Cited

Blatchford, Roy, review of *Dr. White, Books for Keeps,* May, 1999, p. 23.

DeCandido, GraceAnne A., review of *With Love: Ten Heartwarming Stories of Chimpanzees in the Wild, Booklist,* April 15, 1998, p. 1438.

Review of *Dr. White, Publishers Weekly,* March 1, 1999, p. 69.

Goodall, Jane, interview in *Publishers Weekly,* January 25, 1993, p. 68.

Kevles, Bettyann, review of *The Chimpanzees of Gombe: Patterns of Behavior, Los Angeles Times Book Review,* December 28, 1986.

Majkut, Denise R., review of *In the Shadow of Man, Best Sellers,* November 15, 1971.

Marshall, Arwen, review of *Dr. White, School Library Journal,* March, 1999, p. 175.

Wilford, John Noble, review of *In the Shadow of Man, New York Times,* November 26, 1971.

For More Information See

BOOKS

Burby, Liza N., *Jane Goodall: Leading Animal Behaviorist,* Rosen, 1997.

Chessen, Betsy and Pamela Chanko, *Jane Goodall and Her Chimpanzees,* Scholastic, 1999.

Coerr, Eleanor B., *Jane Goodall,* Putnam, 1976.

Ferber, Elizabeth, *A Life with Animals: Jane Goodall,* illustrated by Kees de Kiefte, Benchmark, 1997.

Fox, Mary Virginia, *Jane Goodall: Living Chimp Style,* illustrated by Nona Hegen, Dillon, 1981.

Fromer, Julie, *Jane Goodall, Living with the Chimps,* illustrated by Antonio Castro, Twenty-First Century Books (Frederick, MD), 1992.

Fuchs, Carol A., *Jane Goodall: The Chimpanzee's Friend,* illustrated by Robin Richisson, Rourke (Vero Beach, FL), 1993.

Green, Timothy, *The Restless Spirit: Profiles in Adventure,* Walker & Co., 1970.

Lucas, Eileen, *Jane Goodall, Friend of the Chimps,* Millbrook, 1992.

Meachum, Virginia, *Jane Goodall, Protector of Chimpanzees,* Enslow, 1997.

Pettit, Jayne, *Jane Goodall: Pioneer Researcher,* Franklin Watts, 1999.

Pratt, Paula Bryant, *Jane Goodall,* Lucent (San Diego), 1997.

Senn, J. A., *Jane Goodall, Naturalist,* Blackbirch Press (Woodbridge, CT), 1993.

PERIODICALS

Booklist, January 1, 1972; January 15, 1993, p. 850.

Library Journal, December 1, 1971; March 1, 1972; February 1, 1993, p. 108.

New York Times, August 19, 1986.

New York Times Book Review, August 24, 1986, p. 1; October 1, 1989, p. 35; October 28, 1990, p. 7; June 13, 1993, p. 21.

Publishers Weekly, November 22, 1970; August 9, 1971; October 2, 1972; January 29, 1988, p. 396; March 9, 1998, p. 69.

*   *   *

GOODMAN, Alison 1966-

Personal

Born August 18, 1966, in Melbourne, Australia; daughter of Douglas Matthias (a manufacturer's agent) and Charmaine (a textile teacher; maiden name, Rimmer) Goodman. *Education:* Deakin University, B.A.

Addresses

E-mail—alison@dogstar.wow.aust.com.   *Agent*—Fran Bryson, AMC (Australia) Pty. Ltd., P.O. Box 1034, Carlton, Victoria 3053, Australia.

Career

Writer. Deakin University, Melbourne, Australia, lecturer and tutor in professional writing, 1998—; Victorian Writers Centre, member. University of Ballarat, guest lecturer, 1994; Royal Victorian Institute for the Blind, workshop leader, 1995.

Awards, Honors

Aurealis award, best young adult novel, 1998, and "notable book" citation, Book of the Year Awards, older readers category, Children's Book Council of Australia, 1999, both for *Singing the Dogstar Blues,* which was also short-listed for Talking Book of the Year Award, young people's category, Royal Blind Society, 1999; Shortlist, Cross Pen Prize for Young Adult Fiction, Victorian Premier's Literary Awards, 1999. D. J. O'Hearn memorial fellow, University of Melbourne, 1999.

Alison Goodman

Writings

Singing the Dogstar Blues (novel), HarperCollins (Pymble, Australia), 1998.

Work represented in anthologies, including *The Pattern-maker,* Omnibus Books, 1994; *Shadow Alley,* Omnibus Books, 1995; and *She's Fantastical,* Sybylla Feminist Press, 1995. Contributor of stories and articles to periodicals, including *Eidolon: Science Fiction and Fantasy Journal, Verandah, Pursuit,* and *Age.*

Sidelights

Alison Goodman told *SATA:* "*Singing the Dogstar Blues* is my first novel. It's based on a short story I wrote called 'One Last Zoom at the Buzz Bar,' which is about a girl called Joss Aaronson who steals a time machine and gets thrown into a parallel universe. Joss was such a fun character to write that I decided to write a novel based on her adventures as a time-travel student. Sounds easy, doesn't it? I soon learned that there is a big difference between writing a seven-thousand-word short story and a sixty-thousand-word novel. For one thing, it's hard to believe you'll ever be able to produce sixty-thousand words, let alone mold them into a good story. Like most things, it was just a matter of hanging in there and taking the small steps toward the bigger goal.

"Before I start writing a novel, I can spend up to six months building the plot, developing the characters, and thinking up the first line. Once I've got that first sentence, everything else seems to fall into place. Then I hit the keyboard, and the fun really starts. I love putting all the elements of a novel together. It's like building a huge, multi-layered puzzle.

"When I was studying professional writing at university, comedy wasn't high on the list of desirable talents, so I tried to limit it in my work. I would start off writing straight, serious fiction, but somehow a sense of the ridiculous would always creep in and put a kink in a perfectly good piece of drama. I finally realized that funny was how I wrote, and now I'm very serious about writing comedy."

*   *   *

GRANSTROEM, Brita 1969-
(Brita Granstrom)

Personal

Born July 23, 1969, in Eskilstuna, Sweden; married to Mick Manning (a writer and illustrator); children: Max, Bjoern. *Education:* Attended Oerebro Konstskola; Konstfack (National College of Art, Craft, and Design), Stockholm, Sweden, M.F.A.

Addresses

Contact through publishers.

Career

Illustrator of children's books. Worked in Kenya as a medical illustrator for a flying doctor. *Member:* Society of Authors.

Awards, Honors

Smarties Silver Award, 1996, for *The World's Full of Babies!;* TES Award, 1997, for *What's under the Bed?;* short-listed for Rhone Poulenc Science Prize, 1998, for *Yum-Yum!,* and *How Did I Begin?* and *Science School,* 1999.

Writings

AUTHOR AND ILLUSTRATOR, WITH HUSBAND MICK MANNING

The World Is Full of Babies!, Delacorte (New York City), 1996.
Art School, Kingfisher (New York City), 1996.
Nature Watch, Kingfisher, 1997.
Honk! Honk! A Story of Migration, Kingfisher, 1997.
Yum-Yum!, F. Watts (New York City), 1997.
My Body, Your Body, F. Watts, 1997.
What's Up?, F. Watts, 1997.

Brita Granstroem

Splish, Splash, Splosh!, F. Watts, 1997.
What's under the Bed?, F. Watts, 1997.
How Did I Begin?, F. Watts, 1997.
Nature School, Kingfisher, 1997.
Rainy Day, F. Watts, 1997.
Snowy Day, F. Watts, 1997.
Sunny Day, F. Watts, 1997.
Windy Day, F. Watts, 1997.
Science School, Kingfisher, 1998.
Collect-o-Mania, F. Watts, 1998.
Out There Somewhere, F. Watts, 1998.
What If? A Book about Recycling, F. Watts, 1998.
Wild and Free, F. Watts, 1998.
Drama School, Kingfisher, 1999.
Super School, Kingfisher, 1999.
Let's Build a House!, F. Watts, 1999.
Super Mum, F. Watts, 1999.

Coauthor and illustrator of *Sael Ungen,* Raben & Sjoegren, 1998.

AUTHOR AND ILLUSTRATOR

Ten in the Bed, Candlewick Press (Cambridge, MA), 1996.
Many Hands Counting Book, edited by Gale Pryor, Candlewick Press, 1999.

Other books include *Wof Haer Kommer Jag!* and *Fina och Telefonen,* published by Raben & Sjoegren.

ILLUSTRATOR

Christine Morley and Carole Orbell, *Me and My Pet Dog,* World Book/Two-Can (Chicago, IL), 1996.
Morley and Orbell, *Me and My Pet Cat,* World Book/Two-Can, 1996.
Morley and Orbell, *Me and My Pet Rabbit,* World Book/Two-Can, 1997.
Morley and Orbell, *Me and My Pet Fish,* World Book/Two-Can, 1997.
Pippa Goodhart, *Bed Time,* F. Watts, 1997.
Goodhart, *Morning Time,* F. Watts, 1997.
Goodhart, *Play Time,* F. Watts, 1997.
Goodhart, *Shopping Time,* F. Watts, 1997.
Judy Hindley, *Eyes, Nose, Fingers, and Toes: A First Book about You,* Candlewick Press, 1998.
Manning, *Wash, Scrub, and Brush,* F. Watts, 1999.
Sam McBratney, *Bert's Wonderful News,* Walker and Co. (London, England), 1999.

Illustrator of *Ben's Bring Your Bear Party,* by Martin Waddell, Walker and Co.; and *Kisses Are Little, Smiles Are Wide,* Candlewick Press.

Sidelights

Brita Granstroem told *SATA:* "I do most of my books together with my partner Mick Manning. I love my job. It's a dream come true. When I'm not illustrating children's books, I go out painting. I fill the baby's pram with acrylic paints and go painting on the spot."

GRANSTROM, Brita
See GRANSTROEM, Brita

*   *   *

GUCCIONE, Leslie Davis 1946-
(Kate Chester, Leslie Davis)

Personal

Born December 14, 1946, in Wilmington, DE; daughter of Edward Stowman (a chemical engineer and executive) and Winifred (a homemaker; maiden name, Taylor) Davis II; married Joseph Q. Guccione (an accountant), May 3, 1975; children: Christopher J. (stepson), Amy Mendenhall, Taylor Noyes. *Education:* Studied art with Carolyn Wyeth, 1963-1965; Wilmington Friends School, 1965; attended Institute of European Studies, 1968; Queens College, B.A., 1969. *Politics:* Independent. *Religion:* Episcopalian. *Hobbies and other interests:* Sailing, painting.

Addresses

Agent—Denise Marcil, 685 West End Avenue, New York, NY 10025.

Electronic mail— LDGBooks@worldnet.att.net.

Career

Held various positions in advertising, public relations, and fund raising, 1972-1978; Folk Art Antiques, Duxbury, MA, partner, 1985-1986; writer, 1985—. *Member:* Authors Guild, Duxbury Writer's Workshop, Society of Children's Book Writers & Illustrators, and the Junior League of Summit (NJ).

Awards, Honors

RITA awards finalist, Romance Writers of America, 1985, for *Something Out There;* Best Book, International Readers Association, 1991, and Iowa Teen Choice, 1992, both for *Tell Me How the Wind Sounds;* selected as a Best Books, School Librarians International, 1996, for *Come Morning.*

Writings

FOR YOUNG PEOPLE

(Under name Leslie Davis) *Something Out There,* Pocket Books, 1985.
Tell Me How the Wind Sounds, Scholastic, 1989.
Nobody Listens to Me, Scholastic, 1991.
Come Morning, Lerner Publishing, 1995.

"HEAR NO EVIL" SERIES

(Under name Kate Chester) *Death in the Afternoon,* Scholastic, 1996.
(Under name Kate Chester) *Missing,* Scholastic, 1996.

Leslie Davis Guccione

(Under name Kate Chester) *A Time of Fear,* Scholastic, 1996.
(Under name Kate Chester) *Dead and Buried,* Scholastic, 1997.
(Under name Kate Chester) *Playing with Fire,* Scholastic, 1997.

"CHEERLEADER" SERIES

Moving Up, Scholastic, 1987.
All or Nothing, Scholastic, 1988.
Pretending, Scholastic, 1988.

FOR ADULTS

(Under name Leslie Davis) *A Touch of Scandal,* Avon, 1985.
(Under name Leslie Davis) *The Splintered Moon,* Avon, 1985.
Before the Wind, Silhouette, 1985.
Bittersweet Harvest, Silhouette, 1986.
Still Waters, Silhouette, 1987.
Something in Common, Silhouette, 1987.
Branigan's Touch, Silhouette, 1989.
Private Practice, Silhouette, 1990.
A Gallant Gentleman, Silhouette, 1991.
Rough and Ready, Silhouette, 1992.
A Rock and a Hard Place, Silhouette, 1992.
Derek, Silhouette, 1993.
Major Distractions, Silhouette, 1994.
Branigan's Break, Silhouette, 1995.
Borrowed Baby, Silhouette, 1999.

Has also written copy for the website Petopia.com.

Work in Progress

Fiction for adults and children; a seacoast mystery adventure for middle graders.

Sidelights

Leslie Davis Guccione, award-winning author of more than twenty novels for adults and young readers, told *SATA:* "I grew up as the oldest of four children in a very active family. My dad was a chemical engineer, then in the marketing end of the DuPont Company, so we moved around the East Coast about every three years during my school days. I was in Wilmington, Delaware, for kindergarten through mid-second grade; Wellesley, Massachusetts, for the mid-second to mid-fourth grade; Summit, New Jersey, for grades four through seven; back to Wilmington for eighth to twelfth grade; then off to Charlotte, North Carolina, for college.

"Moving taught me how to make friends. I was glad to stay put after the seventh grade, but in high school I switched from public to private school and had to develop another batch of friendships at sixteen.

"I've always been what my teachers called 'creatively inclined.' That's to say I was full of imagination. I put on plays in my neighborhoods, drew all the time and wrote pretty awful poetry all through school. I was a terrible speller. My fourth grade teacher told me my spelling was atrocious. When I asked her what that meant and she told me to look it up, I, of course, answered that I couldn't because I didn't know how to spell it! (I work on a computer now and Spell Check has been wonderful.)

"My home in Wilmington during the years 1963 to 1965 was not far from Chadds Ford, Pennsylvania, home of the Wyeth family. When I was sixteen I took my portfolio to Carolyn Wyeth and was accepted as a student in her Saturday class. With the exception of her nieces and nephews, I was the youngest student she had ever accepted. Carolyn was the sister of artist Andrew Wyeth and the daughter of N. C. Wyeth, one of America's best illustrators. She taught in his studio.

"I studied with her for two years and my Saturdays were magic. Not only was I painting, I was listening to constant and countless stories of her childhood as one of five children in an enormously talented family. I was there when celebrities and writers would come and interview her.

"After I graduated from Friends School in 1965, I went off to Queens College to major in art, but I also became involved in all aspects of creative writing. I was a member of the literary fraternity Sigma Upsilon and worked on the college's literary magazine. During the summer of 1968, after my junior year, I studied art history and classical music at the Institute of European Studies in Vienna. I traveled with about thirty other students for five weeks before landing in Austria. It was an incredible summer. Robert Kennedy was assassinated

When his father, a freed slave who works for the Underground Railroad, is taken prisoner, twelve-year-old Freedom Newcastle assumes a brave role in the effort to help other slaves escape to freedom in the North. (Cover illustration by Ken Green.)

while I was in Portugal; the Vietnam peace talks were taking place in Paris where the Sorbonne riots had closed the university for the first time in history. (We were the first group of tourists let into the city.) Yet another young person was killed trying to escape over the Berlin Wall while I was there and, after a month of studies in Vienna, we took a weekend in Prague just as the Russians invaded! All of these kinds of adventures and experiences shape my stories and my way of looking at life.

"After a few single years in Boston, I married and moved down to a small New England town on the South Shore. Here I fell in love with the sea. Down here much of life revolves around commercial fishing, lobstering, and the cranberry industry. I've gotten to know the lobstermen, harbormaster, cranberry growers, sailors: the people who make up the daily rhythms of my corner of the world.

"I decided since I was home with small children that I really wanted to put my creative energies into works of fiction. My first book for young adult readers, *Something Out There,* was a romantic mystery, set right out in our harbor. Because I love sailing and know about it, I made my first heroine a teenage sailing instructor and used our town as a model."

Reviewers were quick to compare the novel with Nancy Drew. Kathy Fruitts expressed a viewpoint shared by many when she wrote in *School Library Journal,* "Our 1980s Nancy Drew is Chips . . . ." Full of suspense and excitement—with a good love-story subplot—Guccione's first novel was accepted within the genre on its own merits.

Guccione broke out of what some called a formulaic style with *Tell Me How The Wind Sounds.* Through the protagonist, Amanda, the complexities of communication between new friends, especially when one is deaf, are addressed. A *Kirkus Reviews* contributor described Amanda's character development: "Believably, she works hard to expand her sign vocabulary long before she admits that this shy, difficult, sometimes embarrassing friend 'listen[s] better than people with ears that work [and knows] about things that matter.'" Katherine Bruner applauded the work in *School Library Journal* for how the "interaction between the two young people is powerful and believably constructed," and agreed with *Booklist's* Stephanie Zvirin's opinion of the ending, that "avoidance of a trite 'forever after' ending is a welcome change . . . ."

Guccione explained how she became interested in problems people face when they experience hearing loss: "The son of a friend of mine is profoundly deaf and I began to think about a story with a deaf character, one that would appeal to both hearing-impaired and hearing readers. The result was *Tell Me How the Wind Sounds.* I set the story on Clark's Island, right out in the bay. It is a simple story about a deaf boy whose life is turned upside down when a hearing teenage girl invades his island for the summer. The International Reader Association Young Adult Readers named it one of their best books of 1991. In 1996 I created the 'Hear No Evil' series for Scholastic which featured deaf teenage detective Sara Howell.

"In 1990 my editor at Scholastic read an article about whale watching being harmful to whales in Hawaii and asked if I might like to develop something with that theme, set in New England. I used the whale topic as the vehicle in *Nobody Listens to Me* and wrote about the conflict of two people, a father and daughter, who love each other, yet get caught up in a disagreement over the issue."

The book also won praise from reviewers for tackling a subject that is very real to children, but often overlooked by adults. Robert Hale summarized the key point in his review for *Horn Book:* "Not being listened to when one is being most serious is one of the worst crosses children have to bear." The subject at hand is not important. "What matters is that they be heard." In this case, Mendy took to the streets to protect whales endangered by waters unsettled by heavy boat traffic, to which her father contributed with his sight-seeing boat.

Guccione continued her interview with *SATA:* "I'm always working on more ideas, many of which are requests from my own children. Now I'm thinking again about the Delaware area and hope to write some historical fiction set in the black powder years along the Brandywine River."

The result, in part, was the novel, *Come Morning,* about one family's involvement with the Underground Railroad during the Civil War. Freedom Newcastle, aged twelve, is the son of a freed slave who has romanticized his father's role in the movement. He takes a big step toward maturity when he's forced to help. Ann Burlingame, in a *School Library Journal* review, recognized the novel's "excellent characterization," and recommended it to students studying that era.

Reflecting on her work, Guccione told *SATA:* "My interest in painting and visual expression has a noticeable effect on my style. I write colorful stories, full of description and sense of place."

Works Cited

Bruner, Katharine, review of *Tell Me How the Wind Sounds, School Library Journal,* October, 1989, p. 133.

Burlingame, Ann M., review of *Come Morning, School Library Journal,* November, 1995, p. 100.

Fruitts, Kathy, review of *Something Out There, School Library Journal,* January, 1986, p. 79.

Hale, Robert D., review of *Nobody Listens to Me, The Horn Book Magazine,* May-June, 1991, pp. 364-65.

Review of *Pretending, School Library Journal,* January, 1989, p. 106.

Review of *Tell Me How the Wind Sounds, Kirkus Reviews,* November 15, 1989, p. 1670.

Zvirin, Stephanie, review of *Tell Me How the Wind Sounds, Booklist,* December 1, 1998, p. 735.

For More Information See

PERIODICALS

Booklist, November 1, 1985, p. 397.
Publishers Weekly, July 12, 1991, p. 66.
Voice of Youth Advocates, February, 1986, p. 391.

H–I

HEBERT-COLLINS, Sheila 1948-

Personal

First part of surname is pronounced "A-bear"; born September 30, 1948, in Abbeville, LA; daughter of Irby Hebert (a court clerk) and Lillian Mouton (a homemaker); married Dennis L. Collins (an engineer), August 2, 1969; children: Cooper (son), Cody (daughter).

Sheila Hebert-Collins

Education: Louisiana State University-Baton Rouge, B.S., 1969. *Politics:* Democrat. *Religion:* Catholic.

Addresses

Home—311 Second St., Abbeville, LA 70510. *Office*—Pelican Publishing Company, P.O. Box 3110, Gretna, LA 70054. *E-mail*—kjuntale@acadian.net.

Career

Lower Elementary Teacher in Louisiana, 1969-89; has taken long-term substitute-teaching positions in public and private schools, 1989—. Lecturer and storyteller with the program "Cajun Education"; has visited over 120 schools and libraries. Founder of Les Chaunteurs (French children's singing group). *Member:* Louisiana Retired Teachers, Vermilion Arts Council, Confrerie d' Abbeville.

Writings

Jolie Blonde and the Three Heberts: A Cajun Twist to an Old Tale, Blue Heron (Thibodaux, LA), 1993, Pelican, 1999.

Petite Rouge: A Cajun Twist to an Old Tale, Blue Heron, 1994, Pelican, 1997.

Les Trois Cochon: A Cajun Twist to an Old Tale, illustrated by Patrick Soper, Blue Heron, 1996, Pelican, 1999.

Cendrillon: A Cajun Cinderella, Pelican, 1998.

Jean-Paul Hebert Was There, self published, 1998.

Work in Progress

'T Pousette and 'T Poulette: A Cajun Hansel and Gretel.

Sidelights

Sheila Hebert-Collins told *SATA:* "I was born in the heart of Cajun country, an authentic Cajun. My family and friends all spoke French and were very proud of their heritage. So I grew up with that Cajun pride as well. That Cajun pride motivated me to write my Cajun Fairy Tales, the only way I knew I could keep Cajun culture alive—in books for children. My books include over 30 French words and Cajun sayings, sayings I grew up with . . . .

"I was first published by a small Louisiana publisher who only published Louisiana topics, but children's books were a first. She was pleasantly surprised when our books sold out so quickly, so she encouraged me to write a series. Now I'm on the fifth of the series, but have since signed with Pelican Publishing Co., with worldwide distribution.

"These books have opened up a new life for me. To my mother's delight, my books have brought me back to my home town, Abbeville, living across the street from her. My children were able to attend the very same high school I did and I was able to celebrate my high-school reunion while watching my son lead my alma mater's football team to victory, and my daughter on the homecoming court. Dreams do come true!

"I've gone from teacher, to author, and now storyteller and lecturer. My goal of promoting the Cajun culture has truly been achieved since I have now visited over 120 schools and numerous libraries, reaching over 4000 children."

*   *   *

HICKMAN, Estella (Lee) 1942-

Personal

Born March 16, 1942, in Columbus, OH; daughter of Earl (a teacher of history and athletics) and Irene (a music teacher; maiden name, Blaettnar) Hickman; children: Shawn A. Smith, Shane A. Smith. *Education:* Columbus College of Art and Design, B.F.A., 1972; graduate study at Syracuse University. *Hobbies and other interests:* Going to the theater and opera, horse racing, "smooth jazz," reading, gardening, travel.

Addresses

Home—6121 Beechcroft Rd., Columbus, OH 43229. *Office*—Columbus College of Art and Design, 107 North Ninth St., Columbus, OH 43215. *Electronic mail*—estellasts@aol.com.

Career

WSYX-TV 6, Columbus, OH, art director, 1978-86; School Book Fairs Publishing, Worthington, OH, senior illustrator, 1986-91; Columbus College of Art and Design, Columbus, professor of illustration, c. 1988—. Starlet Studios, illustrator.

Illustrator

Margaret Holland and Craig B. McKee, *Alexandra and the Vanishing Unicorns,* Willowisp Press (Worthington, OH), 1986.

Debby Henwood, *You Can Draw Kittens and Cats,* Willowisp Press, 1987.

Marilyn D. Anderson, *The Bubble Gum Monster,* PAGES Publishing Group, 1987.

Sherry Shahan, *One Sister Too Many,* PAGES Publishing Group, 1987.

Elizabeth Van Steenwyck, *Sarah's Great Idea,* PAGES Publishing Group, 1987.

Shahan, *Baby-Sitting Crack-Up,* PAGES Publishing Group, 1988.

Margaret H. Issacsen-Bright, *Monster Don't Scare Me,* PAGES Publishing Group, 1988.

Michael J. Pellowski, *My Sister the Mess-Up,* PAGES Publishing Group, 1988.

Pellowski, *Triple Trouble,* PAGES Publishing Group, 1988.

Anderson, *The Bubble Gum Monster Strikes Again,* PAGES Publishing Group, 1989.

Janet Adele Bloss, *My Sister the Nightmare,* PAGES Publishing Group, 1989.

Shahan, *There's Something in There,* PAGES Publishing Group, 1989.

Pellowski, *Triple Trouble in Hollywood,* PAGES Publishing Group, 1989.

Peter Rabbit, Willowisp Press, 1990.

Anderson, *Nobody Wants Barkley,* Willowisp Press, 1990.

Bloss, *101 Ways to a Perfect Family,* Willowisp Press, 1990.

Margery Williams, *The Velveteen Rabbit,* Willowisp Press, 1991.

Holland, *Guess Who Learned to Read!,* Willowisp Press, 1991.

Candice F. Ransom, *Hocus-Pocus after School,* Willowisp Press, 1992.

Valerie Cutteridge, *Five Little Monkeys Going to the Zoo,* Seedling Publications (Columbus, OH), 1997.

Betty Erickson, *Big Bad Rex,* Seedling Publications, 1998.

Deborah Williams, *Awful Waffles,* Seedling Publications, 1998.

Work in Progress

Illustrating a new version of *Snow White and the Seven Dwarfs;* a series of illustrations of "Marguerita the Texas mouse"; portfolio pieces on Snow White, Highlander, and Coral and Nessie.

Sidelights

Estella Hickman told *SATA:* "I have been very privileged in the past few years to have introduced many of my students to Seedling Publications, and several of them have been hired to illustrate Seedling's children's books. The new challenge of going for my master's of illustration has opened many new and wonderful avenues that will hopefully lead to many challenging and superior book illustration projects."*

HICKS, Peter 1952-

Personal

Born October 4, 1952, in Brighton, England; son of Thomas (a sales manager) and Josephine (a retail assistant) Hicks; married Geraldine (a nurse), August 3, 1981; children: Tom, Andrew, Johanna. *Education:* St. Mary's College, certificate of education, 1974; The Open University, B.A., 1983; University of Sussex, M.A., 1986; Birkbeck College, University of London, certificate of field archaeology, 1993. *Politics:* Member of the Labour party.

Addresses

Home—169 Surrenden Road, Brighton, BN1 6NN, England. *Office*—Stanley Tech. High School, S. Norwood, London SE25 6AD, England. *Electronic mail*—peterhicks@lineone.net.

Career

Croydon Education Authority, head of faculty, 1988-97, senior teacher, 1997—. MacDonald Books, history consultant, 1998; school governorships, 1985-94; Sussex Archaeological Society, council member, 1993-96; writer, 1993—; Varndean College, adult education tutor, 1994—; University of Sussex, Centre for Continuing

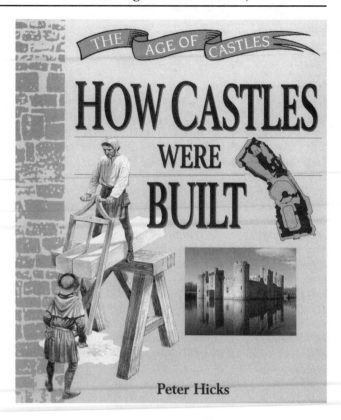

Hicks's book for middle readers describes the design, construction, and uses of various castles in Europe and other parts of the world. (Cover photo by Michael Holford.)

Education tutor, 1994—; *Times Educational Supplement,* archaeology book reviewer, London, 1997—.

Writings

The Aztecs, Thomson Learning (New York), 1993.
The Romans, Wayland (Hove, England), 1993, Thomson, 1994.
Family Life in Saxon Britain, Wayland, 1994.
The Sioux, Thomson, 1994.
Sports and Entertainment, Wayland, 1994, Thomson, 1995.
The Victorians, Wayland, 1995.
Pompeii and Herculaneum, Thomson, 1995.
Troy and Knossos, Thomson, 1996.
The Hidden Past, Raintree Steck-Vaughn, 1997.
Technology in the Time of the Vikings, Wayland, 1997, Raintree, 1998.
How Castles Were Built, Raintree, 1998.
Ancient Greece, Raintree, 1999.

Work in Progress

Gathering research about the Indian Army on the Western Front (1914-15) during World War I.

Sidelights

Peter Hicks told *SATA:* "I was very lucky to have parents who took me to dozens of historical and archaeological sites when I was young. As I got older, I

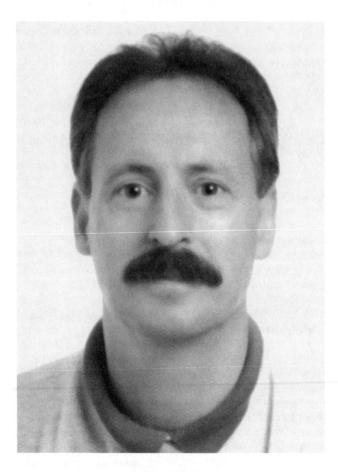

Peter Hicks

became more confident and 'persuaded' them to take me to obscure castles and battlefields! I grew up in Essex, United Kingdom, and traveling by bicycle, alone or with friends, I discovered castles and ancient churches. As a teacher, I am very keen to take pupils out into 'the field.' This has been a hallmark of all the departments and faculties I have worked in.

"In the late 1980s, I trained as a field archaeologist—this was a continuation of an obsession I have had since I was twelve years old, as well as a reaction to the state 'national curriculum' introduced at the same time (which is a bit of a straightjacket). This has allowed me to introduce an archaeological dimension to my teaching. Of course my writing career has allowed me to 'spread the word' to much larger numbers of young people. I hope that the enthusiasm I try to put over in my teaching is present in the books I have written!"

*   *   *

HIRSCH, Odo 19(?)-
[A pseudonym]

Personal

Male.

Addresses

Home—London, England.

Career

Physician. Author of books for adults and children.

Awards, Honors

Short-listed, National Children's Literature Award, Festival Awards for Literature; short-listed, Book of the Year for Younger Readers, Australian Children's Book Council Book of the Year Awards, 1998, both for *Antonio S. and the Mystery of Theodore Guzman.* Patricia Wrightson Prize for Children's Literature, New South Wales Premier's Awards, 1999, for *Antonio S. and the Mystery of Theodore Guzman.*

Writings

Antonio S. and the Mystery of Theodore Guzman, illustrated by Andrew McLean, Allen & Unwin (Carlton North, Australia), 1997.
Bartlett and the Ice Voyage, illustrated by McLean, Allen & Unwin, 1998.
Hazel Green, illustrated by McLean, Allen & Unwin, 1999.

Work in Progress

Bartlett and the City of Gloom and a sequel to *Hazel Green.*

Sidelights

Children's book author Odo Hirsch is shrouded in mystery. According to Virginia Lowe, writing in *Magpies:* "It is widely known that 'Odo Hirsch' is a pseudonym. His name is a secret, but I can reveal it is not someone very famous revealed—he is not HRH Charles Windsor, for instance." Hirsch is also an author of adult fiction, under yet another name, is a physician in London, England, and is highly educated with interests in many fields. He confided to Lowe that while writing fiction has no conflict with his current profession, he said that he does keep confidences and knowing that he wrote fiction might make his customers uneasy. Having said that, what we do know, as the publisher Allan-Unwin's online author profile of Hirsch states: "He now lives in London, and writes excellent books for children. His stories are exciting and funny and give you plenty to think about. They are full of unusual characters who have adventures in interesting places."

Beginning with the award-winning *Antonio S. and the Mystery of Theodore Guzman,* and continuing with *Bartlett and the Ice Voyage,* and *Hazel Green,* Hirsch explores the world of discovery that children delve into to create their own reality. In the first title, Antonio, in a secret room in the rambling mansion where he lives, spies a poster advertising *Hamlet* and becomes intrigued with the process of putting on a play. Encouraged by his magician father and professor mother, and guided by the mysterious neighbor Theodore Guzman, Antonio and his friends set about creating and staging their own production. In his interview with Lowe, Hirsch commented that in *Antonio S.* he "tries to capture certain elements of childhood—elements of inventiveness, discovery, learning, freshness. The book moves from a physical adventure ... to an imaginative one." According to Geraldine Brennan in an article in the *Times Educational Supplement:* "Like the production, the story gets off to a slow start but gathers pace and deserves applause." She also noted that readers of J. K. Rowling's books will like *Antonio S.* Beverly Mathias, writing in *School Librarian,* applauded the magic of the story as well as the gentle pacing of the text "which keeps the reader captivated." High praise also came from *Magpies* reviewer Kevin Steinberger who hailed the book as "a rare junior novel of superb literary quality and classically engaging storytelling."

Hirsch's second children's novel, *Bartlett and the Ice Voyage,* is more of an adventure story, populated with intrepid explorers and a busy young queen who rules seven countries. The tale, which Lowe referred to as a "cross between a fairy tale and a Boys' Own Annual" is a quest set upon by the famous explorer Bartlett and his dashing companion Jacques for an exotic fruit that the queen desires. The adventurers use their inventiveness, desperation, and perseverance in an attempt to grant the queen's request amidst the machinations of petty courtiers who fuel the queen's impatience. Steinberger called *Bartlett and the Ice Voyage* "beautifully crafted with nary a word out of place" as well as a "rare treat."

Unlike *Bartlett,* wherein the plot drives the story, Hirsch considers his third book for children, *Hazel Green,* to be quite different. It is the characters, particularly Hazel herself, who create interest and hold the reader's attention. Hazel is a determined girl with a formidable task—to revive the tradition of having children participate in her city's annual Frogg Day parade. She takes on the uncooperative parade organizer, Mr. Winkel, and is wrongfully accused of stealing the recipe for Chocolate Dippers by Mr. Volio the pastry chef. Fortunately, Hazel has many people behind her, including the mathematician Yak and Mrs. Gluck the floral arranger. Critic Jo Goodman in *Magpies,* called *Hazel Green* "delightful," and stated that "Hirsch deftly establishes a vivid cast of characters."

Speaking to Lynne Babbage in *Reading Time,* Hirsch attributes his ability to write so well for children to being surrounded by a large extended family, and maybe not quite having grown up all the way himself. That, and years of observing people, figuring out what makes them tick, have influenced his writing style. As Hirsch told Virginia Lowe, "what one does with one's influences is to make them into a different mix, that's what makes it original and different."

Works Cited

Babbage, Lynne, "Lunch with Odo Hirsch," *Reading Time,* May, 1999, pp. 2-3.
Brennan, Geraldine, "Dreams Meet Gritty Realism," *Times Educational Supplement,* March 5, 1999.
Goodman, Jo, review of *Hazel Green, Magpies,* March, 1999, p. 32.
Lowe, Virginia, interview with Odo Hirsch, *Magpies,* July, 1998, pp. 14-16.
Mathias, Beverly, review of *Antonio S. and the Mystery of Theodore Guzman, School Librarian,* summer, 1999, p. 89.
Steinberger, Kevin, review of *Bartlett and the Ice Voyage, Magpies,* July, 1998, p. 32.

For More Information See

PERIODICALS

Australian Jewish News, Melbourne edition, September 4, 1998.*

*   *   *

HOBERMAN, Mary Ann 1930-

Personal

Born August 12, 1930, in Stamford, CT; daughter of Milton (a salesman) and Dorothy (maiden name, Miller) Freedman; married Norman Hoberman (an architect, ceramist, and illustrator), February 4, 1951; children: Diane, Perry, Charles, Margaret. *Education:* Smith College, B.A. (magna cum laude), 1951; Yale University, M.A., 1985, postgraduate work in English literature. *Hobbies and other interests:* Biking, gardening, dancing.

Addresses

Home—98 Hunting Ridge Rd., Greenwich, CT 06831. *Agent*—Gina Maccoby Literary Agency, P.O. Box 60, Chappaqua, NY 10514.

Career

Children's poet. Speaker, consultant, and artist-in-the-schools, 1955—; author, 1957—. Fairfield University, Fairfield, CT, adjunct professor, 1980-83; C. G. Jung Center, New York City, program coordinator, 1981; former newspaper reporter and editor in a children's book department. Founder and member of The Pocket People (children's theater group), 1968-75; trustee, Greenwich Library, 1986-91. *Member:* Authors Guild.

Awards, Honors

Book Week Poem award from Children's Book Council, 1976; American Book Award, 1983, for *A House Is a House for Me; The Looking Book* and *A House Is a House for Me* were both selections of the Junior Literary Guild; Children's Books of Distinction list, *Riverbank Review,* 1999, for *The Llama Who Had No Pajama.*

Writings

POETRY FOR CHILDREN

All My Shoes Come in Two's, illustrated by husband, Norman Hoberman, Little, Brown, 1957.
How Do I Go?, illustrated by N. Hoberman, Little, Brown, 1958.

Mary Ann Hoberman

Hello and Good-by, illustrated by N. Hoberman, Little Brown, 1959.

What Jim Knew, illustrated by N. Hoberman, Little, Brown, 1963.

Not Enough Beds for the Babies, illustrated by Helen Spyer, Little, Brown, 1965.

A Little Book of Little Beasts, illustrated by Peter Parnall, Simon & Schuster, 1973.

The Looking Book, illustrated by Jerry Joyner, Viking, 1973.

The Raucous Auk: A Menagerie of Poems, illustrated by Joseph Low, Viking, 1973.

Nuts to You and Nuts to Me: An Alphabet of Poems, illustrated by Ronni Solbert, Knopf, 1974.

I Like Old Clothes, illustrated by Jacqueline Chwast, Knopf, 1976.

Bugs, illustrated by Victoria Chess, Viking, 1976.

A House Is a House for Me, illustrated by Betty Fraser, Viking, 1978.

Yellow Butter, Purple Jelly, Red Jam, Black Bread: Poems, illustrated by Chaya Burstein, Viking, 1981.

The Cozy Book, illustrated by Tony Chen, Viking, 1982, reprinted with illustrations by Betty Fraser, Browndeer Press, 1995.

Mr. and Mrs. Muddle, illustrated by Catharine O'Neill, Little, Brown, 1988.

A Fine Fat Pig, and Other Animal Poems, illustrated by Malcah Zeldis, HarperCollins, 1991.

Fathers, Mothers, Sisters, Brothers: A Collection of Family Poems, illustrated by Marilyn Hafner, Joy Street Books, 1991.

(Editor) *My Song Is Beautiful: Poems and Pictures in Many Voices,* Little, Brown, 1994.

The Seven Silly Eaters, illustrated by Marla Frazee, Harcourt Brace, 1997.

The Llama Who Had No Pajama: 100 Favorite Poems, illustrated by B. Fraser, Harcourt Brace, 1997.

One of Each, illustrated by Marjorie Priceman, Little, Brown, 1997.

(Adapter) *Miss Mary Mack: A Hand-Clapping Rhyme,* illustrated by Nadine Bernard Westcott, Little, Brown, 1998.

And to Think That We Thought That We'd Never Be Friends, illustrated by Kevin Hawkes, Crown, 1999.

The Strange Tale of the Marvelous Mouse Man, illustrated by Laura Forman, Harcourt Brace, 2000.

The Two Sillies, illustrated by Lynne Cravath, Harcourt Brace, 2000.

(Adapter) *The Eensy Weensy Spider,* illustrated by Bernard Westcott, Little, Brown, 2000.

Contributor of poems to numerous anthologies, textbooks, and magazines in the United States and abroad, including *The Southern Poetry Review, Small Pond,* and *Harper's.*

OTHER

Contributor of travel articles to the *New York Times* and *Boston Globe.*

Sidelights

A poet who finds inspiration in writing for children, Mary Ann Hoberman employs playful rhythms and rhymes in her picture books. Celebrating the everyday lives and concerns of children, Hoberman's books deal with animals, pesky little brothers and other family relationships, growing up, the idea of home, and a myriad of other such quotidian subjects, though her handling of such themes is far from commonplace. In *A House Is a House for Me,* which won the American Book Award, Hoberman takes the concept of house and home to the generic level, investigating rabbit hutches, mule sheds, and garages— houses for cars. "Hoberman's own imagination entices the reader/listener to use his imagination, to add more houses for more things," commented Mary Lystad in a critical analysis of Hoberman's work in *St. James Guide to Children's Writers.* It is this teasing of imagination for which Hoberman is best known; her two dozen plus books attest to an imagination ever at work. As *Riverbank Review* noted in its 1999 Children's Books of Distinction awards list, Hoberman's "overriding theme is the joy of playing with words."

Born on August 12, 1930, in Stamford, Connecticut, Hoberman grew up in various towns in the Northeast before returning to Stamford and the house "that is the locus and inspiration for most of my writing for children," as Hoberman noted in *Something about the Author Autobiography Series (SAAS).* The older of two children, Hoberman was often put in charge of her younger brother, a sibling relationship that also found expression in her later writing. One thing was certain in Hoberman's youth: she wanted to become a writer. "I have always wanted to be a writer," Hoberman explained in *SAAS.* "This conviction saved me a lot of career counseling later on in life, but it has always puzzled me. How did I know so early on that that was what I wanted to do with my life?"

Books and words were among her best friends as a young girl and adolescent. She made up rhymes everywhere, especially on the swing where the natural physical rhythm encouraged word play. Graduating from Stamford High School, Hoberman went on to Smith College on the advice of one of her teachers who had graduated from that college. Hoberman was on one of the first post-war junior-year-abroad programs, traveling to France to study in the company of young women from other prestigious schools. Among these was Jacqueline Bouvier, the future Mrs. John F. Kennedy. The year in France was a revelation for Hoberman and only reluctantly did she return to America and her senior year at Smith. But soon she met a senior at Harvard Law School and the two were married within four months.

During the Korean War, both Hoberman and her husband finished school before he was sent off to the military. As luck would have it, he was ultimately stationed in Canada where Hoberman could join him, and there the couple had their first baby. After military service, Hoberman's husband decided to return to college to study architecture. During her husband's studies, Hoberman became a freelance editor at Little, Brown in Boston and also a mother for the second and third times. It was during this time, as a mother giving birth to three children in three years, that Hoberman began playing with rhymes once again. Wheeling the children in the park one day, she came up with a short couplet, "All my shoes / Come in two's," that she turned into her first rhyming picture book, illustrated by her husband. It was a sudden inspiration and something of a lark to put the book together; then she sent it off to an editor at Little, Brown and forgot about it. Months later came the acceptance. Writing in the *New York Times Book Review,* C. Elta Van Norman called *All My Shoes Come in Two's* "a unique treatment of a subject fascinating to the small child." Hoberman was on her way to becoming a children's author.

The Hobermans collaborated on several books, looking at modes of transport in *How Do I Go?,* at greetings in *Hello and Good-by,* and at fantasy worlds in *What Jim Knew.* Generally well received, Hoberman's books of verses for young and very young children began to win a friendly readership. Hoberman worked in a variety of poetic techniques and forms, from free verse to metered poems, from internal rhyme to end rhyme, and from alliteration to the tongue twister. Teaming up with other illustrators, Hoberman has gone on to create award-

winning titles in her verse picture books, and a chapter book, *Mr. and Mrs. Muddle,* about a horse couple who learn the art of compromise.

In the rhyming picture book *The Raucous Auk,* Hoberman's sense of word play is finely honed. Here she deals with familiar animals—the giraffe, the camel, the walrus—as well as those not quite so familiar—the okapi, the panda, and the tapir. Paul Heins, reviewing *The Raucous Auk* in *Horn Book,* declared that "the author's humorously speculative verses lead to Ogden Nash-like conclusions." Heins was referring to verses such as: "The ocelot's a clever cat. / She knowsalot of this and that. / She growsalot of spotted fur / which looks extremely well on her." An alphabet book, *Nuts to You and Nuts to Me,* as well as a counting book, *The Looking Book,* followed.

Of her early work, *A House Is a House for Me* is one of her most popular. Collaborating with illustrator Betty Fraser, Hoberman employed "alternating lines of anapestic trimeter and tetrameter with lots of end and internal rhyme," according to Sharon Elswit in *School Library Journal.* Hoberman created "a rich book," and one that would make kids, according to Elswit, "reach for the colors and chorus the refrain." Harold C. K. Rice called it "an astonishing picture book, one of the best of the year," in the *New York Times Book Review.* In paperback, *A House Is a House for Me* won the American Book Award for picture book paperback. Twenty years later, Hoberman once again teamed up with Fraser for *The Llama Who Had No Pajama,* a collection of one hundred poems. A *Publishers Weekly* reviewer noted that this "inventively illustrated collection brims with enough wordplay and silliness to please a room full of young wordsmiths."

The Cozy Book, first published in 1982 with illustrations by Tony Chen, won a reprise with a 1995 edition, illustrated by Fraser. Of the 1982 book, Brenda Durrin Maloney wrote in *School Library Journal* that just as the author did with the concept of home in *A House Is a House for Me,* Hoberman "stretches the definition of the word *cozy,*" making it include "food, people, feelings, sounds, smells, and more." Hoberman documents a day in the life of a young child from waking up early in the morning to going to bed at night. Of the 1995 edition, with Fraser's illustrations, a *Kirkus Reviews* contributor concluded that the book was "right on mark" as "riotously pell-mell wordplay and as a catalog of a child's world," while Hanna B. Zeiger noted in *Horn Book* that "every page is filled with myriad details," and that the book was "sure to be a favorite."

After taking a hiatus from writing during the 1980s to return to college to complete an advanced degree, Hoberman subsequently came back to writing with renewed vigor. As she noted in *SAAS:* "My sabbatical had done its work; after all those years of academic papers, I was eager to write for children once more." Her *A Fine Fat Pig and Other Animal Poems* features a favorite Hoberman motif—description of animals. Mary Jo Salter, writing in *Washington Post Book World,* found

From The Cozy Book, *written by Hoberman and illustrated by Betty Fraser.*

Hoberman's verse in this collection "irresistibly memorizable." Reviewing *Fathers, Mothers, Sisters, Brothers,* Hoberman's 1991 collection of poems dealing with the family, a writer for *Kirkus Reviews* called the work "wise, witty, and neatly constructed." As Hoberman commented in *SAAS,* the idea for *Fathers, Mothers, Sisters, Brothers* "had been evolving over a lifetime. In the poems I write about many of the feelings I had as a child, of the relationships I experienced and observed, as well as of new kinds of family life and configurations."

A departure for Hoberman was *My Song Is Beautiful,* a collection of multicultural poems from around the world, which she edited. Here are included Eskimo chants, a Chippewa song, a verse from ancient Mexico, as well as lines from A. A. Milne and Nikki Giovanni. A *Publishers Weekly* reviewer called the collection an "outstanding multicultural anthology," and concluded that "this eclectic and joyful volume underscores Hoberman's conviction that 'Every you everywhere in the world is an I; / Every I in the world is a you!'" *Booklist's* Hazel Rochman commented that this "small anthology celebrates diversity, not only in culture, but also in mood and genre." Writing in *School Library Journal,* Dot Minzer called the volume a "first-rate collection that definitely deserves consideration."

Finicky eaters get the Hoberman treatment in *The Seven Silly Eaters,* "a highly comic rhyming romp," according to Barbara Elleman writing in *School Library Journal.* Mrs. Peters, eternally pregnant, would like nothing better than to play her cello in peace, but she is continually at work to feed the disparate appetites of her children, some who like milk, some who like lemonade—but not from a can. Another wants homemade bread, while only creamy oatmeal will satisfy other taste buds. "The combination of food and farce makes for an affectionate rhyming picture book," observed *Booklist's* Rochman. Ann A. Flowers concluded in a *Horn Book* review that the book was a "pleasure for parent and child."

Hoberman returned to the animal kingdom for *One of Each,* featuring a hound dog, and *Miss Mary Mack,* starring a clumsy pachyderm. In the former title, Oliver Tolliver is "a dapper and bewhiskered hound," according to Carol Ann Wilson in *School Library Journal,* who is happy with his home and possessions, of which he has one of each. Inviting the cat, Peggoty Small, to enjoy his home, he is surprised when she finds it all too predictable and boring—there's nothing for her there. Readjusting his singular possessions, he invites Peggoty back, and she suddenly enjoys the new dual-item household. "A 'peachy' offering from a talented team," Wilson concluded in her review. Elizabeth Bush advised in *Bulletin of the Center for Children's Books* that teachers should "run this by the preschool or primary students when it's time to lay down the classroom laws: sharing and caring." Susan Dove Lempke, reviewing the book in *Booklist,* called it a "surefire story-time hit."

Miss Mary is definitely surprised to find an elephant crashing her backyard barbecue in *Miss Mary Mack,* an

Hoberman edited this unique collection of poetry featuring the work of such renowned writers as A. A. Milne and Nikki Giovanni, as well as poems and artwork created by elementary school children.

adaptation of "a favorite hand-clapping rhyme," according to *Booklist's* Stephanie Zvirin. Escaping from the zoo, the rambunctious pachyderm has a great time at the barbecue cum tea party. "Hands will be clapping and toes will be tapping to this spunky rendition of a favorite schoolyard rhyme," declared a reviewer for *Publishers Weekly.* Jane Marino echoed these sentiments in *School Library Journal:* "This high-flying package of fun, complete with music and hand instructions, will have children clapping along in no time."

It is exactly such infectious rhyming and rhythms that have made Hoberman a school favorite. "Children love it," she once told Allen Raymond in *Early Years.* "Adult poetry tossed out rhyme and regular rhythm; that's old hat now. Limericks, light verse—no one does that anymore. If I want to write poetry that way, writing for children is the last bastion."

Works Cited

Bush, Elizabeth, review of *One of Each, Bulletin of the Center for Children's Books,* October, 1997, p. 53.
Review of *The Cozy Book, Kirkus Reviews,* October 15, 1995, p. 1493.
Elleman, Barbara, review of *The Seven Silly Eaters, School Library Journal,* March, 1997, p. 160.
Elswit, Sharon, review of *A House Is a House for Me, School Library Journal,* October, 1978, p. 133.

Now Mary Mack, Mack, Mack,
All dressed in black, black, black,
Has *purple* buttons, buttons, buttons,
Down her back, back, back.

And Elephant, Phant, Phant,
Has shiny rows, rows, rows,
Of silver buttons, buttons, buttons,
Down his nose, nose, nose.

From Miss Mary Mack, *adapted by Hoberman and illustrated by Nadine Bernard Westcott.*

Review of *Fathers, Mothers, Sisters, Brothers: A Collection of Family Poems, Kirkus Reviews,* October 1, 1991, p. 1295.

Flowers, Ann A., review of *The Seven Silly Eaters, Horn Book,* May-June, 1997, p. 308.

Heins, Paul, review of *The Raucous Auk: A Menagerie of Poems, Horn Book,* January-February, 1974, pp. 59-60.

Hoberman, Mary Ann, *All My Shoes Come in Two's,* Little, Brown, 1957.

Hoberman, Mary Ann, *The Raucous Auk: A Menagerie of Poems,* Viking, 1973.

Hoberman, Mary Ann, *My Song Is Beautiful: Poems and Pictures in Many Voices,* Little, Brown, 1994.

Hoberman, Mary Ann, essay in *Something about the Author Autobiography Series,* Volume 18, Gale, 1994, pp. 113-131.

Lempke, Susan Dove, review of *One of Each, Booklist,* November 1, 1997, p. 466.

Review of *The Llama Who Had No Pajama, Publishers Weekly,* November 23, 1998, p. 97.

Review of *The Llama Who Had No Pajama, Riverbank Reviews,* spring, 1999, p. 22.

Lystad, Mary, "Hoberman, Mary Ann," *St. James Guide to Children's Writers,* edited by Sara Pendergast and Tom Pendergast, St. James Press, 1999, pp. 506-08.

Maloney, Brenda Durrin, review of *The Cozy Book, School Library Journal,* January, 1983, pp. 60-61.

Marino, Jane, review of *Miss Mary Mack, School Library Journal,* May, 1998, p. 117.

Minzer, Dot, review of *My Song Is Beautiful: Poems and Pictures in Many Voices, School Library Journal,* June, 1994, p. 119.

Review of *Miss Mary Mack, Publishers Weekly,* April 20, 1998, p. 65.

Review of *My Song Is Beautiful: Poems and Pictures in Many Voices, Publishers Weekly,* May 9, 1994, p. 73.

Raymond, Allen, "Mary Ann Hoberman: Fun-loving Poet, Student of Literature . . . ," *Early Years,* January, 1985, pp. 23-4.

Rice, Harold C. K., "Good Looking," *New York Times Book Review,* December 10, 1978, pp. 72-73, 93.

Rochman, Hazel, review of *My Song Is Beautiful: Poems and Pictures in Many Voices, Booklist,* June 1, 1994, p. 1828.

Rochman, Hazel, review of *The Seven Silly Eaters, Booklist,* March 1, 1997, p. 1172.

Salter, Mary Jo, "Peaceable Kingdom," *Washington Post Book World,* May 12, 1991, p. 18.

Van Norman, C. Elta, "Slippers with Zippers," *New York Times Book Review,* May 26, 1957, p. 26.

Wilson, Carol Ann, review of *One of Each, School Library Journal,* September, 1997, p. 183.

Zeiger, Hanna B., review of *The Cozy Book, Horn Book,* January-February, 1996, p. 98.

Zvirin, Stephanie, review of *Miss Mary Mack, Booklist,* March 15, 1998, p. 1245.

For More Information See

BOOKS

Authors of Books for Young People, Scarecrow Press, 1990.
Children's Books and Their Creators, edited by Anita Silvey, Houghton, 1995.
Children's Literature Review, Volume 22, Gale, 1991, pp. 107-115.
Holmes Holtze, Sally, essay in *Sixth Book of Junior Authors,* H. W. Wilson, 1989, pp. 132-133.

PERIODICALS

Bulletin of the Center for Children's Books, April, 1994, p. 261; May, 1997, pp. 324-25.
Kirkus Reviews, February 1, 1997, p. 223.
New York Times Book Review, July 6, 1997, p. 16.
School Library Journal, April, 1998, p. 118.*

—Sketch by *J. Sydney Jones*

*   *   *

HORNE, Richard (George Anthony) 1960-
(Harry Horse)

Personal

Born May 9, 1960, in Earlsdon, Coventry, Warwickshire, England; son of Henry Derek (a chartered surveyor) and Josephine Anne (a homemaker; maiden name, Moody) Horne; married Amanda Grace Williamson (an artist), March 23, 1990. *Education:* Attended Wrekin College. *Politics:* Liberal. *Religion:* Church of England. *Hobbies and other interests:* Playing the banjo.

Addresses

Home—The Old School House, Loch Awe, By Dalmally, Argyllshire, Scotland PA33 1 AQ. *Office*—c/o Penguin Children's Books, 27 Wrights Lane, London W8 5 TZ, England. *Agent*—Caroline Sheldon, 71 Hillgate Place, London W8 7SS, England.

Career

Illustrator/cartoonist. Candlemaker Row, Edinburgh, Scotland, and Silvermills Lane, Edinburgh, Scotland, book illustrator, 1977-80; Symington Mains, Fountainhall, The Borders, Scotland, book illustrator, 1980-83. *Scotland on Sunday,* political cartoonist, 1987-93. Writer and illustrator of children's books.

Awards, Honors

Writer of the Year Award, Scottish Arts Council, 1984, for *The Ogopogo;* Smarties Gold Award, Book Trust (England), 1998, for *The Last Gold Diggers;* Kinderjury Award, 1998, for *The Last Polar Bears.*

Writings

SELF-ILLUSTRATED

The Ogopogo, or, My Journey with the Loch Ness Monster, MacDonald (Loanhead, UK), 1981.
The Last Polar Bears, Viking (London), 1993.
A Friend for Little Bear, Candlewick (Cambridge, MA), 1996.
The Last Gold Diggers, Puffin (London), 1998.
The Last Cowboys, Puffin, 1999.

ILLUSTRATOR

Michael Mullin, *Magus the Lollipopman,* Canongate (Edinburgh), 1981.
David Hamilton, *The Good Golf Guide to Scotland,* Canongate, 1982, published as *The Scottish Golf Guide,* Canongate, 1985.
Robert Louis Stevenson, *The Strange Case of Dr. Jekyll & Mr. Hyde,* Canongate, 1986, Dufour Editons (Chester Springs, PA), 1987.
Stuart McDonald, *The Adventures of Endill Swift,* Canongate, 1990.
M. C. Strong, *The Great Rock Discography,* Canongate, 1994.
Yefim Druts and Alexei Gessler, *Russian Gypsy Tales,* Trafalgar Square (North Pomfret, VT), 1995.
(Editor) Susan Price, *Horror Stories,* Larousse Kingfisher Chambers, 1995.
M. C. Strong, *The Wee Rock Discography,* Canongate, 1996.
Jim Dodge, *Fup,* Rebel, Inc., 1997.
Dick King-Smith, *Noah's Brother,* Puffin, 1998.
Dick King-Smith, *Tumbleweed,* Puffin, 1998.
Dick King-Smith, *Toby Man,* Penguin, 1998.
Higglety Pigglety Pop (collected poems), Walker, 1999.
Margaret Mahy, *A Villain's Night Out,* Puffin, 1999.
Tony Mitton, *What's the Time Mr. Wolf?,* Walker, 1999.
Dick King-Smith, *Julius Caesar's Goat,* Penguin, 1999.
Dorothy van Woerhom, *Maths Together Green Set: Abu Ali Counts His Donkeys,* Walker, 1999.

Horne has contributed cartoons to numerous publications, including *The Guardian, The Sunday Telegraph,* and *The New Yorker.* Contributes a weekly cartoon to *The Scotsmen* called *Horsebox.* Writer and designer of *Drowned God,* a CD-rom computer game published by Time Warner, 1996.

Adaptations

The Last Polar Bears was adapted for Telemagination/ITV, 2000.

Work in Progress

The Snowbird and *Letters from an Idiot,* 2000; *The Last Polar Bears* (picture book), for Penguin, 2000; *Roo in Rabbit World,* for Penguin, 2001.

Sidelights

Richard Horne told *SATA:* "I wanted to become an illustrator at a ridiculously precocious age. I was seven

From **A Friend for Little Bear,** *written and illustrated by Richard Horne.*

when I first told my parents that I wanted to illustrate books when I grew up. Their reaction to this news was not what I had anticipated. It was to become a source of conflict for the next ten years, culminating with me running away from home at the age of seventeen to pursue my chosen career.

"I had no formal art training, as I was unable to attend art college without my parents' help. So I began work in Edinburgh as a staff illustrator on a magazine called *City Lynx*. I was nineteen when I illustrated *Magus the Lollipopman*, a delightful story by the Irish writer, Michael Mullin. Two years later, I wrote my first book, and it contained many of the threads that I have revisited in my work—namely, an old man's last journey on this earth."

Horne's self-illustrated book, *The Last Polar Bears,* details the story of an adventurous grandfather and his dog, Roo, who are on a journey to seek the last polar bears. The tale is uniquely told through a collection of

letters from the grandfather in the Arctic to his grandchild back home. This frequently humorous tale also addresses serious issues like the hazards of such a journey, as well as larger issues such as pollution and global warming. Horne's venture into authorship met with an enthusiastic reception by such critics as George Hunt and Janet Tayler. Hunt, a reviewer for *Books for Keeps,* commented on Horne's line drawings, dubbing them "sprightly and facetious," and continued on to say that the author created an "original atmosphere" in the story. *School Librarian* critic Tayler praised the artwork, raving "I love the delightful illustrations ... that accompany the text as Grandfather's sketches in his letters."

A Friend for Little Bear, also written and illustrated by Horne, features Little Bear stranded alone on a deserted island. Wishing for a playmate, the lonesome bear searches through mounds of toys before discovering that a true friend is all that he needs. This heartwarming tale imparts valuable truths about friendship to all readers, children and adults alike. Patricia Mahoney Brown, writing in *School Library Journal,* paid tribute to the book, terming it an "effective springboard for discussions on friendship, values, materialism, loneliness, and happiness . . . ." A critic for *Kirkus Reviews* also thought that the book was a worthy effort, remarking that it "has a message, one worth repeating," and noted Horne's "sweet, engaging" drawings.

Works Cited

Brown, Patricia Mahoney, review of *A Friend for Little Bear, School Library Journal,* September, 1996, p. 180.
Review of *A Friend for Little Bear, Kirkus Reviews,* July 15, 1996, p. 1049.
Hunt, George, review of *The Last Polar Bears, Books for Keeps,* January, 1997, pp. 21-22.
Tayler, Janet, review of *The Last Polar Bears, School Librarian,* February, 1994, p. 21.

For More Information See

PERIODICALS

Carousel, spring, 1999, p. 30.
School Librarian, autumn, 1999, pp. 136, 145.*

*   *   *

HORSE, Harry
See HORNE, Richard (George Anthony)

*   *   *

HOWE, James 1946-

Personal

Born August 2, 1946, in Oneida, NY; son of Lee Arthur (a clergyman) and Lonnelle (a teacher; maiden name, Crossley) Howe; married Deborah Smith (a writer and actress), September 28, 1969 (died, June 3, 1978); married Betsy Imershein (a photographer), April 5, 1981; children: (second marriage) Zoe. *Education:* Boston University, B.F.A., 1968; Hunter College of the City University of New York, M.A., 1977. *Hobbies and other interests:* Bicycling, hiking, skiing, movies, theater, traveling, reading.

Addresses

Agent—Amy Berkower, Writers House Inc., 21 West 26th St., New York, NY 10010.

Career

Freelance actor and director, 1971-75; Lucy Kroll Agency, New York City, literary agent, 1976-81; children's writer, 1981—. Member of advisory board, Hospice of St. Vincent's Hospital, 1979-81, and Ethnic Heritage Program, Henry Street Settlement, 1980-83; member of board of trustees, Village Temple, 1980-85; member of board of directors, Hastings Creative Arts Council, 1991—. *Military service:* Civilian public service, 1968-70. *Member:* Authors Guild, PEN American Center, Mystery Writers of America, Society of Children's Book Writers and Illustrators, Writers Guild of America, East.

Awards, Honors

Notable book citation, American Library Association (ALA), 1979, and Pacific Northwest Young Readers' Choice Award, 1982, both for *Bunnicula: A Rabbit-Tale of Mystery; Bunnicula* has also received twelve other Children's Choice awards from various states, including Florida, Hawaii, Illinois, and Vermont, and a listing among *Booklist's* "Fifty All-Time Favorite Children's Books"; Honor Book in Nonfiction, *Boston Globe-Horn Book,* notable book citation, ALA, and Children's Book of the Year citation, Library of Congress, all 1981, and nonfiction nominee, American Book Award in Children's Books (now National Book Award), 1982, all for *The Hospital Book;* CRABbery honor book, 1984, for *The Celery Stalks at Midnight;* Volunteer State award, 1984, for *Howliday Inn;* Washington Irving Younger Fiction award, and runner-up, Colorado Children's Book Award, both 1988, and both for *There's a Monster under My Bed;* Garden State Children's Book Award for Younger Fiction, 1990, for *Nighty-Nightmare;* North Dakota Children's Choice Picture Book, 1992, for *Harold and Chester in Scared Silly: A Halloween Treat.*

James Howe

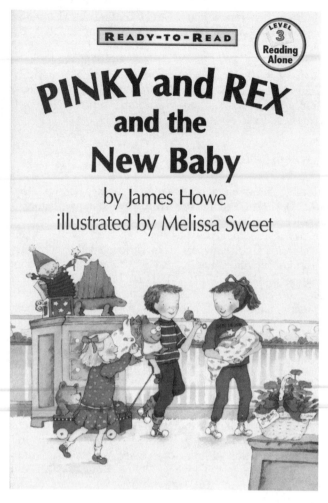

READY-TO-READ

LEVEL 3 Reading Alone

PINKY and REX and the New Baby

by James Howe
illustrated by Melissa Sweet

After her family adopts a new baby, Rex must face the joys and challenges of being a big sister while she maintains her long-standing connection to her best friend, Pinky. (Cover illustration by Melissa Sweet.)

Howe's works have been cited by such periodicals as *School Library Journal* and *Booklist,* and by such organizations as the Junior Literary Guild, the American Booksellers Association, the Child Study Children's Book Committee, the Children's Book Council, the National Science Teachers Association, and the International Reading Association; they have also received numerous other children's choice awards.

Writings

FOR CHILDREN

(With Deborah Howe) *Teddy Bear's Scrapbook,* illustrated by David S. Rose, Atheneum, 1980.
The Hospital Book (nonfiction), photographs by Mal Warshaw, Crown, 1981, Morrow, 1994.
Annie Joins the Circus (spin-off from movie *Annie*), illustrated by Leonard Shortall, Random House, 1982.
The Case of the Missing Mother, illustrated by William Cleaver, Random House, 1983.
A Night without Stars, Atheneum, 1983.

The Muppet Guide to Magnificent Manners; Featuring Jim Henson's Muppets, illustrated by Peter Elwell, Random House, 1984.
How the Ewoks Saved the Trees: An Old Ewok Legend (spin-off from movie *Return of the Jedi*), illustrated by Walter Velez, Random House, 1984.
Morgan's Zoo, illustrated by Leslie Morrill, Atheneum, 1984.
The Day the Teacher Went Bananas (picture book), illustrated by Lillian Hoban, Dutton, 1984.
Mister Tinker in Oz ("Brand-New Oz" adventure series), illustrated by D. Rose, Random House, 1985.
When You Go to Kindergarten, photographs by wife Betsy Imershein, Knopf, 1986, revised second edition, Morrow, 1994.
There's a Monster under My Bed (picture book), illustrated by D. Rose, Atheneum, 1986.
A Love Note for Baby Piggy, Marvel, 1986.
(Reteller) *Babes in Toyland* (adaptation of 1903 operetta by Victor Herbert and Glen MacDonough), illustrated by Allen Atkinson, Gulliver Books, 1986.
(Reteller) *The Secret Garden* (adaptation of the classic by Frances Hodgson Burnett), illustrated by Thomas B. Allen, Random House, 1987.
I Wish I Were a Butterfly (picture book), illustrated by Ed Young, Gulliver Books, 1987.
Carol Burnett: The Sound of Laughter ("Women of Our Time" series), illustrated by Robert Masheris, Viking, 1987.
(Adaptor) *Dances with Wolves: A Story for Children* (adapted from the screenplay by Michael Blake), Newmarket Press, 1991.
Creepy-Crawly Birthday, Avon, 1992.
There's a Dragon in My Sleeping Bag, illustrations by D. Rose, Macmillan, 1994.
The New Nick Kramer, or My Life as a Baby-Sitter, Hyperion, 1995.
Horace and Morris but Mostly Dolores, illustrated by Amy Walrod, Atheneum, 1997.
The Watcher, Atheneum, 1997.

"BUNNICULA" SERIES

(With D. Howe) *Bunnicula: A Rabbit-Tale of Mystery,* illustrated by Alan Daniel, Atheneum, 1979.
Howliday Inn, illustrated by Lynn Munsinger, Atheneum, 1982.
The Celery Stalks at Midnight, illustrated by Leslie Morrill, Atheneum, 1983.
Nighty-Nightmare, illustrated by L. Morrill, Atheneum, 1987.
Harold and Chester in the Fright before Christmas, illustrated by L. Morrill, Morrow, 1988.
Harold and Chester in Scared Silly: A Halloween Treat, illustrated by L. Morrill, Morrow, 1989.
Harold and Chester in Hot Fudge, illustrated by L. Morrill, Morrow, 1990.
Harold and Chester in Creepy-Crawly Birthday, illustrated by L. Morrill, Morrow, 1991.
Return to Howliday Inn, illustrated by A. Daniel, Atheneum, 1992.
The Bunnicula Fun Book, illustrations by A. Daniel, Morrow, 1993.

Rabbit-Cadabra!, illustrations by A. Daniel, Morrow, 1993.

Bunnicula Escapes!: A Pop-Up Adventure, illustrated by A. and Lea Daniel, paper engineering by Vicki Teague-Cooper, Tupelo Books, 1994.

Bunnicula Strikes Again!, Atheneum, 1999.

"SEBASTIAN BARTH" MYSTERY SERIES

What Eric Knew, Atheneum, 1985.
Stage Fright, Atheneum, 1986.
Eat Your Poison, Dear, Atheneum, 1986.
Dew Drop Dead, Atheneum, 1990.

"PINKY AND REX" SERIES

Pinky and Rex, illustrated by Melissa Sweet, Atheneum, 1990.

Pinky and Rex Get Married, illustrated by M. Sweet, Atheneum, 1990.

Pinky and Rex and the Spelling Bee, illustrated by M. Sweet, Atheneum, 1991.

Pinky and Rex and the Mean Old Witch, illustrated by M. Sweet, Atheneum, 1991.

Pinky and Rex Go to Camp, illustrated by M. Sweet, Atheneum, 1992.

Pinky and Rex and the New Baby, illustrated by M. Sweet, Macmillan, 1993.

Pinky and Rex and the Double-Dad Weekend, illustrated by M. Sweet, Atheneum, 1995.

Pinky and Rex and the Bully, illustrated by M. Sweet, Atheneum, 1996.

Pinky and Rex and the New Neighbors, illustrated by M. Sweet, Atheneum, 1997.

Pinky and Rex and the Perfect Pumpkin, illustrated by M. Sweet, Atheneum, 1998.

Pinky and Rex and the School Play, illustrated by M. Sweet, Atheneum, 1998.

OTHER

My Life as a Babysitter (television play), The Disney Channel, 1990.

Playing with Words, photographs by Michael Craine, R. C. Owen, 1994.

(Compiler with William A. Stephany) *The McGraw-Hill Book of Drama,* McGraw-Hill, 1995.

Also compiler of *365 New Words-a-Year Shoelace Calendar for Kids,* Workman Publishing, 1983-85. Contributor to *Horn Book* and *School Library Journal.*

Some of Howe's works have been translated into French, German, Swedish, Danish, Italian, Japanese, Spanish, and Dutch.

Adaptations

Bunnicula has been adapted into an animated television movie, produced by Ruby-Spears Productions, ABC, 1982, a sound recording, narrated by Lou Jacobi, Caedmon Records, 1982, and a videocassette, World Vision Home Video; *Howliday Inn* has been adapted into a sound recording, narrated by Jacobi, Caedmon Records, 1984; *The Celery Stalks at Midnight* has been adapted into a sound recording, 1987; *Nighty-Nightmare* has been adapted into a sound recording, narrated by George S. Irving, Caedmon, 1988.

Sidelights

"Humor is the most precious gift I can give to my reader," James Howe once noted in *Horn Book.* Howe, a writer of fiction, nonfiction, and picture books, gives mightily of that gift in all his works, relating laugh-out-loud tales of vampire bunnies and talking pets in his "Bunnicula" series, and sometimes painfully funny coming-of-age stories in his non-series middle-grade novels. He also serves up close friendship in the chapter-book series, "Pinky and Rex," and mystery with an often humorous twist in his series for junior high readers, "Sebastian Barth." In addition, Howe has also penned picture books and novels, many of which are movie spin-offs. However, with his 1997 novel, *The Watcher,* a serious novel about child abuse, Howe moved into new literary territory.

Born in Oneida, New York, in 1946, Howe grew up in a family that loved words. As a child he began what has become his trademark—wordplay, but as a youngster such verbal pyrotechnics were an attempt to win the attention of his three older brothers. Words became such a fixation for him, that he thought for sure he would be an actor when he grew up. At Boston University he earned a degree in fine arts, working afterward as an actor and director for several years before returning to graduate school where a seminar in playwriting rekindled his childhood love of words. For several years, he also worked as a literary agent in New York City, so that by the time he and his first wife, Deborah, thought of collaborating on a children's book, he was familiar with the world of publishing.

The first collaborative effort led to publication of *Bunnicula: A Rabbit-Tale of Mystery,* winner of a Dorothy Canfield Fisher Award, and an instant success with young readers. The story revolves around Chester, an arrogant, lofty cat who relishes horror stories, and Harold, a lumbering, shaggy dog who narrates the tale under the pseudonym Harold X. (to protect the innocent). The sleuths team up when their owners, the Monroes, innocently adopt a bunny abandoned at a movie theater and name it Bunnicula, after the chilling film *Dracula* that had been playing in a local theater. Convinced that Bunnicula is really a vampire rabbit—it does have oddly-shaped teeth resembling fangs *and* the vegetables in the house have been mysteriously drained of their color soon after Bunnicula's arrival—the cat-and-dog twosome attempt to warn the unsuspecting Monroes. *Bunnicula's* "stylish, exuberant make-believe," observed a reviewer in *Publishers Weekly,* arises from the Howe's "unreined imagination and . . . glinting sense of humor." Zena Sutherland, reviewing the first book in the series in *Bulletin of the Center for Children's Books,* summed up its appeal by noting that "the plot is less important in the story than the style." Sutherland went on to characterize that style as "blithe, sophisticated, and distinguished for the wit and humor of the dialogue."

"Bunnicula" soon evolved into a series, with the completion of such light-hearted and comic tales as *Howliday Inn, The Celery Stalks at Midnight, Nighty-Nightmare, Harold and Chester in Creepy-Crawly Birthday, Return to Howliday Inn,* and *Bunnicula Strikes Again!* Chateau Bow-Wow provides the locale for *Howliday Inn* (so named because Chester is convinced it shelters werewolves). In the story, Chester and Harold are lodged at a boarding house from which cats and dogs strangely disappear almost daily. Frantic when Louise, the French poodle, vanishes, the distressed pair fears the work of a villainous murderer. "Wonderfully witty dialogue and irresistible characters" fill the story, decided a *Publishers Weekly* reviewer. *The Celery Stalks at Midnight* follows the duo's efforts to track Bunnicula, who has disappeared from his cage in the Monroe house. Along with Howie, a tiny pup who insists Chester is his "pop," the three also join forces to destroy (puncture with toothpicks) the vegetables Chester is sure have been transformed into killer zombies by the vampire rabbit.

Most reviewers especially praised the slapstick humor and abundant puns that fill *Celery:* "Hare today, gone tomorrow," quips young Howie to his reluctant feline father. Or, "a vampire," explains Harold to the naive puppy, "is the person who calls the rules during a baseball game." And, "I just had a thought," says the agitated Chester to Harold. "What if Bunnicula's met up with one of his own kind? You know how they multiply . . . ." "Well, I don't really," the bumbling dog earnestly replies, "but if they're like everybody else these days, they probably use those little pocket calculators."

In a 1993 addition to the series, *Rabbit-Cadabra!,* one of several picture-book spin-offs to the antics of Harold and Chester, the Amazing Karlovsky is coming to town and the Monroe boys are excited. Chester and Harold, however, are having second thoughts about the show: the rabbit displayed in publicity posters looks awfully like Bunnicula, the faux or maybe all-too-real vampire bunny. In an attempt to ward off an invasion of vampire bunnies coming out of the magician's hat, they wield garlic pizza and steal the show, revealing the magician to be none other than the Monroes' cousin Charlie. A *Kirkus Reviews* contributor concluded that the story is "[p]redictable, but fans will love it," while Kay Weisman writing in *Booklist* called it an "appealing story."

The "Sebastian Barth" mystery series is a bit more plot-oriented, relating four sleuthing tales about a junior high fledgling detective whose exploits lead him into both dangerous and humorous situations. A flu epidemic at school is actually a case of food poisoning, Sebastian discovers in *Eat Your Poison.* Sebastian suspects, among others, the cafeteria manager. In the fourth book of the series, *Dew Drop Dead,* Howe inserts serious elements in a tale of a discovered body, looking at the issue of homelessness in the process of telling an old-fashioned, fast-paced yarn. In *Stage Fright,* Howe was able to blend his own love for the theater when he has Sebastian desiring to work with a famous actress.

Another popular series from Howe is "Pinky and Rex," written for younger readers just advancing to chapter books. Eleven strong and growing, the series features two young best friends whose relationship is lovingly detailed in a series of small yet piquant and telling mini-adventures. In the debut title, *Pinky and Rex,* the duo test their new friendship over a pink dinosaur. Pinky has twenty-seven stuffed animals and Rex has twenty-seven dinosaurs. So when they see a one-of-a-kind pink dinosaur in the museum gift shop, they need a little help from Pinky's annoying little sister, Amanda, to solve their problem. In this opening title, it is discovered where the two get their names: Pinky is named for his favorite color, while Rex is named after a dinosaur. In the second title, *Pinky and Rex Get Married,* Pinky has a great idea. Lonely when Rex attends a wedding and is not there to play with him, he decides that they too will get married. That way they won't have to spend another day apart.

In *Pinky and Rex and the Spelling Bee,* the desire to win at a spelling bee is mixed with the embarrassment of a peeing accident, while fears about summer camp are broached in *Pinky and Rex Go to Camp.* When a new baby is adopted by Rex's parents in *Pinky and Rex and the New Baby,* Rex displays a bit of sibling rivalry. Nervous lest she be forgotten with the new baby in the house, she rushes around trying to become indispensable; in the process, however, she completely forgets her old friend, Pinky. Feeling neglected, Pinky in turn brings a present for Matthew, the new baby: a soccer ball. Pinky tells Rex that she will have to break the ball in for the baby. Rex's mother recognizes the signals if Rex does not, and sends her daughter out to play with Pinky. *Booklist's* Janice Del Negro commented that this chapter book would be "a solid, useful purchase for collections serving children who are learning to read, as well as transitional readers." A contributor to *Kirkus Reviews* called this book "another strong entry" and one that is noteworthy for its "lively, believable dialogue and realistic situation that gently tests the likable pair's mettle." Valerie F. Patterson noted in *School Library Journal* that those ready for chapter books "will appreciate this gentle story of two friends who really care about each other."

A long-awaited camping trip is rained out in *Pinky and Rex and the Double-Dad Weekend,* but the two friends and their dads have a good weekend anyway, "camping in." Lauren Peterson noted in a *Booklist* review of this title that it "is perfect for young readers starting to make the difficult transition to chapter books." Pinky has to reconsider his nickname in *Pinky and Rex and the School Bully.* When the school bully calls him a sissy because of his nickname, and the fact that he likes the color pink and playing with girls, Pinky begins to wonder how well he is fitting into the scheme of things at school. Mrs. Morgan, a friendly neighbor, has sage advice for him about the dangers of changing yourself just to fit in. "In discussing bullies and insecurity, Howe takes on two conflicts familiar to children and handles them with a sure touch," commented Carolyn Phelan in a *Booklist* review. Marilyn Taniguchi, reviewing this title in *School Library Journal,* remarked that the author "affirms that boys (and girls) can be whatever they want to be," and went on to note that the author "fashions engaging characters" who are both "realistic" and "childlike."

Kindly Mrs. Morgan moves away in *Pinky and Rex and the New Neighbors,* and the two friends fear that the new neighbor will not be so nice. A pumpkin hunt forms the backdrop for familial rivalries and a clash between Rex and Pinky in *Pinky and Rex and the Perfect Pumpkin. Booklist's* Phelan felt that "the children's rift and reconciliation are handled with more realism and finesse than in most books for this age group." More jealousy is disruptive to the friendship in *Pinky and Rex and the School Play,* when Rex wins the starring role instead of Pinky. All is well, however, when Pinky becomes the assistant director.

In addition to his series books and picture books, Howe is well recognized as a novelist for middle-grade readers as well as young adults. His breezy dialogue comes into play with *The New Nick Kramer, or My Life as a Baby-Sitter,* a spin-off of a script Howe wrote for the Disney Channel. Nick desperately wants to beat popular Mitch in anything; he finally settles on Jennifer, betting Mitch that she will ask him to a girl-ask-guy dance. To convince shallow Jennifer that he is not just another macho guy, Nick takes a babysitting class. The subsequent babysitting job he takes, and the girl he meets as a result, make all bets moot. Carrie A. Guarria noted in *School Library Journal* that "Nick's first-person narrative adds believability" to the story, as do the "ploys he erroneously uses to gain Jennifer's trust and companionship." Writing in the *New York Times Book Review,* Robin Tzannes commented that Howe "tells Nick Kramer's story with remarkably natural dialogue and a hilarity that owes a great deal to television sitcoms, making this book hard for kids to put down."

A different approach was taken with *The Watcher,* a "somber, ambitious novel (about child abuse)," according to Stephanie Zvirin in *Booklist.* Employing three different narrative viewpoints, Howe tells the story of a solitary teenage girl whose best friend at an island resort beach seems to be her notebook. Called the Watcher by others at the beach for her habit of watching the families and seemingly recording her impressions in the notebook, the young girl, Margaret, focuses on one family in particular, weaving herself fancifully into their lives. Other narrative viewpoints come from Evan, who is afraid his parents are divorcing, and the lifeguard Chris, who is trying to find his place in his family and the world. Chris and Evan ultimately and unwittingly witness Margaret's abuse at the hands of her father, holding her head under water. Leigh Ann Jones, reviewing the novel in *School Library Journal,* had high praise: "*The Watcher* is a novel so powerful," Jones wrote, "that even after the last page is read, and Margaret is mercifully saved, her story may be reflected upon again and again." Nancy Thackaberry noted in *Voice of Youth Advocates* that "fans of Howe's middle-level books will not be shocked or disappointed by his

realistic fiction. He handles these more mature topics in a way that bridges the younger reader to YA literature."

Whether writing goofy tales of "Bunnicula," bracingly humorous picture books, or hard-hitting YA literature, Howe first and foremost knows how to draw his readers in, to entertain. "Howe's books are clever, often spoofs, and filled with contemporary references that entertain," commented Jane Anne Hannigan in a critical analysis of his work in *St. James Guide to Children's Writers.* "In the end," Howe once commented in *Horn Book,* "my primary responsibility as a writer is to the hidden child in the reader and in myself, and to the belief that— though we are years apart—when I open my mouth to speak, the child will understand. Because in that hidden part of ourselves, we are one."

Works Cited

Review of *Bunnicula: A Rabbit-Tale of Mystery, Publishers Weekly,* March 19, 1979, p. 94.

Del Negro, Janice, review of *Pinky and Rex and the New Baby, Booklist,* March 1, 1998, p. 1230.

Guarria, Carrie A., review of *The New Nick Kramer, or My Life as a Baby-Sitter, School Library Journal,* January, 1996, p. 108.

Hannigan, Jane Anne, "Howe, James," *St. James Guide to Children's Writers,* edited by Sara Pendergast and Tom Pendergast, St. James Press, 1999, pp. 525-27.

Howe, James, *The Celery Stalks at Midnight,* illustrated by Leslie Morrill, Atheneum, 1983, pp. 7, 20, 48.

Howe, James, "Writing for the Hidden Child," *Horn Book,* March-April, 1985, pp. 156-61.

Review of *Howliday Inn, Publishers Weekly,* March 19, 1982, p. 71.

Jones, Leigh Ann, review of *The Watcher, School Library Journal,* May, 1997, p. 134.

Patterson, Valerie F., review of *Pinky and Rex and the New Baby, School Library Journal,* June, 1993, p. 76.

Peterson, Lauren, review of *Pinky and Rex and the Double-Dad Weekend, Booklist,* April 15, 1995, p. 1500.

Phelan, Carolyn, review of *Pinky and Rex and the Bully, Booklist,* April 1, 1996, p. 1364.

Phelan, Carolyn, review of *Pinky and Rex and the Perfect Pumpkin, Booklist,* September 1, 1998, p. 119.

Review of *Pinky and Rex and the New Baby, Kirkus Reviews,* March 15, 1993, p. 372.

Review of *Rabbit-Cadabra!, Kirkus Reviews,* May 1, 1995, p. 599.

Sutherland, Zena, review of *Bunnicula: A Rabbit-Tale of Mystery, Bulletin of the Center for Children's Books,* July-August, 1979, p. 192.

Taniguchi, Marilyn, review of *Pinky and Rex and the Bully, School Library Journal,* April, 1996, p. 110.

Thackaberry, Nancy, review of *The Watcher, Voice of Youth Advocates,* August, 1997, p. 185.

Tzannes, Robin, review of *The New Nick Kramer, or My Life as a Baby-Sitter, New York Times Book Review,* November 12, 1995, p. 49.

Weisman, Kay, review of *Rabbit-Cadabra!, Booklist,* April 15, 1993, p. 1523.

Zvirin, Stephanie, review of *The Watcher, Booklist,* June 1 & 15, 1997, p. 1685.

For More Information See

BOOKS

Children's Literature Review, Volume 9, Gale, 1985, pp. 54-60.
Sixth Book of Junior Authors and Illustrators, edited by Sally Holmes Holtze, H. W. Wilson, 1989, pp. 135-37.

PERIODICALS

Booklist, April 15, 1990, p. 1631; August, 1994, p. 2046; December 15, 1994, p. 757; December 15, 1995, p. 704; May 1, 1998, p. 1524; February 15, 1999, p. 1063; September, 1994, p. 46.
Bulletin of the Center for Children's Books, July-August, 1997, pp. 398-99.
Horn Book, March-April, 1990, pp. 178-83.
New York Times Book Review, May 17, 1992.
Kirkus Reviews, November 15, 1994, p. 1531; January 1, 1996, p. 69; January 15, 1998, p. 112.
Kliatt, September, 1999, p. 17.
Publishers Weekly, April 13, 1992; February 15, 1999, p. 107.
School Library Journal, November, 1987, p. 91; April, 1990, p. 120; April, 1993, pp. 96-97; August, 1994, p. 150; March, 1995, pp. 181-82; March, 1999, p. 176.*

—*Sketch by J. Sydney Jones*

*   *   *

Shelley Hrdlitschka

HRDLITSCHKA, Shelley 1956-

Personal

Surname is pronounced Herd-*litch*-ka; born July 22, 1956, in Vancouver, British Columbia, Canada; daughter of Robert and Vivienne (Lyon) Frampton; married Peter Hrdlitschka (a manager of a construction company), 1977; children: Danielle, Cara, Kyla. *Education:* Simon Fraser University, teaching certificate. *Religion:* Unitarian-Universalist.

Addresses

Home and office—3950 Frames Pl., North Vancouver, British Columbia, Canada V7G 2M4. *Electronic mail*—hrdlitschka@home.com.

Career

Elementary schoolteacher in Delta, British Columbia, 1979-86; currently, writer. *Member:* Writers Union of Canada, Canadian Society of Children's Authors, Illustrators, and Performers, Children's Writers and Illustrators of British Columbia.

Awards, Honors

Our Choice Award, Canadian Children's Book Centre.

Writings

Beans on Toast, illustrated by Ljuba Levstek, Orca Book Publishers (Victoria, British Columbia), 1998.
Disconnected, Orca, 1998.

Newspaper columnist. Contributor of articles and reviews to magazines.

Work in Progress

A sequel to *Disconnected,* entitled *Tangled Web,* for Orca.

Sidelights

Shelley Hrdlitschka told *SATA:* "I discovered my love of children's literature while teaching elementary school, so, while on a parenting leave, I decided to try writing children's stories myself. It took ten long years before I landed my first book contract, but the wait made it that much more rewarding. The second book contract came six months after the first! I've written and published many parenting articles, book reviews, and newspaper columns, but I focus solely on teen fiction now.

"I never did get back to teaching, but I now enjoy visiting schools and libraries and talking to students about the writing process and about the value of perseverance—setting goals and sticking to them.

"Although my story ideas usually come from my own experiences, my three daughters help me with the details, reminding me that fourteen-year-old boys don't usually drink coffee, and they don't say things like 'cute' any more. If a young person writes to me and gives me feedback on my books, I keep their name to use in a future story. That's the little prize they get for going to the trouble of letting me know how they liked my story!"

*   *   *

HUBALEK, Linda K. 1954-

Personal

Born March 7, 1954, in Lindsborg, KS; married. *Education:* Kansas State University, B.A., 1976.

Addresses

Office—Butterfield Books, Inc., P.O. Box 407, Lindsborg, KS 67456.

Career

Butterfield Books, Inc., Lindsborg, KS, owner, publisher, and writer, 1992—. Formerly operated a wholesale floral business.

Writings

Butter in the Well: A Scandinavian Woman's Tale of Life on the Prairie, Hearth Publishing (Hillsboro, KS), 1992, Butterfield Books, 1994.
Praerieblomman: The Prairie Blossoms for an Immigrant's Daughter, Hearth Publishing, 1993, Butterfield Books, 1994.
Egg Gravy: Authentic Recipes from the Butter in the Well Series, Hearth Publishing, 1994, Butterfield Books, 1994.
Looking Back: The Final Tale of Life on the Prairie, Butterfield Books, 1994.
Trail of Thread: A Woman's Westward Journey, Butterfield Books, 1995.
Thimble of Soil: A Woman's Quest for Land, Butterfield Books, 1996.
Stitch of Courage: A Woman's Fight for Freedom, Butterfield Books, 1996.
Planting Dreams: A Swedish Immigrant's Journey to America, Butterfield Books, 1997.
Cultivating Hope: Homesteading on the Great Plains, Butterfield Books, 1998.
Harvesting Faith: Life on the Changing Prairie, Butterfield Books, 1999.

Adaptations

The novel *Praerieblomman* was released as a sound recording by Hearth Publishing in 1994.

Linda K. Hubalek

Sidelights

Linda K. Hubalak told *SATA:* "A door may close in your life, but a window will open instead. My chance came unexpectedly when my husband was transferred from his job in the Midwest to the West Coast. I had to sell my wholesale floral business and find a new career. Homesick for my family and the farmland of the Midwest, I turned to writing about what I missed, and the inspiration was kindled to write about my ancestors and the land they homesteaded.

"Although the story of my family is in my first book, I found the most information about Kajsa Svensson Runeberg, the Swedish woman who homesteaded the farm where I grew up. Even though Kajsa was not a direct relative, she and her descendants have always played a significant role in my life.

"After much research and writing, my first book, *Butter in the Well,* was published in 1992. People were fascinated with the pioneer stories of the immigrant homesteader and asked, 'What happened to the family on the farm?' What resulted were the books *Praerieblomman, Egg Gravy,* and *Looking Back.*

"*Trail of Thread* is about the women who arrived when the Kansas Territory first opened. *Thimble of Soil* continues their stories during the 'bleeding Kansas' era.

The third book in the series, *Stitch of Courage,* pertains to the Civil War years.

"The next series begins with *Planting Dreams,* focusing on Swedish ancestors who migrated to Kansas in 1869. It continues with *Cultivating Hope* and *Harvesting Faith.* These three books trace my family's journey and the homesteading of their farm."

*   *   *

HUTCHINS, Pat 1942-

Personal

Born June 18, 1942, in Yorkshire, England; daughter of Edward (a soldier) and Lilian (maiden name, Crawford) Goundry; married Laurence Hutchins (a film director), July 21, 1965; children: Morgan, Sam. *Education:* Attended Darlington School of Art, 1958-60, and Leeds College of Art, 1960-64.

Addresses

Home—75 Flask Walk, London NW3 1ET, England.

Career

J. Walter Thompson (advertising agency), London, England, assistant art director, 1963-65; author and illustrator of children's books, 1966—.

Pat Hutchins

Awards, Honors

Notable Book, American Library Association, and illustration honor, *Boston Globe/Horn Book,* both 1968, both for *Rosie's Walk;* best illustrated book, *New York Times,* and picture book honor, Spring Book Festival, both 1971, Children's Book Showcase title, 1972, and Brooklyn Art Books for Children award, 1973, all for *Changes, Changes;* Kate Greenaway Medal, 1974, for *The Wind Blew;* illustration honor list, International Board on Books for Young People, 1974, for *Titch;* Kate Greenaway Medal commendation, 1979, for *One-Eyed Jake;* Best Books, *School Library Journal,* 1980, for *The Tale of Thomas Mead;* runner-up, Kurt Maschler Award, 1986, for *The Doorbell Rang.*

Writings

FOR CHILDREN; AUTHOR AND ILLUSTRATOR

Rosie's Walk, Macmillan, 1968.
Tom and Sam, Macmillan, 1968.
The Surprise Party, Macmillan, 1969.
Clocks and More Clocks, Macmillan, 1970.
Changes, Changes, Macmillan, 1971.
Titch, Macmillan, 1971.
Good-night, Owl!, Macmillan, 1972.
The Wind Blew, Macmillan, 1974.
The Silver Christmas Tree, Macmillan, 1974.
Don't Forget the Bacon!, Greenwillow, 1976.
The Best Train Set Ever, Greenwillow, 1978.
Happy Birthday, Sam, Greenwillow, 1978.
One-Eyed Jake, Greenwillow, 1979.
The Tale of Thomas Mead, Greenwillow, 1980.
One Hunter, Greenwillow, 1982.
You'll Soon Grow into Them, Titch, Greenwillow, 1983.
King Henry's Palace, Greenwillow, 1983.
The Very Worst Monster, Greenwillow, 1985.
The Doorbell Rang, Greenwillow, 1986.
Where's the Baby?, Greenwillow, 1986.
Which Witch Is Which?, Greenwillow, 1989.
What Game Shall We Play?, Greenwillow, 1990.
Tidy Titch, Greenwillow, 1991.
Silly Billy, Greenwillow, 1992.
My Best Friend, Greenwillow, 1992.
Little Pink Pig, Greenwillow, 1993.
Three-Star Billy, Greenwillow, 1994.
Titch and Daisy, Greenwillow, 1996.
Shrinking Mouse, Greenwillow, 1997.
It's My Birthday!, Greenwillow, 1999.
Ten Red Apples, Greenwillow, 2000.

TV TIE-IN BOARDBOOK SERIES

It's Bedtime, Titch, Red Fox, 1998.
It's Christmas, Titch, Red Fox, 1998.
Titch Dresses Up, Red Fox, 1998.
Titch's Snowy Day, Red Fox, 1998.
Count with Titch, Red Fox, 1999.
Gardener Titch, Red Fox, 1999.
Tidy Up, Titch, Red Fox, 1999.
Where's Tailcat, Titch?, Red Fox, 1999.

FOR CHILDREN; ILLUSTRATED BY LAURENCE HUTCHINS

The House That Sailed Away, Greenwillow, 1975.

Follow That Bus!, Greenwillow, 1977.
The Mona Lisa Mystery, Greenwillow, 1981.
The Curse of the Egyptian Mummy, Greenwillow, 1983.
Rats!, Greenwillow, 1989.

OTHER

Creator of a thirteen-part model-animated series based on her "Titch" characters, released in England in 1997.

Adaptations

Rosie's Walk, The Surprise Party, Clocks and More Clocks, and *Changes, Changes,* were adapted as film-strips by Weston Woods; *The Tale of Thomas Mead* was adapted as a filmstrip produced by Westport Communications; *The House That Sailed Away* was adapted for television in England; and *The Curse of the Egyptian Mummy* was adapted as a stage production, 1991.

Sidelights

Pat Hutchins is a gifted British author and illustrator of picture books for preschoolers and children in the primary grades. Known especially for her lean texts and vivid artwork, Hutchins creates books full of optimism, humor, and simplicity; telling tales of animals, monster children, inventive children, lazy children, and shy children. Often taking inspiration from her siblings as well as from her own two sons, Hutchins has penned over thirty picture-book titles as well as five chapter books for beginning readers. In her picture books, such as the award-winning *Rosie's Walk, Changes, Changes, The Doorbell Rang, One-Eyed Jake, Titch,* and *The Wind Blew,* Hutchins marries sparse language and evocative illustrations which are often filled with messages not conveyed in the text. Hutchins is particularly fond of two motifs—a lively family of monsters and a shy boy named Titch—and has patterned several books after each. She is also fond of country motifs, no doubt inspired by her own childhood in northern England.

Born in 1942 in Yorkshire, Hutchins grew up in that region, far removed from the "Big Smoke," as the locals called London. One of seven children, she and her siblings spent their free days out roaming the country-side. Christmas, despite hardships, was always a festive occasion for the family, as Huthins's mother managed to put away money all year long to buy her children gifts. Potato picking in bleak November helped the finances before the holiday season, with the entire family pitching in. A local couple took young Hutchins under their wing, making their cottage something of an open house to her. She repaid their kindness years later by using their cottage as the backdrop for illustrations in *The Wind Blew.*

As Hutchins once told *Contemporary Authors New Revision Series* (*CANR*): "I was brought up in a small village in Yorkshire, the second youngest of seven children. As I loved drawing, I would wander round the countryside with my drawing book under my arm and my pet crow on my shoulder (he was too lazy to fly),

and while he searched for grubs, I sketched. Books were my other love, so it was inevitable that I would go to art school and study illustration." At age sixteen, Hutchins won a scholarship to the local art school, Darlington School of Art, where she felt completely in her element. Here she found other young men and women who, as she recalled in an essay for *Something about the Author Autobiography Series* (*SAAS*), "got just as excited as I did about the patterns clouds made, the different colours in the sky, and even the way light changed the tones of grey on the giant structures at the local steelworks." After two years at Darlington, Hutchins enrolled in a program at Leeds College of Art, where she majored in illustration, determining to go into children's book illustration. Upon graduation she and a friend headed south, much to the horror of her local village, to the smoke of London. Hutchins soon discovered, however, that her portfolio still needed work to attract editors. She took a job as an illustrator in an advertising firm, where she met her husband, an art director at the time. The two fell in love, married, and with a new posting in New York for her husband, set up house in a small apartment in Greenwich Village.

"I think our stay in New York was one of the happiest and most creative periods in my life," Hutchins wrote in *SAAS.* In New York, Hutchins shopped an improved portfolio to American publishers and happily made the acquaintance of Susan Hirschman, then head of the children's book department at Macmillan's. Hirschman convinced her to try to write her own story, and Hutchins turned to what she knew best, the country. Her resulting story about a hen called Rosie and a silent fox that follows her around the farmyard was full of complicated text which she ultimately pared down to a scant thirty-two words. "As the fox was silent," Hutchins noted in *SAAS,* "I decided not to mention him in the story at all. That way the reader is one jump ahead of the heroine, Rosie. They know she is being followed. She doesn't." This device, typical in adult novels, proved to be a winner with young audiences as well. *Rosie's Walk* won Hutchins a wide readership as well as an American Library Association notable book citation.

Other early award-winning titles include *Changes, Changes* and *The Wind Blew,* the latter of which captured the prestigious Kate Greenaway Medal in 1974. Hutchins has created learning books, such as *Clocks and More Clocks* and *The Doorbell Rang,* which explore counting and math; and cautionary tales about the values of sharing in *One-Eyed Jake* and the dangers of illiteracy in *Tale of Thomas Mead.* As her own children progressed past the picture-book stage, Hutchins also tried her hand at chapter books full of action, silliness, and turn-the-page breathlessness. Five such titles flowed from her prolific pen, three of them—*Follow That Bus!, The Mona Lisa Mystery,* and *The Curse of the Egyptian Mummy*—mysteries built around camping or school field trips which turn both humorous and dangerous. *Rats!,* about the humorous consequences of allowing a young boy to keep a rodent pet, was her last such chapter book. More popular in England than in America, the first of the series, *The House That Sailed Away,* was adapted for British television. As her children got older, however, Hutchins felt she was no longer in touch with the dialogue and language appropriate to such an age group, and returned to her low-text picture book format.

With her 1971 picture book, *Titch,* Hutchins began a series of books that has culminated in a television series employing model-animated characters. A character based partly on her first son, Morgan, and on her own younger brother, Titch is the youngest of three children and always comes in a poor third to the older brother and sister. Titch's moment of triumph, however, comes when he turns a tiny seed into a mighty plant in the family gardening project. Mary M. Burns, writing in *Horn Book,* called *Titch* a "childlike picture-story which blends economy of text with bright, uncomplicated illustrations," and concluded that Hutchins provided "imaginative realism for pre-schoolers which is reassuring, but never condescending." Margaret Meek, reviewing the picture book in *School Librarian,* observed that the "text and drawings match with artistic deliberation," declaring that this "is what learning to read should be about."

Hutchins reprised Titch in 1983's *You'll Soon Grow into Them, Titch,* in 1991's *Tidy Titch,* and in 1996's *Titch and Daisy.* In the second book of the series, Titch is tired of hand-me-downs, clothes that are always too big when he first gets them, but into which he soon will grow. But finally Titch's day has come: he and his father go out shopping, and Titch returns with a brand-new sweater, trousers, and socks. And when Mother comes home with a new baby boy, Titch now has someone to whom he can hand over his old clothes. Jill Bennett, reviewing *You'll Soon Grow into Them, Titch* in *The Signal Review,* noted that once again, Hutchins "offers beginners the chance to learn one of the untaught reading lessons: the words are not all; what isn't being said can matter a great deal." B. Clark, reviewing the story in *The Junior Bookshelf,* felt that though the tale was "slight," it is "brought to life as always by Pat Hutchins's illustrations."

Tidy Titch portrays the title character helping his older brother and sister to clean their rooms, only to discover that his own room has grown messier with all their unwanted toys. And in *Titch and Daisy,* young Titch is shy about attending a party with children he does not know, but assurances that his friend Daisy will be attending convince him to go. When he does not see her at the party, he takes refuge first behind a sofa, then in a cupboard, and finally under a table where he finds Daisy, one step ahead of him all along. Together, the two feel confident enough to participate in the party festivities. *Booklist's* Carolyn Phelan commented that the "double-page illustrations feature clean, spare ink lines filled with bright, clear colors," while Carolyn Noah observed in *School Library Journal* that this "winsome case of mistaken location focuses on the importance of friendship" and "will be welcomed by youngsters who follow Titch's growth and development." Hanna B. Zeiger, reviewing *Titch and Daisy* in *Horn Book,* concluded that the "gouache illustrations,

effectively set against white space, are vintage Pat Hutchins," and that perceptive readers would spot Daisy hiding in different locations in each double-page spread. Again, Hutchins employed her classic "less is more" technique: readers see what the text does not provide and what the main character is unaware of. Zeiger concluded that the book was a "pleasant portrayal of young children's dilemma when facing a new situation."

Another series of picture books focuses on the antics of a family of monsters. These books, drolly humorous and ultimately uplifting, include *The Very Worst Monster, Where's the Baby?, Silly Billy, Three-Star Billy,* and *It's My Birthday!.* Writing in *SAAS* of her inspiration for *The Very Worst Monster,* Hutchins recalled that "I wanted to do a humorous book about a baby brother or sister being given away. But jealousy is a very strong emotion, and a real child giving its sibling away isn't funny. I wanted the book to be a reassuring book, not something that might make children feel guilty about their feelings of jealousy. If I made the family a family of monsters I could distance the reader from reality, so they could laugh at the situation. Monsters are supposed to do terrible things—but monsters aren't real. I chose to do the illustrations in soft watercolors, so although they are obviously monsters, they're quite harmless ones."

In *The Very Worst Monster,* the girl monster, Hazel, is applauded for her efforts in giving her baby brother away, for this makes her the worst monster of all—quite a compliment in monster society. But baby Billy is returned when the family who has received him find the baby impossible to handle. Reviewing this title in *Bulletin of the Center for Children's Books,* Zena Sutherland noted that "given Hutchins's light touch and humor, the appeal of the subject, and the combining of two sure-fire ideas (sibling dethronement and the worst-is-the-best) this could hardly fail to be amusing and popular." Nancy Schmidtmann declared in a *School Library Journal* review that this was a "monstrously wonderful addition to any picture book collection."

Hutchins was able to incorporate into her monster series an earlier idea she had about an overactive baby who gets itself lost. Considered too edgy as a realistic tale, such a story fit perfectly into the antics of the family of green monsters. In *Where's the Baby?,* young Billy "is blithely traipsing through the house wreaking havoc as he goes," according to Leda Schubert in *School Library Journal.* Each of Billy's disasters is met by words of praise from his Grandma, with text in rhyming couplets. The monster family returns in *Silly Billy,* in which Billy continually interrupts Hazel and the family as they are playing a board game. Billy wants to copy everything Hazel does, and she ultimately tricks him into sleeping while she finishes her game of Monsternopoly. "The child-appeal quotient here is very high," noted Janice Del Negro in *Booklist,* mostly because, as Del Negro pointed out, "children with a baby brother or sister will recognize themselves in the charming, simple story." Shirley Dacey noted in *Magpies* that *Silly Billy* was of "the same high quality in both text and illustration as [Hutchins's] previous works."

Billy makes further appearances in *Three-Star Billy* and *It's My Birthday!* In the former title, "Reverse psychology tames a young monster's temper," according to a *Publishers Weekly* contributor. Pea-green Billy, with his fang-like teeth, does not care much for nursery school, and throws both fits and paint to prove his point. His teacher, instead of getting mad at him, awards him a star for each such outburst, finally winning Billy over. *Booklist*'s Hazel Rochman concluded that "joy is in the slapstick and the mischief and the power of the small raging monster who is loved without question." In *It's My Birthday!*, Billy is back, ready for birthday surprises. Any suggestion of sharing his new presents with party guests is stiffly denied by the greedy monster. However, there is one gift Billy cannot play with on his own, and now in need of cooperation and sharing by the other kids, Billy has the tables turned on him. Gay Lynn Van Vleck, reviewing the book in *School Library Journal*, noted especially the full-color art, and decided that with "its arresting colors and gentle lesson, this tale will be a super storytime selection."

Hutchins returned to more domestic and bucolic matters in several picture books of the 1990s. In *My Best Friend* she "captures the simple elements of a child's life in a heartwarming story, steeped in truth," according to *Booklist*'s Deborah Abbott. An overnight visit reveals the deep friendship between two little girls in a book that is a "must" for story hours, Abbott concluded. A critic for *Kirkus Reviews* called *My Best Friend* a "deceptively simple story with real insight, refreshing as a bright spring day." Hutchins celebrates animals of the farm and countryside in *Little Pink Pig* and *Shrinking Mouse*. In the former title, a busy little piglet gets separated from his mother and has adventures and misadventures in the farmyard until he is found. *Shrinking Mouse* provides a lesson in perspective as a departing mouse gets smaller and smaller until his friends are frightened that he will disappear altogether. *Booklist*'s Ilene Cooper concluded that the "text is perfectly illustrated by Hutchins's crisp artwork featuring elemental shapings just right for young eyes."

It is Hutchins's ability to capture the "just right" elements in any story, and to blend text with illustration seamlessly and synergistically, that has won her a large following with children and reviewers alike. In a critical analysis of Hutchins's work in *St. James Guide to Children's Writers*, Elaine Moss called the author-artist "a magnet for young listeners and readers." Hutchins told *CANR* that "I like to build my stories up, so the reader can understand what is happening and, in some cases, anticipate what is likely to happen on the next page. I think one can get quite complicated ideas across to small children as long as they are presented in a simple, satisfying way."

Works Cited

Abbott, Deborah, review of *My Best Friend*, *Booklist*, March 15, 1993, pp. 1359-60.

Bennett, Jill, "Picture Books 3 to 7: Learning to Read," *The Signal Review: A Selective Guide to Children's Books*, Volume 2, edited by Nancy Chambers, Thimble Press, 1984, pp. 8-11.

Burns, Mary M. review of *Titch, Horn Book*, March-April, 1972, p. 135.

Clark, B., review of *You'll Soon Grow into Them, Titch, The Junior Bookshelf*, August, 1983, p. 154.

Contemporary Authors New Revision Series, Volume 64, Gale, 1998, pp. 192-93.

Cooper, Ilene, review of *Shrinking Mouse, Booklist*, February 15, 1997, p. 1026.

Dacey, Shirley, review of *Silly Billy, Magpies*, May, 1993, p. 27.

Del Negro, Janice, review of *Silly Billy, Booklist*, January 1, 1993, pp. 808-09.

Hutchins, Pat, essay in *Something about the Author Autobiography Series*, Volume 16, Gale, 1993, pp. 229-42.

Meek, Margaret, review of *Titch, School Librarian*, June, 1972, p. 190.

Moss, Elaine, entry on Hutchins in *St. James Guide to Children's Writers*, edited by Sara Pendergast and Tom Pendergast, St. James Press, 1999, pp. 543-44.

Review of *My Best Friend, Kirkus Reviews*, April 15, 1993, p. 531.

Noah, Carolyn, review of *Titch and Daisy, School Library Journal*, April, 1996, p. 110.

Phelan, Carolyn, review of *Titch and Daisy, Booklist*, April 15, 1996, p. 1445.

Rochman, Hazel, review of *Three-Star Billy, Booklist*, October 1, 1994, p. 333.

Schmidtmann, Nancy, review of *The Very Worst Monster, School Library Journal*, May, 1985, p. 76.

Schubert, Leda, review of *Where's the Baby, School Library Journal*, March, 1988, p. 167.

Sutherland, Zena, review of *The Very Worst Monster, Bulletin of the Center for Children's Books*, April, 1985, p. 149.

Review of *Three-Star Billy, Publishers Weekly*, October 3, 1994, p. 68.

Van Vleck, Gay Lynn, review of *It's My Birthday!, School Library Journal*, March, 1999, p. 176.

Zeiger, Hanna B., review of *Titch and Daisy, Horn Book*, May-June, 1996, p. 325.

For More Information See

BOOKS

Children's Books and Their Creators, edited by Anita Silvey, Houghton, 1995, p. 336.

Children's Literature Review, Volume 20, Gale, 1990, pp. 138-54.

PERIODICALS

Booklist, April 1, 1994, p. 1460.

Horn Book, September-October, 1989, p. 621; May-June, 1997, p. 309.

Junior Bookshelf, December, 1992, pp. 234-35.

Los Angeles Times Book Review, September 13, 1998, p. 8.

School Librarian, August, 1989, p. 123; September, 1990, p. 205; November, 1993, p. 149; August, 1994, p. 132; November, 1994, p. 148; April, 1997, p. 106.

—Sketch by J. Sydney Jones

IVANKO, John D(uane) 1966-

Personal

Born October 1, 1966, in Royal Oak, MI; married Lisa Kivirist (a writer), November 16, 1997. *Education:* University of Michigan, B.B.A.; Pennsylvania State University, M.S., 1997.

Addresses

Home—7843 County Rd. P, Browntown, WI 53522. *Electronic mail*—jivanko@aol.com. *Agent*—(stock photography) Eleventh Hour Stock Photography Agency, Chicago, IL.

Career

Freelance photographer. JDI Enterprises, Inc., Browntown, WI, co-owner of Inn Serendipity (bed and breakfast establishment); worked at an advertising agency prior to 1992. Pennsylvania State University, adjunct lecturer. Global Fund for Children, writer and photo illustrator. Monroe Public Library, member of board of directors, 1999—. *Member:* North American Bluebird Society (coexecutive director).

Awards, Honors

Scholarship, Outdoor Writers Association of America, 1997; Director's Choice Award, 2000 Early Childhood News, National Association for the Education of Young Children, 1999, for *To Be a Kid.*

Writings

AUTHOR AND ILLUSTRATOR

The Least Imperfect Path: A Global Journal for the Future, Paradigm Press Ltd., (Royal Oak, MI), 1996.
(With Maya Ajmera) *To Be a Kid,* Charlesbridge, 1999.

John D. Ivanko collaborated with Maya Ajmera on this multicultural book about the joys and activities shared by children in forty countries around the world. (Cover photo by Jon Warren.)

PHOTOGRAPHER (WITH OTHERS)

Children from Australia to Zimbabwe: A Photographic Journey around the World, Charlesbridge, 1998.
Chicago—Heart and Soul of America, Towery, 1998.
The Power of Pittsburgh, Towery, 1998.
The Illinois Adventure, Gibbs Smith, 1999.
Extraordinary Girls, Charlesbridge, 1999.
Let the Games Begin, Charlesbridge, 1999.

Contributor of articles and photographs to national and international periodicals, including *National Geographic Traveler, Islands, Rotarian, Parade, Scottish Life, Wisconsin Trails, Sky, E—The Environmental Magazine, Earth, Chicago Life,* and *Windy City Sports.*

Work in Progress

Writing and photographing the children's photobook *Come Out to Play!; My Best Friend, the Bluebird,* a conservation education book for children; and *Edible Earth—Recipes and Reflections from our Journey Back to the Land* (co-written with Lisa Kivinst). Also, providing photographs for Kivinst's *Natural Simplicity: Inspirational Post Cards for the Journey of Life.*

Sidelights

John D. Ivanko told *SATA:* "On April Fool's Day, 1992, I jumped off the corporate treadmill at an advertising agency to journey around the world on what has become known as my 'quest for understanding.' One year and twenty-nine countries later, I returned to the United States with more than fifteen-thousand photographic images and stirring accounts of my journey. Then, while serving as an adjunct lecturer at Pennsylvania State University, I completed the text for my first book, *The Least Imperfect Path: A Global Journal for the Future.* This travelogue describes my journey and search for elements of social and ecological change.

"I continued to develop as a professional photographer and writer, contributing to national and international magazines as a freelance journalist. Jaunts to Ecuador, Bolivia, Peru, Scotland, Belize, and Guatemala generated additional material. Before leaving Penn State in 1997, I completed my master's degree in studies related to ecotourism and recreation management.

"I am a regular contributor to the Global Fund for Children, a nonprofit organization committed to teaching children to value diversity and grow into productive, caring citizens of the world through books and other outreach initiatives. I have also donated work to the Empower Nepal Foundation and the Pittsburgh Vintage Grand Prix, the nation's largest all-volunteer organization, and I volunteer website design to the Outdoor Recreation Consortium.

"The joys and hopes of the children I met and the increasingly degraded social and ecological environment in which they must grow has inspired and driven me to contribute to a renewed, positive, and hopeful vision for the future, and also to offer stepping stones for us all to navigate our own journey to a more peaceful, sustainable, and just tomorrow. With the awareness developed through traveling came the responsibility to share and care for a planet and its inhabitants. *To Be a Kid* and the many other projects to which I've had an opportunity to contribute served as a beacon for viewing and living in this remarkable world."

J–K

JUKES, Mavis 1947-

Personal

Born May 3, 1947, in Nyack, NY; daughter of Thomas H. (a scientist) and Marguerite (a teacher; maiden name, Esposito) Jukes; married Robert H. Hudson (a sculptor and painter), July 24, 1976; children: (daughters) River, Amy; (stepsons) Cannon, Case. *Education:* Attended University of Colorado-Boulder, 1965-67; University of California-Berkeley, B.A., 1969, elementary teaching certificate, 1970; Golden Gate University, D.Jur., 1978.

Addresses

Home—Cotati, CA.

Career

Longfellow Elementary School, Berkeley, CA, classroom teacher, 1970-73, art specialist, 1973-75; admitted to the Bar of California, 1979; full-time writer, 1979—. *Member:* California Bar Association.

Awards, Honors

Irma Simonton Black Award for Excellence in Children's Literature, Bank Street College of Education, and Parents' Choice Award, Parents' Choice Foundation, both 1983, both for *No One Is Going to Nashville;* Best Books of the Year, *School Library Journal,* 1983, for *No One Is Going to Nashville,* and 1984, for *Like Jake and Me;* Children's Literature Award, Bay Area Book Reviewers Association, illustration honor, *Boston Globe-Horn Book,* and Newbery Honor book, all 1985, all for *Like Jake and Me.*

Writings

FOR CHILDREN

No One Is Going to Nashville, illustrated by Lloyd Bloom, Knopf, 1983.
Like Jake and Me, illustrated by Bloom, Knopf, 1984.

Mavis Jukes includes anecdotes about her own coming-of-age in the late 1950s in this primarily informational book on bodily changes for girls just reaching puberty. (Cover illustration by Krysten Brooker.)

Blackberries in the Dark, illustrated by Thomas B. Allen, Knopf, 1985.

Lights around the Palm, illustrated by Stacey Schuett, Knopf, 1987.

Getting Even, Knopf, 1988.

Wild Iris Bloom, Knopf, 1992.

I'll See You in My Dreams, illustrated by Stacey Schuett, Knopf, 1993.

It's a Girl Thing: How to Stay Healthy, Safe, and in Charge, illustrated by Debbie Tilley, Knopf, 1996.

Human Interaction with Mrs. Gladys Furley, R.N.: Expecting the Unexpected, Delacorte, 1996.

Growing Up: It's a Girl Thing: Straight Talk about First Bras, First Periods, and Your Changing Body, illustrated by Debbie Tilley, Knopf, 1998.

Planning the Impossible, Delacorte, 1999.

Cinderella 2000, Delacorte, 1999.

FILM SCRIPTS

Mavis Jukes: A Conversation with the Author, Disney Educational Productions, 1989.

(With Patricia McKissack) *Who Owns the Sun* (adapted from *Who Owns the Sun* by Stacey Chbosky), Disney Educational Productions, 1990.

OTHER

(Contributor) Marlo Thomas and others, editors, *Free to Be ... a Family,* Bantam, 1987.

Contributor of a children's story to *Ms.* Also contributor to various reading textbooks.

Adaptations

Blackberries in the Dark and *Like Jake and Me* have been adapted as films for Disney Educational Productions; *Like Jake and Me* is available in both videotape and filmstrip format, Random House, 1984.

Sidelights

Mavis Jukes is an award-winning author of children's books, including the Newbery Honor title *Like Jake and Me.* In many of her works, Jukes highlights nontraditional families, as well as sensitive themes such as divorce and child abuse. Noted for their humor and keen perception, Jukes's books explore the often difficult years of childhood and adolescence through situations that are recognizable to a broad base of young readers. Jukes once commented: "I am motivated to write by experience and observations .... I have never outgrown the urge to make people laugh, and I consider humor to be a powerful tool for survival and in work."

Born in Nyack, New York, in 1947, Jukes was raised in the countryside. A tomboy, she was often found in the company of her older brother, Ken. "Ken's expectations of me were pretty high," Jukes related in an essay for *Something about the Author Autobiography Series* (SAAS), "so he informally enrolled me in his boot camp. (I was the only trainee.) Under his spirited command, I learned to jump out of trees and off roofs, spit, swear, catch and hold a snake, drive a car, truck (and hearse),

chew tobacco—and test-drive a number of vehicles he designed and constructed, including a motorcycle made out of a bicycle and a lawn-mower engine."

Jukes's early literary efforts were limited to what she called writing "really embarrassing poetry" as a seventh grader. When Jukes was a freshman in high school, her family moved to Princeton, New Jersey; two years later, the family moved to California. Jukes eventually attended the University of Colorado-Boulder and the University of California-Berkeley, earning her bachelor's degree in 1969 and an elementary teaching certificate a year later. She taught for five years before marrying painter/sculptor Robert H. Hudson, who had two sons.

After her marriage in the mid-1970s, Jukes aspired to a career in law, but events transpired that would ultimately alter her vocational plans. "In my third year of law school I had a baby, and one day I wrote a story for her," Jukes once commented. "When I saw what I had written, I realized I was a writer. I never questioned it. I just finished law school, took the bar and passed it, and then continued writing."

Her first books, *No One Is Going to Nashville* and *Like Jake and Me,* deal directly with the problems of blending two families, an issue with which Jukes had personal knowledge. In *Nashville,* a young girl named Sonia asks to keep a stray dog that she has found. At first her father refuses, but he relents after the girl's stepmother takes up her cause. A reviewer for the *Bulletin of the Center for Children's Books* noted that *Nashville* is an "effective story" with a lot of "sweetness and warmth."

In *Like Jake and Me,* young Alex must come to accept and be accepted by his stepfather, a muscular, bearded cowboy. *Like Jake and Me* finds its roots in Jukes's early, difficult relationship with her stepson Cannon. As she recounted in *SAAS:* "One night Cannon, Case, Bob, and I all went to the movies in an old-timey theater that had a stage and curtain in front of the screen. Just before the movie was to begin, I turned to Cannon [then age nine] and said 'I'll give you five bucks if you go up there and tap dance in front of all these people.' He said, 'I will if you will.' We both jumped up and ran down the aisle and up the stairs to the stage and started tap-dancing like two dopes. I'll never forget it, ever, because it was the first time Cannon had ever held my hand."

1985's *Blackberries in the Dark* took Jukes three years and many revisions to write. The book describes nine-year-old Austin's first visit to his grandparents' home after the death of his grandfather. For a time, Jukes was concerned with the book's potential impact on its readers. "I had some concerns about whether or not the book would be upsetting to children," she once explained. "As it turns out, the story really doesn't make children cry—only adults! And especially me!"

In a lighter vein, *Lights around the Palm* tells the tale of seven-year-old Emma, who insists that she can talk to the animals on her family's farm. Over time, Emma's previously disdainful ten-year-old brother claims that he, too, can hear the animals talking. While recognizing that *Lights* has many commendable elements, a *Bulletin of the Center for Children's Books* reviewer concluded that the book's ideas "are more intriguing than its execution—the themes and ambiguities crowd out the small and quiet story."

Getting Even and *Wild Iris Bloom* cover the adventures of sensible Maggie and her wild friend Iris. In *Getting Even,* the two pals avenge themselves in humorous ways against the grade-school pest, Corky; in *Wild Iris Bloom,* Iris, angry at being left at home while her parents travel on business, escapes the babysitter's supervision and ends up in trouble. *Wild Iris Bloom* "was a very, very difficult book for me to write," Jukes wrote in *SAAS,* "because it involves an episode where Iris is tricked into a car by a stranger and assaulted, something which happened to me. It took me a long time to complete the story because in order to get it right, I had to confront my past and come to terms with it."

I'll See You in My Dreams is another book that has its roots in Jukes's past; in this case, her relationship with her brother, Ken, an airline pilot, whose tragic death as the result of a brain tumor affected his younger sister deeply. In this picture book, images of flight surround a young girl's attempts to come to terms with the death of a favorite uncle, as she worries about how to say good-bye in a way that reflects the love and respect she has for the dying man. "Jukes looks at a sensitive subject in a fresh, innovative way," noted *School Library Journal* contributor Susan Scheps, "matching the experience to her audience's level of understanding." Calling *I'll See You in My Dreams* a "heartfelt creation" but questioning whether its shift from imaginary happening to reality would cause younger readers confusion, *Bulletin of the Center for Children's Books* critic Betsy Hearne concluded of Jukes's book: "[It is] an eloquently written, undeniably moving, and ultimately adult litany of farewell to a loved one."

Jukes's novels *Human Interaction with Mrs. Gladys Furley, R.N.: Expecting the Unexpected* and *Planning the Impossible* both feature twelve-year-old River, a spunky young heroine who uses common sense to make it through the trials and tribulations of middle school. In *Expecting the Unexpected,* the savvy sixth-grader gets enough information out of the sex-ed class taught by Mrs. Furley (a.k.a. "Furball") to think she sees some of the tell-tale signs of pregnancy in her older sister. *Planning the Impossible* finds River thinking of ways to jump-start her courtship of handsome fellow student D. B., while a clique of obnoxious girls try to thwart her plans. Meanwhile, a scheme to hook Furball up with the father of one of River's best friends keeps the plot in a state of humorous confusion. Calling the sequel to *Expecting the Unexpected* "as fresh, frank, and funny as the first," *Voice of Youth Advocates* reviewer Kellie Shoemaker went on to praise Jukes for the "quirky adult characters, realistic kids, and unpredictable situations" in her "fun story." And Jennifer M. Brabander dubbed the

conclusion of *Planning the Impossible* "a celebration of girl power" in her *Horn Book* review.

In addition to fiction, Jukes has also penned several books intended to aid girls and young women as they go through adolescence. Covering all the bases—from sex education to friendships to boys—her "It's a Girl Thing" books use "examples taken from [Jukes's] own adolescence, including a revealing glimpse into what, in retrospect, she recognizes to be her own battle with issues of self-esteem," according to Cathryn M. Mercier in *St. James Guide to Young Adult Writers.* In *It's a Girl Thing: How to Stay Healthy, Safe, and in Charge,* Jukes gives practical advise on all sorts of girl-only dilemmas—like how to pick your first bra, what to do when your period starts in school, or how to deal with sexual abuse. Praising the author's "been there, done that matter-of-factness about aspects of female existence rarely discussed in literature," *Bulletin of the Center for Children's Books* contributor Deborah Stevenson concluded that "the text's comradely, nonjudgmental approach to a wide range of information makes [*It's a Girl Thing*] ... reassuring and useful." "The text is sometimes humorous," stated *School Library Journal* contributor Martha Gordon, "but always conveys caring, respect, and concern .... A fine and thoughtful effort."

Compiled for slightly younger girls, *Growing Up: It's a Girl Thing: Straight Talk about First Bras, First Periods, and Your Changing Body,* lets pre-adolescents know what's coming down the pike when their bodies start to change during the teen years; it even gives advice on how to avoid the terrible experience of standing in a store checkout line with a package of sanitary pads ... by getting your father to do it! "Jukes's common sense extends to many aspects of girls' health," remarked a critic for *Kirkus Reviews* of the upbeat guide, "reminding them to take good care of their bodies, eat well, and relax—there's plenty of time to think and learn about growing up."

In addition to her own life experiences, Jukes has often listed her education and her children as major influences on her work: "Both teaching and law contributed heavily to my writing," the author once commented. "Teaching woke me up—it was like taking a crash course in reality; law school taught me how to talk fast and straight, but what it really taught me was to pay attention to my inventive nature." In addition to her inventiveness, Jukes is given high marks for her technical ability as a writer. She "uses language in direct and poetic ways to describe fully the realistic worlds of today's children," Mercier concluded in her *St. James Guide to Young Adult Writers* essay. "Her command of dialogue complements masterful character development. Above all, Jukes proves herself a writer of insightful wisdom about the psychological and emotional realities of young people."

Works Cited

Brabander, Jennifer M., review of *Planning the Impossible, Horn Book,* March-April, 1999, p. 209.

Gordon, Martha, review of *It's a Girl Thing: How to Stay Healthy, Safe, and in Charge, School Library Journal,* June, 1996, pp. 142-43.

Review of *Growing Up: It's a Girl Thing: Straight Talk about First Bras, First Periods, and Your Changing Body, Kirkus Reviews,* August 15, 1998, p. 1190.

Hearne, Betsy, review of *I'll See You in My Dreams, Bulletin of the Center for Children's Books,* May, 1993, p. 285.

Jukes, Mavis, essay in *Something about the Author Autobiography Series,* Volume 12, Gale, 1991, pp. 177-91.

Review of *Lights around the Palm, Bulletin of the Center for Children's Books,* December, 1987, p. 67.

Mercier, Cathryn M., essay on Jukes in *St. James Guide to Young Adult Writers,* 3rd edition, St. James Press, 1999, pp. 568-69.

Review of *No One Is Going to Nashville, Bulletin of the Center for Children's Books,* January, 1984, p. 90.

Scheps, Susan, review of *I'll See You in My Dreams, School Library Journal,* March, 1993, p. 180.

Shoemaker, Kellie, review of *Planning the Impossible, Voice of Youth Advocates,* April, 1999, p. 37.

Stevenson, Deborah, review of *It's a Girl Thing: How to Stay Healthy, Safe, and in Charge, Bulletin of the Center for Children's Books,* July-August, 1996, p. 376.

For More Information See

PERIODICALS

Booklist, March 1, 1993, p. 1226.
Kirkus Reviews, February 15, 1993, p. 228.
Kliatt, July, 1996, p. 30.
Publishers Weekly, March 15, 1993, p. 87; February 1, 1999, p. 86.
School Library Journal, August, 1990, p. 116; April, 1999, p. 136.

*   *   *

KELLY, Ralph
See GEIS, Darlene (Stern)

Autobiography Feature

M. E. Kerr

1927-

I grew up always wanting to be a writer. My father was a mayonnaise manufacturer, with a strange habit, for a mayonnaise manufacturer, of reading everything from the Harvard Classics, to all of Dickens, Emerson, Poe, Thoreau, Kipling, and John O'Hara, Sinclair Lewis, John Steinbeck, all the Book-of-the-Month Club selections, plus magazines like *Time, Life, Look,* and *Fortune,* and all the New York City newspapers, along with the local Auburn, New York, *Citizen Advertiser.* I would like to say that it was his love of reading that made me want to be a writer ... and that certainly contributed.

So did English teachers who encouraged me, and librarians who had to pull me out of the stacks at closing time. And there were my favorite writers like Thomas Wolfe, Sherwood Anderson, the Brontës, and our home-town hero, Samuel Hopkins Adams. (I'd pedal past his big house on Owasco Lake, just to see where a real writer lived!) But in my heart, I know who was responsible for this ambition of mine to become a writer: it was my lifelong abettor, still going strong today, my eighty-eight-year-old mother.

One of the most vivid memories of my childhood is of my mother making a phone call. First, she'd tell me to go out and play. I'd pretend to do that, letting the back door slam, hiding right around the corner of the living room, in the hall. She'd have her pack of Kools and the ashtray on the desk, as she gave the number of one of her girlfriends to the operator ... My Mother would begin nearly every conversation the same way: "Wait till you hear this!"

Even today, when I'm finished with a book and sifting through ideas for a new one, I ask myself: Is the idea a "wait till you hear this?"

Saturday nights in summer, my mother'd get out her Chevrolet coupe, and we'd go downtown and park for awhile in various places, beginning outside the one theater in town, the Auburn Palace. My mother would take out her knitting. We'd watch who went into the movies, while my mother did a running commentary. "Don't tell me Lois Gilbert's daughter is still going out with Chippy Palmer? That'll be over as soon as she goes to college and Chippy goes into the plumbing business with his father. Chippy ought to use his common sense and not waste his time and

"M. E. Kerr"

hard-earned money on someone from South Street ... There's Polly Otter by herself again. Carl's probably down at Boysen's Bar ... Loretta Hislop in the same old dress, year after year after year. That's what happens when you marry a man who gambles."

We would stay there until everyone had gotten into the first show, and then we'd slip down to the front of Boysen's Bar, just as it was beginning to get dark.

"I'm right," my mother'd say. "There's Carl Otter's white Buick. He's in there.... Don't tell me the Leonards are *eating* in there! Well, there they are in the window. Of all places to eat dinner, with that stale smell of beer and Carl Otter getting crocked at the bar! I guess it's those dinner specials. Len Leonard has to watch every cent since his accident. Poor Len owes all over town, tells everyone 'The check's in the mail.' The check's in the mail like I'm from Paris, France.... Oh! Oh! There's Eleanor Budd on her way in."

On and on.

Always, before we went home, a swing by the Women's Union, where many single women had apartments, up into the parking lot to see if there were any familiar cars, a good way to tell who was seeing who in the Women's Union.... My mother knew the color, make, and year of everyone's car, and so did all her girlfriends.

Then we'd go up Genesee Street at a crawl, my mother still talking. "The Henrys are eating in their dining room for a change. They must have company.... If I thought it would help, I'd get up on a ladder and paint the trim on the Stewarts' house myself, but nobody's going to get Harry Stewart to care about his house, his lawn, his shrubbery, or anything but bridge!"

Then home ... and a lesson from my mother on the importance of fiction. Fiction, I learned early on, spins off grandly from fact. Our trip downtown would be related over the phone, beginning, "Wait till you hear this! Carl Otter sent poor little Polly off to see *Brother Rat* so he

could have a night on the town, that dear little woman with her face down to her shoes, standing in line by herself while he treats Ellie Budd to old-fashioneds down at Boysen's."

Long before the character in one of Salinger's short stories ever peeked into someone else's bathroom cabinet to inspect its contents, I'd learned from my mother that that was the first thing you did once the bathroom door was closed in other people's homes.

"What are you looking for?" I'd ask.

She'd say, "Shhhh! Run the water!"

I learned that the first thing you look for is prescription medicine, then all the ointments and liquids that tell you what ailments are being treated in the house you're visiting.

My mother taught me all a writer'd need to know about socio/economic/ethnic differences, too.

The Reyersons are very R-I-C-H, she'd say, and if she didn't spell it out, she whispered it: *rich.*

In our little upstate New York town, in the thirties, there were very few Jews, and my mother was never sure "Jew" was all right to say, so she'd instruct me not to go around town calling people "Jews," since my father was in business in that town. I was to say "a person of the Jewish persuasion."

She taught me to cut out all the labels from my coats and jackets, anything I might remove in Second Presbyterian Church on a Sunday morning, so that no one knew that we often bought out-of-town.

My mother'd come from a poor immigrant German family twenty-six miles from Auburn, where she'd been raised in a convent. She'd taken a step up in her marriage, a fact she was always defensive about in Auburn, always proud of in her hometown, Syracuse; and the labels she'd cut out were sewn back in for visits there.

She took an unusual interest in the boys who came to call on me when I was in my early teens. She warned me that if I married a Catholic, there'd be one baby right after the other; that if I married an Italian, I wouldn't be allowed to wash the salad bowl, they just wiped it dry; and that any boy whose father was bald, would be bald himself one day.

When I was around fifteen, I was dating the son of the local undertaker, and my mother said I'd better not marry him, or I'd end up doing all the cosmetic work on the corpses. Don't say I didn't warn you, she'd tell me, it's a family business-*everyone* in an undertaker's family has something to do in a funeral home.

Our small town housed Auburn prison, where executions still took place when I was a child. The identity of the man who pulled the switch was a secret. Eight or nine men would march into the prison on the night of an execution, one of them the actual executioner.

My mother and her girlfriends would be parked outside Auburn prison to watch who went in on one of those nights. When everyone came back to our house after, for cookies and tea, the guessing game would begin. I'd be upstairs, hanging on the banister, listening wide-eyed while they went down the list. Was it Russ from the tobacco store? Kenny Thompson's father? Melanie Rossi's father?—listening to my mother insist, "Never! Not Mike Rossi! Mike wouldn't harm a fly!" Etcetera.

When I was around five or six, there was a high school teacher who rented a small house on our street. She had the wonderful last name of St. Amour. She was a mysterious lady who smoked with a long cigarette holder, played piano, and on summer nights could be heard singing songs like "Ah, Sweet Mystery of Life." She was quite beautiful, in her thirties, never married so far as my mother could figure out. No one knew where she'd come from, and she didn't pal around with the other teachers at school.

At the same time, our mayor was a widower, a dashing fellow who drove around in a black Packard convertible, with the initials PKT-1 on the license plates.

He began seeing Mademoiselle St. Amour, as my mother always referred to her, though she only taught French, was not really from France. The mayor never parked outside of the house, but drove all the way down the driveway and parked behind the house.

"Marijane," my mother'd say, "go down through the fields and see if Mayor Tallent's car is at Mademoiselle St. Amour's."

Why?"

"Just do it! Be sure the license plate reads PKT-1. You don't know a Packard from a Chevrolet!"

A few years later, I got the idea to form a spy club, rounding up several other kids to go out on "missions," to go look in people's windows and report back to my clubhouse what we'd seen, and to list all the cars in the driveways with their license plates.

We were found out when two of us, on a mission over at the Goldmans', tripped over ash cans, the noise alerting the Goldmans that there were intruders in the bushes.

"How'd she ever get that idea?" my mother asked my father. "It's this war talk, talk of German spies loose."

One summer before the war, the family drove across the country to California to visit my mother's sister, Agnes. Aunt Agnes, my mother, and I would go on all the bus tours past movie stars' homes, my mother taking notes so she could write it up in my baby book . . . . We'd go up to Pops Willow Beach, where Agnes said anyone who was anybody went.

"There's Kent Taylor!" my mother whispered, though this famous movie star was all the way down the beach. "Go get his autograph, Marijane!"

"I don't want his autograph!"

"Just do it!" my mother said. "Tell him your name is Ida, and you'd like him to write something for Ida."

Aunt Agnes (an apple never falls far from the tree) said, "Honey, tell him you have a sister named Agnes. Tell him to write something for Agnes."

Second only to gossip about citizens of Auburn, New York, was gossip about Hollywood stars.

Every Wednesday afternoon I waited in suspense for my mother to return from Mr. Billy's Beauty Salon. Mr. Billy also played the organ at Second Presbyterian Church, and he played piano for Laura Bryan's dance classes. He wore a toupee and spats and an Adolphe Menjou mustache, and although he almost never left Auburn, where he looked after his invalid mother, it was never doubted by my mother, her girlfriends, or me that he knew all the Hollywood gossip.

My mother, with her hair newly set, still smelling of lilac Permafix, would recite to me all the latest news: that Jack Benny was in love with Ann Sheridan, breaking Mary Benny's heart; that Joan Crawford's entire face and body were covered with freckles the size of lima beans; and that

Gary Cooper and Marlene Dietrich fell in love filming *Morocco.*

I can still remember sitting in the darkened Palace theater, on one of those occasions when we weren't parked outside watching people go in, unwrapping a Baby Ruth bar in the middle of *Sweethearts,* starring Jeanette Mac-Donald and Nelson Eddy, my mother leaning down to whisper to me, "Mr. Billy says they hate each other! In real life, they don't even speak!"

Soon, a world war was raging. Downstairs in our basement a map of the world was tacked to the wall. My kid brother, fourteen years younger than me, and my father tracked the war with thumbtacks, everything from the battle in North Africa, to the taking of the islands in the Pacific, the invasion of Sicily, the Netherlands, New Guinea, the bombing of Berlin, the evacuation of Cassino—all of it, and my older brother by then was flying off a carrier in Torpedo 9, famous in the Battle of Midway.

But upstairs, in front of a Monopoly board, my mother and I sat listening to the "Lux Radio Theater" or "Grand Central Station," while my mother said things like: "You've landed on my hotels—wait! I think she's going to find out that this Uncle Alan of hers is her real father—hush!" turning up the volume on the Stromberg-Carlson. Or: "Hold it! Don't roll!" her ear bent in the radio's direction. "Oh, no! She's not going to marry *him!* Him? With a prison record?"

Even after I went off to Stuart Hall, in Staunton, Virginia, I was never totally, never even partially invulnerable to what my mother had to say.

Letters from my father would arrive, carefully typed in thin envelopes, filled with consent and advice.

Yes, your mother and I will allow you to go to Richmond for the weekend . . . . Marijane, if you persist with this wish to be a writer then, yes, apply to a journalism school, so you can at least earn your living until you're married. You

Marijane Meaker, a Girl Scout, age ten.

The Meaker family portrait, 1944: standing, Ellis, Jr., Marijane (age sixteen), Ellis, Sr.; seated, Charles and Ida.

won't earn a dime writing stories of your own invention! Writers like that starve! . . . And please, don't apply to The University of Missouri Journalism School, or you'll marry someone from St. Louis, and that's the last we'll see of you on holidays, since wives go home with their husbands . . . . So investigate Syracuse University near us, where there's a fine school.

But it was the fat envelope with the unruly handwriting I saved to open in my room, by myself, sitting atop the Bates bedspread, eager to take it all in, words running together, misspelled, no punctuation except for exclamation points.

Well Marijane the McIntees house blew up from the furnace all their things out on the lawn for everyone to see and I mean everything! But Robert Annan in a marines uniform said say hi to you in church and did you like school his pimples gone very sharp as youd say. But Buddy Smith came home a lootenant on leave and Mildred Spring dropped him just like that war or no war for some sailor no one knows the family of in Penn Yann she'll regret it all her life and next door Margie Waterhouse dating a sailor who claims to be from Maine but who knows if thats true.

Recently, I visited my mother, just outside Auburn, in a place called Presbyterian Manor, where she lives now with eight other old women and one old man. There's a view of Skaneateles Lake, where we'd go summers past to hear band concerts in the park, and she's right next to Krebs' Restaurant. On the days the family'd go there for

dinner in the thirties and forties, my mother would always warn in the morning: "Don't eat anything all day! You know the size of their portions! Only Gertie Lord can eat everything they put down in front of you at Krebs." (Gertie Lord was Auburn's fat lady.)

Most of my mother's girlfriends are gone now. But she still reads every word of the *Auburn Citizen,* and in two minutes can tell me what happened to any of my schoolmates of forty and fifty years ago, how many children and grandchildren they have, who's divorced and who recently advertised for a maid, or put the house up for sale.

She sat with her television on, telling me how badly she felt that young Alan Thicke's show was cancelled on top of the fact his wife, the soap star, was divorcing him, and they have these two nice boys. But no one, she told me flatly, can compete with "Johnny." "Johnny," she insisted, bounced right back no matter what happened in his marriages, and then she leaned forward and said, "Shhhh! Do you hear that?"

"What?"

She turned down the volume with her remote control paddle. "Did you hear that, Marijane? That's Eunice Tutton outside the door, seeing if we're in here. As soon as we leave, she'll be in this room, in a second, to look in my closet."

"Why?"

"*Why?* She counts my dresses. She's always trying to find out if I've got more dresses than she has."

She struggled to her feet, balancing herself on her cane, as we prepared to go for a walk. "Well, let her, poor old Eunice. She's ninety-two. That's all she's got to think about: how many dresses I have."

We walked outside into a beautiful autumn afternoon. "I can tell you right now, Marijane," she said, "when no one's listening, that I didn't like your book *Me Me Me Me Me* at all!"

That was my latest book then, my teenage autobiography, with generous mention of the family.

"I don't know why you want to tell everyone's business," she continued. "I try to go back and figure out why you never liked things like knitting, with all the knitting I did, or where this writing idea ever came from in the first place . . . . Look across the street now, Marijane. See that bent-over old man? (Don't let him see you looking, or he'll see me and start over here!) That's Dave Daw. Remember when you went to high school with Cathy, and he ran off with Gloria Alexander? Years ago! Gloria never brought Dave any happiness, with her hair falling out, chasing off to scalp specialists. God's punishment! . . . Anyway," my mother continued, "you were always up in your room writing those stories. It was all those books your father had everywhere in the house . . . . You're your father's daughter, all right."

At the University of Missouri, where I went despite my father's warning that if I did go there, I'd end up marrying someone from Missouri, I switched my major from journalism to English . . . partly because I failed Economics, which one had to pass to get into J-School, and partly because I realized I didn't want anything to do with writing fact. I wanted to make up my own facts. I wanted to do creative writing.

It was the end of World War II, and Columbia, Missouri, was a real college town, filled with kids right off the farm, or coming from little towns like Bolivar and Poplar Bluff, plus an abundance of young men straight out of the service. Girls who'd never been any farther than St. Louis or Kansas City were matched on blind dates with fellows who'd fought in Okinawa, or already seen London and Paris, as sorority/fraternity life commenced. My very first week there I went with some classmates to a popular hangout called The Shack, and learned the game of Chug-a-Lug, which was a beer drinking contest, in which you drained your full glass in one breath, while everyone sang "Here's to Marijane, she's true blue, she's a drinker through and through!"

Although it was very much a party campus in those postwar years, it was still the end of the 1940s, and there were rules: a time to be in at night, no men above the first floor in a sorority house, no alcoholic beverages ... and in our sorority, Alpha Delta Pi, dating men who were not in fraternities was frowned on. They were called "independents"; they were unwelcome (though tolerated) at major sorority functions.

I found someone to date (and fall in love with) who gave my father far more to worry about than the boy from St. Louis or Kansas City whom he'd envisioned. George was from Hungary originally, a Jew who'd barely managed to escape the Nazis in his teens by being smuggled into Venezuela.

By the time he arrived on the Missouri campus, he was an ardent Communist. He was the furthest thing from a Joe College type there was. He didn't drink, or smoke, or go out for sports, or go down to any of the campus hangouts to sing and play after classes, and he didn't own a pair of jeans or a tie ... and he was more interested in reading Karl Marx and Lenin than Thomas Wolfe or Sinclair Lewis. He was SERIOUS.

George would show up at the Alpha Delta Pi sorority house in his dark pants and turtleneck sweater, with a briefcase filled with Communist propaganda, and spend any rare free time he had lecturing me on the class struggle and dialectical materialism. He wasn't around a lot because he was working his way through college as a counterman and also as a Spanish teacher at Stephens College ... but he was there often enough to irritate my sorority sisters, and to delight me.

Under his spell, I joined the Communist party, and voted for Henry Wallace for President of the United States, the only one in Cayuga County, New York, to do so.

I stayed on for summer sessions, too, because of George, and although he'd politicized me, he hadn't cured me of my wish to be a writer.

I wrote story after story, sending them off to New York-based magazines, accumulating so many rejection slips that I attended a sorority masquerade party as a rejection slip, wearing a black slip with rejections from all the magazines pinned to it.

Because George was so busy, I made many friends to spend my spare time with, most of them would-be writers, few of them sorority/fraternity people.

One of them was a young man named Ernest Leogrande, who ultimately became a writer for the New York *Daily News.* Ernie was my closest confidant, until his death

in 1985, and from the time I first met him on the train to St. Louis, en route to the university for my freshman year, he stayed in my life, moving to New York City when I did, never living too far from where I lived .... In nearly every book I wrote, there was a character called Ernie Leogrande. He was my good luck charm, and by the time I was M. E. Kerr, writing for teenagers, he was my adviser on contemporary music, since he covered all the rock concerts for the *News.*

Afternoons in Columbia, Ernie and I and other "writers" sat in coffee shops talking about F. Scott Fitzgerald, and Hemingway, and the "new" writer Carson McCullers, and dreamed of going to New York City, and getting published.

Evenings, by phone, or in the university library, George and I talked about getting married and going to Venezuela, or back to Hungary. "If you marry me," George promised, "you'll have something consequential to write about: a *real* life, not this playpen here in the United States."

I was definitely torn.

No one was more typically American than I was, coming from small-town life, probably more privileged than most girls, worrying as I grew up about little more than how to get a bigger allowance so I could buy more clothes or the latest Glen Miller records.

If George had helped to raise my consciousness about the *real* world, he hadn't been able to totally convince me that all the things American I loved—our literature, our music, our holidays and customs—were all little more than a Capitalist/Wall Street plot against the working people. I couldn't imagine moving away from everything and everyone I loved .... But I couldn't imagine letting him go, either.

To this day, I believe it was my mother who solved my problem, though she sort of denies it. ("I don't know what you're talking about," she says, with a thin little smile.) Somehow, George came to the attention of "the authorities" shortly after my mother and my father came to Columbia for a visit. At the time, my mother's only comment about George was. "He's going to land you in Russia if he has his way, and he's shorter than you are!"

She may or may not have written a letter to the FBI, but the FBI visited George a few weeks later, filled with questions about his affiliations, and his future plans. Around that same time, there were many witch-hunts going on in the country, rumors of faculty members in large universities being Communists. George would laugh about it, saying they always looked in the wrong places: investigated political science teachers, when the real party members were in the agriculture school, for example.

It was also around this time that Whittaker Chambers was accusing Alger Hiss of having been a Communist when he worked for the State Department in the thirties. Also, Communist party members were being arrested for advocating the overthrow of the government.

The pressure was very much on George. He felt he had to leave the country immediately. There was no money to take me with him, even if I had gotten up the courage to go.

In my book *Me, Me, Me, Me, Me,* I describe his leaving, as well as his letter to me many years later when, disillusioned by what he found in Hungary, he'd escaped with his wife and children .... I also describe in that book, our last meeting, in 1968 in my New York City apartment, when he came one night for dinner, catching me up on his new life as a journalist in Caracas.

In 1949, I arrived in New York City, with several sorority sisters, bent on a career as a writer.

In those days, New York City was still a place where you could take a subway at night and not fear getting mugged. You could also find a two-bedroom apartment for $150 a month, if you wanted to live in Washington Heights, where the four of us found ours.

My roommates all got good jobs in advertising publishing, because they knew shorthand. In those days, a good job, for a female, was a job as a secretary, at about fifty dollars a week.

I had never been able to master shorthand, though I had studied it at my father's insistence.... My first job was at Dutton Publishing Company, as something like an assistant to the file clerk, at thirty-two dollars a week.

I can still remember the woman who trained me saying: "When you answer the phone, tell whoever's calling your name, Marijane Meaker," as though I might not know my own name.

My job had no real title. I worked in the art department, in the bull pen, carrying my lunch every day in a paper sack, after a long subway ride with two station changes; it took me an hour to get down to lower New York from Washington Heights in hose, heels, hat, and gloves.

I remember once passing an editor's office, where a sort of scruffy character was seated talking to the editor about "Truman." I thought, "That guy knows President Truman?" because he was saying things about seeing Truman, talking with Truman.... It was one of Dutton's authors, Gore Vidal, speaking of Truman Capote. Vidal was younger then, not successful yet, wearing an old camel-hair coat, and hair longer than most men wore it in those days.

I wasn't worth the thirty-two dollars Dutton paid me to file letters and answer phones and carry things from one floor to another. My own work came first with me. I was always sitting there scratching out short stories and poems. I think the only time I looked up was when an author came into the area to discuss the artwork on his/her cover. I was in awe of all the authors. I remember one young, tough fellow who never liked his covers, who always gave the art director a hard time. He was Mickey Spillane, not too well known yet.

Life away from the office, up in Washington Heights, was busy on weekends with boyfriends who chipped in fifty cents apiece for Sunday pot roast dinners.

Friday and Saturday nights we'd go to places like the Old Garden, on West Twenty-ninth Street, the Jumbo Shop on West Eighth Street, or Albert French Restaurant on University Place, where you could have dinner for $2.50. If we couldn't afford that, we'd eat dinner in, and go out later to drink beer at Joe King's Rathskeller (draught beer was ten cents a glass) or listen to jazz at Nick's in Greenwich Village, or hang out at Arthur's in the Village, where occasionally actors and writers from the Circle in the Square Theater would come in for drinks. I remember

seeing Tennessee Williams there one night, and Geraldine Page, and Marlon Brando, and a TV star called Wally Cox.

Although we lived in Washington Heights, we always seemed to head to the Village on weekends, or someplace "downtown" where we thought "the action" was.

Always, there was talk of writing.... One of my roommates worked on a confession magazine, and for awhile I churned out confessions, selling several at $250 apiece, but not considering them real sales, because they were made-to-order stories about unfortunate females who didn't know that the men they married were dope addicts or bigamists or second cousins.

Another roommate had a boyfriend who wanted to write westerns, and she would make pots of coffee for him weekend nights while he borrowed my typewriter. I'd come home and find a sheet of paper in my Smith-Corona with a beginning story: "Mungo was back in town, and so was the smell of gunfire." Exhausted from his stint at my typewriter, David would be asleep on our couch, and as the rest of us came in from our dates, we would have heated discussions about whether or not we'd let him sleep there. How would it look to our neighbors, a man overnight in our apartment?

Dutton soon found me out, and fired me for not doing my work, and I went from Dutton to a series of flunkie jobs, everything from a proofreader on *The Review of Gastroenterology,* to a clerk at Compton Advertising Agency, to a reader at Fawcett Publications.

Not knowing shorthand was my great curse, and my great blessing. I was inept. Time and time again I was asked to turn in my key to the Ladies' Room, and report to the front office for my final paycheck.

All the while I was going from job to job, I was writing stories and sending them out. When I couldn't find a literary agent to represent me, I took the money from a sale to a confession magazine, and had stationery printed up: Marijane Meaker, Literary Agent.... I began sending stories out under pseudonyms, with Marijane Meaker raving about her new discoveries, to various editors.

On April 20, 1951, a letter came in the mail from the *Ladies' Home Journal,* to Marijane Meaker, Literary Agent, saying they were going to buy Laura Winston's story "devotedly, Patrick Henry Casebolt."

The $750 from that sale launched me on my writing career.

I never worked at a full-time job again.

Bruce Gould, then the editor of *Ladies' Home Journal,* liked the story so much, he came to interview me in New York City about a position opening up on the magazine, as a columnist for young people. It meant I would have to go to Philadelphia to live. I declined, but I also admitted that I was both Laura Winston and Marijane Meaker. Gould decided to plug that issue of the magazine with this story of a young writer posing as her own agent. He managed to get me on several radio shows, including one conducted by the then-famous Mary Margaret McBride.

That publicity came to the attention of an editor named Dick Carroll. He was launching a new original paperback series called Gold Medal Books, published by Fawcett Publications. He'd heard me say on the radio that I'd once worked for Fawcett in some menial capacity.

"How about trying a novel for our new line?" he asked me. "How about a book on boarding school life?" (My story for the *Ladies' Home Journal* was set in a boarding school.)

"How about one on sorority life?" I suggested.

"Give me a few chapters and an outline," said Dick, "and if you do well, maybe I can get you an advance."

I went to work on it, and in a few months sent him the result.

He called me for lunch, and as we taxied to the restaurant we went under the ramp near Grand Central Station, and in that dark tunnel he told me: "We're taking your story. I'm advancing you $2000," and then we emerged into the sunlight of Park Avenue. I was now under contract for my first novel, a paperback original which came to be called, not by my title *Sorority Girl,* but by one Dick thought up, *Spring Fire,* an idea he'd gotten from *The Fires of Spring,* a fast-selling novel by James Michener.

Spring Fire was an instant paperback success, selling 1,463,917 copies in 1952, more than *The Damned* by John D. MacDonald or *My Cousin Rachel* by Daphne du Maurier, both published that same year in the U.S.

Long out of print now, *Spring Fire* enabled me to become a full-time freelance novelist, enjoy a trip to Europe, and get my first apartment, sans roommates, on East Ninety-fourth Street, off Fifth Avenue, where I would live for eight years.

The apartment building at 23 East Ninety-fourth was very small, only two apartments per floor, five floors altogether.

About a year after I moved in, a new tenant moved across the hall.

He rang my bell one day to tell me that he worked at the Frick Museum, and was not home during the day to receive deliveries. Would I accept a small drum for him?

A drum? I hated the whole idea—that just across the way there'd be some drummer. He'd neglected to point out that it was a drum of china and crystal, sent from his home in Omaha, Nebraska.

He was a man a few years older than me, tall, sandy-haired, an art historian who'd graduated recently from Princeton.

Thus began a very close friendship, that still remains today, with Tom Baird. We began spending most of our free time together, and I always think that one day he looked over my shoulder as I was working at the typewriter, and told himself "I can do that." Because Thomas Baird soon became an author, as well as an art historian, beginning with a short story called "Remember, Remember," which I sold for him (I was still a half-hearted literary agent) . . . the first story I ever sold for a legitimate client. In 1962, his first novel, *Triumphal Entry,* was

Meaker with Ernest Leogrande, East Hampton, New York, 1982.

published. Today he has eleven novels to his credit, two of them young adult novels.

I think of my New York years (1949-1973) as the best of times!

I began taking courses at The New School, in everything from writing to adolescent psychology, and there I made another friend, who would open up new worlds to me. She was a professor there named Martha Wolfenstein, married then to Nathan Leites of the famous Rand Corporation, which I always thought of as "the think tank," there were so many brilliant minds employed there. Through Martha and Nathan, I met New York's psychoanalysts (Martha was a child analyst), and many sociologists, political scientists, and anthropologists (including Margaret Mead) I'd have never had the opportunity to even glimpse as a mere beginning writer.

And I read all of Freud, under Martha's formidable influence, and began subscribing to *The International Journal of Psychoanalysis, The Psychoanalytic Study of the Child,* plus reading everything by Reik, Stekel, Kubie, Mahler, Fromm, Ernest Jones, on and on and on.

It was the fifties, a time when many young people in New York City were undergoing lengthy psychoanalyses. I always think my friendship with Martha spared me that process (and expense). I got it by osmosis.

Certainly this friendship, and its resultant interest in what makes people tick, enhanced my writing, for I had moved into suspense novels, whydunits instead of whodunits, writing as Vin Packer. This move was motivated solely because I'd heard that the *New York Times* mystery and suspense columnist, Anthony Boucher, would review paperbacks as well as hardcovers.

As Vin Packer, I wrote nineteen novels of suspense, all paperback originals, encouraged by Boucher's good reviews of my work. I particularly liked to fictionalize famous contemporary murder cases like the "Wolf Whistle" Mississippi murder of the young black boy Emmett Till, and the Fraeden-Wepman matricide. A good many of my stories were told from the point of view of a teenager, again probably Martha's influence, since many of her patients were young adults ... and she often discussed their problems with me, without ever identifying anyone under her care.

The fact that I wrote many novels about teenagers would come up in conversation years later, when I became friends with a writer named Louise Fitzhugh.

Louise was an artist turned writer, who had done a very successful book called *Harriet the Spy.* It was published by Harper and Row as a "young adult" book. I had never heard of such a category.

Meaker (left) on the "Mary Margaret McBride Show,"

"You'd be a good young adult writer," Louise would tell me, "since you're always writing about kids."

"But not from their viewpoint," I'd answer, and I'd dismiss her suggestions that I should try to write for this field.

I went on to hardcover, eventually, as Marijane Meaker, writing first a nonfiction study of famous suicides for Doubleday, called *Sudden Endings.*

I suppose it was natural to move from homicide to suicide, since suicide is often described as self-directed homicide.

My book on the subject studied the lives of everyone from Arshile Gorky, to Ernest Hemingway, to James Forrestal, Robert Young, the railroad magnate, Virginia Woolf, Joseph Goebbels, Hart Crane, etcetera, and I learned two important facts while I was researching the material. The first fact was that while I could locate a famous person in every field from business to art, I could not find a famous sports figure or a famous musician who had ever committed suicide (this was before our rock stars came along). The second fact I learned was that since I was not an authority of any kind, only a reporter, I was not allowed by my editor to comment on the first fact, or speculate about it. I was told I had "no editorial excuse" to make anything of this discovery.

I found this most dismaying, and I also found an abundance of errors I had made when the galleys were returned to me. I was not a very careful researcher. I seemed to hate facts.

I quickly decided I would stick with fiction. There I could invent and speculate. I went on to do the obligatory family novel that I guess every young writer must get out of his/her system.

It was a terrible bomb called *Hometown,* and the only attention it got was in upstate New York, where my aunt was busy getting it out of the local library, and various other relatives were decrying its publication.

It was described by *Publishers Weekly* as "a long, boring novel, all the more surprising because it comes from the facile pen of Vin Packer." I was beginning to believe that my real name was a jinx, though ultimately I went on to publish a successful novel called *Shockproof Sydney Skate* as Marijane Meaker. It became a Literary Guild alternate, and a selection of the Book Find Club, and the paperback money was exceptional, enough eventually to buy me the house I live in today, in East Hampton, New York.

Again, my friend Louise Fitzhugh was nudging me about writing a novel for young adults. Again, she reminded me that my protagonist, Sydney Skate, was a teenager.

Louise, by that time, was interested in writing mystery and suspense. She thought that maybe if we traded typewriters, a young adult book would emerge for me, and my typewriter would produce for her a crime story.

We laughed about it. I took a look at some of these young adult novels and decided I could never write one ... *until* I picked up one called *The Pigman* by Paul Zindel.

Right around that same time, I'd just finished participating in an experiment, whereby writers went into high schools, taking over English classes for one day a month, trying to get kids interested in writing.

I'd been assigned to some classes at Central Commercial High School, in New York City, on Forty-second Street. These kids worked half a day and went to school half a day. They were wild, unruly, wonderful kids who didn't give a fig for reading, but who responded to writing assignments with great vigor and originality.

The star of one of my classes was a very fat black girl nicknamed "Tiny."

She wrote really grotesque stories, about things like a woman going swimming and accidentally swallowing strange eggs in the water, and giving birth to red snakes.

I always "published" Tiny's stories in the little mimeographed magazines we ran off for the kids. One day her mother appeared, complaining that Tiny's stories were hideous and that I was encouraging her to write "weird."

While we discussed this, I learned that Tiny's mother was an ardent do-gooder who worked with her small church helping drug addicts. Tiny would come home from school to an empty apartment, fix herself something to eat, watch TV, and wait for her mom to come home from her churchwork. Then they'd eat dinner, her mom would go back to her good works, and Tiny would eat and watch TV.

Tiny was getting to be enormous. She was also glued to the TV all the while she was alone.

In other words, while Tiny's mom was putting out the fire in the house across the street, her own house was on fire.

I was thinking a lot about this.

A book was coming to me.

I had just read Zindel's books.

That was the birth of my first book for young adults. Tiny translated into "Dinky," and since I knew that this story could be told about any family, black or white, rich or poor, I decided to stick close to home. I'd just moved to Brooklyn Heights, which abounded with lawyers because the courts were right nearby. I set my story there, and made

Tom Baird, East Hampton, New York, 1984.

Marijane Meaker, honorary Doctor of Literature from Long Island University.

Dinky's mother a middle-class lawyer's wife who was involved in rehabilitating dope addicts.

The result was *Dinky Hocker Shoots Smack.*

Since I love pseudonyms, I decided to call myself M. E. Kerr, a play on my last name, Meaker.

Since I had done well with the paperback sale of *Shockproof Sydney Skate,* I thought of this book for young adults as a little sideline, an indulgence. I only received $2000 from Harper and Row for it. I didn't expect to make much more on the paperback sale.

To my astonishment, this "sideline" made money. The paperback sale was enormous. It was optioned for the movies (many times) and ultimately made into an afternoon special. It is still going strong today.

I decided to take a second look at this new, to me, young adult category. I was in my forties, by then, and not very interested any longer in murder and crime. The passion I had brought to that interest was waning, as I became more mellow, more liable to see the light in the dark, or the light *and* the dark. As I looked back on my life, things seemed funnier to me than they used to. *I* seemed funnier to me than I used to, and so did a lot of what I'd "suffered."

Miraculously, as I sat down to make notes for possible future stories, things that happened to me long ago came back clear as a bell, and ringing, and making me smile and

shake my head as I realized I had stories in me about *me*— no longer disguised as a homicidal maniac, or a twisted criminal bent on a scam, but as the small-town kid I'd been, so typically American and middle class and yes, vulnerable, but not as tragic and complicated as I used to imagine.

So I had a new identity for myself in middle age: M. E. Kerr.

I also moved to a new place, East Hampton, on Long Island, New York, which would eventually become Seaview, New York, in many of my novels. My old hometown, Auburn, would appear from time to time as Cayuta, New York.

I've never married nor had children, and I've lately thought this has been a great asset. If I'd had children, I'm sure I would have been tempted to keep them tied to something in an upstairs room, so no harm would come to them. I think the youngster in me remains vivid because I've never raised any children to compete with her, or compare with her, and I have not had to pace the floor nights worrying where they are or with whom, and what has happened to the family car.

Again, these experiences come to me through osmosis. When I first moved to East Hampton, a sweet seventeen-year-old kid next door to me was going through his first love affair with a very rich girl who spent summers in our community. His family disapproved of this girl; his dad was a policeman, and Kippy was brought up strictly. He was working as a soda jerk the summer he met this rather sophisticated young lady. He had a new bicycle; she had a new Porsche.

Kippy would come over to my house, agonizing about what to wear, what fork to pick up on the table when he was invited to her house for lunch. She had a butler. She lived by the ocean. She was a year older than Kippy. She'd gone to high school in European boarding schools.

That same summer, I was reading a book by Howard Blum called *Wanted: The Search for Nazis in America.*

That book, and what Kippy was going through, became all mixed together, until finally I sat down to write a novel called *Gentlehands.*

Gentlehands was about a boy in Kippy's situation, who looked up a grandfather the family was estranged from, in order to impress this girl. The erudite, opera-loving grandfather proved to be a Nazi war criminal the Immigration Service was investigating.

Of any book I've ever written, *Gentlehands* was the easiest. It poured from my typewriter as though a tape was inside with the whole story put down on it.

Another time, I'd gone to a local high school football game. At halftime I'd watched a pretty blond girl run up to the pom-pom cheerleaders, greeting them as though she hadn't seen them in a long time. She was carrying something in her arms, in a blanket. Behind her, a tall black guy was waiting for her, not joining in the reunion.

When this blond girl unfolded the blanket, there was a tiny black baby gurgling up at everyone.

I was standing beside my dentist's wife, and I said something about supposing that was inevitable in a community where there were blacks and whites going to school together: intermarriage.

She said, "Ah, but that's not the real story. The real story is the anger black girls here have because white girls date 'their men.'" She said many of the black boys were sports heroes, and the white girls went out with them, but white boys didn't in turn date black girls.

This incident, on an ordinary autumn afternoon, was the background for a book called *Love Is a Missing Person.* It was the story of a girl whose sister fell in love with a black boy, and ran off with him at the end of the novel. Not a lot of local teachers and parents were thrilled about this Kerr, but it has elicited many letters from kids familiar with the problem of interracial dating.

Sometimes my ideas come from the past, and I update them. That was true of my book about boarding school life called *Is That You, Miss Blue?* Nearly everything that happened in that story, happened to me when I was attending Stuart Hall. A present-day Stuart Hall student wrote to tell me she liked the book, " . . . but boarding schools just aren't that strict anymore." I think it was a valid criticism.

I had always hesitated writing a book for kids set in the forties, when I was growing up. I remembered how I hated reading "historical" novels, when I was a kid. Still, the years during World War II haunt me, and I am filled with stories about what happened to teenage girls back then. There have been so many, many stories about what went on in the lives of young men . . . so few about "us."

Finally, I decided to tackle the problem by attempting a novel that would begin in the forties and end in the eighties. I didn't want to write a long three-generational type thing, so I came up with a new approach, for me. I wrote three short stories about the same characters: one set in the forties, told from the first person; one set in the sixties, told from the third person; the last, a letter in the second person, written by a boy to his dad, set in the eighties.

The three stories, read together, are a novel.

I called this *I Stay Near You*—one story in three.

One great advantage in writing for kids is keeping up with the times. I've developed a very enthusiastic interest in today's music. I listen faithfully to the top ten, and I follow all the groups from pop to rock to heavy metal. I'm an MTV watcher, mesmerized by all the groups from Police, Duran Duran, Wham!, Van Halen, and Aztec Camera, to Twisted Sister, Kiss, and Motley Crue. Some of the videos I love, and some I really hate, but all of them teach me about kids today. It's a whole new world for me, one I probably wouldn't have investigated if I wasn't a Y.A. writer.

When I first moved to East Hampton, I missed New York City a lot. Three months of the year our little village jumps with tourists and summer people, the likes of Paul McCartney, Mick Jagger, Lauren Bacall and Alan Alda, but the rest of the year we are a sleepy little place without an industry or very much going on. And I missed the easy access to other writers, the chance to meet casually with someone who wasn't a weekend house guest, to talk about the latest books, and what's going on in the publishing world.

I decided to form a writers' workshop, by putting an ad in the paper to see what interest there was out there. I would lead this workshop. It would be a nonprofit undertaking, benefiting the Springs Scholarship Fund, "Springs" being the section of East Hampton where I live. I arranged for us to meet at a place called Ashawagh Hall, a community center near me.

The response was quick and most enthusiastic. We had to turn some people away, we had so many signed up. Thus, The Ashawagh Hall Writers' Workshop was born. We meet once a week for two hours, fall and spring sessions running for twelve weeks at a time. Our group age ranges from the early twenties to the seventies, twenty members in all, everyone from the minister at the Amagansett Presbyterian Church, to the bartender from a hotel in Sag Harbor, to a famous artist's wife, a beautiful young girl who only writes horror stories, and local teachers, a real estate salesperson, a retired editor, etcetera.

We're going into our third year.

Probably none of us would have ever met each other socially, but all of us are focused on each other's work, as well as what's current, and what's being published in the various genres from suspense to literary. We have our own literary agency, though no one has to pay a ten- or fifteen-percent fee . . . and each semester we try to take in one or two new members.

I have few interests that aren't related to writing.

I read like a fat person eats. I read everything from magazines like *Time, The Rolling Stone, Interview, New York Magazine, Redbook, Fortune, Business Week, Vanity Fair, Woman's Day,* and *Ms.* to the best-sellers—Anne Tyler (a particular favorite), Raymond Carver, Elmore Leonard, Eudora Welty, Robert Cormier, Alice Munro,

Bobbie Ann Mason, Alice Walker, Joyce Carol Oates, Barbara Pym—on and on and on. And I reread wonderful Carson McCullers. I love poetry, too—Yeats and Auden and Kastner and Rilke and Wakoski and Leo Connellan.

I watch a good deal of television, talk shows and news programs like Ted Koppel's. I'm a movie fan ... I guess I'm just a media freak.

Long ago, despite my WASP training, I learned that motion isn't work, that sitting at the typewriter when you have no clear idea of what you want to write, is wasted time. When I'm "stuck" between novels, I mostly read, walk by the ocean, and complain that I can't work to other writers who complain back that they are finding what they're working on too hard, impossible, or not worth it.

The hardest book I ever wrote was one called *Little Little,* about teenage dwarfs. I don't know why it was so difficult, except I couldn't seem to get much humor into it, and what was there often seemed too dark.... Another thing was that I was afraid to tell *anyone* I was writing a book for young adults about dwarfs. I was afraid of the reaction, and of being discouraged by it. So I kept it to myself as I started the story over and over again, worked on it up to about fifty pages, then abandoned it. It seemed unworkable after several years of trying.

One day I decided to write an essay about it for the Long Island section of the *New York Times.* It would be about the one story I wanted to write but couldn't.

In the middle of this essay, I stopped, and started the book again, and this time finished it.

Maybe it is my favorite book, not because I think it's better than the rest, but because it was such a struggle. Maybe a parent, who's finally raised a particularly difficult child, feels this same affection and pride when that kid turns out okay.

I love writing, and I particularly love writing for young adults. I know other young-adult writers who claim that their books arc just slotted into that category, and claim

there's no difference between an adult novel and a young-adult one.... I beg to disagree. When I write for young adults I know they're still wrestling with very important problems like winning and losing, not feeling accepted or accepting, prejudice, love—all the things adults ultimately get hardened to, and forgetful of. I know my audience hasn't yet made up their minds about everything, that they're still vulnerable and open to suggestion and able to change their minds.... Give me that kind of an audience any day!

Update

When I speak with kids in schools, I like to ask them if they can guess the one subject I steer clear of writing about? Nobody ever guesses that it's rock music. I tell them although I am a great fan of rock 'n roll and many rock stars, if I were to mention Tom Petty & The Heartbreakers, for example, or 98 Degrees, N'Sync or Bon Jovi, three or four years from now teenagers reading my books might say "Who are they?" Nothing dates a book quicker than mention of today's pop music. Too bad, because I love it!

But there was one book which I wrote feeling it was not only appropriate to include talk of Sting, Madonna, Bruce Springsteen, etcetera, it was also not going to matter a few years down the line, because surely my subject matter would date the book, anyway.

This was in the early eighties when a young neighbor of mine came back to his family not only to tell them he was gay, but also to tell them he had an illness that was fatal. A cruel joke spread through our town: "There's good news and there's bad news. The bad news is I'm gay. The good news is I'm dying."

The illness Jim (not his real name) had was known then as GRID. Gay-related Immune Deficiency. As I was writing my story about a young man like Jim, who'd grown up hiding his sexual orientation, not wanting to shame his family or be estranged in his small community, GRID became knows as AIDS.

I had gotten the idea to call my novel *Night Kites* one Fourth of July when I was attending a town fireworks display, and noticing all the green collars people were wearing around their necks, as disco dancers sometimes wear things that glow in the dark. I thought of fixing a kite with something like that, so it could fly in the dark. A night kite, I thought ... and then the image came to me as a metaphor for people who are different. I could see a scene ... Jim walking along the beach with the much younger kid sister who adored him, trying to tell her not that he was gay—what would that mean to a four-year-old?—but wanting to say something about not everybody being the same. "Most kites go up in the daytime ... but some are night kites, and they fly in the dark, alone, on their own, and they're not afraid to be different."

My appreciation of rock musicians has led to the knowledge that a great majority of them were yesterday's losers—unhappy kids who didn't fit in or belong—it's all through their music. And today, many of them are our night kites—our wonderful, creative mavericks.

So rock lore was sprinkled liberally through the book ... and I went with the title *Night Kites.* It was the first book about AIDS, adult or young adult, which featured a protagonist who was a male homosexual. Begun in 1984

"M. E. Kerr"

and published in 1986, there was considerable hostility toward the book because of its subject. There were requests from schools not to speak about it when I gave presentations, and even I had misgivings in the beginning about burdening teachers with a book which provoked too many hard questions.

Unfortunately, as time passed, AIDS remained and became a great enough health risk for information concerning it to be mainstreamed. The schools could not ignore it. And then there was some hostility which went all the way in the other direction. Why hadn't I mentioned condoms? (Condoms? In a YA book in the early eighties?) Why hadn't I spoken up against premarital sex? And finally, did the romantic image of a night kite suggest that male promiscuity was desirable?

Ah, well, there are always our critics there to try and steer us back on the path.

After the agony of writing *Night Kites,* even as many dear friends were being diagnosed with AIDS, I decided that whatever I wrote next would be light, non-controversial, fun. And I thought of my old suspense career, of how I had liked writing capers, so I made up my mind to do a series.

I decided to star a young man whose dad had once been a police detective, from whom he'd learned many tricks. Not coincidentally, some of these "tricks" had been told to me by the policeman I moved next door to when I bought my first house in East Hampton. He and his whole family had already provided ample material for *Gentlehands.*

Now I was ready to profit again from propinquity—for how would I have ever know so many things about small-town police life without Bill?

What I wanted to do was think of a name for my young man which would work in the books' titles. I decided on John Fell. There are many things you can do with Fell, beginning with a book called that. Next, *Fell Back ...* followed by *Fell Down.* And I was ready to do *Fell in Love, Fell Away,* on and on until *Fell Over* or *Fell Dead.*

Then my editor, Robert O. Warren at HarperCollins, suggested that *Fell* was not exactly *falling* off the shelves. I, of course, argued that they were not on the shelves to fall off. But sales were disappointing, and ultimately I abandoned Fell after the third book.

It was somewhere around that time, too, when I decided that I would like to write fantasy for a younger age ... and I remembered a proposed picture book Harper had turned down just as a young editor named Nola Thacker remembered it. She'd worked at Harper and liked the book, and she had moved on to Scholastic. After she discussed this with her boss, an editor I think of as *Ann Reit* (who's never wrong), a proposal was made that I might write a book for kids using another name than Kerr. I'd always felt that Harper helped build the Kerr name, and I'd always been happy there.

The Scholastic offer also provided me with an opportunity to see how I'd do as an unknown, and to work with Reit who is sharp and creative. Although I didn't claim to be a first novelist, since I felt that wouldn't be fair, I did change my pseudonym to Mary James.

Shoebag, instead of becoming a picture book, became a short novel. It was inspired by Franz Kafka's *Metamorphosis* in which a man woke up one morning changed into a cockroach. His horrified family wanted nothing to do with such a dirty insect.

I had always thought that if a cockroach had one day awakened as a human, his family would be equally repelled.

And so, after inventing the idea that roaches are always named after their places of birth, I began the story of Shoebag, and his mother, Under The Toaster ... and his father, Drainboard.

Happily, *Shoebag* was successful, and ultimately followed by a sequel, *Shoebag Returns.*

There are two other Scholastic books, as well, and then I went back to being Kerr, and wrote a book about the Gulf War called *Linger.*

It was inspired by a newspaper photo of a handsome young man who'd joined the Marines to learn a trade of some kind, but soon found himself fighting in Saudi Arabia. He was hit by "friendly fire" and left deaf with a mutilated face and a bad leg.

That war of the American flags and the yellow ribbons was the only one *then* which our kids could remember. It came on TV like a Nintendo game, glitzy and exciting, with no body bags to depress us, nor any estimations of how many people we killed, or how many of our own men and women were killed. It just looked like some faraway night sport, and in a short while it was over, we won, life went on. At least it did for most people, and those who were killed or ruined were not a great subject of interest to anyone but their loved ones.

I hoped *Linger* would help them be remembered, and make kids think twice about the idea of a stint in the Marines to learn a trade ... as well as about what war really means.

I had always wanted to write a book about a lesbian teenager who doesn't have to worry over anyone finding out what she is, for there would be no way for her to pretend she was anything else. I didn't want her to be a savvy kid who didn't care what anyone thought, and I didn't think of her as a big city kid, where she'd have access to others like her.

I could never come up with the right focus until a summer of horrific floods in the Midwest.... A farmer was quoted in the *New York Times* as saying about the Mississippi: "Why did they ever try to fool with nature, and use those levees to make that river into a stream? You can't force things to be what they're not." I had gone to the University of Missouri and visited many friends with farms, so I knew the terrain, and when I read that man's words, I knew I had a metaphor: the river.

In my research I came upon a sign I saw marking the highest point of the floodgate back in 1973. A quote from Mark Twain.

> *One who knows the Mississippi will promptly aver that 10,000 River Commissions cannot tame that stream ... cannot say to it Go here or Go there and make it obey ... cannot bar its path with an obstruction, which it will tear down, dance over and laugh at.*

In *Deliver Us from Evie,* Evie is a very masculine girl, with no talent or inclination to try and be more feminine. Once her mother begins to realize that the rumors about

Evie are true, she says: "If Evie *is* a lesbian, she's got a bigger problem than some other girl would have who isn't so stereotypical.... It's bad enough to look that way, but it's awful to look it and be it. Then you're what everyone's always thought one of those females look like."

Evie, who is having a romance with a feminine girl named Patty, tells her mother, "Patty likes me the way I am. She likes me in pants with my hair slicked back. She likes me in my bomber jacket, and she likes me taking long steps, sinking my hands in my pocket, and all the other stuff you say I shouldn't do.... Some of us look it, Mom! I know you so-called normal people would like it better if we looked as much like all of you as possible, but some of us don't, can't, and never will. And some others of us go for the ones who don't, can't, and never will."

One of the reasons I chose to make Evie a butch stereotype was to address the tendency of the majority to accept those members of minority groups who appear most like *them.* The lighter skinned black over the darker. The male homosexual no one would ever know was gay. The Jewish girl with the bobbed nose (almost a rite of passage in my small town in the '50s—before Barbra Streisand came along as a role model to change some young women's minds about "nose jobs.") Gloria Steinem as a feminist more palpable than Betty Friedan.

I've been writing professionally now for fifty years come 2000. It has been my sole support and the only constant in my life. (My longtime friend Tom Baird died of a heart attack ten years ago, and so many of my contemporaries have also been visited by the Great Flyswatter In The Sky). It is no wonder that I have always thought of writing about writing. *Blood on the Forehead* is that book, the title coming from an old saying of Gene Fowler's: "Writing is easy. All you have to do is sit there and wait until the drops of blood appear on your forehead."

Of course, the title is hyperbole, but I've always felt that good writing *is* hard work, which is not to say you can't love hard work. There's little satisfaction for me in things that are easy (some of my best friends aren't easy), although looking back makes things seem easier than they were. Juxtaposing the old Beatles' song, "Yesterday," I've always wanted to title a story "The Easy Game of Yesterday."

Blood on the Forehead talks about how some of my ideas came for books like *Gentlehands* and *Little Little,* as well as for short stories, which I seldom get the chance to write unless an anthologist requests one. There simply isn't a market anymore for shorts.

One of my greatest pleasures continues to be the Ashawagh Writers' Workshop which I founded back in the early eighties. How we've grown! In a day when writers are all threatened by big conglomerates swallowing up our small-town bookshops, by talk of the death of midlist books, by all the gloomy philosophies and forecasts regarding publishing, we are thriving: in spirit, and in practical matters like book contracts.

Many of us have been with the workshop since its beginning, and every Thursday night we climb the stairs to the attic of Ashawagh Hall, for a two-hour session reading our writing, talking about the latest books, sharing them with each other, passing on publishing gossip, and breaking open champagne for every new sale a writer makes. Most of our writers produce adult novels, but we have a few young adult authors and some who write memoirs. This year alone we have *The Hampton Affair, The Irish Cottage Murders,* and *Who I Am Keeps Happening* already in bookstores or soon to be. And I have just finished a YA called *What Became of Her.*

When I was a young, young writer and poor, I knew a very rich woman who had a leather doll which was dear to her beyond belief. The doll's name was Wambly. He traveled with her. His clothes were tailor made. When they ate in restaurants, a high chair was procured for Wambly. If she was playing tennis, he was on the bench in his tennis whites and cashmere blazer. If she was skiing, he was in a

A meeting of the Ashawagh Hall Writers' Workshop, 1984.

backpack on the slopes with her in his wool cap and shades.... She could not fathom life without Wambly.

Meanwhile *I* would watch them and wonder what if I dollnapped Wambly? What if I wrote her a ransom note for a lot of money, threatening to destroy Wambly if she didn't pay up?

Of course she would pay. There was no question she would.

One day I went to the dentist and there in the waiting room Wambly sat. I thought: "Take him! Think of all the writing you can do if you have a nice cushion! Is dollnapping such a big offense? Of course not! And she'll dine out on the story of the day someone took Wambly!"

But I didn't do it.

Wambly and she are now safely ensconced in graves which are part of their private seventeen plot area in the Sag Harbor cemetery, each with a headstone. Part of writing is making happen what you might not have been able to make happen in life. And so in *What Became of Her,* I dollnap Wambly.

One of the great rewards of writing is seeing dreams realized. Another is being appreciated. Not only did I receive an honorary Doctor of Literature from Long Island University, but I also have been given three lifetime achievement awards: the Margaret Edwards Award, the New York State Librarians' Knickerbocker Award, and an award from the Publishing Triangle.

To my astonishment and pleasure, a young graduate student at Columbia University, Michelle Koh, chose me to be the subject of a website she created. The M. E. Kerr/Mary James website at http://www.columbia.edu/~msk28/

I still live on a Dead End street with the ominous name Deep Six Drive, but that's okay, because I've always been an optimist. You'd have to be to begin announcing in your pre-teens that someday you were going to be a writer.

Writings

YOUNG ADULT FICTION; UNDER PSEUDONYM M. E. KERR

Dinky Hocker Shoots Smack!, Harper, 1972.
If I Love You, Am I Trapped Forever?, Harper, 1973.
The Son of Someone Famous, Harper, 1974.
Is That You, Miss Blue?, Harper, 1975.
Love Is a Missing Person, Harper, 1975.
I'll Love You When You're More Like Me, Harper, 1977.
Gentlehands, Harper, 1978.
Little Little, Harper, 1981.
What I Really Think of You, Harper, 1982.
Him She Loves?, Harper, 1984.
I Stay Near You: 1 Story in 3, Harper, 1985.
Night Kites, Harper, 1986.
Fell, Harper, 1989.
Fell Back, Harper, 1989.
Fell Down, HarperCollins, 1991.
Linger, HarperCollins, 1993.
Deliver Us From Evie, HarperCollins, 1994.
"Hello," I Lied, HarperCollins, 1997.
What Became of Her, Harper, 2000.

FICTION UNDER NAME M. J. MEAKER

Hometown, Doubleday, 1967.
Game of Survival, New American Library, 1968.
Shockproof Sydney Skate, Little, Brown, 1972.

FICTION; UNDER PSEUDONYM MARY JAMES

Shoebag, Scholastic, 1990.
The Shuteyes, Scholastic, 1993.
Frankenlouse, Scholastic, 1994.
Shoebag Returns, Scholastic, 1996.

NONFICTION

Me, Me, Me, Me, Me: Not a Novel (autobiography), Harper, 1983.
Blood on the Forehead: What I Know About Writing, HarperCollins, 1998.

ADULT FICTION; UNDER PSEUDONYM VIN PACKER

Dark Intruder, Gold Medal Books, 1952.
Spring Fire, Gold Medal Books, 1952.
Look Back to Love, Gold Medal Books, 1953.
Come Destroy Me, Gold Medal Books, 1954.
Whisper His Sin, Gold Medal Books, 1954.
The Thrill Kids, Gold Medal Books, 1955.
Dark Don't Catch Me, Gold Medal Books, 1956.
The Young and the Violent, Gold Medal Books, 1956.
Three-Day Terror, Gold Medal Books, 1957.
The Evil Friendship, Gold Medal Books, 1958.
5:45 to Suburbia, Gold Medal Books, 1958.
The Twisted Ones, Gold Medal Books, 1959.
The Damnation of Adam Blessing, Gold Medal Books, 1961.
The Girl on the Best-Seller List, Gold Medal Books, 1961.
Something in the Shadows, Gold Medal Books, 1961.
Intimate Victims, Gold Medal Books, 1962.
Alone at Night, Gold Medal Books, 1963.
The Hare in March, New American Library, 1967.
Don't Rely on Gemini, Delacorte, 1969.

*ADULT NONFICTION; UNDER PSEUDONYM ANN ALDRICH
EXCEPT AS NOTED*

We Walk Alone, Gold Medal Books, 1955.
We Too Must Love, Gold Medal Books, 1958.
Carol, in a Thousand Cities, Gold Medal Books, 1960.
We Two Won't Last, Gold Medal Books, 1963.
(Under name M. J. Meaker) *Sudden Endings,* Doubleday, 1964, paperback edition published under pseudonym Vin Packer, Fawcett, 1964.
Take a Lesbian to Lunch, MacFadden-Bartell, 1972.

KUSKIN, Karla 1932-
(Nicholas J. Charles)

Personal

Born July 17, 1932, in New York, NY; daughter of Sidney T. (in advertising) and Mitzi (maiden name, Salzman) Seidman; married Charles M. Kuskin (a musician), December 4, 1955 (divorced, August, 1987); married William L. Bell, July 24, 1989; children: (first marriage) Nicholas, Julia. *Education:* Attended Antioch College, 1950-53; Yale University, B.F.A., 1955.

Addresses

Home—96 Joralemon St., Brooklyn, NY 11201.

Career

Writer and illustrator. Conducts poetry and writing workshops. Worked variously as an assistant to a fashion photographer, a design underling, and in advertising, "many, many years ago."

Awards, Honors

American Institute of Graphic Arts Book Show awards, 1955-57, for *Roar and More,* 1958-60, for *Square as a House,* and 1958, for *In the Middle of the Trees;* Children's Book Award, International Reading Association, 1976, for *Near the Window Tree: Poems and Notes;* Children's Book Showcase selection, Children's Book Council, 1976, for *Near the Window Tree: Poems and Notes,* and 1977, for *A Boy Had a Mother Who Bought Him a Hat;* award for excellence in poetry for children, National Council of Teachers of English, 1979; New York Academy of Sciences Children's Science Book Award, 1980, for *A Space Story;* American Library Association Award, 1980, for *Dogs & Dragons, Trees & Dreams: A Collection of Poems;* named Outstanding Brooklyn Author, 1981; *The Philharmonic Gets Dressed* was named a best illustrated book by the *New York Times,* 1982; American Library Association Award, 1982, and National Book Award nomination, 1983, both for *The Philharmonic Gets Dressed;* Parents' Choice Award for Literature, 1986, for *The Dallas Titans Get Ready for Bed,* and 1987, for *Jerusalem Shining Still;* Parenting-Reading Magic Award, 1992, for *Soap Soup;* Parents' Choice Humor Book award, 1993, for *A Great Miracle Happened There;* John S. Burroughs Science Award, 1994, for *City Dog;* Children's Books of Distinction Award, *Riverbank Review,* 1999, for *The Sky Is Always in the Sky.*

Writings

CHILDREN'S BOOKS

A Space Story, illustrated by Marc Simont, Harper, 1978.
The Philharmonic Gets Dressed, illustrated by Simont, Harper, 1982.
The Dallas Titans Get Ready for Bed, illustrated by Simont, Harper, 1986.

Jerusalem, Shining Still, illustrated by David Frampton, Harper, 1987.
A Great Miracle Happened There: A Chanukah Story, illustrated by Robert Andrew Parker, Willa Perlman Books, 1993.
City Noise, illustrated by Renee Flower, HarperCollins, 1994.
Patchwork Island, illustrated by Petra Mathers, HarperCollins, 1994.
Paul, paintings by Milton Avery, HarperCollins, 1994.
Thoughts, Pictures, and Words, photographs by Nicholas Kuskin, R. C. Owen, 1995.
The Upstairs Cat, illustrated by Howard Fine, Clarion Books, 1997.
The Sky Is Always in the Sky, illustrated by Isabelle Dervaux, Laura Geringer Books, 1998.
I Am Me, illustrated by Dyanna Wolcott, Simon & Schuster, 2000.

Jerusalem, Shining Still has been recorded on audio cassette.

SELF-ILLUSTRATED CHILDREN'S BOOKS

Roar and More, Harper, 1956, revised edition, HarperCollins, 1990.
James and the Rain, Harper, 1957, illustrated by Reg Cartwright, Simon & Schuster, 1995.
In the Middle of the Trees (poems), Harper, 1958.
The Animals and the Ark, Harper, 1958.

Karla Kuskin

Just Like Everyone Else, Harper, 1959.
Which Horse Is William?, Harper, 1959.
Square as a House, Harper, 1960.
The Bear Who Saw the Spring, Harper, 1961.
All Sizes of Noises, Harper, 1962.
Alexander Soames: His Poems, Harper, 1962.
(Under pseudonym Nicholas J. Charles) *How Do You Get
　　from Here to There?,* Macmillan, 1962.
ABCDEFGHIJKLMNOPQRSTUVWXYZ, Harper, 1963.
The Rose on My Cake (poems), Harper, 1964.
Sand and Snow, Harper, 1965.
(Under pseudonym Nicholas J. Charles) *Jane Anne June
　　Spoon and Her Very Adventurous Search for the
　　Moon,* Norton, 1966.
The Walk the Mouse Girls Took, Harper, 1967.
Watson, the Smartest Dog in the U.S.A., Harper, 1968.
In the Flaky Frosty Morning, Harper, 1969.
Any Me I Want to Be: Poems, Harper, 1972.
What Did You Bring Me?, Harper, 1973.
Near the Window Tree: Poems and Notes, Harper, 1975.
A Boy Had a Mother Who Bought Him a Hat, Houghton,
　　1976.
Herbert Hated Being Small, Houghton, 1979.
Dogs & Dragons, Trees & Dreams: A Collection of Poems,
　　Harper 1980.
Night Again, Little, Brown, 1981.
Something Sleeping in the Hall, Harper, 1985.
Soap Soup, HarperCollins, 1992.
City Dog, Clarion Books, 1994.

ILLUSTRATOR

Violette Viertel and John Viertel, *Xingu,* Macmillan, 1959.
Mitzi S. Seidman, *Who Woke the Sun,* Macmillan, 1960.
Jean Lee Latham and Bee Lewi, *The Dog That Lost His
　　Family,* Macmillan, 1961.
Margaret Mealy and Norman Mealy, *Sing for Joy,* Seabury,
　　1961.
Virginia Cary Hudson, *O Ye Jigs and Juleps!,* Macmillan,
　　1962.
Rhoda Levine, *Harrison Loved His Umbrella,* Atheneum,
　　1964.
Hudson, *Credos & Quips,* Macmillan, 1964.
Gladys Schmitt, *Boris, the Lopsided Bear,* Collier Books,
　　1966.
Marguerita Rudolph, *Look at Me,* McGraw, 1967.
Sherry Kafka, *Big Enough,* Putnam, 1970.
Marie Winn, editor, and Allan Miller, music arranger, *What
　　Shall We Do and Allee Galloo!,* Harper, 1970.
Marcia Brown, *Stone Soup,* Great Books Foundation, 1984.
Joan Grant, *The Monster Who Grew Small,* Great Books
　　Foundation, 1984.
Ellen Babbit, *The Monkey and the Crocodile,* Great Books
　　Foundation, 1984.

OTHER

Contributor of essays and reviews to books and periodicals, including *The State of the Language,* University of
California Press, *Saturday Review, House and Garden,
Parents, Choice, New York Times, Los Angeles Times,*
and *Village Voice.*

Author of screenplays, including *What Do You Mean by
Design?* and *An Electric Talking Picture,* both 1973.

Author and narrator of filmstrip *Poetry Explained by
Karla Kuskin,* Weston Woods, 1980. An interview with
the author entitled *A Talk with Karla Kuskin* has been
produced by Tim Podell Productions.

Adaptations

The Philharmonic Gets Dressed was adapted for film by
Sarson Productions.

Sidelights

Karla Kuskin is an award-winning author and illustrator
whose nearly four dozen publications include verse
picture books written by her, illustrated by her, or those
she has both written and illustrated. She first achieved
popularity with the 1956 publication of *Roar and More,*
and has gone on to pen such award-winning and popular
titles as *In the Middle of the Trees, The Philharmonic
Gets Dressed, Soap Soup, The Dallas Titans Get Ready
for Bed,* and *The Sky Is Always in the Sky.* Additionally,
she is the recipient of a National Council of Teachers of
English Poetry prize for her body of work, writes often
in poetry and verse, and she is well known for her witty,
alliterative style that serves well at read-aloud time. Her
artwork is equally whimsical. "I write for children,"
Kuskin noted in *Something about the Author Autobiography Series* (SAAS), "because of a close bond I have
with my own childhood. There is an understanding, a
way of seeing things that I have never completely
outgrown, that is still a part of me."

Kuskin's childhood was spent largely in New York City.
The only child of Mitzi and Sidney Seidman, "I was the
focus of a lot of approving attention and scrutiny,"
Kuskin remarked in *SAAS.* "I preferred the attention. But
my mother, a dry cleaner's daughter, has always had the
ability to spot an imperfection in the material at fifty
feet. While I was often highly praised, I was also
continually judged by that eye and have inherited the
same sharp vision." Kuskin's love of words began early,
and a first poem—transcribed by her mother when the
fledgling author was four—describes the hydrangea
bushes outside the front door of the country house where
the family lived for a year. But New York was and
continues to be Kuskin's backdrop, as "difficult, alarm-
ing, marvelous, and ugly" as it sometimes is. Her father
was in advertising, though he had dreams of journalism,
and her mother gave up a stage career for photography
which she gave up with the birth of her daughter. "I
promised myself that when I grew up I would not give
up a job for my family but would combine the two,"
Kuskin noted in *SAAS.* "I was determined that my
children should never feel that they had kept me from
work I wanted to do."

From an early age that work meant writing and drawing.
She formed an early, "almost magical belief in the
power of words on paper," she commented in *SAAS.* "To
write things down, preserve the moment in words, has
always been a necessity." Likewise there was an early
attachment to paper of all sorts. "There is nothing like an
unmarked surface waiting to be marked." Her education,

at private schools in New York, helped foster this love of words, as did her parents. Both at home and at school, poetry reading was a daily activity. As a child, her favorite poets included Alfred Noyes, Robert Frost, along with the humorous verses of Ogden Nash, Don Marquis, A. A. Milne, and the *Mother Goose* volumes. T. S. Eliot became an inspiration, as were e.e. cummings, Yeats, and Auden. "Literature was neither dry or dusty," she recalled of her school years in *SAAS*. "It was a fascinating part of our lives."

During adolescence Kuskin was short, thin, and did not feel very popular among her peers. She wrote in her *SAAS* essay that "reading and writing had always been among my favorite pastimes; in high school they became my refuge. I would come home in the afternoon, get myself milk and cookies, and fall into the world of whatever book I was reading at the moment." Kuskin spent a considerable amount of time at the Hudson Street Library located very close to her home. She also endeavored, with the support of various dedicated teachers, to write her own poems and short stories.

"I was not really sure, in those days, how I could best express myself," she elaborated in *SAAS*. "I knew that I enjoyed writing, drawing, painting; but when I graduated from high school in 1950 I had no idea what work I was really suited for and what work was really suited to me." Kuskin entered a work-study program at Antioch College where she hoped that a sampling of jobs would help her make a career. Through her work she gradually developed an interest in the field of graphic arts and, in 1953, transferred to Yale University's School of Fine Arts. Kuskin's final requirement before receiving her bachelor's degree from Yale was to create and print a book using a small press that had recently been purchased by the university.

"The subject of my slim book, *Roar and More,* was animals and their noises," she explained in *SAAS*, "a subject well-suited to typographical illustration." *Roar and More* was soon accepted for publication, though in a slightly different form than the original; a number of colors were eliminated and the linoleum cuts were changed to drawings. Despite the alterations the book fared well with critics and young readers, won an award from the American Institute of Graphic Arts, and was reprinted in a much more colorful edition in 1990. Reviewing the 1956 edition in the *New York Times Book Review,* George A. Woods called the book "a spirited romp" and "satisfyingly unconventional."

This initial publication pointed her in the right career direction. About this same time, Kuskin married a freelance oboist. She worked on a magazine, for a photographer and in advertising during the first year of her marriage. A forced vacation due to a bout of hepatitis gave her the free time to play with ideas and a rainy stay on Cape Cod provided the inspiration for *James and the Rain,* "one of the best read-aloud stories for very young children to appear in a long, long time," according to a critic in *Publishers Weekly.* The story of a young boy who sets out to discover what various

animals do when it rains, *James and the Rain* begins with a simple description: "James pressed his nose against the pane / And saw a million drops of rain / The earth was wet / The sky was grey / It looked like it would rain all day." The book was republished in 1995 with illustrations by Reg Cartwright.

In the early 1960s, Kuskin had two children, Nicholas and Julia. Her experiences as a parent became a source of topics for some of her books. *The Bear Who Saw the Spring,* for example, was written when Kuskin was pregnant with her first child, Nicholas, and contemplating motherhood. The story focuses on a knowledgeable, older bear who teaches a young dog about the seasons of the year; the relationship of the two characters is similar to that of a parent and child. *Sand and Snow,* about a boy who loves the winter and a girl who loves the summer, was dedicated to Kuskin's infant daughter Julia. And *Alexander Soames, His Poems,* a book Kuskin acknowledges was partly inspired by her children, recounts a conversation between a mother and her son Alex, who will only speak in verse despite his mother's repeated requests that he express himself in prose. Critiquing the last title, Ellen Lewis Buell noted in the *New York Times Book Review* that "Kuskin's fantasy about a small boy who speaks only in rhymes is as amusing as its title's promise." Buell went on to remark that the verses "are good nonsense, lighthearted, swiftly paced."

Kuskin also draws upon vivid memories of her own youth as themes for her books. Growing up in New York City, Kuskin reflected in *SAAS*, "there was ... the sense of being a small child in big places that was very much a part of my childhood. And I was determined to remember those places and those feelings. I vowed to myself that I would never forget what it was like to be a child as I grew older. Frustration, pleasure, what I saw as injustices, all made me promise this to myself." Kuskin has been lauded for knowing "what is worth saving and what is important to children," according to Alvina Treut Burrows in *Language Arts*. "Her pictures and her verse and poetry," the reviewer continued, "are brimming over with the experiences of children growing up in a big city."

Kuskin's great respect for education and her love of poetry have motivated her to visit schools and try to help children in writing their own verse. She stresses a different approach in the way she writes for children and the way children should write poetry themselves. "When I write I often rhyme," Kuskin remarked in *Language Arts,* "and I'm very much concerned with rhythm because children love the sound and swing of both. But when children write, I try to discourage them from rhyming because I think it's such a hurdle. It freezes all the originality they have, and they use someone else's rhymes. It's too hard. And yet their images are so original." The author encourages children to write verses by paying attention to their surroundings, concentrating on descriptions and experiences, and writing what they have imagined in short, easy lines rather than worrying about perfect sentences and paragraphs.

Kuskin has also employed an educational technique in some of her poetry collections. In *Dogs & Dragons, Trees & Dreams: A Collection of Poems,* for example, Kuskin adds notes to each poem, explaining her inspiration for the particular verse and encouraging the reader to write his own poetry. Critics lauded the author for including her commentary; *Washington Post Book World* contributor Rose Styron thought that *Dogs & Dragons, Trees & Dreams* "works nicely" and praised Kuskin's "variety, wit and unfailing sensitivity" in addressing children.

In addition to teaching children to read, write, and appreciate poetry, Kuskin's self-illustrated books contain appealing pictures that serve to emphasize her themes. Her early books, such as *All Sizes of Noises*—an assortment of everyday sounds translated into visual representations—display Kuskin's belief that "the best picture book is a unity, a good marriage in which pictures and words love, honor, and obey each other," she wrote in *SAAS.* Her 1994 self-illustrated *City Dog* is an example of this meticulous blending of art with text. The story of a city dog's first trip to the country, this book "is a verbal and visual romp," as poetry and motion take over, according to Betsy Hearne writing in *Bulletin of the Center for Children's Books.* Hearne went on to note that "words and pictures that at first glance appear naive accrue a rhythmic warmth that deepens with each runthrough." Mary Lou Budd concluded in *School Library Journal* that *City Dog* was replete "with the imagery one has come to expect from Kuskin," and was "a treat."

While Kuskin's self-illustrated books far outnumber those illustrated by others, she has no compunctions about working with other artists when the story requires it. "For many years," Kuskin noted in *SAAS,* "I assumed that I would illustrate whatever I wrote." In the late 1970s, however, the author asked Marc Simont to illustrate *A Space Story,* a book about the solar system that won an award from the New York Academy of Sciences. Her later collaborations with Simont and then David Frampton are among her most popular and acclaimed books. After *A Space Story,* Simont illustrated the well-received *The Philharmonic Gets Dressed,* which earned Kuskin several awards, including one from the American Library Association, and an inclusion on the short-list for the American Book Award. The book describes the pre-performance activities of one hundred and five orchestra members; their preparations include bathing, shaving, powdering, hair drying, and dressing before they finally play a concert.

A similar topic is addressed in Kuskin and Simont's third collaboration, *The Dallas Titans Get Ready for Bed.* After a difficult game, forty-five members of a victorious football team retreat to the locker room until the coach tells them they must go home and rest for practice the next morning. As reluctantly as a child who wishes to avoid an early bedtime, each player removes layers of football gear, takes a shower, dresses in street clothes, and leaves for home. Though Molly Ivins commented in the *New York Times Book Review* that

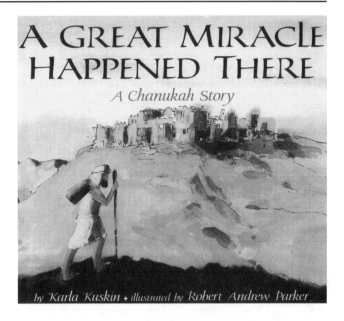

A Christian boy spends the first night of Chanukah at the home of his Jewish friend, and the boys are told the story of the Jews' fight for religious freedom. (Cover illustration by Robert Andrew Parker.)

The Dallas Titans Get Ready for Bed is "a much better book for boys than for girls," she described it as "neat" and "funny." And *Horn Book* contributor Hanna B. Zeiger found the story "a totally original and very funny behind-the-scenes look at a large organization."

For *Jerusalem, Shining Still,* a book she wrote after an official invitation in 1982 to the city, Kuskin chose a woodcut artist named David Frampton to provide illustrations. Recounting three thousand years of the history of Jerusalem, Israel, was a challenging task for the author. She spent a considerable amount of time thinking about her visit there and deciding what elements of the city and its past she would include in her book. "I wrote and cut and cut and wrote and condensed that long history into seven and a half pages," she related in *SAAS.* Kuskin eventually chose Jerusalem's survival and growth despite frequent attacks by foreigners as the theme of *Jerusalem, Shining Still,* and she was praised for making the city's complex history more accessible to children.

Chanukah is the topic of Kuskin's 1993 *A Great Miracle Happened There,* with illustrations by Robert Andrew Parker. With a prose text, the book tells the story of a young Christian boy spending his first Chanukah with a Jewish family and the questions the children ask about the tradition. A reviewer for *School Library Journal* felt that it was a "book worth sharing for many seasons to come." A *Kirkus Reviews* contributor called the book an "unusually thoughtful account of the events celebrated during Chanukah." The 1994 picture book, *Paul,* is the result of an unusual collaboration. For this book, Kuskin wrote a text for illustrations created by the noted American painter Milton Avery, completed in 1946 for a book that was never published. The manuscript had been lost, and Kuskin's job was to weave a story from the series of fantastical double-spread illustrations. She constructed one depicting a young boy's search for his magical grandmother.

Patchwork Island, illustrated by Petra Mathers, is a story-poem about a mother who stitches a quilt for her toddler; the resulting quilt is filled with images from her Canadian island home. Heide Piehler commented in *School Library Journal* that the "sense of warmth and security that the patchwork symbolizes is evident in both illustrations and narrative." Somewhat similar to her first title, *Roar and More,* is Kuskin's *City Noise,* an "exuberant explosion of colors and shapes" accompanying a "rhyming, energetic poem," according to Mary Rinato Berman in *School Library Journal.* A tin can held to a little girl's ear becomes a magical conch shell, relating all the strange sounds of the city. A critic writing in *Publishers Weekly* felt that illustrator Renee Flower and Kuskin "seize on urban cacophony and turn

it into a celebration of life itself in this dynamic picture book." Kuskin recreates a veritable ocean of city sounds: "Squalling / Calling / Crashing / Rushing / ... Cars and garbage / Reds and greens / Girls and women / Men / Machines . . . ." A *Kirkus Reviews* contributor called the book an "exuberant poem that captures the hubbub of urban life."

Kuskin tells the tale of two fighting cats in verse in *The Upstairs Cat,* illustrated by Howard Fine, and in the 1998 *The Sky Is Always in the Sky,* illustrated by Isabelle Dervaux, she collects thirty-six of her poems previously published in other books. Reviewing the latter title, *Booklist's* Hazel Rochman noted that there "is a wonderful physical immediacy to this selection of poems," and concluded that it was a "great collection for reading aloud at home, in the library, and in the classroom." *Riverbank Review* listed it among its 1999 Children's Books of Distinction awards, noting the

Kuskin provided both text and illustrations for this lively picture book about a dog's first trip to the country. (Cover illustration by Kuskin.)

"[f]unny and intelligent" nature of the poems that act as a representative sampling of Kuskin's body of work.

Though many of Kuskin's works have earned her acclaim and awards, the author believes, as she wrote in *SAAS,* that "basically one works for oneself. It is the process that keeps you going much more than the little patches of appreciation you may have the good fortune to stumble into here and there .... Anyone can succeed gracefully. The trick is learning how to fail. I find failure as frightening, discouraging, and unpleasant as everyone else does, but I am quite sure that the ability to survive it, to get up and begin again, is as necessary as a good idea, a reasonable portion of talent, and a disciplined mind."

But beyond such a work ethic, Kuskin also possesses a unique gift. As Judson Knight and Margaret F. Maxwell concluded in a critical study of Kuskin's work in *St. James Guide to Children's Writers,* "Kuskin's most successful poems are those which capture the essence of childish experience; her ability to think herself into a child's skin ... is due to the fact that she draws for her inspiration on memories of her own childhood. That she has been able to distill these memories into simple yet lighthearted verses, which at their best are exquisite in their evocation of her small themes, is Kuskin's lasting talent."

Works Cited

Berman, Mary Rinato, review of *City Noise, School Library Journal,* November, 1994, p. 98.

Budd, Mary Lou, review of *City Dog, School Library Journal,* March, 1994, p. 202.

Buell, Ellen Lewis, review of *Alexander Soames, New York Times Book Review,* May 5, 1963, p. 22.

Burrows, Alvina Treut, "Profile: Karla Kuskin," *Language Arts,* November-December, 1979, pp. 934-40.

Review of *City Noise, Publishers Weekly,* July 18, 1994, p. 244.

Review of *City Noise, Kirkus Reviews,* October 15, 1994, p. 1409.

Review of *A Great Miracle Happened There, School Library Journal,* October, 1993, p. 45.

Review of *A Great Miracle Happened There, Kirkus Reviews,* November 1, 1993, p. 1394.

Hearne, Betsy, review of *City Dog, Bulletin of the Center for Children's Books,* May 22, 1994, p. 292.

Ivins, Molly, review of *The Dallas Titans Get Ready for Bed, New York Times Book Review,* November 9, 1986, p. 40.

Review of *James and the Rain, Publishers Weekly,* July 22, 1957, p. 67.

Knight, Judson, and Margaret F. Maxwell, "Kuskin, Karla," *St. James Guide to Children's Writers,* edited by Sara Pendergast and Tom Pendergast, St. James Press, 1999, pp. 613-15.

Kuskin, Karla, *James and the Rain,* Harper, 1957.

Kuskin, Karla, *Something about the Author Autobiography Series,* Volume 3, 1987, pp. 115-130.

Kuskin, Karla, *City Noise,* HarperCollins, 1994.

Kuskin selected the poems for this compilation from her many popular collections. (Cover illustration by Isabelle Dervaux.)

Piehler, Heide, review of *Patchwork Island, School Library Journal,* July, 1994, p. 95.

Rochman, Hazel, review of *The Sky Is Always in the Sky, Booklist,* March 15, 1998, p. 1628.

Review of *The Sky Is Always in the Sky, Riverbank Review,* spring, 1999, p. 23.

Styron, Rose, review of *A Pocketful of Rhyme: "Dogs & Dragons, Trees & Dreams: A Collection of Poems, Washington Post Book World,* March 8, 1981, pp. 10-11.

Woods, George A., "From Snarls to Purrs," *New York Times Book Review,* November 18, 1956, p. 49.

Zeiger, Hanna B., review of *The Dallas Titans Get Ready for Bed, Horn Book,* November-December, 1986, pp. 737-38.

For More Information See

BOOKS

Children's Literature Review, Volume 4, Gale, 1982.

Children's Books and Their Creators, edited by Anita Silvey, Houghton, 1995.

Hopkins, Lee Bennett, *Pass the Poetry Please,* Citation Press, 1976.

PERIODICALS

Booklist, September 15, 1993, p. 154; March 1, 1994, p. 1270; May 15, 1994, p. 1681; June 1, 1994, p. 1840; June 1, 1995, p. 1787; August, 1995, p. 1943.
Bulletin of the Center for Children's Books, June, 1994, pp. 324-25; July-August, 1995, p. 378.
Horn Book, July-August, 1995, pp. 476-77.
Kirkus Reviews, May 1, 1998, p. 660.

New York Times Book Review, August 17, 1986; May 22, 1994, p. 22; July 19, 1998, p. 24.
Publishers Weekly, October 13, 1997, p. 74.
Riverbank Review, fall, 1999, pp. 19-21.
School Library Journal, September, 1995, pp. 194-95; December, 1997, pp. 95-96; July, 1998, p. 89.

—*Sketch by J. Sydney Jones*

L

LEAH, Devorah
See DEVORAH-LEAH

*   *   *

LEWIS, Cynthia Copeland 1960-

Personal

Born June 2, 1960, in New Milford, CT; daughter of A. Clayton (a business executive) and Sharlene J. (a homemaker) Copeland; married Thomas J. Lewis (a scientist), December 23, 1983; Children: Anya Brooke, Alexandra Paige, Aaron Avery. *Education:* Smith College, B.A., 1982. *Politics:* Republican. *Religion:* United Church of Christ.

Addresses

Home and Office—18 Acrebrook Rd., Keene, NH 03431.

Career

Writer and Illustrator. Has worked as a newspaper reporter, editor and graphic artist. Volunteer for school associations (classroom assistant, PTA vice president) and church groups.

Writings

FOR CHILDREN, EXCEPT AS NOTED

Hello, Alexander Graham Bell Speaking, Dillon Press, 1991.
Teen Suicide: Too Young To Die (young adult), Enslow, 1994.
Dilly's Big Sister Diary, Millbrook, 1998.
Dilly's Summer Camp Diary, Millbrook, 1999.

OTHER

Mother's First Year, Betterway Publications, 1989, Berkley, 1992.

Cynthia Copeland Lewis

(With Thomas J. Lewis) *Best Hikes With Children In Vermont, New Hampshire and Maine,* The Mountaineers, 1991, second edition, 2000.
(With Thomas J. Lewis) *Best Hikes With Children in Connecticut, Massachusetts and Rhode Island,* The Mountaineers, 1991, second edition, 1999.
(With Thomas J. Lewis) *Best Hikes with Children in the Catskills and Hudson River Valley,* The Mountaineers, 1992.
Really Important Stuff My Kids Have Taught Me, Workman Publishing, 1994.
(With Thomas J. Lewis and Carolyn Bradley) *In-Line Skate New England,* Countryman Press, 1997.

Also author of "Mother Knows Best" Page-A-Day calendar (for 2000), Workman, 1999. Contributor to periodicals, including *American Baby Magazine* and *Family Circle.*

Work in Progress

Illustrations for books on the five senses, including *Your Tongue Can Tell* and *Follow Your Nose,* written by Vicki Cobb, for Millbrook Press; a third "Dilly" book, for Millbrook Press; two chapter books of historical fiction for middle graders; young-adult books on tattooing and body piercing and diet fads. Also contracted to write another "Mother Knows Best" Page-A-Day calendar, for Workman.

Sidelights

Cynthia Copeland Lewis told *SATA:* "I have been interested in writing since I was able to. When I was in seventh grade, my English teacher, Mrs. Schultz, took me aside one day and told me that she thought I should be a writer. She contacted a reporter named Leslie Jacobs who worked for our local newspaper and asked if she would be willing to mentor a young writer. She agreed, and I learned a great deal that year, attending local events and town meetings with Leslie, writing articles (with her help) and taking photographs, a few of which made it into the newspaper.

"A decade later, after graduating from college, I began my professional career as a newspaper reporter. My other early jobs included working as an editor in a corporate publications department and as a graphic artist creating corporate logos and brochures. I also spent a year or so working for a small publishing company where I drew coloring books, designed greeting cards, and edited children's puzzle magazines.

"When I had my first child in 1986, I knew I wanted to be an 'at-home mom.' I began writing my first book, *Mother's First Year,* when my daughter was 18 months old. I wrote about all of the changes that occur in a woman's life after she becomes a mother. I sent a letter and sample chapter to one publisher and signed a contract not long after. Of course, not all of my books found interested publishers so quickly.

"My children—I now have three—have inspired many of my projects, including the recent 'Dilly' books (*Dilly's Big Sister Diary* and *Dilly's Summer Camp Diary*). My daughter Alexandra portrayed Dilly in the photographs that appear in the books and provided me with third-grade insights and ideas that added authenticity to Dilly's voice."

LIN, Grace 1974-

Personal

Born May 17, 1974; daughter of Jer-shang (a doctor) and Lin-Lin (Yang) Lin. *Education:* Rhode Island School of Design, B.F.A., 1996.

Addresses

Home—213 Summer St., Somerville, MA 02144. *Office*—P.O. Box 401036, North Cambridge, MA 02140. *E-mail*—gracelin@concentric.net.

Career

Freelance illustrator, 1997—. *Member:* Society of Children's Book Writers and Illustrators.

Illustrator

(And author) *The Ugly Vegetables,* Charlesbridge (Watertown, MA), 1999.
They Did It First!, McGraw, 1999.
Shelley Gill and Deborah Tobola, *The Big Buck Adventure,* Charlesbridge, 1999.

Grace Lin

Work in Progress

Illustrations for *Round Is a Mooncake,* for Chronicle Books, and *We Eat Rice,* for Lee & Low.

Sidelights

Grace Lin told *SATA:* "My most vivid memory of childhood is lying on the living room floor reading a book. I would sprawl next to my mother's banana plant (big plant!) and read. My mother would call throughout the house, 'Grace, where are you? Clean your room!' I would cosy up closer to the banana plant, which hid me from view, and continue reading.

"It's this love of books that has been a constant in my life. When I became old enough to think about the future, I wanted to be either an Olympic figure-skater or a book illustrator. When I realized that I fell down every time I tried to lift one foot off the ice, my direction became clear.

"Now I write and illustrate books that I wish I could have had when I was younger. As a child, I was hungry for books with an Asian-American character. I wanted the main character to be someone just like me. Back then, the few books with Asian characters were folktales, not something that fit into my contemporary life. It's much better now, but I don't forget the desire I had.

"I hope my books bring some joy into the world and, maybe, make someone smile and think: 'This book is about me.'"

For More Information See

PERIODICALS

Kirkus Reviews, June 15, 1999, p. 966.
Publishers Weekly, July 5, 1999, p. 69.

*   *   *

LONDON, Jane
See GEIS, Darlene (Stern)

*   *   *

LOWRY, Lois 1937-

Personal

Born March 20, 1937, in Honolulu, HI; daughter of Robert E. (a dentist) and Katharine (a teacher; maiden name, Landis) Hammersberg; married Donald Grey Lowry (an attorney), June 11, 1956 (divorced, 1977); children: Alix, Grey (deceased), Kristin, Benjamin. *Education:* Attended Brown University, 1954-56; University of Southern Maine, B.A., 1972, also graduate study. *Politics:* Democrat. *Religion:* Episcopalian.

Lois Lowry

Addresses

Home—34 Hancock St., Boston, MA 02114; and Sanbornton, NH. *Agent*—c/o Wendy Schmalz, Harold Ober Associates, 40 East 49th St., New York, NY 10017.

Career

Freelance writer and photographer, 1972—. *Member:* Society of Children's Book Writers and Illustrators, PEN American Center, Authors Guild, MacDowell Colony (fellow).

Awards, Honors

Children's Literature Award, International Reading Association, and Notable Book, American Library Association (ALA), both 1978, and state children's choice awards from Massachusetts and California, all for *A Summer to Die;* Children's Book of the Year, Child Study Association of America, and Notable Book, ALA, both 1979, both for *Anastasia Krupnik;* Notable Book, ALA, 1980, and Honor List, International Board on Books for Young People, 1982, both for *Autumn Street;* Notable Book, ALA, 1981, and American Book Award nomination (juvenile paperback category), 1983, both for *Anastasia Again!;* Notable Book citation, ALA, 1983, for *The One Hundredth Thing about Caroline;* Children's Book of the Year, Child Study Association of America, 1986, for *Us and Uncle Fraud;* New Jersey children's choice award, 1986, for *Anastasia, Ask Your Analyst;* Golden Kite Award, Society of Children's Book Writers and Illustrators, Child Study Award,

Children's Book Committee of Bank Street College, and *Boston Globe/Horn Book* Award, all 1987, all for *Rabble Starkey;* Newbery Medal, ALA, Sidney Taylor Award, National Jewish Libraries, and National Jewish Book Award, all 1990, all for *Number the Stars;* Newbery Medal, ALA, 1993, for *The Giver;* RA/CBC Children's Choice citation, 1997, for *See You Around, Sam!*

Writings

FOR CHILDREN; NOVELS

A Summer to Die, illustrated by Jenny Oliver, Houghton, 1977.

Find a Stranger, Say Goodbye, Houghton, 1978.

Anastasia Krupnik, Houghton, 1979.

Autumn Street, Houghton, 1979.

Anastasia Again!, Houghton, 1981.

Anastasia at Your Service, Houghton, 1982.

Taking Care of Terrific, Houghton, 1983.

The One Hundredth Thing about Caroline, Houghton, 1983.

Anastasia, Ask Your Analyst, Houghton, 1984.

Us and Uncle Fraud, Houghton, 1984.

Anastasia on Her Own, Houghton, 1985.

Switcharound, Houghton, 1985.

Anastasia Has the Answers, Houghton, 1986.

Rabble Starkey, Houghton, 1987.

Anastasia's Chosen Career, Houghton, 1987.

All about Sam, illustrated by Diane De Groat, Houghton, 1988.

Number the Stars, Houghton, 1989.

Your Move, J.P.!, Houghton, 1990.

Anastasia at This Address, Houghton, 1991.

Attaboy, Sam!, Houghton, 1992.

The Giver, Houghton, 1993.

Anastasia, Absolutely, Houghton, 1995.

See You Around, Sam!, Houghton, 1996.

Stay!: Keeper's Story, illustrated by True Kelley, Houghton, 1997.

Looking Back, Houghton, 1998.

Zooman Sam, Houghton, 1999.

OTHER

Black American Literature (textbook), J. Weston Walsh, 1973.

Literature of the American Revolution (textbook), J. Weston Walsh, 1974.

(Photographer) Frederick H. Lewis, *Here in Kennebunkport,* Durrell, 1978.

(And photographer) *Looking Back: A Photographic Memoir* (autobiography), Houghton, 1998.

Also author of introduction to *Dear Author: Students Write about the Books That Changed Their Lives,* Conari Press, 1995. Contributor of stories, articles, and photographs to periodicals, including *Redbook, Yankee,* and *Downeast.*

Adaptations

Find a Stranger, Say Goodbye was made into the Afterschool Special "I Don't Know Who I Am," 1980;

Taking Care of Terrific was televised on "Wonderworks," 1988. *Anastasia at Your Service* was recorded on audiocassette, Learning Library, 1984; *Anastasia Krupnik* was made into a filmstrip, Cheshire, 1987.

Work in Progress

Companion volume to *The Giver,* for Houghton.

Sidelights

"The most important things to me in my own life, as well as in my books, are human relationships of all kinds," Lois Lowry once commented. "Although my books deal largely with families, I also attach a great deal of importance to friendships. Those are the things young people should pay attention to in their lives." Lowry's ability to explore young people's lives and relationships—in works both funny and serious—has made her one of today's most popular and critically acclaimed authors for young teens. Whether writing about the everyday trials and tribulations of Anastasia Krupnik or the extraordinary courage shown by children living in oppressive societies, Lowry spins a compelling story containing characters with whom young readers can identify. As Brad Owens commented in the *Christian Science Monitor,* "author Lois Lowry has a sensitive way of taking problems seriously without ever being shallow or leaning too far over into despair."

Lowry was born in 1937 in Honolulu, Hawaii, where her father was stationed as a dentist with the army. Shortly before the Pearl Harbor bombing caused the United States to enter World War II, Lowry and family moved to the mainland. She and her mother and siblings spent the duration of the war with her mother's family in the Amish area of Pennsylvania. "I remember all these relatively normal Christmases with trees, presents, turkeys, and carols, except that they had this enormous hole in them because there was never any father," Lowry once commented. This feeling of loss during her early life, she explained, is "probably why I've written a terrific father figure into almost all of my books—sort of a fantasy of mine while growing up."

Lowry was an eager student, and learned to read at the age of three. "I became aware that letters had sounds and if you put them together they made words, and if you put the words together they made stories," she remembered in her *Something about the Author Autobiography Series* (*SAAS*) essay. Her skill set her apart from other children in her class, however: "I hate[d] the games they play[ed]: one in particular, where they pretend[ed] to be elephants, holding their arms like trunks, and lumbering about in a line while the teacher play[ed] elephant-marching music on the piano. I refuse[d]. I [sat] in a corner of the classroom instead, reading. An intellectual snob at the age of three." She was skipped from first to third grade, where she still excelled in reading but found some trouble with math. "I [was] humbled. For the remainder of my official academic life I [was] the youngest, usually the smallest, in every grade, and the

Spunky and rebellious Anastasia Krupnik, the heroine of Lowry's popular series, is introduced to readers in this 1979 novel. (Cover illustration by Diane DeGroat.)

one who suffer[ed] from math anxiety long before the term [was] invented."

Nevertheless, Lowry enjoyed a "quiet, well-ordered, predictable, safe, and happy" childhood. She used her imagination to turn her experiences into stories, discovering that "even my own naivete seems bearable as long as it has a form, a substance, and a narrative," as she recalled in *SAAS*. She excelled at school, although she found little to interest her in extracurricular activities, whose committees and rules had no appeal. "Somehow, it all [began] to seem like that dumb elephant-marching game the kids had played back in nursery school," she remembered. "I prefer to be on my own, and usually manage[d] to be." By the time she graduated from high school at sixteen, she had the ambition of being a novelist. She entered Pembroke College, the women's branch of Brown University, and began to study writing.

The 1950s, however, were a time when most women were expected to find a husband at school, not a career. Lowry married a naval officer at nineteen, and dropped out of college to raise a family. "In 1963 I was twenty-six years old," she related in her autobiographical essay.

"I had four children under the age of five. Come to think of it, so did my husband; but he also, by then, had a law degree from Harvard, so I think he got a little better end of the bargain than I did. I don't blame him, or anyone, for that. I blame the mindless culture of the fifties, which did a lot of damage to decent people's lives." As her children grew older, she had the opportunity to return to college, and this time completed her degree. She also discovered an interest in photography and set up a darkroom in her basement. She began publishing short stories in magazines, and wrote a couple of literature textbooks. She grew out of the role of wife and homemaker and was divorced in 1977, just as she was starting a career of her own.

In 1977, Lowry published her first children's novel, written at the suggestion of an editor who had read some of her short stories. *A Summer to Die* portrays thirteen-year-old Meg's struggle to come to terms with her older sister's fatal illness. When the reader is first introduced to the Chalmers family, Meg is jealous of the vivacious and pretty Molly. The family has just moved to the country and Meg must now share a room with her older sister. At first she is resentful when Molly's illness makes her the focus of their parents' attention; gradually, however, Meg comes to realize that Molly is not going to recover. With the aid of some new friends—an older neighbor who encourages her interest in photography and a young couple expecting a baby—Meg tries to accept and find meaning in her family's adversity.

Calling *A Summer to Die* "a remarkable first novel," *Horn Book* contributor Mary M. Burns hailed the "finesse with which [the author] limns her characters." *Junior Bookshelf* reviewer Mary Hobbs similarly remarked that "the family relationships are closely, often humorously, observed," and added that "the writing is beautifully unobtrusive, yet bracing and compelling." Linda R. Silver praised Lowry's skill with setting and character, and concluded in *School Library Journal* that the "story captures the mysteries of living and dying without manipulating the reader's emotions, providing understanding and a comforting sense of completion." Tragically, Lowry's sympathy for Meg and Molly was drawn from her own experience. Her older sister, Helen, died of cancer when Lowry was twenty-five. "[*A Summer to Die*] was not strictly autobiographical," she once commented. "I changed a lot, but when my mother read the book she recognized the characters as my sister and me. She knew that the circumstances in the book were very different, but the characters had great veracity for her."

After publishing her second novel, about an adopted girl's search for her natural mother, Lowry produced the first book in what has become one of the most popular series in children's literature. *Anastasia Krupnik* appeared in 1979, and its spirited, impetuous, and irreverent heroine has entertained readers with several humorous adventures since then. Memories of Lowry's own childhood, as well as her experiences as a parent, have inspired many of Anastasia's escapades. "Until I was about twelve I thought my parents were terrific, wise,

In Lowry's Newbery-winning novel, ten-year-old Annemarie tells the story of her family's involvement in the WWII resistance movement in Nazi-occupied Denmark.

wonderful, beautiful, loving, and well-dressed," the author confessed. "By age twelve and a half, they turned into stupid boring people with whom I did not want to be seen in public.... That happens to all kids, and to the kids in my books as well."

In Anastasia's debut, the ten-year-old protagonist faces numerous comic predicaments, including a crush on a boy who is always dribbling an imaginary basketball and the anticipated arrival of a baby sibling. Lowry "masterfully captures the heart and mind of a perceptive fourth grader," noted *Booklist's* Barbara Elleman, who also praised the "tightly strung" plot and "superbly developed" characters. Ann A. Flowers highlighted Anastasia's parents as "among the most humorous, sensible, and understanding ... to be found in recent children's fiction" and added in her *Horn Book* review that "Anastasia herself is an amusing and engaging heroine." "The writing is lively, funny, and above all, intelligent," Zena Sutherland asserted in the *Bulletin of the Center for*

Children's Books. The family relationships are "superbly drawn, and the dialogue is a delight. In fact," the critic concluded, "the whole book is a delight."

The 1980s saw Lowry produce six more titles detailing the adventures of "one of the most intriguing female protagonists to appear in children's books since the advent of Harriet the spy," as Mary M. Burns described Anastasia in *Horn Book*. In 1981's *Anastasia Again!*, the heroine must deal with her precocious baby brother Sam as well as a move to the suburbs. "Lowry's prose, timing and on-target humor combine to give this protagonist credibility, and she's no less precise with secondary characters," Marilyn Kaye stated in *School Library Journal*. Anastasia is twelve in 1982's *Anastasia at Your Service*, in which she takes a summer job serving as a maid to a rich, elderly neighbor. When the woman turns out to be a classmate's grandmother, Anastasia must scheme to spare herself the embarrassment of working at her peer's birthday party. Reviewers again praised the author's portrayal of a close and supportive yet comic family, as well as the skillfully drawn characters and realistic dialogue. "Lowry's right on target in capturing the thoughts and emotions of a twelve-year-old girl," noted Barbara Elleman in a *Booklist* review, "and, on a broader scale, in proving herself as one of the consistently top children's writers in both appeal and quality."

In *Anastasia, Ask Your Analyst,* the heroine is suffering from the typical trials of turning thirteen, such as finding her family terribly embarrassing. She attributes it to "hormones" and talks out her problems to a bust of Sigmund Freud when her parents tell her she doesn't need a therapist. Like the previous books in the series, "this is up-beat, funny, and sophisticatedly witty," according to *Bulletin of the Center for Children's Books* writer Zena Sutherland, who added that "the characters are solidly conceived, the writing style and dialogue both polished and effervescent." *Anastasia on Her Own* has the heroine managing the household during her mother's absence, sometimes with less-than-successful results. Calling the work "the best [Anastasia] sequel yet," *Horn Book's* Ann A. Flowers stated that Lowry's "Anastasia Krupnik books furnish the solid, funny, staple reading that [Beverly Cleary's] Ramona stories give to younger readers."

Anastasia Has the Answers provides "a sixth witty and perceptive novel" in the series, a *Kirkus Reviews* critic commented. The heroine's newly acquired journalistic techniques are used to recount her struggles in gym class and her efforts at matchmaking. The result, said the *Kirkus Reviews* writer, is a "deft portrayal of the emotional ups and downs of being thirteen [which] is right on target." "Once again," Mary M. Burns asserted in *Horn Book,* "Anastasia Krupnik proves herself a true original among the galaxy of memorable characters in children's literature." A need for more self-confidence leads to a modeling course in *Anastasia's Chosen Career,* in which the thirteen year old makes a new friend and re-evaluates an old one. "Lowry gives readers a fine mixture of wit and wisdom, offering funny adolescent dialogue that is true to their interests and language, and the insight of an affectionate and perceptive observer of the human scene," Dudley B. Carlson concluded in *School Library Journal.*

While Anastasia's adventures have enchanted her many fans, Lowry has not overlooked other outlets for her comic talents. In 1983 she published *The One Hundredth Thing about Caroline,* the first in a series about the sometimes-fighting, sometimes-cooperating siblings Caroline and J. P. Tate. In this novel, eleven-year-old Caroline is certain that their upstairs neighbor is out to kill her and J. P. in order to get close to their divorced mother. As Caroline and her friend Stacy try to unravel the mystery, even "genius" older brother J. P. joins in the act. "As demonstrated in her 'Anastasia' books, Lowry's style is bright, fast-paced and funny, with skillfully drawn, believable characters," Kathleen Brachmann commented in *School Library Journal.* In 1985's *Switcharound,* J. P. and Caroline are united by their disappointment at being sent to stay with their father and his new family for the summer. Instead of spending time at the Natural History Museum, Caroline is left to babysit their younger half-siblings, including the pathetic Poochie. Similarly, J. P. has to postpone a computer project and coach his dad's Little League team instead. How the two plot their revenge and learn an unexpected lesson provides entertaining reading. Maria B. Salvadore observed in *School Library Journal* that "again, Lowry has created realistic, likable characters in plausible, humorous situations," while a *Publishers Weekly* reviewer likewise concluded that *Switcharound* rates "another A+ for the latest in an unbroken list of superb novels."

Older brother J. P. is the star of 1990's *Your Move, J. P.!,* in which the seventh grader experiences his first crush. J. P. spins a web of lies in order to impress lovely Angela Galsworthy, but only ends up trapping himself. "The author makes the most of the humor in J. P.'s antics but maintains a rueful sympathy throughout for his plight and for his eventual admission of truth," Ethel R. Twitchell noted in *Horn Book.* "Lowry's story is awash in real emotion yet able to make fun of itself at the same time," *Booklist*'s Ilene Cooper remarked, comparing the novel favorably with Betsy Byars's popular "Bingo Brown" books. Ruth Ann Smith made a similar comparison, and stated in *Bulletin of the Center for Children's Books* that "Lowry's brand of comic realism combines a keen sense of the absurd with a sympathetic understanding of early adolescent angst."

Along with her successes in comic fiction, the 1980s saw Lowry continue to produce novels with more serious themes, similar to her first book. *Autumn Street* is based on the author's experiences growing up in the 1940s, and provides "a reading experience that touches the heart," according to *School Library Journal* contributor Marilyn Singer. *Us and Uncle Fraud* is a more dramatic story of the "superb companionship between brother and sister in their search for treasure," as Lyn Littlefield Hoopes described it in the *Christian Science Monitor.* Lowry earned particularly good notices—as well as *Boston Globe/Horn Book* and Golden Kite

Awards—for 1987's *Rabble Starkey.* Twelve-year-old Parable Ann, better known as "Rabble," was born when her mother was just fourteen. Her father left shortly after, and Rabble's mother, Sweet Hosanna, now supports them by working as a live-in housekeeper and babysitter for the Bigelow family. Rabble has found a best friend in Veronica Bigelow, also twelve, and now that Mrs. Bigelow has been hospitalized for mental illness the two families are enjoying some peaceful, happy times. The two girls befriend an elderly neighbor, the local bully begins to take a romantic interest in Veronica, and Sweet Hosanna decides to go back to school.

With a setting in the rural West Virginia Appalachians, *Rabble Starkey* makes "a surprising and invigorating change from [the author's] usual, but always admirable, suburban, middle-class protagonists," Ann A. Flowers remarked in *Horn Book.* By the end of the novel, when Mrs. Bigelow is well enough to return home and the Starkeys decide to leave, "Rabble discovers it is love, not convention, that shapes a family, and love can come from many directions and take many forms," Betsy Hearne observed in the *Christian Science Monitor.* Lowry "is adept at portraying the nuances of relationships and emotions," a *Kirkus Reviews* critic stated, adding that in this novel "she presents a lively cast of characters in an unusual plot, skillfully handled." As Flowers concluded, Rabble's character is "an agreeable and distinct personality. In fact, we feel that we know all the characters immediately and intimately—a tribute to Lois Lowry's skill as a novelist."

While Lowry's books have always received good reviews, in the 1990s she has come to be recognized as one of the finest authors writing for young adolescents today. Not only have her "Anastasia" books continued to grow in popularity, but her more serious works have earned her two Newbery Medals—the highest accolade available to an American children's book writer. Her first Newbery came in 1990 for *Number the Stars,* a fact-based story set against the backdrop of Nazi-occupied Denmark. Nazi Germany invaded Denmark shortly after the start of World War II, and pursued the same policy of deportation of Jews that they enforced at home. In Lowry's story, ten-year-old Annemarie Johansen and her family are drawn into the resistance movement, shuttling Jews from Denmark into neutral Sweden. For most Danish Jews, this protection by their gentile neighbors was the only thing that prevented them from being sent to the Nazi death camps.

Lowry's novel does not focus on the horrors of war, however, but instead views events from the perspective of a child. Annemarie still worries about school and enjoys flowers and kittens, even as her family takes in her Jewish friend Ellen and protects her from the Nazis by disguising her as Annemarie's late sister. By presenting events from Annemarie's point of view, Lowry creates "a moving and satisfying story of heroism in war time which is totally accessible to young readers," Louise L. Sherman remarked in *School Library Journal.* She added that the novel "brings the war to a child's level of understanding, suggesting but not detailing its horrors." *New York Times Book Review* contributor Edith Milton, however, felt that this viewpoint "keeps us at too great a distance to see clearly either the scale of the evil or the magnitude of the courage from which this story springs." But *Horn Book*'s Mary M. Burns found Lowry's approach perfectly suited to her audience. "Lois Lowry belongs to the select group that has mastered the art of writing for this [preadolescent] audience," Burns wrote, for "she draws the reader into the intensity of the situation as a child of Annemarie's age might perceive it." The critic concluded that "the whole work is seamless, compelling, and memorable—impossible to put down; difficult to forget."

Lowry received the prestigious Newbery Medal a second time for her 1993 novel *The Giver*. In this radical departure from her previous works, Lowry creates a futuristic utopian world where every aspect of life—birth, death, families, career choices, emotions, even the weather—is strictly controlled in order to create a safe and comfortable community with no fear or violence. Jonas is twelve years old and is looking forward to an important rite of passage: the ceremony in which he, along with all children his age, will be assigned a life's vocation. Jonas is bewildered when he is skipped during the ceremony, but it is because he has been selected for a unique position. Jonas will become the new Receiver, the prestigious and powerful person who holds all the memories of the community. In his lessons with the old Receiver, whom Jonas calls the Giver, Jonas begins learning about the things—memories, emotions, and knowledge—that the community has given up in favor of peacefulness. At first, these memories are pleasant: images of snow, colors, feelings of love. But then Jonas encounters the darker aspects of human experience—war, death, and pain—and discovers that community members who are "Released" are actually being euthanized. This discovery leads Jonas to escape from the community with his young foster brother Gabriel. In an interestingly ambiguous ending, readers can decide for themselves whether the boys have safely reached "Elsewhere," been intercepted by their community's security forces, or died from hunger and exposure.

While some reviewers believed younger readers might be disappointed by the ambiguous ending, Lowry maintained that there is no single "right" ending to the novel. As she said in her Newbery Medal acceptance speech, reprinted in *Horn Book:* "There's a right one for each of us, and it depends on our own beliefs, on our own hopes . . . . Most of the young readers who have written to me have perceived the magic of the circular journey. The truth that we go out and come back, and that what we come back to is changed, and so are we." *Five Owls* contributor Gary D. Schmidt found the ending most appropriate, explaining that with it "the reader must do what Jonas must now do for the first time: make a choice." "The challenge of the ambiguity is appropriate for the stature of this intricately constructed masterwork," Patty Campbell stated in *Horn Book,* and called *The Giver* "a book so unlike what has gone before, so rich in levels of meaning, so daring in complexity of

symbol and metaphor, so challenging in the ambiguity of its conclusion, that we are left with all our neat little everyday categories and judgments hanging useless." Karen Ray, in a *New York Times Book Review* appraisal, found *The Giver* to be "powerful and provocative," while a *Kirkus Reviews* critic similarly concluded: "Wrought with admirable skill—the emptiness and menace underlying this Utopia emerge step by inexorable step: a richly provocative novel."

Along with her more serious novels, Lowry has continued to write new works exploring the lives of Anastasia Krupnik and her family. "I have the feeling she's going to go on forever—or until I get sick of her, which hasn't happened yet. I'm still very fond of her and her whole family," the author once remarked. In 1988 she published the first of a new series presenting events from the point of view of Anastasia's bright little brother. *All about Sam* spans Sam's early life, and finds its humor in the innocent misunderstandings of childhood. "Once again Lowry shows that she knows exactly how children think and feel and what they find funny," Trev Jones observed in *School Library Journal*. In *Attaboy, Sam!* the precocious preschooler's attempts to make a homemade gift for his mother's birthday turn into disaster. "While Lowry snags readers with her teasing style, exaggeration, and gimmickry," Marcia Hupp stated in *School Library Journal,* "she holds them with an unerring sense of humor and a sure sense of her audience." In *See You Around, Sam!* "Lowry looks deep into the I'm-running-away! scenario to invest an old story with truth, vigor, and laughs," as Roger Sutton summarized in *Horn Book. School Library Journal* contributor Starr LaTronica similarly hailed Sam's latest adventure as a worthy installment in a series distinguished for its "cast of multi-dimensional, quirky, but very believable characters and their humorous, astute observations."

Irrepressible Anastasia is up to more antics in 1991's *Anastasia at This Address.* Interested by a magazine personal ad describing a wealthy, boyish twenty-eight year old, she responds with just a little stretching of the truth: she becomes twenty-two instead of thirteen, and sends an old photo of her mother to her new pen pal. A role in the wedding of a friend's sister provides a surprising outcome to Anastasia's correspondence. The whole contains "more on-target predicaments and laugh-aloud funny dialogue from Lowry," wrote a *Kirkus Reviews* critic, adding that "all the splendidly realized characters continue to grow." "Anastasia is thoroughly delightful here," Stephanie Zvirin similarly observed in *Booklist,* concluding that this "delightful, funny book" will "leave readers chuckling out loud."

Anastasia, Absolutely, appearing in 1995, focuses on the struggles of the thirteen-year-old heroine as she faces moral issues in both her schoolwork and in real life. In her eighth-grade values class, Anastasia worries about whether she has provided appropriate responses to hypothetical scenarios about what she would do if she saw someone shoplifting, or if she could give one of her own kidneys to save a sibling's life. Moral responsibility becomes a more substantial concern when one morning while walking the dog and mailing a letter, she accidentally deposits the bag containing the dog droppings into the mailbox. Anastasia worries that her mistake might be considered a federal offense—tampering with the mail—and agonizes over what she should do. When she finally confesses, she discovers that she is a hero because the "package" she placed in the mailbox was responsible for neutralizing a bomb that had been set there. While observing that "Anastasia's still funny," *Bulletin of the Center for Children's Books* writer Deborah Stevenson noted that "this is a shallow sitcom plot without a shred of plausibility to it." Michael Cart, however, observed in the *New York Times Book Review* that "it's not plot that principally distinguishes this series." Praising the author for the "artistic integrity" and "literary strengths" she brings to her humorous fiction, the critic explained that it is "wonderfully obvious that Ms. Lowry appreciates the power that a humorous view of life lends her readers in their dealing with adversity." Anastasia's "believably flourishing functional family" is "perhaps the greatest of Ms. Lowry's successes in this series," Cart added, concluding that "Anastasia is a winner. Long may her series flourish."

Lowry explores the difficulties of family life from a different perspective in the 1997 novel *Stay!: Keeper's Story*. In the manner of a Victorian adventure story, the mongrel dog Keeper tells his own story directly to the reader. At first he is known as Lucky, and his human companion is a homeless man named Jack. After Jack's death, Lucky is taken in by a photographer who names him Pal. Pal's life as a TV star doesn't provide him with love and affection, however, so he runs away and ends up with a little girl named Emily. As Keeper, the canine hero finally finds the true home he has been searching for. Throughout Keeper's narration, "the author proves she is as well versed in animal behavior as in human sensibilities," a *Publishers Weekly* critic observed. "The versatile Lowry proves a dab hand at the animal saga," Roger Sutton remarked in *Horn Book*, and concluded that "this one practically sits up and begs to be read aloud."

In her autobiographical essay, Lowry shared how writing has been more than just a career for her: "Though my earliest memory includes the futility of comfort, my subsequent memories of anguish are always comforted by an ability to shape them into bearable proportions. Now I deal with the frustrations, fears, and disappointments of life by making stories out of them: by examining them, tipping them upside down and inside out, arranging them in an order that makes sense, weaving them through with details and holding them up to the light." The idea that these stories can also move and teach the young people who read them also provides strong motivation. As Lowry once remarked: "When I write, I draw a great deal from my own past. There is a satisfying sense of continuity, for me, in the realization that my own experiences, fictionalized, touch young readers in subtle and very personal ways."

Works Cited

Review of *Anastasia at This Address, Kirkus Reviews,* March 15, 1991, p. 396.

Review of *Anastasia Has the Answers, Kirkus Reviews,* April 1, 1986, pp. 546-47.

Brachmann, Kathleen, review of *The One Hundredth Thing about Caroline, School Library Journal,* October, 1983, p. 160.

Burns, Mary M., review of *Anastasia Again!, Horn Book,* October, 1981, pp. 535-36.

Burns, review of *Anastasia Has the Answers, Horn Book,* May-June, 1986, pp. 327-28.

Burns, review of *Number the Stars, Horn Book,* May-June, 1989, p. 371.

Burns, review of *A Summer to Die, Horn Book,* August, 1977, p. 451.

Campbell, Patty, "The Sand in the Oyster," *Horn Book,* November-December, 1993, pp. 717-21.

Carlson, Dudley B., review of *Anastasia's Chosen Career, School Library Journal,* September, 1987, p. 180.

Cart, Michael, review of *Anastasia, Absolutely, New York Times Book Review,* January 14, 1996, p. 23.

Cooper, Ilene, review of *Your Move, J. P.!, Booklist,* March 1, 1990, p. 1345.

Elleman, Barbara, review of *Anastasia at Your Service, Booklist,* September 1, 1982, p. 46.

Elleman, review of *Anastasia Krupnik, Booklist,* October 15, 1979, p. 354.

Flowers, Ann A., review of *Anastasia Krupnik, Horn Book,* December, 1979, p. 663.

Flowers, review of *Anastasia on Her Own, Horn Book,* September-October, 1985, pp. 556-57.

Flowers, review of *Rabble Starkey, Horn Book,* July-August, 1987, pp. 463-65.

Review of *The Giver, Kirkus Reviews,* March 1, 1993, p. 301.

Hearne, Betsy, "Families Shaped by Love, Not Convention," *Christian Science Monitor,* May 1, 1987, pp. B3-B4.

Hobbs, Mary, review of *A Summer to Die, Junior Bookshelf,* August, 1979, pp. 224-25.

Hoopes, Lyn Littlefield, review of *Us and Uncle Fraud, Christian Science Monitor,* March 1, 1985, p. 65.

Hupp, Marcia, review of *Attaboy, Sam!, School Library Journal,* May, 1992, p. 114.

Jones, Trev, review of *All about Sam, School Library Journal,* August, 1988, p. 96.

Kaye, Marilyn, review of *Anastasia Again!, School Library Journal,* October, 1981, p. 144.

LaTronica, Starr, review of *See You Around, Sam!, School Library Journal,* October, 1996, p. 102.

Lowry, Lois, essay in *Something About the Author Autobiography Series,* Volume 3, Gale, 1986, pp. 131-46.

Lowry, interview in *Authors and Artists for Young Adults,* Volume 5, Gale, 1990, pp. 129-40.

Lowry, "Newbery Medal Acceptance," *Horn Book,* July-August, 1994, pp. 414-22.

Milton, Edith, "Escape from Copenhagen," *New York Times Book Review,* May 21, 1989, p. 32.

Owens, Brad, review of *Anastasia Krupnik, Christian Science Monitor,* January 14, 1980, p. B6.

Review of *Rabble Starkey, Kirkus Reviews,* March 1, 1987, p. 374.

Ray, Karen, review of *The Giver, New York Times Book Review,* October 31, 1993, p. 26.

Salvadore, Maria B., review of *Switcharound, School Library Journal,* February, 1986, p. 87.

Schmidt, Gary D., review of *The Giver, Five Owls,* September-October, 1993, pp. 14-15.

Sherman, Louise L., review of *Number the Stars, School Library Journal,* March, 1989, p. 177.

Silver, Linda R., review of *A Summer to Die, School Library Journal,* May, 1977, pp. 62-63.

Singer, Marilyn, review of *Autumn Street, School Library Journal,* April, 1980, pp. 125-26.

Smith, Ruth Ann, review of *Your Move, J. P.!, Bulletin of the Center for Children's Books,* March, 1990, p. 169.

Review of *Stay!: Keeper's Story, Publishers Weekly,* July 28, 1997, p. 75.

Stevenson, Deborah, review of *Anastasia, Absolutely, Bulletin of the Center for Children's Books,* September, 1995, pp. 20-21.

Sutherland, Zena, review of *Anastasia, Ask Your Analyst, Bulletin of the Center for Children's Books,* May, 1984, p. 169.

Sutherland, review of *Anastasia Krupnik, Bulletin of the Center for Children's Books,* January, 1980, p. 99.

Sutton, Roger, review of *See You Around, Sam!, Horn Book,* September-October, 1996, p. 597.

Sutton, review of *Stay!: Keeper's Story, Horn Book,* January-February, 1998, pp. 76-77.

Review of *Switcharound, Publishers Weekly,* November 8, 1985, p. 60.

Twitchell, Ethel R., review of *Your Move, J. P.!, Horn Book,* March-April, 1990, pp. 201-02.

Zvirin, Stephanie, review of *Anastasia at This Address, Booklist,* April 1, 1991, p. 1564.

For More Information See

BOOKS

Children's Literature Review, Gale, Volume 6, 1984, pp. 192-96, Volume 46, 1997, pp. 25-50.

Contemporary Authors New Revision Series (includes interview), Volume 13, Gale, 1984, pp. 333-36.

Dictionary of Literary Biography, Volume 52: *American Writers for Children since 1960: Fiction,* Gale, 1987, pp. 249-61.

Lowry, Lois, *Looking Back: A Photographic Memoir,* Houghton, 1998.

PERIODICALS

Booklist, April 15, 1980, p. 1206; September 1, 1987, pp. 66-67; March 1, 1989, p. 1194; April 15, 1993, p. 1506.

Bulletin of the Center for Children's Books, May, 1985, p. 70; October, 1988, pp. 46-47; April, 1993, p. 257; November, 1996, p. 105; January, 1998, p. 165; September, 1999, p. 21.

Five Owls, April, 1989, pp. 59-60.

Horn Book, June, 1978, p. 258; December, 1982, p. 650; December, 1983, p. 711; June, 1984, pp. 330-31; January, 1988, pp. 29-31; July, 1990, pp. 412-21.

Junior Bookshelf, August, 1980, p. 194.

Journal of Youth Services in Libraries, fall, 1996, pp. 39-40, 49.

Kirkus Reviews, March 1, 1992, p. 326.

New York Times Book Review, February 28, 1982, p. 31; August 5, 1984, p. 14; September 14, 1986, p. 37.

Publishers Weekly, March 13, 1987, p. 86.

School Librarian, February, 1995, pp. 31-32.

School Library Journal, May, 1986, p. 94; January, 1990, p. 9.

Signal, May, 1980, pp. 119-22.

Voice of Youth Advocates, August, 1985, p. 186; April, 1988, p. 26; August, 1993, p. 167; December, 1995, p. 304.

Washington Post Book World, May 9, 1993, p. 15.

—Sketch by Diane Telgen

M

MAHONY, Elizabeth Winthrop
See WINTHROP Elizabeth

*   *   *

MACDONALD, Caroline 1948-1997

OBITUARY NOTICE—See index for *SATA* sketch: Born October 1, 1948, in Taranaki, New Zealand; died after suffering from cancer, on July 24, 1997, in Australia. Children's fantasy and science fiction writer. Macdonald worked in various office jobs before turning to writing in 1982. She was the author of novels and short stories for young adults and children for most of her career. She also served as editor of teaching materials for Deakin University, in Geelong, Australia, from 1984 to 1988. Her first book was *Elephant Rock* (1984), followed by a science fiction novel about extraterrestrials, *Visitors* (1984). Other writings by Macdonald include *Yellow Boarding House* (1985), *Joseph's Boat* (1988), *Earthgames* (1988), a post-ecological disaster novel called *The Lake at the End of the World* (1988), *Speaking to Miranda* (1992), a dark fantasy collection titled *Hostilities: Nine Bizarre Stories* (1991), *Eye Witness* (1992), a horror novel titled *Secret Lives* (1993), *Spider Mansion* (1994), and *Through the Witch's Window* (1997), a young adult fantasy. Macdonald was the recipient of the New Zealand Literary Fund Choysa Bursary (1983), the Esther Glen Medal from the New Zealand Library Association (1984), the New Zealand Children's Book of the Year Award for *Visitors* (1985), and the Children's Book Council of Australia Book of the Year Honour Prize and the Alan Marshall Prize for Children's Literature (Victorian Premier's Literary Awards), both for *The Lake at the End of the World* (1989). One critic has noted that: "Although she is usually considered a science fiction writer, Macdonald has garnered praise for the accuracy and depth of the human relationships she depicts, as well as for the subtlety and craft of her stories' construction."

OBITUARIES AND OTHER SOURCES:

PERIODICALS

Canberra Times, October 19, 1997.
Locus, September, 1997, p. 78.

—*Robert Reginald and Mary A. Burgess*

*   *   *

MAILLU, David G. 1939-
(Vigad G. Mulila)

Personal

Born October, 19, 1939, in Kilungu, Kenya; son of Joseph Mulandi (a peasant) and Esther Kavuli; married, wife's name Hannelore (a social worker), 1971; children: Christine Mwende (with another woman prior to marriage), Elizabeth Kavuli (with wife). *Education:* High school diploma, Machakos Technical School; other certificates from correspondence schools.

Addresses

Office—c/o Jomo Kenyatta Foundation, Enterprise Rd., P.O. Box 30533, Nairobi, Kenya.

Career

Voice of Kenya (radio station), graphic designer, 1964-73; writer, 1974—. Established Comb Books (a publishing company).

Awards, Honors

Jomo Kenyatta Prize for Literature, 1992, for *Broken Drum.*

Writings

FOR YOUNG PEOPLE

Kisalu and His Fruit Garden and Other Stories, East African Publishing House (Nairobi, Kenya), 1972.

Kaana Ngy'a, Heinemann Educational Books (Nairobi), 1983.

The Poor Child, Heinemann Kenya, 1988.

Mbengo and the Princess, Maillu, 1989.

The Last Hunter, Jomo Kenyatta Foundation, 1992.

Journey into Fairyland, Jomo Kenyatta Foundation, 1992.

The Lion and the Hare, Jomo Kenyatta Foundation, 1992.

The Orphan and His Goat Friend, Jomo Kenyatta Foundation, 1993.

Princess Kalala and the Ugly Bird, Jomo Kenyatta Foundation, 1993.

The Priceless Gift, East African Educational Publishers, 1993.

Sasa and Sisi, Jomo Kenyatta Foundation, 1995.

Dancing Zebra, Jomo Kenyatta Foundation, 1995.

The Lost Brother, Jomo Kenyatta Foundation, 1995.

OTHER WRITINGS

Ki Kyambonie: Kikamba Nthimo/Muandiki (poetry), Comb Books (Nairobi), 1972.

Unfit for Human Consumption (novella), Comb Books, 1973.

My Dear Bottle (poem), Comb Books, 1973.

Troubles (novella), Comb Books, 1974.

After 4:30 (poem), Comb Books, 1974, revised edition, Maillu (Nairobi), 1987.

The Kommon Man (novella), Comb Books, 1975-76.

Kujenga na Kubomoa, Comb Books, 1976.

No!, Comb Books, 1976.

Dear Monika (fictional letter), Comb Books, 1976.

Dear Daughter (fictional letter), Comb Books, 1976.

(As Vigad G. Mulila) *English Punctuation* (textbook), Comb Books, 1978.

(As Vigad G. Mulila) *English Spelling and Words Frequently Confused* (textbook), Comb Books, 1978.

Kadosa, Maillu Publishers (Machakos, Kenya), 1979.

Jese Kristo (drama), National Theatre Company and Maillu Publishers, 1979, performed at Kenya National Theatre, October 19, 1979.

Hit of Love/Wendo Ndikilo, Maillu Publishers, 1980.

For Mbatha and Rabeka (novel), Macmillan (London), 1980.

Benni Kamba 009 in The Equatorial Assignment (novel), Macmillan, 1980.

Looking for Mother, Bookwise (Nairobi), 1981.

The Ayah, Heinemann, 1986.

Benni Kamba 009 in Operation DXT (novel), Heinemann Educational Books, 1986.

Untouchable (novel), Maillu, 1987.

The Thorns of Life, Macmillan, 1988.

Our Kind of Polygamy (essay), Heinemann Kenya, 1988.

Pragmatic Leadership: Evaluation of Kenya's Cultural and Political Development, Featuring Daniel arap Moi, President of Republic of Kenya (essay), Maillu, 1988.

The Principles of Nyayo Philosophy (textbook), Maillu, 1989.

My Dear Mariana: Kumya Ivu, Maillu, 1989.

How to Look for the Right Boyfriend (nonfiction), Maillu, 1989.

The Black Adam and Eve (essay), Maillu, 1989.

P.O. Box I Love You Via My Heart (novel), Maillu, 1989.

Without Kiinua Mgongo (novella), Maillu, 1989.

Kusoma na Kuandika, Maillu, 1989.

Anayekukeep (novella), Maillu), 1990.

Broken Drum (novel), Jomo Kenyatta Foundation and Maillu (Nairobi), 1991.

African Indigenous Political Ideology: Africa's Cultural Interpretation of Democracy, Maillu, 1997.

Sidelights

The prolific author of fiction, nonfiction, and works for young readers, David G. Maillu is among the most popular novelists in Kenya. Although he did not hail from a literary family—he was the eldest of six children born to illiterate farmers—Maillu made up for this disadvantage early on. Before he started school, older friends taught him to read. Maillu performed at a high level academically, and with his talent and determination he earned diplomas by correspondence when other learning opportunities were not available locally.

One of Maillu's diplomas enabled him to secure a position as a graphic designer for the Voice of Kenya radio station, a job he held for ten years. Hoping to pursue a career as a writer, Maillu surveyed the reading public and found that average readers were interested in such topics as human relations, marriage, sex, religion, money, politics, and drinking. He would focus on these topics in his literature for the masses. In 1972, Maillu founded his own publishing company, Comb Books. After his short novel *Unfit for Human Consumption,* about a man's drinking and womanizing, became a popular success the following year, Maillu turned to writing full time.

During the 1970s and 1980s, Maillu published his own works through a series of self-owned publishing operations. As his fame grew, he also published works with mainstream publishers, such as his James Bond-type novels, *Benni Kamba 009 in The Equatorial Assignment* and *Benni Kamba 009 in Operation DXT,* the love story *For Mbatha and Rabe,* for Macmillan, and a tale about the mistreatment of female servants for Heinemann titled *The Ayah.* For *Broken Drum,* his fictional history of the Kamba, Maillu won the Jomo Kenyatta Prize for Literature in 1992. Harking back to his first published work—the children's book *Kisalu and His Fruit Garden*—Maillu published a series of children's fables for the Jomo Kenyatta Foundation, the country's main publisher of books for school children.

For More Information See

BOOKS

Dictionary of Literary Biography, Volume 157: *Twentieth Century Caribbean and Black African Writers,* Gale (Detroit), 1996.

Mwongera, Elizabeth and Richard Arden, "Approaches and Techniques in Teaching Literature to Secondary

School Students," in *The Role of Language and Literature in the School Curriculum,* British Council (Nairobi), 1991.*

*   *   *

McKEE, Tim 1970-

Personal

Born April 13, 1970, in New York City; son of James J. (a lawyer) and Doris (a marketing representative; maiden name, Brown) McKee. *Education:* Princeton University, B.A., 1992; University of Missouri School of Journalism, M.A., 1998.

Addresses

Home—Northern California. *E-mail*— tsmckee@ yahoo.com.

Career

Writer. Teacher, history and English, Barnato Park High School, Johannesburg, South Africa, 1992-94, 1996-97. Mutual Assistance Network, Sacramento, CA, grant writer, 1998-99.

Awards, Honors

Best Books, *School Library Journal,* Editor's Choice, *Booklist,* Lasting Connection, *Booklinks,* and Capitol Choices Noteworthy Book for Children, all 1998, and Notable Children's Trade Book in the Field of Social Studies, National Council for Social Studies-Children's Book Council, Skipping Stones Honor Award, Children's Literature Choice List, Nonfiction Honor List, *Voice of Youth Advocates,* Honor Book, Jane Addams Children's Book Award, Notable Children's Book, American Library Association (ALA), and Best Book for Young Adults, ALA, all 1999, all for *No More Strangers Now.*

Writings

No More Strangers Now: Young Voices from a New South Africa, illustrated with photographs by Anne Blackshaw, DK Ink, 1998.

Work in Progress

A book for young people that explores issues of race, reconciliation and growing up in America.

Sidelights

Tim McKee told *SATA:* "I write with the belief that storytellers play a pivotal role in the way we perceive the world around us; because the world is too vast to have direct contact with all of its people and places, I believe we turn to stories to make sense of that which we don't experience firsthand ourselves.

Tim McKee

"Unfortunately, sometimes the stories we hear do more to build stereotypes and separate us than to help us understand how we are connected. Whether a fairy tale, a television news piece or a book, our stories often teach us that the people who live 'over there' (over railroad tracks, over oceans, over racial or gender lines) are fundamentally different from us.

"I write to undermine this sense of 'other'; to build bridges between readers and those places and peoples they seek to understand; to make the alien feel more familiar. I write about and for young people because I believe they speak with a directness and honesty that adults all too often cover up or 'doublespeak' our way around.

"In the case of *No More Strangers Now,* I was driven by my passion to broaden American teenagers' understanding of their counterparts in South Africa. I knew from living there that life in South Africa was far more complicated, interesting and inspiring than media stories about crime and violence or books about lions and rhinos suggested. I believed, and continue to believe, that we in America live in a society rife with inequality and injustice, and that we have much to learn from the way other societies, including South Africa, confront these issues.

"The fact that *No More Strangers Now* is being used so widely in American junior high and high schools confirms my suspicion that teenagers here are hungry for stories that bring them closer to teens from other countries. I am confident that this same sense of openness will apply to stories from America's own rich tapestry, which I hope to explore in subsequent books.

"Although the non-fiction first-person narrative is my primary medium, I write poetry and short fiction to build bridges between people as well. Through painting portraits of characters, setting scenes and creating landscapes of emotion, I endeavor to speak to a reader through a shared feeling or experience; to tap into the irrefutable fact that we are all connected by the incredible beauty and profound sadness that both come with being human."

For More Information See

PERIODICALS

Horn Book, September-October, 1998, pp. 621-22.

MEAKER, Marijane (Agnes)
  See Kerr M.E.

*   *   *

MILLS, Adam
  See STANLEY, George Edward

*   *   *

MULILA, Vigad G.
  See MAILLU, David G.

O

OLUONYE, Mary N(kechi) 1955-

Personal

Born October 4, 1955, in Cleveland, OH; daughter of Gabriel Ikemefuna (a civil engineer) and Dorothy Mae (a registered nurse; maiden name, Cole) Oluonye; married Dr. Menoni Ize-Iyamu, 1980 (divorced 1991); children: Izosa. *Education:* University of Windsor, B.S., 1978. *Religion:* Christian.

Addresses

Home— 2435 Noble Road, Cleveland Heights, OH 44121. *Electronic mail*—o-squared@juno.com.

Career

Children's Services Associate, Shaker Heights Public Library, Shaker Heights, OH, 1998—.

Writings

Nigeria, Lerner, 1998.
South Africa, Lerner, 1999.

Work in Progress

Madagascar, for Lerner.

Sidelights

Mary Oluonye told *SATA:* "Ever since I was a child, reading has been my favorite thing to do. Wanting to write just came about naturally because of my love of books of all kinds. I also have a great respect for writers.

"While growing up in both Nigeria and the U.S., I was often asked questions, or heard comments made about Africa, and specifically about Nigeria, that led me to believe that many people have wrong ideas about a country like Nigeria. But people asked questions, and that meant that they were interested in the answers. So I

Mary N. Oluonye

decided to write a book to give people, especially children, an idea of what Nigeria is really like.

"I wish I could travel all around the world, but since I can't right now, the next best thing is to read about different people, lands and cultures. This is what led me to write the children's books on the countries of South Africa and Madagascar.

"The type of writing I do involves research. I spend a lot of time on research, and I am always on the look-out for people from other cultures. I want to learn from them;

learn about their culture, providing that they want to share the information, of course."

* * *

O'NEILL, Amanda 1951-

Personal

Born April 20, 1951, at St. Leonards-on-sea, Sussex, England; daughter of Ron (a teacher) and Kay (a teacher; maiden name, Abbott) Harrison; partner of Richard O'Neill (a writer); children: Conor Howard. *Education:* London College of Music, Associateship, 1969; Exeter University, B.A., 1972, M.A., 1978; University of London Institute of Education, Diploma in Educational Administration. *Hobbies and other interests:* Natural history, pets, arts and crafts, Arthurian studies, medieval literature, history, mythology.

Addresses

Home—8 Milford Rd., Leicester, LE2 3F9 England. *Agent*—(Literary) David O'Leary Literary Agency, 10 Lansdowne Court, Lansdowne Rise, London, W11 2NR England.

Career

Freelance writer and editor, 1986—. Hillcroft Adult Education College, De Montfort University, educational administrator, 1976-96. Copyeditor for firms including Longmans, Constable, Collins and Heinemann: subjects include African poetry, history, social policy, technology, trampolining; consultant on several children's information CD-Roms for firms including First Information and Dorling Kindersley.

Amanda O'Neill

Awards, Honors

Shortlisted for Junior Information Book Award, *Times Educational Supplement* Books and Resources Awards, 1997, for *I Wonder Why Snakes Shed Their Skins.*

Writings

Mitchell Beazley Pocket Guide to Cats, Mitchell Beazley International Ltd., 1991.
Ancient Times, Mitchell Beazley, 1992.
Biblical Times, Mitchell Beazley, 1992.
Gods and Demons, Mitchell Beazley, 1993.
I Wonder Why Spiders Spin Webs, Kingfisher, 1995.
The Art of Chinese Watercolours, Parragon, 1995.
The Life and Works of Munch, Parragon, 1996.
I Wonder Why Snakes Shed Their Skins, Kingfisher, 1996.
I Wonder Why Vultures are Bald, Kingfisher, 1997.
Best-Ever Book of Cats, Kingfisher, 1998.
Best-Ever Book of Dogs, Kingfisher, 1999.

OTHER

(Editor) *The Complete Encyclopedia of Needlework and Sewing Techniques,* New Burlington Books, 1989.
(Editor) *The Complete Book of the Dog,* Chartwell Books, 1989.
(Editor) *The Complete Book of the Cat,* Chartwell Books, 1989.
(Editor) *The Decorative Arts 1890-1990,* Gallery Books, 1990.
(With Richard O'Neill) *Your 1995 Horoscope,* Parragon, 1994.
(With Maureen Stanford) *The Teddy Bear Book,* Simon & Schuster, 1994.

Contributor to *Lands and Peoples,* Mitchell Beazley, 1989-90; *The New Europe,* Mitchell Beazley, 1992; *Larousse Desk Reference Encyclopedia,* Kingfisher, 1995; and *Dorling Kindersley Children's Encyclopedia,* Dorling Kindersley, 1997 (CD-Rom). Also indexer for a variety of works, including *Best American Beers, Harley Davidson Encyclopedia, Tropical Fish Encyclopedia,* Kingfisher's *Zoom In On History* series, cooking books, craft books, and others; contributor of articles on pet-keeping and wildlife to animal magazines, including *Wild About Animals* and *Dogs Monthly.*

Work in Progress

Complete Book of Dog & Puppy Care, for Salamander Books.

Sidelights

Amanda O'Neill told *SATA:* "Although I've written on a range of subjects, history and animals are my favorites. I've been animal-mad since childhood, and am now lucky enough to have a twelve-year-old son who encourages me to fill the house with livestock. He was responsible for the arrival of Giant African Snails, Madagascar Hissing Cockroaches and assorted rabbits, guinea pigs, hamsters, gerbils, mice and fish. We also have an evil black cat and five dogs (four Chihuahuas

and a Yorkie cross). We take an interest in animal
rescue, and three of our dogs are rescues."

P

PAULSEN, Gary 1939-

Personal

Born May 17, 1939, in Minneapolis, MN; son of Oscar (an army officer) and Eunice Paulsen; married third wife, Ruth Ellen Wright (an artist), May 5, 1971; children: (third marriage) James Wright; two children from first marriage. *Education:* Attended Bemidji College, 1957-58, and University of Colorado, 1976. *Politics:* "As Russian author Alexander Solzhenitsyn has said, 'If we limit ourselves to political structures we are not artists.'" *Religion:* "I believe in spiritual progress."

Addresses

Home—New Mexico. *Agent*—Jennifer Flannery, 34-36 28th St., No. 5, Long Island City, NY 11106.

Career

Writer since the 1960s. Has also worked as a teacher, field engineer, editor, soldier, actor, director, farmer, rancher, truck driver, trapper, professional archer, migrant farm worker, singer, and sailor. *Military service:* U.S. Army, 1959-62; became sergeant.

Awards, Honors

Society of Midland Authors Book Award, 1985, for *Tracker;* Parents' Choice Award, Parents' Choice Foundation, 1985, Newbery Honor Book citation, 1986, and Children's Book of the Year Award, Child Study Association of America, 1986, all for *Dogsong;* Newbery Honor Book citation, 1988, *Booklist* Editor's Choice citation, 1988, and Dorothy Canfield Fisher Children's Book Award, 1989, all for *Hatchet; Parenting* magazine Reading-Magic Award, Teachers' Choice Award from International Reading Association (IRA), and Best Books of the Year citation from *Learning* magazine, all 1990, all for *The Voyage of the Frog;* Newbery Honor Book citation, Judy Lopez Memorial Award, and *Parenting* magazine Best Book of the Year

Gary Paulsen

citation, all 1990, all for *The Winter Room;* Parents' Choice Award, 1991, for *The Boy Who Owned the School;* ALAN Award, 1991; *Booklist* Editor's Choice citation, Society of Midland Authors Book Award, and Spur Award from Western Writers of America, all 1991, all for *Woodsong;* Spur Award, 1993, for *The Haymeadow; Booklist* "Books for Youth Top of the List" citation, 1993, for *Harris and Me;* "Children's Choice for 1994" citations, IRA/Children's Book Council, 1994, for *Nightjohn* and *Dogteam;* Children's Literature Award finalist, PEN Center USA West, 1994, for *Sisters/Hermanas;* Margaret A. Edwards Award for lifetime achievement in writing for young adults, 1997;

YALSA Best Books for Young Adults, 1998, for *The Schernoff Discoveries.*

Many of Paulsen's books have been selected as American Library Association (ALA) Best Books for Young Adults, ALA Notable Children's Books, National Council of Teachers of English (NCTE) Notable Books in the Language Arts, *School Library Journal* Best Books of the Year, Notable Children's Books in the Social Studies, and New York Library Books for the Teen Age Reader. In addition, several of his books have won or been nominated for state awards, including the Wisconsin Golden Archer Award, North Dakota Flicker Tale Children's Book Award, Colorado Blue Spruce Young Adult Award, Maryland Black-Eyed Susan Book Award, and Illinois Rebecca Caudill Young Readers Book Award.

Writings

JUVENILE FICTION

Mr. Tucket, illustrated by Noel Sickles, Funk & Wagnalls, 1968.
The C. B. Radio Caper, illustrated by John Asquith, Raintree, 1977.
The Curse of the Cobra, illustrated by Asquith, Raintree, 1977.
Winterkill, T Nelson, 1977.
The Foxman, T Nelson, 1977.
Tiltawhirl John, T Nelson, 1977.
The Golden Stick, illustrated by Jerry Scott, Raintree, 1977.
The Night the White Deer Died, T. Nelson, 1978.
(With Ray Peekner) *The Green Recruit,* Independence Press, 1978.
The Spitball Gang, Elsevier, 1980.
Popcorn Days and Buttermilk Nights, Lodestar Books, 1983.
Dancing Carl, Bradbury, 1983.
Tracker, Bradbury, 1984.
Dogsong, Bradbury, 1985.
Sentries, Bradbury, 1986.
The Crossing, Orchard, 1987.
Hatchet, Bradbury, 1987.
The Island, Orchard, 1988.
The Voyage of the Frog, Orchard, 1989.
The Winter Room, Orchard, 1989.
The Boy Who Owned the School, Orchard, 1990.
Canyons, Delacorte, 1990.
Woodsong, illustrated by wife, Ruth W. Paulsen, Bradbury, 1990.
The Cookcamp, Orchard, 1991.
The River, Delacorte, 1991.
The Monument, Delacorte, 1991.
The Haymeadow, Delacorte, 1992.
Christmas Sonata, illustrated by Leslie Bowman, Delacorte, 1992.
Nightjohn, Delacorte, 1993.
Sisters/Hermanas, Harcourt, 1993.
Dogteam, illustrated by R. W. Paulsen, Delacorte, 1993.
Harris and Me: A Summer Remembered, Harcourt, 1993.
The Car, Harcourt, 1994.
The Tortilla Factory, paintings by R. W. Paulsen, Harcourt, 1995.

Call Me Francis Tucket, Delacorte, 1995.
The Tent: A Parable in One Sitting, Harcourt, 1995.
The Rifle, Harcourt, 1995.
Brian's Winter, Delacorte, 1996.
Worksong, illustrated by R. W. Paulsen, Harcourt, 1997.
Tucket's Ride, Delacorte, 1997.
The Schernoff Discoveries, Delacorte, 1997.
Sarny, a Life Remembered, Delacorte, 1997.
The Transall Saga, Delacorte, 1998.
Soldier's Heart: A Novel of the Civil War, Delacorte, 1998.
Canoe Days, illustrated by R. W. Paulsen, Doubleday, 1999.
The White Fox Chronicles, Delacorte, 1999.
Brian's Return, Delacorte, 1999.
Alida's Song, Delacorte, 1999.
Tucket's Gold, Delacorte, 1999.

"CULPEPPER ADVENTURES" SERIES; PUBLISHED BY DELL

The Case of the Dirty Bird, 1992.
Dunc's Doll, 1992.
Culpepper's Cannon, 1992.
Dunc Gets Tweaked, 1992.
Dunc's Halloween, 1992.
Dunc Breaks the Record, 1992.
Dunc and the Flaming Ghost, 1992.
Amos Gets Famous, 1993.
Dunc and Amos Hit the Big Top, 1993.
Dunc's Dump, 1993.
Dunc and the Scam Artist, 1993.
Dunc and Amos and the Red Tattoos, 1993.
The Wild Culpepper Cruise, 1993.
Dunc's Undercover Christmas, 1993.
Dunc and the Haunted House, 1993.
Cowpokes and Desperadoes, 1994.
Prince Amos, 1994.
Coach Amos, 1994.
Dunc and the Greased Sticks of Doom, Dell, 1994.
Amos's Killer Concert Caper, Dell, 1994.
Amos Gets Married, Dell, 1995.
Amos Goes Bananas, Dell, 1995.
Dunc and Amos Go to the Dogs, Dell, 1996.
Amos and the Vampire, Dell, 1996.
Amos and the Chameleon Caper, Dell, 1996.
Super Amos, Dell, 1997.
Dunc and Amos on Thin Ice, Dell, 1997.
Amos Binder, Secret Agent, Dell, 1997.

"GARY PAULSEN WORLD OF ADVENTURE" SERIES

The Legend of Red Horse Cavern, Dell, 1994.
Escape from Fire Mountain, Dell, 1995.
The Rock Jockeys, Dell, 1995.
Danger on Midnight River, Dell, 1995.
Hook 'Em Snotty!, Dell, 1995.
Rodomonte's Revenge, Dell, 1995.
The Gorgon Slayer, Dell, 1995.
Captive!, Dell, 1996.
Project: A Perfect New World, Dell, 1996.
Skydive!, Dell, 1996.
The Treasure of El Patron, Dell, 1996.
The Seventh Crystal, Dell, 1996.
The Creature of Black Water Lake, Dell, 1997.
The Grizzly, Dell, 1997.
Thunder Valley, Dell, 1998.

Curse of the Ruins, Dell, 1998.
Time Benders, Dell, 1998.
Flight of the Hawk, Dell, 1998.

JUVENILE NONFICTION

(With Dan Theis) *Martin Luther King: The Man Who Climbed the Mountain,* Raintree, 1976.
The Small Ones, illustrated by K. Goff, photographs by Wilford Miller, Raintree, 1976.
The Grass-Eaters: Real Animals, illustrated by Goff, photographs by Miller, Raintree, 1976.
Dribbling, Shooting, and Scoring Sometimes, photographs by Heinz Kluetmeier, Raintree, 1976.
Hitting, Pitching, and Running Maybe, photographs by Kluetmeier, Raintree, 1976.
Tackling, Running, and Kicking—Now and Again, photographs by Kluetmeier, Raintree, 1977.
Riding, Roping, and Bulldogging—Almost, photographs by Kluetmeier, Raintree, 1977.
Careers in an Airport, photographs by R. Nye, Raintree, 1977.
Running, Jumping, and Throwing—If You Can, photographs by Kluetmeier, Raintree, 1978.
Forehanding and Backhanding—If You're Lucky, photographs by Kluetmeier, Raintree, 1978.
(With John Morris) *Hiking and Backpacking,* illustrated by R. W. Paulsen, Simon & Schuster, 1978.
(With Morris) *Canoeing, Kayaking, and Rafting,* illustrated by John Peterson and Jack Storholm, Simon & Schuster, 1979.
Downhill, Hotdogging and Cross-Country—If the Snow Isn't Sticky, photographs by Kluetmeier and Willis Wood, Raintree, 1979.
Facing Off, Checking and Goaltending—Perhaps, photographs by Kluetmeier and Melchior DiGiacomo, Raintree, 1979.
Going Very Fast in a Circle—If You Don't Run Out of Gas, photographs by Kluetmeier and Bob D'Olivo, Raintree, 1979.
Launching, Floating High and Landing—If Your Pilot Light Doesn't Go Out, photographs by Kluetmeier, Raintree, 1979, published as *Full of Hot Air: Launching, Floating High, and Landing,* photographs by Mary A. Heltshe, Delacorte, 1993.
Pummeling, Falling and Getting Up—Sometimes, photographs by Kluetmeier and Joe DiMaggio, Raintree, 1979.
Track, Enduro and Motocross—Unless You Fall Over, photographs by Kluetmeier, Raintree, 1979.
(With Art Browne, Jr.) *TV and Movie Animals,* Messner, 1980.
Sailing: From Jibs to Jibing, illustrated by R. W. Paulsen, Messner, 1981.
Father Water, Mother Woods: Essays on Fishing and Hunting in the North Woods, illustrated by R. W. Paulsen, Delacorte, 1994.
My Life in Dog's Years, drawings by R. W. Paulsen, Delacorte, 1998.

FICTION FOR ADULTS

The Implosion Effect, Major Books, 1976.
The Death Specialists, Major Books, 1976.
C. B. Jockey, Major Books, 1977.

The Sweeper, Harlequin, 1981.
Campkill, Pinnacle Books, 1981.
Clutterkill, Harlequin, 1982.
Murphy, Walker, 1987.
Murphy's Gold, Walker, 1988.
The Madonna Stories, Van Vliet, 1988.
Murphy's Herd, Walker, 1989.
(With Brian Burks) *Murphy's Stand,* Walker, 1993.
(With B. Burks) *Murphy's Ambush,* Walker, 1995.
(With B. Burks) *Murphy's Trail,* Walker, 1996.

PLAYS

Communications (one-act), produced in New Mexico, 1974.
Together-Apart (one-act), produced in Denver, CO, at Changing Scene Theater, 1976.

OTHER

(With Raymond Friday Locke) *The Special War,* Sirkay, 1966.
Some Birds Don't Fly, Rand McNally, 1969.
The Building a New, Buying an Old, Remodeling a Used, Comprehensive Home and Shelter Book, Prentice-Hall, 1976.
Farm: A History and Celebration of the American Farmer, Prentice-Hall, 1977.
Successful Home Repair, Structures, 1978.
Money-Saving Home Repair Guide, Ideals, 1981.
Beat the System: A Survival Guide, Pinnacle Books, 1983.
Kill Fee, Donald I. Fine, Inc., 1990.
Night Rituals, Bantam, 1991.
Clabbered Dirt, Sweet Grass (adult nonfiction), illustrated by R. W. Paulsen, Harcourt, 1992.
Eastern Sun, Winter Moon (adult nonfiction), Harcourt, 1993.
Winterdance: The Fine Madness of Running the Iditarod (adult nonfiction), Harcourt, 1994.
Puppies, Dogs, and Blue Northers: Reflections on Being raised by a Pack of Sled Dogs (adult nonfiction), Harcourt, 1996.
Pilgrimage on a Steel Ride: A Memoir about Men and Motorcycles (adult nonfiction), Harcourt, 1997.

Also author of the introduction to *The Call of the Wild,* by Jack London, illustrated by Barry Moser, Macmillan, 1994. Author of numerous short stories and articles. Paulsen's works have been published in German, Japanese, Danish, Dutch, Russian, Norwegian, Italian, Spanish, French, Swedish, and Chinese.

Adaptations

Dogsong has been released as a filmstrip with cassette, Random House/Miller-Brody, 1986; *Hatchet* has been released as a filmstrip with cassette, Random House, 1988; *Woodsong* has been released as an audiocassette, Bantam Audio, 1991; *Canyons, Hatchet,* and *The River* have been released as audiocassettes, all read by Peter Coyote, Bantam Audio, 1992; *The Haymeadow* and *The Monument* have been released as audiocassettes, both Bantam Audio, 1992.

In this Newbery Honor Book by Paulsen, a fourteen-year-old Eskimo boy's arduous dogsled trek across the Alaskan wilderness becomes a quest for self-discovery. (Cover illustration by Neil Waldman.)

Work in Progress

Books in the "Gary Paulsen World of Adventure" series.

Sidelights

A writer of popular and finely wrought young adult novels and nonfiction with sales totaling more than three million worldwide, Gary Paulsen has joined a select group of YA writers, receiving the 1997 Margaret A. Edwards Award honoring an author's lifetime achievement in writing books for teens. The Young Adult Library Services Association of the American Library Association, in choosing Paulsen, cited the diverse nature of his work as well as its page-turning quality: "From quiet introspective memoirs to edge-of-the-seat adventures, Paulsen grabs and holds the attention of his readers. The theme of survival is woven throughout, whether it is living through a plane crash or living in an abusive, alcoholic household." The selection committee

noted six titles specifically: *Dancing Carl, Hatchet, The Crossing, The Winter Room, Woodsong,* and *Canyons.* But they could have included dozens more titles—the prolific Paulsen has nearly one-hundred-and-fifty books to his credit. The committee could have cited Paulsen's own favorite, and one of his three Newbery Honor Books, *Dogsong;* or other popular YA titles such as *The Haymeadow, The Monument, Nightjohn, Sentries,* or *Alida's Song.* Paulsen's body of work provides many choices.

In prose lean and echoing of Hemingway, Paulsen has created powerful young adult fiction, often set in wilderness or rural areas and featuring teenagers who arrive at self-awareness by way of experiences in nature—through challenging tests of their own survival instincts—or through the ministrations of understanding adults. A former resident of northern Minnesota, Paulsen writes from his first-hand knowledge of the outdoors and from his experiences as a hunter, trapper, and even a dogsledder in the grueling Alaska Iditarod race. Paulsen displays an "extraordinary ability to picture for the reader how man's comprehension of life can be transformed with the lessons of nature," writes Evie Wilson in *Voice of Youth Advocates.* "With humor and psychological genius, Paulsen develops strong adolescent characters who lend new power to youth's plea to be allowed to apply individual skills in their risk-taking." In addition to writing young adult fiction, Paulsen has also authored numerous picture books with his illustrator wife, books of children's nonfiction, as well as two plays and many works of adult fiction and nonfiction.

Paulsen was born in Minnesota in 1939, the son of first-generation Danish and Swedish parents. During his childhood, he saw little of his father, who served in the military in Europe during World War II, and little of his mother, who worked in a Chicago ammunitions factory. "I was reared by my grandmother and several aunts," he once told *SATA.* "I first saw my father when I was seven in the Philippines where my parents and I lived from 1946 to 1949." Writing of that experience a half century later in *Riverbank Review,* Paulsen noted that he "lived essentially as a street child in Manila, because my parents were alcoholics and I was not supervised. The effect was profound and lasting."

When the family returned to the United States, Paulsen suffered from being continually uprooted. "We moved around constantly . . . . The longest time I spent in one school was for about five months," Paulsen told *SATA.* "I was an 'Army brat,' and it was a miserable life. School was a nightmare because I was unbelievably shy, and terrible at sports . . . . I wound up skipping most of the ninth grade." In addition to problems at school, he faced many ordeals at home. "My father drank a lot, and there would be terrible arguments," he noted. Eventually Paulsen was sent again to live with relatives and worked to support himself with jobs as a newspaper boy and as a pin-setter in a bowling alley.

Things began to change for the better during his teen years. He found security and support with his grand-

In this wilderness survival story—also the sequel to Paulsen's **Mr. Tucket**—*the young Francis continues his journey through the American West, this time with two orphans in tow. (Cover illustration by Jos. A. Smith.)*

mother and aunts—"safety nets" as he described them in his interview. A turning point in his life came one sub-zero winter day when, as he was walking past the public library, he decided to stop in to warm himself. "To my absolute astonishment the librarian walked up to me and asked if I wanted a library card," he related. "When she handed me the card, she handed me the world. I can't even describe how liberating it was. She recommended westerns and science fiction but every now and then would slip in a classic. I roared through everything she gave me and in the summer read a book a day. It was as though I had been dying of thirst and the librarian had handed me a five-gallon bucket of water. I drank and drank."

After just barely graduating from high school in Thief River Falls, Minnesota, in 1959, Paulsen attended Bemidji College in Minnesota, for two years, paying for his tuition with money he'd earned as a trapper for the state of Minnesota. But when he flunked out of college, he joined the U.S. Army, serving from 1959 to 1962, and working with missiles. After his tour of duty in the Army was completed, he took extension courses to become a certified field engineer, finding work in the aerospace departments of the Bendix and Lockheed corporations. There it occurred to him that he might try and become a writer. "I'd finished reading a magazine article on flight-testing ... and thought, *gad,* what a way to make a living—writing about something you like and getting paid for it!" he told F. Serdahely in *Writer's Digest.* "I remembered writing some of my past reports, some fictionalized versions I'd included. And I thought: 'What the hell, I *am* an engineering writer.' But, conversely, I also realized I didn't know a thing about writing *professionally.* After several hours of hard thinking, a way to learn came to me. All I had to do was go to work editing a magazine."

Creating a fictitious resume, Paulsen was able to obtain an associate editor position on a men's magazine in Hollywood, California. Although it soon became apparent to his employers that he had no editorial experience, he told *SATA* that "they could see I was serious about wanting to learn, and they were willing to teach me." He spent nearly a year with the magazine, finding it "the best of all possible ways to learn about writing. It probably did more to improve my craft and ability than any other single event in my life." Still living in California, Paulsen also found work as a film extra (he once played a drunken Indian in a movie called *Flap*), and took up sculpting as a hobby, once winning first prize in an exhibition.

Paulsen's first book, *The Special War,* was published in 1966, and he soon proved himself to be one of the most prolific authors in the United States. In little over a decade, working mainly out of northern Minnesota—where he moved after becoming disillusioned with Hollywood—he published nearly forty books and close to two hundred articles and stories for magazines. Among Paulsen's diverse titles were a number of children's nonfiction books about animals, a biography of Martin Luther King, Jr., several humorous titles under the "Sports on the Light Side" series published by Raintree Press, two plays, adult fiction and nonfiction, as well as some initial ventures into juvenile fiction. On a bet with a friend, he once wrote eleven articles and short stories inside four days and sold all of them.

His prolific output was interrupted by a libel lawsuit brought against his 1977 young adult novel *Winterkill,* the powerful story of a semi-delinquent boy befriended by a hard-bitten cop named Duda in a small Minnesota town. Paulsen eventually won the case, but, as he noted, "the whole situation was so nasty and ugly that I stopped writing. I wanted nothing more to do with publishing and burned my bridges, so to speak." Unable to earn any other type of living, he went back to trapping for the state of Minnesota, working a sixty-mile line on foot or skis.

To help Paulsen in his hunting job, a friend gave him a team of sled dogs, a gift which ultimately had a profound influence on Paulsen. "One day, about mid-night, we were crossing Clear Water Lake, which is about three miles long," Paulsen recounts. "There was a full moon shining so brightly on the snow you could read by it. There was no one around, and all I could hear was the rhythm of the dogs' breathing as they pulled the sled." The intensity of the moment prompted an impulsive seven-day trip by Paulsen through northern Minnesota. "I didn't go home—my wife was frantic—I didn't check lines, I just ran the dogs.... For food, we had a few beaver carcasses.... I was initiated into this incredibly ancient and very beautiful bond, and it was as if everything that had happened to me before ceased to exist." Paulsen afterwards made a resolution to permanently give up hunting and trapping, and proceeded to pursue dogsled racing as a hobby. He went so far as to enter the grueling twelve-hundred-mile Iditarod race in Alaska, an experience which later provided the basis for his award-winning novel, *Dogsong.*

Paulsen's acclaimed young adult fiction—all written since the 1980s—often centers around teenage characters who arrive at an understanding of themselves and their world through pivotal experiences with nature. His writing has been praised for its almost poetic effect, and he is also credited with creating vivid descriptions of his characters' emotional states. His 1984 novel, *Tracker,* tells about a thirteen-year-old boy who faces his first season of deer hunting alone as his grandfather lies dying of cancer. Ronald A. Jobe praised the novel in *Language Arts* as "powerfully written," adding that "[Paulsen] explores with the reader the innermost frustrations, hurts, and fears of the young boy." Of special interest to Paulsen in writing *Tracker* was exploring the almost "mystical relationship that develops between the hunter and the hunted," as he remarked in his interview. "It's a relationship with its own integrity, not to be violated.... At a certain point, the animal senses death coming and accepts it. This acceptance of death is something I was trying to write about in *Tracker.*"

Tracker was the first of several of Paulsen's books to receive wide critical and popular recognition. *Dogsong,* a Newbery Medal Honor book, is a rite-of-passage novel about a young Inuit boy (Russel) who wishes to abandon the increasingly modern ways of his people. Through the guidance of a tribal elder, Russel learns to bow-hunt and dogsled, and eventually leads his own pack of dogs on a trip across Alaska and back. "While the language of [*Dogsong*] is lyrical, Paulsen recognizes the reality of Russel's world—the dirty smoke and the stinking yellow fur of the bear," writes Nel Ward in *Voice of Youth Advocates.* "He also recognizes the reality of killing to save lives, and of dreaming to save sanity, in the communion between present and past, life and death, reality and imagination, in this majestic exploration into the Alaskan wilderness by a master author who knows his subject well." The author further explores racing over snow with a band of dogs in the 1993 picture book, *Dogteam.* Also reminiscent of this running-for-your-life theme is the 1991 *Canyons,* in which two boys across a century prove themselves, the modern boy forced to mount a challenging run through a desert-like canyon.

The hero of four Paulsen novels faces survival in the dead of winter in this 1996 work. (Cover illustration by Neal McPheeters.)

Perhaps Paulsen's most popular creation is the 1987 novel, *Hatchet,* also a Newbery Honor Book. *Hatchet* tells the story of a thirteen-year-old thoroughly modern boy (Brian) who is forced to survive alone in the Canadian woods after a plane crash. Like Russel in *Dogsong, Hatchet*'s hero is also transformed by the wilderness. "By the time he is rescued, Brian is permanently changed," notes Suzanne Rahn in *Twentieth-Century Children's Writers;* "he is far more observant and thoughtful, and knows what is really important in his life." As noted in *Children's Books and Their Creators,* "*Hatchet* has rapidly become one of the most popular adventure stories of all time," combining "elementary language with a riveting plot to produce a book both comprehensible and enjoyable for those children who frequently equate reading with frustration."

Hatchet was so popular with readers that they demanded, and won, three sequels: *The River, Brian's Winter,* and *Brian's Return.* In the first of these, government researchers want to learn Brian's survival tactics, so they

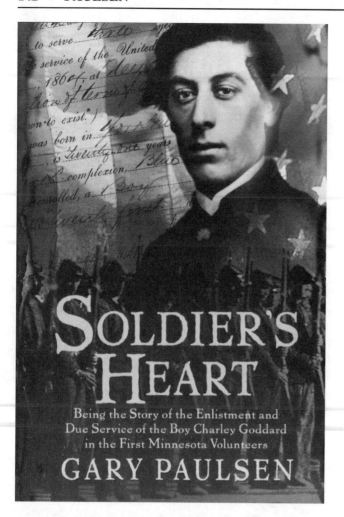

Paulsen's novel is based on the life of Charley Goddard, a real Civil War soldier who joins the Union Army at age fifteen, witnesses the atrocities of war, and comes home physically and psychologically scarred. (Cover illustration by Ericka Meltzer O'Rourke.)

have him reenact the near tragedy. Dropped off near a Canadian lake with a young psychologist named Derek, things go fine at first until lightning strikes the camp and Derek is left in a coma. It is up to Brian to get them both a hundred miles down river to civilization and help. A critic in *Kirkus Reviews* praised the "lyrically described details of Brian's adventure," though many critics found the plot premise somewhat unbelievable.

In *Brian's Winter,* Paulsen further responded to the wishes of his young readers, once again testing Brian against the wilderness, but now in deadly winter. This time out, Paulsen did not attempt to stretch plot conventions as in *The River,* but simply provided an alternative ending to *Hatchet:* What if Brian had not been rescued before winter came? This time, Brian finds a survival kit in the crashed plane giving him a bit more of a chance against the cold, but still it is basically him against the elements—including a seven-hundred-pound moose. "Paulsen writes with the authoritative particularity of someone who knows the woods," commented Hazel Rochman in a *Booklist* review of *Brian's Winter.*

"This docunovel is for outdoors lovers and also for all of those adventurers snug at home in a centrally heated high-rise." Helen Turner concluded in *Voice of Youth Advocates* that *Brian's Winter,* like *Hatchet* before it, was "a great adventure story." A final encore to the series of books was provided with the 1999 *Brian's Return,* in which Brian, now sixteen and unable to fit back into so-called civilization, plans to return to the woods, the only place he feels at home. Less of an action-adventure novel than a paean to nature, *Brian's Return* "is bold, confident and persuasive, its transcendental themes are powerfully seductive," according to a *Publishers Weekly* reviewer.

Paulsen tells of a different kind of growing up in *Harris and Me: A Summer Remembered.* Instead of the main character reaching maturity while struggling in the wilderness, in *Harris* the unnamed protagonist discovers a sense of belonging while spending a summer on his relatives' farm. A child of abusive and alcoholic parents, the young narrator is sent to live with another set of relations—his uncle's family—and there he meets the reckless Harris, who leads him in escapades involving playing Tarzan in the loft of the barn and using pig pens as the stage for G.I. Joe games. "Through it all," explained a reviewer for *Bulletin of the Center for Children's Books,* "the lonely hero imperceptibly learns about belonging." In *Voice of Youth Advocates,* Penny Blubaugh pointed out that "for the first time in his life [the narrator] finds himself surrounded by love."

Similar in concept are the ALA Best Book for Young Adults, *The Cookcamp,* and its 1999 sequel, *Alida's Song.* Recreating his own childhood experience, Paulsen tells a tale of a young boy sent to his grandmother, a voyage of salvation for the youthful protagonist. In the first title, the boy comes from Chicago to the woods of Minnesota where his grandmother is working as a cook for road builders. In *Alida's Song,* the nameless protagonist is now fourteen and sliding into trouble until he again spends a summer with his grandmother on the farm where she now cooks for two elderly brothers. Escaping the alcoholism at home, he finds love and renewal in the simple surroundings and in nature. A *Publishers Weekly* critic described the book as "Paulsen's classic blend of emotion and ruggedness, as satisfying as ever." Such reworking of his own private history is one of Paulsen's hallmarks. Looking at life as a literal gem, he can turn said gem, gazing at a new facet, a new angle of approach for old stories, mining and re-mining his own lode of stories endlessly.

Paulsen relates his own tale of survival in *Eastern Sun, Winter Moon,* a story several reviewers have called shocking, painful, and vividly told. The author opens his account during World War II; his military officer father is stationed in Manila, while his attractive, promiscuous mother (who raises the young Paulsen) resides in Chicago, fending off her loneliness by drinking and seeking the company of other men. In 1945, mother and son travel to the Philippines to join Paulsen's father. While on board ship, both Paulsen and his mother are witnesses to brutal horror, as they watch a plane crash into the ocean, and its defenseless passengers savagely torn apart in the shark-infested waters. More violence ensues after the family is reunited: The young Paulsen slices his tongue in an accident, and he witnesses a man being mutilated after he is hit by the wreckage from a typhoon. *Eastern Sun, Winter Moon* is "an indelible account of a childhood lived on the edge, hallmarked by Paulsen's sinewy writing, purity of voice, and, especially, by his bedrock honesty," declared a critic for *Kirkus Reviews*. In the *Los Angeles Times Book Review*, Tim Winton assessed the autobiography as a "raw portrayal of a child thrown into the horrors of war and the adult world."

Further memoirs from Paulsen include *Winterdance,* which chronicles the Iditarod race, *Puppies, Dogs, and Blue Northers* and *My Life in Dog Years,* both of which are full of stories of the dogs that have accompanied Paulsen through his life, *Clabbered Dirt, Sweet Grass,* a memoir of his farm years, and *Pilgrimage on a Steel Ride,* a documentation of a motorcycle trip to Alaska that Paulsen took in the mid-1990s when he discovered he had a heart condition and could no longer go dog-sledding. While most of the remembrances are intended for an adult audience, one of his most powerful memoirs for young readers is *Woodsong,* an autobiographical account of his life in Minnesota and Alaska preparing his sled dogs to run the Iditarod. A reviewer noted in *Horn Book* that the "lure of the wilderness is always a potent draw, and Paulsen evokes its mysteries as well as anyone since Jack London."

Domestic themes are taken up in quiet books such as *The Monument,* about the construction of a Vietnam memorial in a small town, and *The Haymeadow,* in which a young boy proves himself to his father by tending six thousand sheep one summer in Wyoming. *Dancing Carl* is a relatively early Paulsen title, set again in a 1950s Minnesota backwater, in which a disturbed war veteran takes over the local ice rinks and is ultimately brought out of his trauma when he dances on the ice to win the heart of a young woman. Reviewing *Dancing Carl* in *Horn Book,* Dorcas Hand commented that "[f]illed with poetry and with life, the book is not only an insightful, beautifully written story for children but for readers of any age." In *The Winter Room* Paulsen tells another quiet tale of discovery. Set on a farm in the 1930s, the story features the brothers Eldon and Wayne who gather with their family in the stove-warm winter room on cold nights and listen to the stories told by Uncle David. The brothers slowly discover the truth behind their uncle's heroic stories. Reviewing *The Winter Room,* a writer for *Publishers Weekly* noted that "Paulsen never disappoints, and proves his talent again in this remarkably good tale."

In another critically successful book, Paulsen examines the horrors and brutality of slavery. The historically based *Nightjohn* is set in the nineteenth-century South and revolves around Sarny, a young slave girl who, because she has not yet begun to menstruate (and is therefore not yet old enough for breeding purposes), is allowed to remain a "child" for a bit longer. She is all too familiar with the cruel and bloody punishments for slaves caught showing an interest in education, but she is persuaded to learn to read by Nightjohn, a runaway slave who has just been recaptured. Some time later, the eager young student is caught tracing letters in the ground; her vicious master beats her, then vents his anger on Sarny's adopted "mammy," humiliating her by tying her naked to his buggy and whipping her as he forces her to pull him and the vehicle. When Nightjohn confesses that he has been Sarny's teacher, the slave endures his punishment: two of his toes are sliced off. A commentator for *Kirkus Reviews* called *Nightjohn* "a searing picture of slavery" and an "unbearably vivid book." "By the time the book is completed," wrote Frances Bradburn in *Wilson Library Bulletin,* "the revulsion, the horror, the awe, and the triumph are complete." The critic continued, "fortunately for all of us, Gary Paulsen has had the courage to risk censure in order to tell a powerful story in a style only he is capable of." Sarny was reprised as a character in the 1997 *Sarny: A Life Remembered,* in which the former slave narrates her life in 1930 from the ripe old age of 94. A focal point of her story is the fact that she learned to read: this saved her on more than one occasion. "[Sarny's] story makes absorbing reading," concluded Bruce Anne Shook in a *School Library Journal* review of *Sarny.*

Paulsen's concern with literacy is personal: he still believes, as he told David Gale in a *School Library Journal* interview celebrating his Margaret A. Edwards Award, that "there's nothing that has happened to me that would have happened if a librarian hadn't got me to read.... All of our knowledge, everything we are—is locked up in books, and if you can't read, it's lost." Waging a one-writer campaign against illiteracy, Paulsen has consciously crafted his books with clean, spare language in order to attract reluctant readers. He has also created two series, "Culpepper Adventures" and "Gary Paulsen's World of Adventure," geared towards middle-grade reluctant readers. The books in both series are short and action-filled. Amos and Dunc are the two friends in the "Culpepper Adventures," featuring domestic-style mysteries, while the "World of Adventure" tackles stories from kidnapping to skydiving with a varied cast of characters. Additionally, his "Francis Tucket" stories, including *Mr. Tucket, Call Me Francis Tucket, Tucket's Ride,* and *Tucket's Gold,* follow the adventures of an adolescent on a wagon train to the Oregon Territory and provide "stallion-swift" adventure tales, according to a reviewer in *Publishers Weekly.*

Paulsen has shown that he is not a one-trick pony with such diverse titles as the picture books *The Tortilla Factory* and *Worksong,* the bilingual *Sisters/Hermanas,* a story of culture clash told from the points of view of two girls, *The Tent,* about revivalism, *The Schernoff Discoveries,* a humorous novel about a self-confessed geek, and *The Transall Saga,* a "rare venture into middle-grade science fiction," according to John Peters in *School Library Journal.*

Other books of Paulsen's fiction—*Sentries, The Crossing,* and *Soldier's Heart*—have furthered Paulsen's reputation as a leading writer for young adults. Paulsen prefers to write for adolescents because, as he told *SATA*, "[it's] artistically fruitless to write for adults. Adults created the mess which we are struggling to outlive. Adults have their minds set. Art reaches out for newness, and adults aren't new. And adults aren't truthful." His book *Sentries*, a collection of stories, particularly demonstrates his belief that, as he stated, "young people know the score." *Sentries* juxtaposes the stories of four teenagers on the brink of life-important decisions, with the accounts of three soldiers—from different battles throughout history—whose lives have been devastated by war.

A similar juxtaposition is presented in *The Crossing*, in which the lives of Manny, a Mexican orphan living on the U.S. border, and Robert, a sergeant stationed at nearby Ft. Bliss, are inexorably intertwined. Haunted by war experiences, Robert ultimately gives his life to save Manny, in a story that "older children and teenagers will not want to put down," according to a *Kirkus Reviews* critic. Paulsen enlarges on the theme of war in his 1998 *Soldier's Heart: A Novel of the Civil War*. The story of fifteen-year-old Charley Goddard who lies about his age to enlist in the Union Army in 1861, the novel describes "the harrowing realities of war," according to Steven Engelfried in *School Library Journal*. "Paulsen pulls no punches," Engelfried went on, "rendering the young man's experiences in matter-of-fact prose that accentuates the horror." As a young child in the Philippines, Paulsen saw firsthand the effects of war, and his stint in the military introduced him to the fraternity of men for whom war is simply "The Job." When he wrote his Civil War novel about Goddard, he had many of these men in mind as well. A *Publishers Weekly* reviewer concluded that "Paulsen's storytelling is so psychologically true that readers will feel they have lived through Charley's experiences."

It is exactly this empathic power of Paulsen's, the ability to transcend time and space and speak directly to his readers that has made him such a popular and respected author. In awarding the writer the 1997 Margaret A. Edwards Award, the award committee, as noted in *School Library Journal*, commented on this very trait: "With his intense love of the outdoors and crazy courage born of adversity, Paulsen reached young adults everywhere. His writing conveys respect for their intelligence and ability to overcome life's worst realities. As Paulsen himself has said, 'I know if there is any hope at all for the human race, it has to come from young people.'"

Works Cited

Review of *Alida's Song, Publishers Weekly*, May 31, 1999, pp. 94-95.

Behr, Christine C., *Children's Books and Their Creators*, edited by Anita Silvey, Houghton, 1995, pp. 510-11.

Blubaugh, Penny, review of *Harris and Me: A Summer Remembered, Voice of Youth Advocates*, February, 1994, p. 371.

Bradburn, Frances, "Middle Books," *Wilson Library Bulletin*, January, 1993, pp. 87-88.

Review of *Brian's Return, Publishers Weekly*, January 11, 1999, p. 26.

Review of *Call Me Francis Tucket, Publishers Weekly*, July 3, 1995, p. 62.

Review of *The Crossing, Kirkus Reviews*, July 15, 1987, p. 1074.

Review of *Eastern Sun, Winter Moon, Kirkus Reviews*, January 1, 1993, p. 48.

Engelfried, Steve, review of *Soldier's Heart, School Library Journal*, September, 1998, p. 206.

Gale, David, "The Maximum Expression of Being Human," *School Library Journal*, June, 1997, pp. 24-29.

Hand, Dorcas, review of *Dancing Carl, Horn Book*, July-August, 1983, pp. 446-47.

Review of *Harris and Me: A Summer Remembered, Bulletin of the Center for Children's Books*, January, 1994, pp. 164-65.

Jobe, Ronald A., review of *Tracker, Language Arts*, September, 1984, p. 527.

Review of *Nightjohn, Kirkus Reviews*, January 1, 1993, p. 67.

Paulsen, Gary, "The True Face of War," *Riverbank Review*, spring, 1999, pp. 25-26.

Peters, John, review of *The Transall Saga, School Library Journal*, May, 1998, p. 147.

Rahn, Suzanne, entry on Gary Paulsen in *Twentieth-Century Children's Writers*, 3rd edition, St. James Press, 1989, pp. 763-65.

Review of *The River, Kirkus Reviews*, June 15, 1991, p. 792.

Rochman, Hazel, review of *Brian's Winter, Booklist*, December 15, 1995, p. 700.

Serdahely, F., "Prolific Paulsen," *Writer's Digest*, January, 1980.

Shook, Bruce Anne, review of *Sarny, School Library Journal*, September, 1997, p. 224.

Review of *Soldier's Heart, Publishers Weekly*, July 20, 1998, p. 221.

Turner, Helen, review of *Brian's Winter, Voice of Youth Advocates*, February, 1997, p. 332.

Ward, Nel, review of *Dogsong, Voice of Youth Advocates*, December, 1985, pp. 321-22.

Wilson, Evie, review of *The Island, Voice of Youth Advocates*, June, 1988, pp. 89-90.

Review of *The Winter Room, Publishers Weekly*, September 29, 1989, p. 69.

Winton, Tim, "His Own World War," *Los Angeles Times Book Review*, March 21, 1993, pp. 1, 11.

Review of *Woodsong, Horn Book*, November-December, 1990, p. 762.

For More Information See

BOOKS

Children's Literature Review, Volume 19, Gale, 1990.

Drew, Bernard A., *The 100 Most Popular Young Adult Authors: Biographical Sketches and Bibliographies*, Libraries Unlimited, Inc., 1996, pp. 396-403.

Peters, Stephanie True, *Gary Paulsen*, Learning Works, 1999.

Salvner, Gary M., *Presenting Gary Paulsen*, Twayne, 1996.

St. James Guide to Young Adult Writers, edited by Tom Pendergast and Sara Pendergast, St. James Press, 1999, pp. 674-78.

PERIODICALS

ALAN Review, spring, 1994.

Booklist, November 1, 1992, p. 514; December 15, 1992, pp. 727-28; January 15, 1993, p. 850; February 15, 1994, p. 1051; March 15, 1995, p. 1323; July, 1995, p. 1880; December 15, 1996, p. 727; June 1 & 15, 1997, p. 1705; January 1, 1998, p. 799; May 15, 1998, p. 1623.

Bulletin of the Center for Children's Books, February, 1993, pp. 187-88; June, 1995, pp. 356-57; October, 1995, pp. 64-65; July-August, 1997, pp. 406-07; March, 1998, pp. 254-55; September, 1998, p. 26; September, 1999, pp. 26-27.

Kirkus Reviews, June 1, 1999, p. 887; August 15, 1999, p. 1314.

Kliatt, May, 1995, p. 39; March, 1997, p. 12; May, 1998, p. 7; July, 1998, p. 8; September, 1999, p. 12.

Library Journal, February 15, 1993, p. 174.

Publishers Weekly, December 14, 1992, p. 58; January 25, 1993, p. 73; August 30, 1993, p. 94; September 30, 1993, p. 63; March 28, 1994, pp. 70-71; September 2, 1996, p. 132; August 11, 1997, p. 403; May 25, 1998, p. 91.

Reading Time, May, 1999, p. 29.

School Library Journal, October, 1992, p. 43; November, 1992, pp. 97-98; July, 1993, p. 82; August, 1993, pp. 208-9; October, 1993, p. 120; January, 1994, p. 132; May, 1995, p. 122; June, 1995, pp. 112-13; August, 1995, p. 38; February, 1996, p. 102; November, 1996, p. 130; March, 1997, p. 190; March, 1998, p. 238; May, 1998, p. 147; June-July, 1999, p. 99.

Voice of Youth Advocates, April, 1994, p. 29; October, 1994, p. 234; February, 1996, p. 375; February, 1997, p. 352.

Washington Post Book World, December 6, 1992, p. 20; December 20, 1992.

Writer's Digest, July, 1994, pp. 42-44, 65.*

—*Sketch by J. Sydney Jones*

*　　*　　*

PECK, Robert Newton 1928-

Personal

Born February 17, 1928, in Vermont; son of Haven (a farmer) and Lucile (maiden name, Dornburgh) Peck; married Dorothy Anne Houston, 1958; married Sharon Ann Michael (SAM), 1995; children: (first marriage) Christopher Haven, Anne Houston. *Education:* Rollins College, A.B., 1953; Cornell University, graduate coursework in law. *Religion:* Protestant. *Hobbies and other interests:* Playing ragtime piano, sports.

Addresses

Home—500 Sweetwater Club Circle, Longwood, FL 32779.

Career

Writer and farmer. Worked variously as a lumberjack, in a paper mill, as a hog butcher, and as a New York City advertising executive. Director of Rollins College Writers Conference, 1978-1982. Owner of publishing company, Peck Press. Teacher and speaker at conferences. *Military service:* U.S. Army, Infantry, 1945-47; served with 88th Division in Italy, Germany, and France; received commendation.

Awards, Honors

Best Books for Young Adults, American Library Association, and Spring Book Festival Award older honor, *Book World,* both 1973, Media & Methods Maxi Award (paperback), *Media & Methods,* 1975, and Colorado Children's Book Award, 1977, all for *A Day No Pigs Would Die;* outstanding book, *New York Times,* 1973, for *Millie's Boy;* children's book of the year, Child Study Association of America, 1973, for *Millie's Boy,* 1975, for *Bee Tree and Other Stuff,* 1976, for *Hamilton,* and 1987, for *Soup on Ice;* Books for the Teen Age, New York Public Library, 1980 and 1981, for *A Day No Pigs Would Die,* 1980, 1981, and 1982, for *Hang for Treason,* and 1980 and 1982, for *Clunie;* Mark Twain Award, Missouri Association of School Librarians, 1981, for *Soup for President;* Notable Children's Trade Book in the Field of Social Studies, National Council for Social Studies and the Children's Book Council, 1982, for *Justice Lion,* and 1986, for *Spanish Hoof;* Michigan Young Reader's Award, Michigan Council of Teachers,

Robert Newton Peck

The poignant sequel to the best-selling
A DAY NO PIGS WOULD DIE
ROBERT NEWTON PECK

A Part of the Sky

"Will touch readers of all ages." Library Journal

Random House 0-679-88696-6

The sequel to Peck's autobiographical novel **A Day No Pigs Would Die,** *this book continues the story of thirteen-year-old Rob, who struggles, after his father's death, to keep the family together on their small Vermont farm during the Great Depression. (Cover illustration by Mark Hess.)*

1984, for *Soup;* Bologna International Children's Book Fair, 1985, for *Spanish Hoof.*

Writings

FICTION; FOR YOUNG ADULTS

A Day No Pigs Would Die, Knopf, 1972.
Millie's Boy, Knopf, 1973.
Soup, illustrated by Charles Gehm, Knopf, 1974.
Bee Tree and Other Stuff (poems), illustrated by Laura Lydecker, Walker & Co., 1975.
Fawn, Little, Brown, 1975.
Wild Cat, illustrated by Hal Frenck, Holiday House, 1975.
Soup and Me, illustrated by Charles Lilly, Knopf, 1975.
Hamilton, illustrated by Laura Lydecker, Little, Brown, 1976.
Hang for Treason, Doubleday, 1976.

King of Kazoo (musical), illustrated by William Bryan Park, Knopf, 1976.
Rabbits and Redcoats, illustrated by Laura Lydecker, Walker & Co., 1976.
Trig, illustrated by Pamela Johnson, Little, Brown, 1977.
Last Sunday, illustrated by Ben Stahl, Doubleday, 1977.
The King's Iron, Little, Brown, 1977.
Patooie, illustrated by Ted Lewin, Knopf, 1977.
Soup for President, illustrated by Lewin, Knopf, 1978.
Eagle Fur, Knopf, 1978.
Trig Sees Red, illustrated by Pamela Johnson, Little, Brown, 1978.
Mr. Little, illustrated by Ben Stahl, Doubleday, 1979.
Basket Case, Doubleday, 1979.
Hub, illustrated by Ted Lewin, Knopf, 1979.
Clunie, Knopf, 1979.
Trig Goes Ape, illustrated by Pamela Johnson, Little, Brown, 1980.
Soup's Drum, illustrated by Charles Robinson, Knopf, 1980.
Soup on Wheels, illustrated by Robinson, Knopf, 1981.
Justice Lion, Little, Brown, 1981.
Kirk's Law, Doubleday, 1981.
Trig or Treat, illustrated by Pamela Johnson, Little, Brown, 1982.
Banjo, illustrated by Andrew Glass, Knopf, 1982.
The Seminole Seed, Pineapple Press, 1983.
Soup in the Saddle, illustrated by Charles Robinson, Knopf, 1983.
Soup's Goat, illustrated by Robinson, Knopf, 1984.
Dukes, Pineapple Press, 1984.
Jo Silver, Pineapple Press, 1985.
Spanish Hoof, Knopf, 1985.
Soup on Ice, illustrated by Charles Robinson, Knopf, 1985.
Soup on Fire, illustrated by Robinson, Delacorte, 1987.
Soup's Uncle, illustrated by Robinson, Delacorte, 1988.
Hallapoosa, Walker & Co., 1988.
The Horse Hunters, Random House, 1988.
Arly, Walker & Co., 1989.
Soup's Hoop, illustrated by Charles Robinson, Delacorte, 1990.
Higbee's Halloween, Walker & Co., 1990.
Little Soup's Hayride, Dell, 1991.
Little Soup's Birthday, Dell, 1991.
Arly's Run, Walker & Co., 1991.
Soup in Love, Delacorte, 1992.
FortDog July, Walker & Co., 1992.
Little Soup's Turkey, Dell, 1992.
Little Soup's Bunny, Dell, 1993.
A Part of the Sky, Knopf, 1994.
Soup Ahoy, illustrated by Charles Robinson, Knopf, 1995.
Soup 1776, illustrated by Robinson, Knopf, 1995.
Nine Man Tree, Random House, 1998.
Cowboy Ghost, Random House, 1999.

FICTION; FOR ADULTS

The Happy Sadist, Doubleday, 1962.

NONFICTION

Path of Hunters: Animal Struggle in a Meadow, illustrated by Betty Fraser, Knopf, 1973.
Secrets of Successful Fiction, Writer's Digest Books, 1980.

Fiction Is Folks: How to Create Unforgettable Characters,
    Writer's Digest Books, 1983.
My Vermont, Peck Press, 1985.
My Vermont II, Peck Press, 1988.

Also author of songs, television commercials, and
jingles. Adapter of novels *Soup and Me, Soup for
President,* and *Mr. Little* for television's *Afterschool
Specials,* American Broadcasting Companies, Inc.
(ABC-TV).

Adaptations

Soup was adapted for television and broadcast by ABC-
TV, 1978; *A Day No Pigs Would Die* was adapted for
cassette and released by Listening Library.

Sidelights

Beginning with his first title in 1972, *A Day No Pigs
Would Die,* Robert Newton Peck has carved out a
territory in YA fiction for himself. Dissecting the past,
Peck takes readers back to a rural America which honors
the old-fashioned virtues of hard work, self-sufficiency,
and the importance of education. Often set in Vermont,
Peck's stories reflect the influence of Mark Twain's *Tom
Sawyer,* especially so in Peck's humorous set of books
based on the character Soup. But Peck's works also
engage serious themes, portraying adolescents in their
struggles on the cusp of adulthood in such titles as *A
Day No Pigs Would Die* and its 1994 sequel, *A Part of
the Sky,* and in *Millie's Boy, Justice Lion, Spanish Hoof,
Arly,* and *Arly's Run.* Teachers often find a place in
Peck's fiction, serving as supporting and life-affirming
role models, as in *Mr. Little.*

Born in 1928, the seventh child of rural Vermont
farmers, Peck was the first of the family to attend
school, where he fell under the influence of an inspiring
teacher, Miss Kelly, who often makes appearances in his
later fiction in one guise or another. He also formed a
childhood friendship with a young boy named Luther,
nicknamed Soup, who became the centerpiece of further
Peck fiction. Peck's father slaughtered hogs during the
difficult Depression years, and this too would inform his
later writing. A careful sifter of his own experience
when it comes to writing, Peck went from being the first
of his family to even attend grade school, on to attend
college. He earned an A.B. from Rollins College in 1953
and also studied law at Cornell University. Married in
1958, he soon had two children, and pursued a successful career as an advertising executive in New York City.
But by his mid-forties, Peck was ready to try something
different. His love of books drew him to writing.

Peck's first novel, *A Day No Pigs Would Die,* is a semi-
autobiographical account of his family and childhood on
the Vermont farm. Written in three weeks, the tale
portrays a young boy's coming of age when he must kill
his pet pig, learning how to become a man in the eyes of
his Shaker family. Dubbed "charming and simple" by
Christopher Lehmann-Haupt in the *New York Times
Book Review,* the novel became an instant favorite,

especially with reluctant readers, and also won numerous awards for first-time author Peck. Lehmann-Haupt
went on to note that this novel was "a stunning little
dramatization of the brutality of life on a Vermont farm,
of the necessary cruelty of nature, and of one family's
attempt to transcend the hardness of life by accepting it."
This theme of the objective cruelty of nature and man's
need to fit into its pattern is replayed in much of Peck's
fiction and nonfiction alike. Jonathan Yardley, also
writing in the *New York Times Book Review,* remarked
that *A Day No Pigs Would Die* "is sentiment without
sentimentality . . . an honest, unpretentious book." Since
its publication, the novel has found a place on most best-
of-YA lists and is also taught in some college young-
adult literature courses.

Peck reprised the character of Rob Peck from his first
novel over two decades later in real time, but only weeks
after the ending of the first book in fictional time. After
his father's death, young Rob is forced to work at a store
to make payments on the family farm. Most critics felt,
however, that the sequel was not as strong as the initial

*Yoolee Tharp must protect his mother and sister first
from the violent rage of his father and later from a
killer beast that stalks their village. (Cover illustration
by Richard Waldrep.)*

title with its bond between boy and father and evocation of Shaker ideals.

In *Millie's Boy,* Peck tells the story of another boy on the edge of adulthood. Left an orphan after his prostitute mother is killed, 16-year-old Tit Smith is chased by wild dogs when he runs away from the County Work Farm, and then is taken in by a kindly doctor in another tale of Vermont, this time from the turn of the century. A reviewer for *Booklist* noted that the novel contained "well-done characterizations, dialog and ... background," and was "laced with adventure and humor."

In 1974, Peck turned to less serious themes with *Soup,* the story of young Rob and his friend, Soup, who can talk Rob into almost any mischief, from smoking cornsilk to rolling downhill in a barrel. Episodic and filled with humor, the book chronicles life among the poor, rural Vermonters of the 1930s. Critics compared

In Peck's fourteenth book about Soup Vinson and his friend Rob, the two boys uncover the important role of Native Americans in their town's history as the community prepares for its annual Fourth of July celebration. (Cover illustration by Charles Robinson.)

the fare to Tom Sawyer's adventures, and a reviewer for *Booklist* called the first "Soup" title "a series of entertaining, autobiographical recollections." Peck has gone on to pen over a dozen titles in the "Soup" series, all guaranteed to bring reluctant readers into the literacy fold. Though some critics, such as Zena Sutherland, reviewing the 1978 *Soup for President* in *Bulletin of the Center for Children's Books,* found Peck's "corn-fed nostalgia ... just a bit too jolly," others, including Mary M. Burns in *Horn Book,* noted that the adventures of Soup and Rob succeed "primarily as a humorous reminiscence of small-town attitudes and customs in pre-World War II era." Other popular titles in the series include *Soup on Ice,* "a story that portends the real Christmas spirit in subtle style," according to Peggy Forehand in *School Library Journal,* and *Soup 1776,* which *School Library Journal* contributor Connie Pierce called "a blast."

Peck has also reached into more distant time periods for historical fiction. Going back to Colonial and Revolutionary War periods, he crafted further coming-of-age stories in *Eagle Fur, Fawn, Hang for Treason, The King's Iron,* and *Rabbits and Redcoats.* Throughout these tales, Peck's love of history is obvious, as is his depiction of the father-son bond. Additionally, he continued to employ a graphic style of writing well suited to descriptions of often violent circumstances.

With *Clunie* and *Spanish Hoof,* Peck drew female protagonists. The first title deals with a young girl who is mentally disabled, called "simple" by the kids at school. Based on research at an institution, Peck's book was a "moving story, though not altogether free of sentimentality," according to a critic in *Kirkus Reviews.* Reviewing the same novel in the *New York Times Book Review,* Patricia Lee Gauch commented that "Peck has never been more the consummate storyteller than in this book about Clunie Finn, a retarded farm girl caught in a web of adolescent cruelty."

In *Spanish Hoof,* Peck tells "an utterly predictable yet endearingly sweet-'n'-earthy tale of cattle-ranching in Depression-era Florida," according to a critic for *Kirkus Reviews.* Narrated by an eleven-year-old tomboy, Harry (Harriet) Beecher, the story tells of one family's attempt to stay above water financially, and of Harry's sacrifice, selling her horse to help save the ranch. *Booklist's* Karen Stang Hanley concluded that this "rewarding story about a girl's departure from childhood and a loving extended family is ... a natural for independent reading."

Spanish Hoof also introduced a new setting for Peck's novels. Whereas most of his early books are set in Vermont, once he moved to Florida, he began using that location more and more in his fiction. In *Hallapoosa* and *The Horse Hunters,* in *Arly* and its sequel, *Arly's Run,* and in *Nine Man Tree* and the 1999 *Cowboy Ghost,* Peck once again creates moving coming-of-age tales about young boys, but all using Florida as their backdrop. In *Hallapoosa,* Peck presents an orphan brother and sister sent to live with a relative, a justice of the peace in the small southern Florida town of Hallapoosa. Once again taking the Depression as his historical backdrop, Peck weaves a tale involving "murder, a kidnapping, and ... return from the dead," according to a *Kirkus Reviews* contributor, who concluded that "Peck's language is a pungent, evocative pleasure." *The Horse Hunters* once again uses Depression-era Florida for a story of a young boy who discovers his manhood on a wild mustang roundup. Reviewing the novel for *Voice of Youth Advocates,* Allan A. Cuseo felt that this "coming-of-age epic" was "more lethargic" than Peck's other works, but that the author's "usual themes of endurance, freedom of choice, and humankind's basic goodness are affirmed."

In *Arly* and *Arly's Run,* Peck takes the usual character of the supporting teacher and boosts her to another level. Miss Binnie Hoe serves up education as a way to freedom for the children of workers in the factory town of Jailtown, Florida. Young Arly is forced into labor too, as his father falls ill and bills need to be paid. Miss Hoe arranges for Arly's escape from the virtual prison of Jailtown. Jennifer Brown, writing in *Children's Book Review Service,* declared that this "is a powerful book which any caring adult should read," while Katharine Bruner concluded in *School Library Journal* that "Arly's adventures at school, his encounters with evil, his moments of grief and despair, remain vivid long after the last page has been turned." In the sequel, *Arly's Run,* the young boy discovers that freedom is something that must be won anywhere, and he ultimately finds a new home for himself. Kathy Elmore noted in *Voice of Youth Advocates* that his "historical adventure grabs the reader from the first chapter" and would serve as an "eye-opening" introduction to "the plight of migrant workers."

After battling cancer, Peck returned with more fiction in 1998. *Nine Man Tree* is set in 1931 in the backwoods of Florida where "an illiterate dirt-poor family suffers under the rule of an abusive father," according to a *Publishers Weekly* commentator. The son protects sister and mother from the father's drunken rages, but soon an even bigger enemy looms: a giant wild boar that is attacking and eating humans. The father is killed on an expedition to kill the animal and a Calusa Indian dies with the beast he refuses to kill. "A tale full of bite," concluded the reviewer for *Publishers Weekly.* Helen Rosenberg, writing in *Booklist,* remarked that Peck "tells a haunting story in which the wild boar and the abusive father meet similar fates, but it is also an adventure and a ... tale that will have reluctant readers glued to their chairs."

In *Cowboy Ghost,* Peck tells another growing-up story against the backdrop of a Florida cattle drive in the early years of the twentieth century. Young Titus battles Seminoles and bad weather in the 500-mile drive, rising from cook's helper to leader of the drive. William C. Schadt noted in *School Library Journal* that readers would be "entertained by the way Peck portrays the cowboy lifestyle, including his liberal use of folksy, country jargon," and concluded that this was "a good story."

Sixteen-year-old Tee invokes the comforting spirit of the Cowboy Ghost when he must lead a cattle drive through the Florida wilderness. (Cover illustration by Chris Cocozza.)

Good stories are exactly what Peck is known for. Like his favorite teacher, Miss Kelly, Peck himself has become something of an inspiration for young readers, coaxing the reluctant ones with gripping descriptions of action, and enriching all with his evocation of times and places that are now forever lost.

Works Cited

Brown, Jennifer, review of *Arly, Children's Book Review Service,* June, 1989, p. 126.

Bruner, Katharine, review of *Arly, School Library Journal,* June, 1989, p. 108.

Burns, Mary M., review of *Soup for President, Horn Book,* May-June, 1978, pp. 279-80.

Review of *Clunie, Kirkus Reviews,* February 1, 1980, p. 125.

Cuseo, Allan A., review of *The Horse Hunters, Voice of Youth Advocates,* June, 1989, p. 105.

Elmore, Kathy, review of *Arly's Run, Voice of Youth Advocates,* April, 1992, p. 34.

Forehand, Peggy, review of *Soup on Ice, School Library Journal,* October, 1985, p. 192.

Gauch, Patricia Lee, review of _Clunie, New York Times Book Review,_ February 24, 1983, p. 33.

Review of _Hallapoosa, Kirkus Reviews,_ April 15, 1988, p. 567.

Hanley, Karen Stang, review of _Spanish Hoof, Booklist,_ April 15, 1985, p. 1198.

Lehmann-Haupt, Christopher, review of _A Day No Pigs Would Die, New York Times Book Review,_ January 4, 1973, p. 35.

Review of _Millie's Boy, Booklist,_ December 1, 1975, pp. 382-83.

Review of _Nine Man Tree, Publishers Weekly,_ August 17, 1998, p. 73.

Pierce, Connie, review of _Soup 1776, School Library Journal,_ October, 1995, p. 139.

Rosenberg, Helen, review of _Nine Man Tree, Booklist,_ August, 1998, p. 2008.

Schadt, William C., review of _Cowboy Ghost, School Library Journal,_ March, 1999, p. 213.

Review of _Soup, Booklist,_ April 1, 1974, p. 878.

Review of _Spanish Hoof, Kirkus Reviews,_ March 1, 1985, p. J13.

Sutherland, Zena, review of _Soup for President, Bulletin of the Center for Children's Books,_ June, 1978, p. 165.

Yardley, Jonathan, review of _A Day No Pigs Would Die, New York Times Book Review,_ May 13, 1973, p. 37.

For More Information See

BOOKS

Children's Literature Review, Volume 45, Gale, 1997, pp. 93-126.

Fifth Book of Junior Authors and Illustrators, edited by Sally Holmes Holtze, H. W. Wilson, 1983, pp. 240-241.

Peck, Robert Newton, in an essay for _Something about the Author Autobiography Series,_ Volume 1, Gale, 1986, pp. 235-247.

Peck, _Fiction Is Folks,_ Writer's Digest Books, 1983.

St. James Guide to Young Adult Writers, edited by Tom Pendergast and Sara Pendergast, St. James Press, 1999, pp. 683-85.

PERIODICALS

Booklist, June 1, 1994, p. 1799; January 15, 1995, p. 946; February 15, 1996, p. 1036; August, 1997, p. 1920

Horn Book, November-December, 1995, p. 776.

Kirkus Reviews, September 1, 1998, p. 1291.

New York Times, January 4, 1973.

New York Times Book Review, May 13, 1973; November 13, 1994, p. 27.

Publishers Weekly, July 21, 1997, p. 203; January 11, 1999, p. 73.

School Library Journal, March, 1994, p. 183; August, 1994, p. 70; October, 1995, p. 139; November, 1998, p. 126.

ON-LINE

Author's Website at www.athenet.net/~blahnik/rnpeck.

—_Sketch by J. Sydney Jones_

R

REEVES, Jeni 1947-

Personal

First name "Jeni" is a homophonic contraction of given name, Jeanne Claire Legnini; born May 16, 1947, in Geneva, NY; daughter of Joseph A. and Louise (Reale) Legnini; married Stuart G. Reeves (a research scientist), March 6, 1976; children: Tegan Jemma. *Education:* Attended l'Academia degli Belli Arti, Perugia, Italy, 1970-71.

Addresses

Home—420 Teakwood Lane N.E., Cedar Rapids, IA 52402. *Electronic mail*—Reeves84@FYIowa.infi.net. *Agent*—(art representatives) Campbell-Steele Gallery, Marion, IA; Jadite Galleries, New York, NY; Woman-made Gallery, Chicago, IL.

Career

Cornell University, Ithaca, NY, graphic designer and supervisor, 1974-76; Infovision (television production company), London, England, senior graphic designer and illustrator, 1977-80; SPS Design Studio, London, graphic designer and illustrator, 1980-82; painter in Kenya, 1983-86; painter and illustrator in the United States, 1986—. Work represented in exhibitions, including solo shows at the British Council, Nairobi, Kenya, 1986, Jadite Gallery, New York City, 1991, and 1570 Gallery, Rochester, NY, 1994. Also worked as television weather personality and film critic, as vice-president of a film production company, and as a photographer. Scriptwriter for television and film projects.

Illustrator

Thomas Amper, *Booker T. Washington,* Carolrhoda (Minneapolis, MN), 1998.
Fran Sammis, *Colors of Kenya,* Carolrhoda, 1998.
Jane Sutcliffe, *Babe Didrikson Zaharias, All-Around Athlete,* Carolrhoda, 1999.

Jeni Reeves

Jean Patrick, *Strike 'em Out, Jackie!,* Carolrhoda, 1999.

Work in Progress

Researching for: two new book illustration projects for Carolrhoda Books; a biography on abolitionist Frederick Douglass; a picture book on Sacajawea and the Lewis and Clark Expedition; canvases, a suite of paintings, "Ghosts and Listeners," exploring the relationship of man and land through the ruins left behind; "Old Tales for New," a series of paintings of children in contemporary guises of storybook figures; and a series of paintings using television distortion to suggest ambiguity. Also, writing adaptations of folk tales/myths; transcribing a Kenyan memoir.

Sidelights

Jeni Reeves told *SATA:* "I am an American artist and illustrator who has spent a number of years living and working abroad. I studied art and sculpture in Italy and worked in photography, film-making, television, and graphic and illustrative design in the United States and England. Throughout this time I continued to pursue my interests in painting and illustration, exhibiting my work and developing book projects from European folklore. A timely move to Kenya produced a very strong desire to paint the African landscape and its people, culminating first in a solo exhibition in Nairobi and then in New York City. I now live in the American Midwest.

"Although I have only recently started illustrating books, in looking back on my peripatetic career, it appears that almost everything I did prepared me for it. Photography gave me a critical eye and appreciation for composition. Sculpture and painting trained me in realizing form, technique, and color. Experience in film-making and television allowed me to write copy, to work sequentially, making visual images flow into narrative stories. Graphic design taught me to work to a deadline and to work succinctly, using symbolism and basic elements of design to convey messages. Finally, being able to live in various parts of the world broadened my scope of life and excited my interpretation of what I saw.

"My desire to make children's books, however, goes back to my childhood, where a creative family environment encouraged art in every popular form. I would go through reams of papers making sketches for imagined color plates to rival my favorite illustrators: Arthur Rackham, N. C. Wyeth, H. J. Ford, and, yes, Walt Disney. I wrote fairy tales based on my experience as a Catholic school girl, love of Greek mythology, and passion for Rocky and Bulwinkle's 'Fractured Fairy Tales.' It was an interesting mix, which would have been my first real experience with rejection, had I the courage to submit them for publication. As unpublishable as these were, and in spite of all my subsequent worldliness in growing up, I still strive to illustrate stories that appeal to the child in all of us, illuminating those common truths we do, indeed, all share."

For More Information See

PERIODICALS

ArtSpeak, September, 1991.
Finger Lakes, November-December, 1989.

*   *   *

REID BANKS, Lynne 1929-

Personal

Listed in some sources under Banks; born July 31, 1929, in London, England; daughter of James Reid (a doctor) and Muriel Alexander (an actress; maiden name, Marsh); married Chaim Stephenson (a sculptor), 1965; children: Adiel, Gillon, Omri (sons). *Education:* Attended high school in Canada; attended Italia Conti Stage School, London, 1946, and Royal Academy of Dramatic Art, London, 1947-49. *Hobbies and other interests:* Theater, gardening, teaching English as a second language abroad.

Addresses

Home—Dorset, England. *Agent*—Sheila Watson, Watson, Little Ltd., Capo di Monte, Windmill Hill, London NW3 6RJ, England.

Career

Actress in English repertory companies, 1949-54; freelance journalist, London, England, 1954-55; Independent Television News, London, news reporter, 1955-57, scriptwriter, 1958-62; taught English as a foreign language in Israel, 1963-71; writer, 1971—. *Member:* Society of Authors (London), PEN Actors' Equity.

Awards, Honors

Yorkshire Arts Literary Award, 1976, and Best Books for Young Adults, American Library Association, 1977,

Lynne Reid Banks

both for *Dark Quartet;* West Australian Young Readers' Book Award, Library Association of Australia, 1980, for *My Darling Villain;* Outstanding Books of the Year, *New York Times,* 1981, Young Readers' Choice Award, Pacific Northwest Library Association, 1984, California Young Readers' Medal, California Reading Association, 1985, Children's Books of the Year, Child Study Association, 1986, and Young Readers of Virginia Award, Arizona Young Readers' Award, and Rebecca Caudill Young Readers' Books Award, Illinois Association for Media in Education, all 1988, all for *The Indian in the Cupboard;* Parents' Choice Award for Literature, Parents' Choice Foundation, 1986, Notable Books, *New York Times,* 1986, Children's Books of the Year, 1987, and Indian Paintbrush Award, Wyoming Library Association, 1989, all for *The Return of the Indian;* Silver Award, Smarties Prize, 1996, for *Harry the Poisonous Centipede.*

Writings

FOR YOUNG PEOPLE

One More River, Vallentine, Mitchell (London), 1973, Simon & Schuster (New York), 1973, revised edition, Morrow, 1992.

The Adventures of King Midas, illustrated by George Him, Dent (London), 1976, illustrated by Jos. A. Smith, Morrow, 1992.

The Farthest-Away Mountain, illustrated by Victor Ambrus, Abelard-Schuman, 1976, Doubleday, 1977, illustrated by Dave Henderson, Doubleday, 1991.

My Darling Villain, Bodley Head, 1977, Harper, 1977.

Houdini: The Autobiography of a Self-Educated Hamster, illustrated by Terry Riley, Dent, 1978, published in the U.S. as *I, Houdini: The Autobiography of a Self-Educated Hamster,* Doubleday, 1988.

Letters to My Israeli Sons: The Story of Jewish Survival, W. H. Allen (London), 1979, F. Watts, 1980.

The Writing on the Wall, Chatto & Windus (London), 1981, Harper, 1981.

Maura's Angel, illustrated by Robin Jacques, Dent, 1984, Avon, 1998.

The Fairy Rebel, illustrated by William Geldart, Dent, 1985, Doubleday, 1988.

Melusine: A Mystery, Hamilton Children's, 1988, Harper, 1989.

The Magic Hare, illustrated by Hilda Offen, Collins, 1992, illustrated by Barry Moser, Morrow, 1993.

Broken Bridge (sequel to *One More River*), Hamish Hamilton, 1994, Morrow, 1994.

Harry the Poisonous Centipede: A Story to Make You Squirm, illustrated by Tony Ross, Collins, 1996, Morrow, 1997.

Angela and Diabola, illustrated by Klaas Verplancke, HarperCollins (London), 1997, Avon, 1997.

Moses in Egypt (based on the film *Prince of Egypt*), Penguin, 1998.

"INDIAN IN THE CUPBOARD" SERIES; FOR CHILDREN

The Indian in the Cupboard, illustrated by Robin Jacques, Dent, 1980, Doubleday, 1980.

Return of the Indian, illustrated by William Geldart, Dent, 1986, published in the U.S. as *The Return of the Indian,* Doubleday, 1986.

The Secret of the Indian, illustrated by Ted Lewin, Collins, 1989, Doubleday, 1989.

The Mystery of the Cupboard, illustrated by Piers Sanford, Collins, 1993, illustrated by Tom Newsom, Morrow, 1993.

The Indian Trilogy, Lions (London), 1993.

The Key to the Indian, illustrated by James Watling, Avon, 1998, Collins, 1999.

PLAYS

It Never Rains (produced by British Broadcasting Corp. [BBC], 1954), Deane, 1954.

All in a Row, Deane, 1956.

The Killer Dies Twice (three-act), Deane, 1956.

Already It's Tomorrow (produced by BBC, 1962), Samuel French, 1962.

The Unborn, produced in London, England, 1962.

The Wednesday Caller, produced by BBC, 1963.

Last Word on Julie, produced by ATV, 1964.

The Gift (three-act), produced in London, 1965.

The Stowaway (radio play), produced by BBC, 1967.

The Eye of the Beholder, produced by ITV, 1977.

Lame Duck (radio play), produced by BBC, 1978.

Purely from Principal (radio play), produced by BBC, 1985.

The Travels of Yoshi and the Tea-Kettle (for children; produced in London, 1991), Nelson, 1993.

OTHER

The L-Shaped Room, Chatto & Windus, 1960, Simon & Schuster, 1961, revised edition, Longman, 1976.

An End to Running, Chatto & Windus, 1962, published in the U.S. as *House of Hope,* Simon & Schuster, 1962.

Children at the Gate, Chatto & Windus, 1968, Simon & Schuster, 1968.

The Backward Shadow, Chatto & Windus, 1970, Simon & Schuster, 1970.

The Kibbutz: Some Personal Reflections, Anglo-Israel Association (London), 1972.

Two Is Lonely (sequel to *The L-Shaped Room* and *The Backward Shadow*), Chatto & Windus, 1974, Simon & Schuster, 1974.

Sarah and After: The Matriarchs, Bodley Head, 1975, published in the U.S. as *Sarah and After: Five Women Who Founded a Nation,* Doubleday, 1975.

Dark Quartet: The Story of the Brontes, Weidenfeld & Nicholson (London), 1976, Delacorte, 1977.

Path to the Silent Country: Charlotte Bronte's Years of Fame (sequel to *Dark Quartet*), Weidenfeld & Nicholson, 1976, Delacorte, 1977.

Defy the Wilderness, Chatto & Windus, 1981.

Torn Country: An Oral History of the Israeli War of Independence, F. Watts, 1982.

The Warning Bell, Hamish Hamilton, 1984, St. Martin's, 1987.

Casualties, Hamish Hamilton, 1986, St. Martin's, 1987.

Fair Exchange, Piatkus (London), 1998.

Contributor to numerous periodicals, including *Ladies' Home Journal, Observer, Guardian, Sunday Telegraph, Independent,* and *Sunday Times.*

The Indian in the Cupboard and its sequels were translated into some twenty languages.

Adaptations

The L-Shaped Room, starring Leslie Caron, was released by Davis-Royal Films, 1962; all the "Indian in the Cupboard" books have been adapted as audiobooks; *The Indian in the Cupboard* was adapted as a major motion picture, 1995; *The Farthest-Away Mountain, The Fairy Rebel, I, Houdini, The Adventures of King Midas, Harry the Poisonous Centipede,* and *Angela and Diabola* were all adapted as audiobooks, narrated by Reid Banks, Listening Library, 1994-99.

Work in Progress

Alice-by-Accident, for Avon; *The Further Adventures of Harry the Poisonous Centipede,* for HarperCollins.

Sidelights

While British author Lynne Reid Banks has written about a number of complex subjects—single parenthood, war, the Middle East, Zionism—she is best known to young audiences for imaginative stories such as *The Indian in the Cupboard, The Adventures of King Midas,* and *Melusine.* Many of Reid Banks's titles for younger readers, such as the "Indian" books, feature magic as a central theme. Teen readers are attracted to works such as *The Writing on the Wall,* in which Reid Banks deals with typical teenage problems, including dating, drugs, and family relationships. Reid Banks often draws on personal experience for her writing. "I have learned a fundamental lesson," she wrote in an essay for the *Sixth Book of Junior Authors and Illustrators.* "Nothing is ever wasted. And for a writer, there's something more: nothing one ever experiences or feels is wasted. Even the bad things, the negative emotions . . . . While one is suffering them, I mean at the time, a little voice is saying 'Hold on to it. Remember.' Because one day you may need it."

Born in London in 1929, Reid Banks had her childhood interrupted by World War II, when she and her mother were evacuated to Saskatchewan, Canada, for five years. "Since my mother was evacuated with me, I was very happy, and though we were poor, I hardly noticed it, except that I couldn't have trendy clothes," the author noted in an interview with Marc Caplan for *Authors and Artists for Young Adults (AAYA).* "I didn't really realise what the war meant, or the terrible things that had been happening, until I got back to England, at the very formative age of fifteen. I found my city in ruins, and learned what had been happening to my family, left behind, and in Europe, to the Jews. I felt like a deserter." The experience marked the author for life.

Reid Banks originally planned on being an actress like her mother, and to train for what she hoped would be a glamorous career, she attended the Royal Academy of Dramatic Art in London. "I adored every minute of it . . . . I was going to take the theater world by storm!," she noted in her *Junior Authors* essay. However, the demand for actresses was slight, and Reid Banks found it difficult to make a living. After five years as an actress in low-paying provincial repertory theaters, Reid Banks found a more stable and more lucrative job as a television writer and reporter. At the same time, she wrote plays for stage, radio, and television, many of which were produced, and worked on her first novel.

Written for adult readers, *The L-Shaped Room* became Reid Banks's first literary success. The book chronicles the life of unmarried, twenty-seven-year-old Jane Graham, who goes to live in run-down lodgings when she becomes pregnant. Reid Banks eventually wrote two more novels featuring Jane Graham, *The Backward Shadow* and *Two Is Lonely,* and has continued to write fiction for adults in between the children's books that have become the basis of her career as a writer. As she told Chris Stephenson in *Carousel,* "from about 1985, children's books took over."

The positive critical response to *The L-Shaped Room* provided Reid Banks with the means to accomplish another dream, as she recounted in her *AAYA* interview: "Throughout my late teens and twenties, when Israel was going through its early traumas [as a newly formed modern nation], I had a great desire to go there." In 1960 she traveled to Israel, and subsequently she met the man who would become her husband, sculptor Chaim Stephenson; what had started as a series of visits became a residency. "Living in a kibbutz, working the land, teaching and having my babies in that 'alien' country that I came to love so much, was a sublimation for my lingering feelings of guilt for having missed the War," the author maintained.

Reid Banks and her family returned to England in 1972, and she published her first young-adult book in 1973—*One More River,* the story of Lesley, a pampered Canadian girl attempting to adjust to life in an Israeli kibbutz. The sequel to *One More River,* titled *Broken Bridge,* appeared in 1994. With Lesley now grown up and still living in the kibbutz, the story involves questions about her choice of lifestyle after her nephew is killed by an Arab terrorist during a visit to Jerusalem, a tragedy compounded by the fact that Lesley's daughter Nili witnessed the murder but will not divulge the terrorist's identity. In this novel, Reid Banks "pos[es] some tough questions about the Mideast struggle and the motivations and actions of the Israeli people," according to *Booklist* contributor Jeanne Triner.

Since the early 1970s, Reid Banks has delighted scores of young fans with tales of magical kings, brave fairies, toys that come to life, and intrepid hamsters, hares, and centipedes. In *I, Houdini: The Autobiography of a Self-Educated Hamster,* she spins a yarn about a hamster that enjoys escaping from his cage to cause all manner of mischief in the house where his owners—three brothers—live. In *The Farthest-Away Mountain,* fourteen-year-old Dakin is a feisty young woman who sets out to accomplish her three goals: to reach the distant mountains, to meet a gargoyle, and to marry a prince. While accomplishing the first two goals, Dakin comes to realize that a prince need not have a princely character, and thus abandons her search for royalty in favor of a trusted friend. Within an imaginative plot and fantastic setting, Reid Banks "makes every character come alive, capturing the nuances of their natures, their pettiness, jealousy and fears through ... [both] voices ... and ... actions," according to *School Library Journal* contributor Edith Ching.

Magic again appears in *Maura's Angel.* Eleven-year-old Maura lives in Belfast in Northern Ireland, where violence between Protestant and Catholic factions still persists. With her brother in jail and her father in hiding for being a member of the I.R.A., Maura and her mother attempt to keep the household together, until one day when Maura encounters, during a bomb blast, her angel: a young girl who could be her twin, who goes by the name of Angela. While Maura gets used to Angela, Angela becomes accustomed to being human, encountering the feelings of happiness and sorrow she had not experienced in heaven. "It is [Angela's] desperate wish to make things right for Maura's family ... that brings about terrible consequences," noted *School Library Journal* contributor Eva Mitnik of a story that will cause young readers to reflect on its message about the value in life's hardships "long after they turn the final page."

In *Angela and Diabola* Reid Banks plays up the fantasy elements of pure good and evil. Twin sisters Angela and Diabola are opposites; as their names would suggest, one is very, very good, while the other is awful. In fact, after killing the family cat and getting her mother put in jail, the girls' parents decide that the best that can be done is to keep Diabola in a cage when she is not closely supervised. Unfortunately, as readers might suspect, steel bars do little to suppress the evil child, who turns to telekinesis as a way of spreading her wickedness. In true storybook fashion, the two sisters ultimately do battle, with Angela coming out the victor, although slightly altered. Comparing the book to the work of Roald Dahl in her *School Library Journal* review, Anne Connor called *Angela and Diabola* "an absurd look at human nature [that] is often bitingly funny," while a *Publishers Weekly* contributor noted that Reid Banks's "expansive storytelling and comic exaggeration produce high kid appeal."

Among Reid Banks's most popular works for children are *The Indian in the Cupboard* and its sequels: *Return of the Indian, The Secret of the Indian, The Mystery of the Cupboard,* and *The Key to the Indian.* In each volume, young Omri's plastic toy figurines come to life every time they are locked in a small metal cupboard with a lead key. Omri soon discovers that his favorite toy, a small plastic Indian figure named Little Bear, has, when brought to life, a taste for adventure—sometimes with near-disastrous results. Other characters, which

New York Times Book Review contributor Michael Dorris described as "plucky, albeit creaky cultural stereotypes, ever predictable and true to the dictates of their sex, ethnic group, or time," include a cowboy, a British nurse, a soldier, a saloon-bar hostess, and a little horse.

A reviewer for the *Times Literary Supplement* found *The Indian in the Cupboard* "original, lively, compulsive writing" that "will well stand through repeated readings." Sequels from that original novel allow Omri to discover the history behind the cupboard, which has been in his family for many years. In *The Mystery of the Cupboard,* in which Omri and his family inherit an old house in the Dorset countryside, Omri discovers a notebook written by his great aunt that reveals the cupboard's secret, and meets a host of new tiny characters. While noting that the book's efforts to explain the "science" behind the cupboard's transformational ability fall short, Dorris added that "the exercise itself has provided Ms. Banks an excuse and the context to devise a stunning, full-blown tale" about Omri's great-great aunt, "a vivid, arresting personality, a woman consumed by jealousy and recrimination" whose own story will fascinate readers. *The Key to the Indian* finds Omri sharing his secret with his father, who joins his son in an effort to help Little Bear and his Iroquois tribe survive the efforts of early American settlers to defeat them. "Readers will revel in all of the details of this book, from the intricate workings of the magic to the solutions Omri finds to [transportation] problems," according to Eva Mitnik in *School Library Journal.*

While Reid Banks enjoys writing for audiences of all ages—her most recent adult novel, *Fair Exchange,* was published in 1998—she is especially fond of writing stories for younger readers. "Writing for young people is a much pleasanter, and easier, thing than writing for adults," she commented in her interview with Caplan. "I especially enjoy writing wish-fulfillment tales for younger children in which real, everyday life co-exists with magic .... In the end, one has to write what one wants to write, or what one is commissioned to write, and hope for the best. You can't win 'em all."

Works Cited

Review of *Angela and Diabola, Publishers Weekly,* May 25, 1998, p. 92.

Ching, Edith, review of *The Farthest-Away Mountain, School Library Journal,* July, 1997, p. 56.

Connor, Anne, review of *Angela and Diabola, School Library Journal,* July, 1997, p. 90.

Dorris, Michael, "A Boy and His Box, Batteries Not Needed," *New York Times Book Review,* May 16, 1993.

Review of *The Indian in the Cupboard, Times Literary Supplement,* November 21, 1980.

Mitnik, Eva, review of *The Key to the Indian, School Library Journal,* December, 1998, p. 118.

Mitnik, review of *Maura's Angel, School Library Journal,* August, 1998, p. 160.

Reid Banks, Lynne, essay in *Sixth Book of Junior Authors and Illustrators,* edited by Sally Holmes Holtze, Wilson, 1989, pp. 22-24.

Reid Banks, interview with Marc Caplan published in *Authors and Artists for Young Adults,* Volume 6, Gale, 1991, pp. 189-94.

Stephenson, Chris, interview with Reid Banks in *Carousel,* spring, 1999, p. 32.

Triner, Jeanne, review of *Broken Bridge, Booklist,* March 15, 1995, p. 1321-22.

For More Information See

BOOKS

Children's Literature Review, Volume 24, Gale, 1991, pp. 186-200.

Twentieth-Century Young Adult Writers, St. James Press, 1994.

PERIODICALS

Horn Book, September-October, 1993, p. 483.

Publishers Weekly, February 20, 1995, pp. 206-07; June 9, 1997, p. 46; October 26, 1998, p. 66.

School Library Journal, June, 1993, p. 102; April, 1994, p. 88; April, 1995, p. 150; September, 1997, p. 172.

Stone Soup, September-October, 1996, pp. 26-28.

* * *

RORABACK, Robin (Ellan) 1964-

Personal

Born January 30, 1964, in Sharon, CT; daughter of Robert Donald (an electrician) and Barbara Rose (Marks) Roraback. *Education:* Northwestern Connecticut Community Technical College, A.S., 1985; Rhode Island School of Design, B.F.A., 1988. *Hobbies and other interests:* Pottery, photography, hiking, reading.

Addresses

Home and office—299 Taconic Rd., Salisbury, CT 06068. *Agent*—Carol Bancroft, Carol Bancroft and Friends, 121 Dodgingtown Rd., P.O. Box 266, Bethel, CT 06801.

Career

Housatonic Day Care Center, Lakeville, CT, preschool teacher, 1988—. *Member:* Society of Children's Book Writers and Illustrators.

Illustrator

Anne W. Philips, *Enough,* McGraw (New York City), 1998.

John Herman, *Red, White, and Blue: The Story of the American Flag,* Grosset (New York City), 1998.

Ziporah Hildebrant, *This Is Our Seder,* Holiday House (New York City), 1999.

Work in Progress

Writing books.

Sidelights

Robin Roraback told *SATA:* "From the time I got my first library card at age six, I have loved books. I always knew I wanted to illustrate them someday.

"I use all sorts of resources for my illustrations. I go to tag sales, looking for interesting objects to include in illustrations. I look through magazines and take photographs and long walks with my dogs—always looking for colors, objects, and characters for my illustrations. I often use my family, which includes four cats and three dogs, as models.

"I have many favorite illustrators, including Lizbeth Zwerger, David Small, Erik Blegvad, Ernest Shepard, Beatrix Potter, Marcia Sewall, Sue Truesdell, Margot Apple, Robert McCloskey, Jessie Willcox Smith, and Donald Carrick."

For More Information See

PERIODICALS

Booklist, March 1, 1999, p. 1216.
Publishers Weekly, February 22, 1999, p. 86.

Robin Roraback provided the lively illustrations for Ziporah Hildebrandt's **This Is Our Seder,** *which presents the most basic concepts and celebratory aspects of Passover. (Cover illustration by Roraback.)*

ROSS, Clare 1975-
(Clare Good)

Personal

Born September 23, 1975, in Sydney, Australia; daughter of Lester (a farmer) and Maureen (a cleaner) Good; married Simon Ross (an engineer), March 20, 1999. *Education:* University of Canberra, B.A.; St. Mary's College Gunnedah, Higher School Certificate.

Addresses

Home—4 Arndell St., Macquarie, Australian Capital Territory, 2614 Australia.

Career

Australian Gas Association, Canberra, Australian Capital Territory, Administrative Secretary, 1999—.

Writings

Here Comes the Rain, Scholastic Australia, 1999.

Sidelights

Clare Ross told *SATA:* "My first book, *Here Comes the Rain,* was written about my parents' beef cattle farm—'Woodlands.' I was lucky enough to grow up in outback Australia where I developed a great love of animals and a respect for the beautiful but harsh Australian landscape. I now work in the city but plan to return to farm life. I write about what I know and what I love. Teaching children about the land and sharing my experiences with them is the aim of my writing."

Clare Ross

S–T

SAUVAIN, Philip Arthur 1933-

Personal

Born March 28, 1933, in Burton on Trent, Staffordshire, England; son of Alan (an education officer) and Norah (a teacher; maiden name, Humphreys) Sauvain; married June Maureen Spenceley (a teacher), July 27, 1963; children: Richard Philip, Rachel Anne. *Education:* Cambridge University, M.A. (with honors), 1956; University of London, postgraduate certificate in education, 1957.

Addresses

Home and Office—70 Finborough Rd., Stowmarket, Suffolk 1P14 1PU, England.

Philip Arthur Sauvain

Career

Writer, 1974—. Steyning Grammar School, Sussex, England, head of geography department, 1957-61; Penistone Grammar School, Sheffield, England, head of geography department, 1961-63; James Graham College, Leeds, England, senior lecturer in geography, 1963-68; Charlotte Mason College of Education, Ambleside, England, head of environmental studies department, 1968-74. *Member:* Incorporated Society of Authors, Playwrights, and Composers. Member of committee of Educational Writer's Group, 1978.

Awards, Honors

Honorary senior scholar of Emmanuel College, Cambridge, 1956; Runner-up, *Times Educational Supplement* Information Book Award, 1975, for *Looking around in Town and Country.*

Writings

NONFICTION

A Map Reading Companion, Hulton Educational Publications, 1961.

A Geographical Field Study Companion, Hulton Educational Publications, 1964.

The First Men on the Moon, Hulton Educational Publications, 1972.

The Great Wall of China, Hulton Educational Publications, 1972.

Looking around in Town and Country, F. Watts (New York City), 1975.

Looking Back, F. Watts, 1975.

Junior Guide to Arundel Castle, F. Watts, 1978.

Certificate Mapwork, Hulton Educational Publications, 1979.

Macmillan Local Studies Kit, Macmillan, 1979.

First Elements of Geography: The British Isles, Hulton Educational Publications, 1980.

(With Michael Carrier) *Topics for Discussion and Language Practice: Books I and II,* Hulton Educational Publications, 1980.

The World about Us: Science Discussion Pictures, Pack 1, Macmillan, 1981.

Britain's Living Heritage, Batsford (London), 1982.

The World about Us: Science Discussion Pictures, Pack 2, Macmillan, 1983.

Theatre, Bell & Hyman (London), 1983.

Modern World History 1919 Onwards, Hulton Educational Publications, 1983.

The Modern World since 1917, Blackwell Scientific Publications, 1983.

British Social and Economic History, Blackwell Scientific Publications, 1985.

European and World History 1815-1919, Hulton Educational Publications, 1985.

France and the French, Blackwell Scientific Publications, 1985.

How History Began, Piper (Boston), 1985.

About Castles and Crusaders, Piper, 1986.

British Economic and Social History, Book I: 1700-1870, Stanley Thornes (Cheltenham, Gloucestershire), 1987.

British Economic and Social History, Book II: 1850 to the Present Day, Stanley Thornes, 1987.

Skills for Geography, Stanley Thornes, 1989.

The Modern World: 1914-1980, Stanley Thornes, 1989.

Holidays and Pastimes, Wayland (Sussex), 1991.

Work, Wayland 1991.

Communications, Schuster Young Books, 1992.

The Era of the Second World War, Stanley Thornes, 1993.

Robert Scott in the Antarctic, illustrated by Gibbons and Fred Anderson, Zoe, 1993.

The Tudors and Stuarts, Wayland, 1995.

Easter, Wayland, 1997.

"ENVIRONMENTAL STUDIES" SERIES

Exploring at Home, Hulton Educational Publications, 1966.

Exploring Britain, Hulton Educational Publications, 1966.

Exploring the World, Hulton Educational Publications, 1967.

"DISCOVERY" SERIES

About the Weather, Macmillan, 1970.

Along a Road, Macmillan, 1970.

In a Garden, Macmillan, 1970.

Near Your Home, Macmillan, 1970.

Where You Live, Macmillan, 1970.

Where You Go to School, Macmillan, 1970.

"LIVELY HISTORY" SERIES

Lively History, Volume 1: Lord and Peasant: Old Stone Age to 1485 A.D., Hulton Educational Publications, 1970.

Lively History, Volume 2: Town and Country: 1485-1789, Hulton Educational Publications, 1971.

Lively History, Volume 3: Empire, City and Industry: 1789-1901, Hulton Educational Publications, 1973.

Lively History, Volume 4: Conflict, Science and Society: The Twentieth Century, Hulton Educational Publications, 1973.

"PRACTICAL GEOGRAPHY" SERIES

Practical Geography, Volume 1: Pictures and Plans, Hulton Educational Publications, 1970.

Practical Geography, Volume 2: Facts, Maps, and Places, Hulton Educational Publications, 1970.

Practical Geography, Volume 3: Man and Environment, Hulton Educational Publications, 1971.

Practical Geography, Volume 4: Advanced Techniques and Statistics, Hulton Educational Publications, 1972.

"BREAKAWAY" SERIES

Finding a Job and Settling Down, Hulton Educational Publications, 1973.

People with Problems, Hulton Educational Publications, 1973.

Keeping the Peace, Hulton Educational Publications, 1974.

Living in Towns, Hulton Educational Publications, 1974.

Vanishing World, Hulton Educational Publications, 1974.

World of Adventure, Hulton Educational Publications, 1974.

Enjoying Ourselves, Hulton Educational Publications, 1976.

Where the Money Goes, Hulton Educational Publications, 1976.

"EXPLORING THE WORLD OF MAN" SERIES

Man the Builder, Hulton Educational Publications, 1973.

Man the Farmer, Hulton Educational Publications, 1973.

Man the Traveller, Hulton Educational Publications, 1973.

Man the Manufacturer, Hulton Educational Publications, 1974.

Man the Pleasure Lover, Hulton Educational Publications, 1974.

Man the Warrior, Hulton Educational Publications, 1974.

Man the Discoverer, Hulton Educational Publications, 1975.

Man the Citizen, Hulton Educational Publications, 1976.

Man the Artist, Hulton Educational Publications, 1977.

Man the Thinker, Hulton Educational Publications, 1977.

"FIRST LOOK" SERIES

Maps and How to Read Them, F. Watts, 1973.

Winds, F. Watts, 1975.

Dinosaurs, F. Watts, 1976.

Discoveries and Inventions before the Age of Steam, F. Watts, 1977.

Rain, F. Watts, 1978.

Snow and Ice, F. Watts, 1978.

"ENVIRONMENT BOOK" SERIES

By Land, Sea, and Air, Macmillan, 1974.

On a Farm, F. Watts, 1974.

On a Holiday, F. Watts, 1974.

Under Your Feet, F. Watts, 1974.

Back in the Past, F. Watts, 1978.

Dial 999, F. Watts, 1978.

In Town, F. Watts, 1978.

Made in Britain, F. Watts, 1978.

"IMAGINING THE PAST" SERIES

A Castle, Macmillan, 1976.

A Medieval Town, Macmillan, 1976.

An Abbey, Macmillan, 1976.

A Tudor Mansion, Macmillan, 1976.

Prehistoric Britain, Macmillan, 1976.

Roman Britain, Macmillan, 1976.

A Georgian Town, Macmillan, 1980.
An Eighteenth-Century Village, Macmillan, 1980.
A Regency Coaching Inn, Macmillan, 1980.
A Victorian Factory Town, Macmillan, 1980.
Stuart Britain, Macmillan, 1980.
The Victorian Seaside, Macmillan, 1980.

"LOOKING AROUND" CARDS SERIES

Houses and Towns, F. Watts, 1978.
Villages and Farms, F. Watts, 1978.
Hills and Coasts, F. Watts, 1979.
Valleys and Routeways, F. Watts, 1979

"STORY OF BRITAIN" SERIES

Britain in the Middle Ages, Macmillan, 1980.
Early Britain, Macmillan, 1980.
From Nelson to the Present, Macmillan, 1980.
Tudors, Stuarts, and Georgians, Macmillan, 1980.

"HISTORY OF BRITAIN" SERIES

Before 1066, Macmillan, 1982.
Henry VII to George III, Macmillan, 1982.
Modern Times, Macmillan, 1982.
The Middle Ages, Macmillan, 1982.

"NEW GEOGRAPHIES" SERIES

Europe, Hulton Educational Publications, 1983.
North America and the USSR, Hulton Educational Publications, 1983.
Teacher's Handbook, Hulton Educational Publications, 1983.
The British Isles, Hulton Educational Publications, 1983.
The Developing World, Hulton Educational Publications, 1983.

"JUNIOR GEOGRAPHY" SERIES

About the World, Macmillan, 1983.
At Home and Around, Macmillan, 1983.
How We Live, Macmillan, 1983.
In Britain Now, Macmillan, 1983.

"NEW HISTORIES" SERIES

Crown and Parliament, Hulton Educational Publications, 1984.
Serf and Crusader, Hulton Educational Publications, 1984.
Tribes and Tribunes, Hulton Educational Publications, 1984.
Forge and Factory, Hulton Educational Publications, 1985.
Teachers' Handbook, Hulton Educational Publications, 1985.
War and Peace, Hulton Educational Publications, 1985.

"WHAT TO LOOK FOR" SERIES

At the Country House, Longman (Watford), 1986.
At the Castle, Longman, 1986.
At the Cathedral, Longman, 1986.
At the Roman Fort and Villa, Longman, 1986.

"EXPLORING ENERGY" SERIES

Carrying Energy, Macmillan, 1987.
Oil and Natural Gas, Macmillan, 1987.
Wind and Water Power, Macmillan, 1987.
Wood and Coal, Macmillan, 1987.

"SKILLS FOR HISTORY" SERIES

British and European History, Stanley Thornes, 1988.
British Economic and Social History, Stanley Thornes, 1988.
Modern World History, Stanley Thornes, 1988.
(With Nigel Shepley and Stuart Archer) *Skills for Standard Grade History,* Stanley Thornes, 1990.

"WORLD OF WORK" SERIES

Airport, Macmillan Education, 1989.
Mine, Macmillan Education, 1989.
Ship, Macmillan Education, 1989.

"HOW WE BUILD" SERIES BOOKS

Roads, Macmillan, 1989.
Skyscrapers, Macmillan, 1989.
Tunnels, Macmillan, 1989.

"EXPLORING THE PAST" SERIES

Old World, Stanley Thomas, 1991.
Changing World, Stanley Thomas, 1992.
Expanding World, Stanley Thomas, 1993.

"THE WAY IT WORKS" SERIES

Air, Heinemann Children's Reference (Exeter, NH), 1992.
Motion, Heinemann Children's Reference, 1992.
Water, Heinemann Children's Reference, 1992.

"GREAT BATTLE AND SEIGES" SERIES

El Alamein, Wayland, 1992.
Hastings, Wayland, 1992.
Midway, Wayland, 1993.
Waterloo, Wayland, 1993.

"HISTORY DETECTIVE" SERIES

Over 200 Years Ago: In Ancient Greece, illustrated by Graham Humphreys, Zoe, 1992.
Over 1,600 Years Ago: In the Roman Empire, illustrated by Harry Clow, Zoe, 1992.
Over 450 Years Ago: In the New World, illustrated by Eric Rowe, Zoe, 1993.
Over 3,000 Years Ago: In Ancient Egypt, illustrated by Eric Rowe, Zoe, 1993.

"TARGET GEOGRAPHY" SERIES

Big Book, Ward Lock Educational, 1994.
Near and Far, Ward Lock Educational, 1994.
Look Around, Ward Lock Educational, 1994.
Using the Land, Ward Lock Educational, 1994.
Maps and Places, Ward Lock Educational, 1994.
At Home and Abroad, Ward Lock Educational, 1994.
Around the World, Ward Lock Educational, 1994.
At Home and in Britain, Ward Lock Educational, 1994.
About Our World, Ward Lock Educational, 1994.
Our Earth, Ward Lock Educational, 1994.
Teacher's Guide: KS1/KS2, Ward Lock Educational, 1995.
Key Stage 3: Book 1, Ward Lock Educational, 1995.
Key Stage 3: Book 2, Ward Lock Educational, 1995.
Key Stage 3: Book 3, Ward Lock Educational, 1996.

"GEOGRAPHY DETECTIVE" SERIES

Rainforests, Zoe, 1996.
Seas and Oceans, Zoe, 1996.

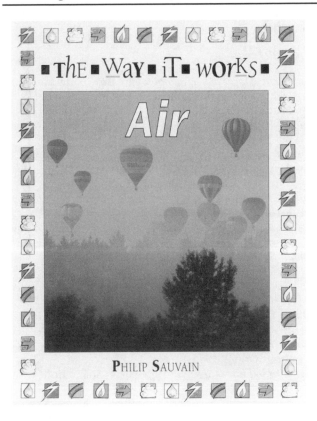

Sauvain's 1992 work discusses the properties and uses of air and how it affects all things that fly.

Mountains, Zoe, 1996.
Rivers and Valleys, Zoe, 1996.

"FAMOUS LIVES" SERIES

Saints, Wayland, 1996.
Kings and Queens, Wayland, 1996.

"BRITAIN SINCE 1930" SERIES

Life at Home, Wayland, 1995.
Leisure Time, Wayland, 1996.
Life at Work, Wayland, 1996.
The Advance of Technology, Wayland, 1996.

"KEY HISTORY FOR GCSE" SERIES

Key Themes of the Twentieth Century, Stanley Thornes, 1996.
Key Themes of the Twentieth Century: Teacher's Guide, Stanley Thornes, 1996.
Germany in the Twentieth Century, Stanley Thornes, 1997.
Germany in the Twentieth Century: Teacher's Guide, Stanley Thornes, 1997.
Vietnam, Stanley Thornes, 1997.
Vietnam: Teacher's Guide, Stanley Thornes, 1997.

Contributor of articles to periodicals, including *Times Educational Supplement, Teachers World, Child Education, Pictorial Education,* and *British Heritage.* Edited *Collins School Database* diaries for older children, 1988-93.

Sidelights

Philip Arthur Sauvain's book *Looking around in Town and Country* is filled with information for young readers. The author explores towns, coasts, railways, and other locations. He describes buildings along the way and explains the purposes of objects encountered. Designed as a pictorial guide to the environment of the British Isles, the book offers several indexes for young readers of varied levels of understanding. Sauvain drew on his experience as a teacher of environmental studies when preparing the work.

Sauvain followed *Looking around in Town and Country* with *Looking Back,* a pictorial encyclopedia to British history that highlights the key events, personalities, and facets of everyday life in the past. The author used his own color transparencies to show children the many buildings, relics, and monuments still seen today in all parts of Britain.

Sauvain commented: "I always find it helpful to envisage the final layout of words and pictures at the time of writing the text. For some time now I have been photographing many of the characteristic features that illustrate the history and geography of the British Isles and Western Europe. My color transparencies and

Sauvain and illustrator Eric Rowe collaborated on this book about the impact of Columbus's arrival in the New World on Native-American civilizations. (Cover illustration by Rowe.)

monochrome prints illustrate most of the books I have written. Indeed, some of my work, such as a set of science-discussion pictures for five- to seven-year-olds, has been largely photographic.

"I first started to write in response to a challenge from an old acquaintance who said, 'Why not write a book for schools?' It was also something of a family tradition. My father and my maternal grandfather (G. A. Humphreys) had both written school textbooks in the 1930s, and my great-grandfather Aime Louis Sauvain wrote a French textbook, *Presque mot a mot,* in 1887.

"Writing and preparing materials for use by children in schools is one of the essential, but least glamorous, branches of authorship. It imposes certain constraints that many general writers might find particularly irksome, such as restricted vocabulary and writing within strict word limits to the page.

"I shall always remember the day my first book appeared in November, 1961, because I drove into the back of a vehicle half an hour after receiving my complimentary copies through the post!"

For More Information See

PERIODICALS

Educational Development Centre Review, January, 1972.
Growing Point, September, 1975; November, 1977; September, 1978; February, 1979.
School Librarian, November, 1992, pp. 153; February, 1993, pp. 34.
School Library Journal, January, 1993, pp. 110+; February, 1993, p. 104; March, 1993, p. 203; July, 1993, p. 95; August, 1993, p. 182; March, 1994, p. 23.
Times Educational Supplement, July 24, 1970; June 8, 1973.

*   *   *

SIMON, Francesca 1955-

Personal

Born February 23, 1955, in St. Louis, MO; daughter of Mayo (a writer) and Sondra (a teacher) Simon; married Martin Stamp (a computer programmer and analyst), June 22, 1986; children: Joshua. *Education:* Yale University, B.A., 1977; Oxford University, M.A., with honors, 1979. *Hobbies and other interests:* Reading, theater, playing the violin, playing with my son.

Addresses

Agent—Rosemary Sandberg, 6 Bayley St., London WC1B 3HB, England. *E-mail*—marst@cix.co.uk.

Career

Freelance journalist, 1980-1993; writer of children's books, 1992—. *Member:* Trollope Society.

Writings

FOR CHILDREN

But What Does the Hippopotamus Say?, illustrated by Helen Floate, Macmillan (London, England), 1994, Harcourt (New York), 1994.
Horrid Henry, Orion (London, England), 1994, illustrated by Tony Ross, Hyperion (New York), 1999.
Rosie's Swing, Hazar, 1994.
Higgledy Piggledy, the Hen Who Loved to Dance, illustrated by Elisabeth Moseng, Collins, 1995.
Horrid Henry and the Secret Club, illustrated by Tony Ross, Orion, 1995.
Cafe at the Edge of the Moon, illustrated by Keren Ludlow, Orion, 1996.
Spider School, illustrated by Peta Coplans, Orion, 1996, Dial, 1996.
The Topsy-Turvies, illustrated by Keren Ludlow, Dial, 1996.
What's That Noise?, illustrated by David Melling, Hodder, 1996, Barron's Educational Series, 1996.
Horrid Henry and the Tooth Fairy, illustrated by Tony Ross, Orion, 1996.
Big Class, Little Class, illustrated by Sonia Holleyman, Orion, 1996.
When the Moon Comes Out, illustrated by Joanne Kossoff, Macmillan, 1997.
Moo Baa Baa Quack: Seven Farmyard Stories, illustrated by Emily Bolam, Orion, 1997, Atheneum, 1998.

Francesca Simon

Camels Don't Ski, illustrated by Ailie Busby, Levinson, 1998, Sterling Publications, 1998.

Horrid Henry Strikes it Rich, illustrated by Tony Ross, Dolphin (London, England), 1998.

Where Are You?, illustrated by David Melling, Peachtree Publishing (Atlanta, GA), 1998.

Calling All Toddlers, illustrated by Susan Winter, Orion, 1998, Orchard, 1999.

Helping Hercules, illustrated by Ros Coward, Orion, 1999.

Hugo and the Bullyfrogs, illustrated by Caroline Jayne Church, David & Charles (Newton Abbot, England), 1999.

Contributor of articles to magazines, including *Cosmopolitan, Vogue,* and *Parents' Magazine.*

Work in Progress

Horrid Henry's Haunted House, for Dolphin; *Toddler Times,* illustrated by Susan Winter, *Miaow Miaow Bow Wow,* illustrated by Emily Bolam, and *"Don't be Horrid, Henry,"* illustrated by Kevin McAleenan, all for Orion.

Sidelights

Francesca Simon is an author of picture and chapter books for preschoolers and primary graders. "I started writing children's books in 1989 after the birth of my son, Joshua," Simon recalled. "Suddenly all I was reading was books for children, and I started, to my surprise, to get ideas. I wrote my first story when Joshua was four weeks old. I sent it off to a publisher and promptly received a scathing reply. They not only hated the story, but clearly thought a warped mind had produced it. I stopped writing immediately.

"One day, however, when my son was a year and a half and we'd been reading a lot of animal-noise books, he asked me what noise a caterpillar made. I thought, 'Wouldn't it be a great idea to do an animal noise book based on all the unusual animals kids see in books, like yaks and camels and giraffes?' That became my first book, *But What Does the Hippopotamus Say?*

"All my ideas start from similar small incidents, often sparked by Joshua. For example, one of my favourite picture books, *The Topsy-Turvies,* is about an upside-down family who eat with their feet, draw on walls rather than paper, sleep in their clothes, and wear pyjamas outside. This grew out of a game I played with Josh called the 'no' game where I would forbid him to sit in a chair, go down a slide, or eat with a fork.

"I have quite an impish sense of humour, a good memory for childhood emotions, and a logical mind, which I've discovered are useful qualities for a children's author. But I'm also aware that if Josh hadn't asked me about caterpillar noises I never would have found that out."

A book about the sounds animals make, *But What Does the Hippopotamus Say?* features unusual animals like

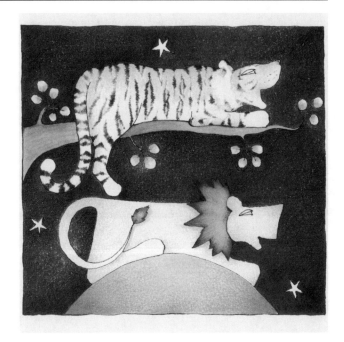

From **But What Does the Hippopotamus Say?**, *written by Francesca Simon and illustrated by Helen Floate.*

the hippo, yak, giraffe, and kangaroo, along with the more familiar cat, pig, and sheep. *Wilson Library Bulletin* contributors Donnarae MacCann and Olga Richard asserted that the book "is an ideal noisemaker since it invites participation." A *Kirkus Reviews* contributor similarly maintained that Simon gives children "a feeling of accomplishment by including them," and dubbed the work "a good book for introducing young children to a wider range of animals than the usual farm variety." Linda Wicher, reviewing *But What Does the Hippopotamus Say?* for *School Library Journal,* called the book an "off-beat offering."

Simon's *Horrid Henry* has evolved into a series of tales about a boy whose bad behavior is a contrast to that of his brother, Perfect Peter. Henry's dislike for his angelic younger sibling inspires him to new heights of outlandishness in his pranks. Nevertheless, as Cherie Gladstone noted in *School Librarian,* Henry seems to win in all situations with "anarchic humour and ... glee." *Sunday Times Bookshop* contributor Nicolette Jones asserted: "When it comes to books that break the rules adults normally impose—always a source of delight for children—Francesca Simon's 'Horrid Henry' books are required reading." In one of the more recent additions to the series, *Horrid Henry Strikes it Rich,* Henry even manages to *sell* his brother.

Simon introduces other memorable and spunky young protagonists in *Cafe at the Edge of the Moon* and *Spider School.* In *Cafe at the Edge of the Moon,* Janey daydreams her way to a moon eatery where she eats dessert first, pours ketchup on her fruit, and generally enjoys a world without parents and rules. A reviewer for *Junior Bookshelf* declared that young children with older or younger brothers "or rather fussy parents—will understand Janey's frustrations." Ann Treneman, reviewing the book in the *Times Educational Supplement,* called Janey "a wild sort of child" who would make a good friend for her own six-year-old. Kate wakes up on the wrong side of the bed in *Spider School.* It's her first day of school, she can't find her new clothes, and she is forced to wear last year's, which are too small and dirty. Late for class, she runs to the new school to find a dungeon-like classroom ruled by a gorilla teacher wearing pearls. There are no books, and the other kids are zombies. When spiders are served in the cafeteria, Kate leads a revolt. She later awakens from her nightmare, gets up on the right side of the bed to a sunny day, steps into her new clothes, and is ultimately welcomed in her real school by an ideal teacher. *School Library Journal* reviewer Lisa S. Murphy said it is "an enjoyable story for children who have already had a positive school experience—preschoolers may have serious qualms!" "The lesson about the value of a positive attitude gains force by the mildness of its delivery," wrote a *Publishers Weekly* reviewer.

The Topsy-Turvies relates the adventures of a 1960s-style family who live life upside down, sleeping in the kitchen, dining in the bedroom, sleeping during the day, and waking at midnight to pursue their activities in their pajamas. When a neighbor asks them to babysit, they oblige and rearrange her house according to their own style. "Simon's delightful story is told with sophisticated, genuine humor, a superb mix of good intentions and sheer outrageousness," wrote a *Kirkus Reviews* critic. Annabel Gibb, reviewing *The Topsy-Turvies* for *Books for Keeps,* maintained that it "provides good material for discussion of convention and difference."

Works Cited

Review of *But What Does the Hippopotamus Say?, Kirkus Reviews,* September 15, 1994, p. 1281.

Review of *Cafe at the Edge of the Moon, Junior Bookshelf,* December, 1996, pp. 240-41.

Gibb, Annabel, review of *The Topsy-Turvies, Books for Keeps,* September, 1997, p. 20.

Gladstone, Cherie, review of *Horrid Henry, School Librarian,* November, 1994, p. 154.

Jones, Nicolette, review of *Horrid Henry Strikes it Rich, Sunday Times Bookshop,* June 21, 1998.

MacCann, Donnarae, and Olga Richard, review of *But What Does the Hippopotamus Say?, Wilson Library Bulletin,* January, 1995, p. 120.

Murphy, Lisa S., review of *Spider School, School Library Journal,* September, 1996, p. 191.

Review of *Spider School, Publishers Weekly,* September 9, 1996, p. 83.

Review of *The Topsy-Turvies, Kirkus Reviews,* May 1, 1996, p. 693.

Treneman, Ann, review of *Cafe at the Edge of the Moon, Times Educational Supplement,* March 21, 1997, p. 9.

Wicher, Linda, review of *But What Does the Hippopotamus Say?, School Library Journal,* February, 1995, p. 82.

For More Information See

PERIODICALS

Books for Keeps, March, 1998, p. 18.
Magpies, July, 1996, p. 27.
Publishers Weekly, January 11, 1999, p. 70, 72.
School Librarian, autumn, 1998, pp. 129-30; spring, 1999, p. 20.
School Library Journal, May, 1999, p. 97.

*   *   *

SPIRES, Elizabeth, 1952-

Personal

Born May 28, 1952, in Lancaster, OH; daughter of Richard C. (in grounds maintenance) and Sue (maiden name, Wagner) Spires; married Madison Smartt Bell (a novelist), June 15, 1985; children: Celia Dovell Bell. *Education:* Vassar College, B.A., 1974; Johns Hopkins University, M.A., 1979. *Hobbies and other interests:* Reading, playing the hammer dulcimer, and snorkeling.

Addresses

Office—Department of English, Goucher College, Towson, MD 21204. *Agent*—Jane Gelfman, Gelfman Scheid-

Elizabeth Spires

er Literary Agents, 250 West 57th Street, New York, NY 10107, 212-245-1993.

Career

Charles E. Merrill Publishing Co., Columbus, OH, assistant editor, 1976-1977; freelance writer, 1977-1981; Washington College, Chestertown, MD, visiting assistant professor of English, 1981; Loyola College, Baltimore, MD, adjunct assistant professor of English and poet in residence, 1981-1982; Johns Hopkins University, Baltimore, visiting associate professor in writing seminars, 1984-1985, 1988-1992; Goucher College, Towson, MD, professor of English and chair for distinguished achievement, 1996-1999, writer in residence, 1982-1986, 1988-1995. *Member:* Poetry Society of America.

Awards, Honors

Academy of American Poets' Prize, 1974; *Mademoiselle* magazine College Poetry Prize, 1974; W. K. Rose Fellowship, Vassar College, 1976; Individual Artist's Grant, Ohio Arts Council, 1978; Pushcart Prize, Pushcart Press, 1981, 1995; Ingram Merrill Foundation Award, 1981; Artist's Fellowship, Maryland State Arts Council, 1982, 1989; National Endowment for the Arts Fellowship, 1981, 1992; Amy Lowell Traveling Poetry Scholarship, Harvard University, 1986-1987; Sara Teasdale Poetry Award, Wellesley College, 1990; Towson State University Prize for Literature, 1992; Guggenheim Fellowship in Poetry, 1992; Whiting Writers Award, 1996; Witter Bynner Prize for Poetry, American Academy of Arts & Letters, 1998.

Writings

FOR CHILDREN

The Falling Star, illustrated by Carlo A. Michelini, C. E. Merrill, 1981.
Count With Me, C. E. Merrill, 1981.
The Wheels Go Round, C. E. Merrill, 1981.
Simon's Adventure, illustrated by Judy Hand, Antioch Publishing, 1982.
Top Bananas, Antioch Publishing, 1982.
Things That Go Fast, illustrated by Jean Rudegeair, Antioch Publishing, 1982.
With One White Wing: Puzzles in Poems and Pictures, illustrated by Erik Blegvad, McElderry Books, 1995.
Riddle Road: Puzzles in Poems and Pictures, illustrated by Erik Blegvad, McElderry Books, 1999.
The Mouse of Amherst: A Tale of Young Readers, illustrated by Claire A. Nivola, Farrar Straus & Giroux, 1999.

POETRY COLLECTIONS; ADULT

Boardwalk, Bits Press, 1980.
Globe, Wesleyan University Press, 1981.
Swan's Island, Holt, Rinehart, and Winston, 1985.
Annonciade, Viking Penguin, 1989.
Worldling, W. W. Norton, 1995.

In With One White Wing, *illustrated by Erik Blegvad, Spires offers twenty-six original word games and picture puzzles geared for young readers.*

OTHER

W. D. Snodgrass, An Interview, Northouse & Northouse, 1988.
(Edited by Elizabeth Spires) *The Instant of Knowing: Lectures, Criticism, and Occasional Prose,* by Josephine Jacobsen, University of Michigan Press, 1998.

Contributor of poems to anthologies, including *The Best American Poetry,* 1989, 1990, 1991, and 1992; and to periodicals, including *Antaeus, New Yorker, New Republic, Mademoiselle, Poetry, American Poetry Review, Yale Review, Partisan Review, New Criterion,* and *Paris Review.*

Work in Progress

A book of poems for adults; retelling of Greek and Roman myths; and a picture book titled *The Big Meow,* forthcoming from Candlewick Press.

Sidelights

Elizabeth Spires told *SATA:* "As a child, I was a classic 'bookworm,' haunting my small-town library on a daily basis and reading a book a day during summer vacations. By the time I was twelve, I had decided to be a writer. My original plan, influenced by my admiration for Flannery O'Connor, was to become a short-story writer. Instead, in college at Vassar, I began writing poetry seriously. This has led to my publishing several collections of poetry for adult readers. My daughter, Celia, who is now eight, defined poetry one day (very appropriately, I thought) as 'playing with words.' I have 'played with words' in my writing for children in two picture books of riddles.

"I'm an Anglophile by nature, particularly interested in English literature and literary landmarks. Living in England in 1986-87 gave me a different perspective on the United States and allowed me to see it in a fresher way. Being outside my native country pushed me toward thinking more about global problems, such as the ever-present threat of war, and about cultural differences and idiosyncrasies. I've also been thinking a lot about the future, what life ten or twenty or thirty years from now will be like, both for myself as an individual, and for society as a whole."

Worldling, Spires's fifth collection of poetry, deals with motherhood, mortality, and questions about the soul's physical existence. Poems chronicle the poet's pregnancy, along with her daughter's birth and early life. Reviewers, including Donna Seaman for *Booklist,* generally praised the work. Seaman described Spires's experience of motherhood as "a vivifying series of poems about conception, expectancy, and birth.... There's something ... quietly spiritual." Another reviewer, Christine Stenstrom of *Library Journal,* characterized Spires's work as having "a gossamer touch that draws the reader into the compelling rhythm of her struggle to come to terms with her own life."

Spires teamed with veteran illustrator Erik Blegvad to produce two children's books of riddles. The first, *With One White Wing,* is a verbal/visual collaboration that offers the reader clues to solve the twenty-six puzzles contained therein. Deborah Stevenson's review for *Bulletin of the Center for Children's Books* described the collection as "inventive," generally agreeing with Carolyn Phelan's assessment in *Booklist* that the material provides "a relief from the puns and groaners that fill most riddle books...." Another reviewer, Campbell Geeslin for the *New York Times,* added that the musical quality of Spires's free-form verses make the riddles "fun to read out loud."

Four years later, in 1999, the poet and illustrator again joined forces and produced, *Riddle Road: Puzzles in Poems and Pictures.* Also lively and entertaining, a *Kirkus Reviews* contributor noted that: "The game-like quality of the book demands attention to meaning ... and helps children have fun actively reading not only words but pictures."

Inspired by a fondness for Emily Dickinson's poetry, Spires invented a mouse named Emmaline to help introduce Dickinson's work to young readers. *The Mouse of Amherst,* illustrated by Claire A. Nivola, intersperses Emmaline's poems with those of Dickinson

(as well as facts about that poet's life), and close-call encounters with cats and other mouse predators. *Booklist* reviewer Susan Dove Lempke declared it a "charmer," which conveys the "idea of the relationship formed between a poet and a reader."

Spires shared thoughts about her motivations to write *The Mouse of Amherst* with *SATA.* "I now think the story was motivated by questions of poetic inspiration, friendship, and apprenticeship, themes in my own life. That's thinking of it in purely adult terms. I hope that children who read the story will identify with Emmaline, the novice poet, and perhaps be inspired to write some poems themselves."

Works Cited

Geeslin, Campbell, review of *With One White Wing, New York Times,* April 7, 1996.

Lempke, Susan Dove, review of *The Mouse of Amherst, Booklist,* March 15, 1999, p. 1330.

Phelan, Carolyn, review of *With One White Wing, Booklist,* October 1, 1995, p. 325.

Review of *Riddle Road: Puzzles in Poems and Pictures, Kirkus Reviews,* May 15, 1999, p. 806.

Seaman, Donna, review of *Worldling, Booklist,* November 15, 1995, p. 533.

Stenstrom, Christine, review of *Worldling, Library Journal,* November 15, 1995, p. 79.

Stevenson, Deborah, review of *With One White Wing, Bulletin of the Center for Children's Books,* February, 1966, p. 205.

For More Information See

PERIODICALS

Horn Book, January-February, 1996, p. 88.
Kirkus Reviews, August 15, 1995, p. 1194.
New Criterion, December, 1995.
New York Times Book Review, July 18, 1999, p. 24.
Publishers Weekly, October 23, 1995, p. 66.
School Library Journal, September, 1995, p. 197.

*   *   *

STANLEY, George Edward 1942-
(M. T. Coffin, Adam Mills, Stuart Symons)

Personal

Born July 15, 1942, in Memphis, TX; son of Joseph (a farmer) and Cellie (a nurse; maiden name, Lowe) Stanley; married Gwen Meshew (a Slavic specialist), June 29, 1974; children: James Edward, Charles Albert Andrew. *Education:* Texas Tech University, B.A., 1965, M.S., 1967; University of Port Elizabeth, South Africa, D. Litt., 1974. *Politics:* Democrat. *Religion:* Baptist.

George Edward Stanley

Addresses

Home: 5527 Eisenhower Dr., Lawton, OK 73505. *Office:* Department of English, Foreign Languages, and Journalism, Cameron University, 2800 West Gore, Lawton, OK 73505. *Agent:* Susan Cohen, Writers House, Inc., 21 West 26th St., New York, NY 10010.

Career

East Texas State University, Commerce, instructor in English as a foreign language, 1967-1969; University of Kansas, Lawrence, instructor in English as a foreign language, 1969-1970; Cameron University, Lawton, OK, instructor, 1970-1973, assistant professor, 1973-1976, associate professor, 1976-1979, professor of Arabic, French, and Turkish, 1979—, chairman of department of English, Foreign Languages, and Journalism, 1984—. Fulbright lecturer at University of Chad, 1973. Director, annual Writers of Children's Literature Conference co-sponsored by Cameron University and the Society of Children's Book Writers; member of faculty, Institute of Children's Literature, Redding Ridge, CT, 1986-1992; member of faculty, Writer's Digest School, Cincinnati, OH, 1992—.

Member: Mystery Writers of America, Society of Children's Book Writers and Illustrators, Modern Language Association, American Association of Teachers of Arabic, American Association of Teachers of Turkic Languages.

Awards, Honors

Distinguished Faculty Award from Phi Kappa Phi, 1974; Member of the Year Award from the Society of Children's Book Writers, 1979; Oklahoma Writers Hall of Fame, 1994.

Writings

CHILDREN'S FICTION

Mini-Mysteries, Saturday Evening Post Co., 1979.
The Crime Lab, illustrated by Andrew Glass, Avon, 1980.
The Case of the Clever Marathon Cheat, Meadowbrook, 1985.
The Ukrainian Egg Mystery, Avon, 1986.
The Codebreaker Kids!, Avon, 1987.
The Italian Spaghetti Mystery, Avon, 1987.
(Under collective pseudonym Laura Lee Hope) *The New Bobbsey Twins: The Case of the Runaway Money,* Simon and Schuster, 1987.
The Mexican Tamale Mystery, Avon, 1988.
(Under the collective pseudonym Laura Lee Hope) *The Bobbsey Twins: The Mystery on the Mississippi,* Simon and Schuster, 1988.
The Codebreaker Kids Return, Avon, 1989.
Hershell Cobwell and the Miraculous Tattoo, Avon, 1991.
Rats in the Attic: And Other Stories to Make Your Skin Crawl, Avon, 1994.
Happy Deathday to You: And Other Stories to Give You Nightmares, Avon, 1995.
Ghost Horse (Road to Reading Series), Mile 5, Golden Books, 2000.
Snake Camp (Road to Reading Series), Mile 4, Golden Books, 2000.

"SCAREDY CATS" SERIES

The Day the Ants Got Really Mad, Simon and Schuster, 1996.
There's a Shark in the Swimming Pool!, Simon and Schuster, 1996.
Mrs. O'Dell's Third-Grade Class Is Shrinking, Simon and Schuster, 1996.
Bugs for Breakfast, Simon and Schuster, 1996.
Who Invited Aliens to My Slumber Party?, Simon and Schuster, 1997.
The New Kid in School Is a Vampire Bat, Simon and Schuster, 1997.
A Werewolf Followed Me Home, Simon and Schuster, 1997.
The Vampire Kittens of Count Dracula, Simon and Schuster, 1997.

"SPINETINGLERS" SERIES; UNDER NAME M. T. COFFIN

Billy Baker's Dog Won't Stay Buried!, Avon, 1995
Where Have All the Parents Gone?, Avon, 1995.
Check It Out and Die!, Avon, 1995.
Don't Go to the Principal's Office, Avon, 1996.
The Dead Kid Did It!, Avon, 1996.
Pet Store, Avon, 1996.
Escape From the Haunted Museum, Avon, 1996.
The Curse of the Cheerleaders, Avon, 1997.
Circus F.R.E.A.K.S, Avon, 1997.

This first episode in Stanley's "Scaredy Cats" series is about a family whose new house is built on the biggest anthill in the world. (Cover illustration by Sal Murdocca.)

"THIRD GRADE DETECTIVES" SERIES

The Secret of the Left-handed Envelope, Simon and Schuster, 2000.

The Mystery of the Pretty Pink Handkerchief, Simon and Schuster, 2000.

The Hair-raising Clue in the Tomato Patch, Simon and Schuster, 2000.

The Message from the Talking Cobweb, Simon and Schuster, 2000.

"THE KATIE LYNN COOKIE COMPANY" SERIES

The Secret Ingredient, illustrated by Linda Dockey Graves, Random House, 1999.

Frogs' Legs for Dinner, illustrated by Linda Dockey Graves, Random House, 2000.

The Battle of the Bakers, illustrated by Linda Dockey Graves, Random House, 2000.

Bottled Up!, Random House, 2001.

"TWIN CONNECTION" SERIES; UNDER PSEUDONYM ADAM MILLS

Hot Pursuit, Ballantine, 1989.
On the Run, Ballantine, 1989.

Right on Target, Ballantine, 1989.
Secret Ballot, Ballantine, 1989.
Dangerous Play, Ballantine, 1989.
Skyjack!, Ballantine, 1989.
High-Tech Heist, Ballantine, 1989.
Cold Chills, Ballantine, 1989.

RADIO PLAYS; ALL PRODUCED BY BRITISH BROADCASTING CORPORATION

The Reclassified Child, 1974.
Another Football Season, 1974.
Better English, 1975.

OTHER

Writing Short Stories for Young People, Writer's Digest, 1987.

Also author of "Mini-Mystery Series," a monthly short story in *Child Life Mystery and Science Fiction,* 1977—. Contributor of short stories under pseudonym Stuart Symons to *Espionage.* Also contributor of articles, stories, and reviews to scholarly journals and popular magazines for adults and children, including *Texas Outlook, English Studies in Africa, Linguistics, Bulletin of the Society of Children's Book Writers, Darling, Women's Choice, Children's Playmate, Health Explorer, Junior Medical Detective,* and *Jack and Jill.*

Sidelights

"When I was growing up in the small town of Memphis, Texas, in the late 1940s and early 1950s, I discovered that I had two passions: mysteries and movies. I read all the mysteries in the public library and went to all the Saturday afternoon matinees, mainly to see the serials. There were two movie houses in Memphis and I would walk to town several times a week just to see the new movie posters. Since I was allowed to go to the movies only on Saturday afternoons, I missed a lot of the great films of those years, but have since been able to buy video tapes of most of the ones that I never got to see and can now watch them anytime I want to! (I also collect movie posters!) Two of my favorite movies from that period are *The Bat* and *Home Sweet Homicide,* because they both have mystery writers as the main characters.

"As I grew older, my interests broadened, of course, and I began studying foreign languages. (Actually, I have always liked anything 'foreign.') In college, I majored in French and Portuguese and minored in German, and I went the route of the typical college professor as far as writing is concerned: I began writing very esoteric articles about linguistics that I doubt many people read.

"When it came time to work on my doctorate, I decided to follow another one of my dreams: going to Africa. I went to South Africa, to the University of Port Elizabeth, to research the problems the Xhosa have learning English and Afrikaans. Following my work in South Africa, I accepted a Fulbright professorship to the University of N'Djamena in Chad, Central Africa. It was there that I began writing fiction (something else I had always wanted to do) and I sold my first radio play to the British Broadcasting World Service in London.

"I grew up reading mysteries and wanting to write mysteries. I never got over Nancy Drew, the Dana Girls, or the Hardy Boys. If Nancy Drew had been a forensic scientist, I might be in a different occupation today. But she wasn't and that's why I created Dr. Constance Daniels, head of the Forensic Science laboratory of the Bay City Police Department. Dr. Daniels first appeared in *Child Life* magazine. Later, I introduced a new, younger character in the series, Marie-Claire Verlaine, and moved the locale to Paris, but the forensic science solutions remained. If I had known someone like Dr. Daniels, or Marie-Claire, when I was studying biology, chemistry, and physics, I might have excelled in science."

Inspired, in part, by those memories, Stanley wrote *The Codebreaker Kids,* a novel about three enterprising kids who start a business encoding and decoding messages for would-be spies. In what *School Library Journal* reviewer Elaine Knight called an "off-the-wall but very funny spy mystery," the three friends become enmeshed in both sides of tricky situations. Diane Roback's review for *Publishers Weekly* found the humor far-fetched, but the inclusion of real codes good for the reader in "[t]his fast-paced caper" with "Dinky's careful instructions for using them" a fine embellishment.

Reviewers gave *The Italian Spaghetti Mystery* better marks for mystery than humor. Blair Christolon's review for *School Library Journal* found the plot of a private school headmistress and her students'—cum summer performers—search for Mr. Spaghetti Man and his spaghetti-making secret to be "evenly paced and the conclusion clever," despite "primitive sound effects" and "corny" humor. Writing again for *Publishers Weekly,* Diane Roback declared the sequel to *The Ukrainian Egg Mystery* "wacky."

Hershell Cobwell and the Miraculous Tattoo places a series of crazy events in a different context, illustrating the lengths to which one boy goes to get attention and approval from his peers. A reviewer in *Booklist* dubbed it "a cautionary tale, filled with zestful humor."

During the same interview with *SATA,* Stanley went on to say: "There was a long period of time in my life when I wrote only one short story a month. Looking back on that period now, I can't honestly tell you why that's all I did, but it was, and I was perfectly satisfied. It filled my need to be a published writer, but the need then probably wasn't as great as it has since become, and I think that's a normal development. We develop into writers. For some of us it's absolutely necessary that we take it easy and let ourselves evolve into writers. I used to wonder how some of my friends wrote several different stories and books at the same time. I thought I'd never be able to do that, but I was able, and I am able.

"As I developed, I got to the point where I began getting ideas for other stories and other series and other

characters. I'd been working long enough with some of my editors that I felt quite comfortable in suggesting these new ideas to them. Some of them were accepted. Some weren't. Some even became the basis for entire magazines. At one time, I had seven series running at the same time (some stayed longer in the magazines than others), but soon the evolutionary process took over and I got to the point where I wanted to write books, too."

One area Stanley explored was the story meant to be read aloud. In the case of *Rats in the Attic: And Other Stories to Make Your Skin Crawl,* the best place for reading is suggested to be a campfire. Reviewer Larry Prater told readers of *Kliatt* that "middle schoolers will ... revel in the soft-core gore and mayhem" of the stories, which involve kids who flirt with danger and the supernatural and pay dearly.

Stanley also shared his views about the role of an author. "Writing for young people carries with it a great responsibility. Some young person is actually going to read what you've written and be influenced by it. Keeping this in mind can be helpful because it makes you want to put your best foot forward and produce not only something that you'll be proud of, but something that the young reader will never forget, whether it carries a lesson for life or simply recounts an exciting adventure.

"It's very important that you perceive yourself as a young person; this is one of the secrets of writing for them. You have to live what he is living and feel what he is feeling. You have to understand a young person's emotions, fears, disappointments, triumphs. You have to understand what it means to score that soccer goal or not to score it. You have to understand what it means to make one hundred percent on a spelling quiz. You have to understand what it means not to understand math. You have to understand what it means not to be able to play football, either because you're too small or because your parents won't let you. You have to understand what it means to have to wait for Christmas or a birthday party. You almost have to become the character you're writing about.

"One of the great things about writing for young people is that they're interested in learning about everything. This can't help but inspire the writer to reach greater heights. You want to teach them, to entertain them, to make them read what you've written. It's quite mind-boggling, frankly, when they come up to you and tell you that they really enjoy reading your stories."

With these thoughts in mind, Stanley began the "Scaredy Cat" series with *The Day the Ants Got Really Mad.* Intended for children of early-grade-school age, the book tells how Michael, a boy about the same age, copes with the discovery that his family's home is built on the world's largest anthill. Maura Bresnahan's review in *School Library Journal* said that Stanley's informative story about ants "combines humor and a semi-scary situation" in a way "children will find immensely entertaining."

"I very much dislike a lot of what is being written today for children. I think most children are looking for something that will excite them and carry them off to other worlds. They can see enough realism on the nightly news to last them a lifetime. Give them something they can look forward to, something that will stir their sense of adventure and make them want to become the best in whatever they finally end up doing. But don't forget to make them laugh!

"I am married, and my wife (who teaches German and Russian) and I have two wonderful boys, James and Charles. They are the delights of our lives. I think that I would probably have written for children anyway because I seem to have a fixation for the eight-to-twelve-year-old period of my life, but having children makes writing for them that much more exciting for me. I am not, however, my sons' favorite author! (I'm working on that!)

"I spend my spare time reading, learning new languages, watching foreign films, and just trying to keep my head above the water. My wife tells me that I can't relax; actually, I'm relaxing when I'm busy. It's when I'm not busy that I start getting uptight!"

Works Cited

Bresnahan, Maura, review of *The Day the Ants Got Really Mad,* illustrated by Sal Murdocca, *School Library Journal,* August, 1996, p. 130.

Christolon, Blair, review of *The Italian Spaghetti Mystery, School Library Journal,* June-July, 1987, p. 101.

Review of *Hershell Cobwell and the Miraculous Tattoo, Booklist,* March 15, 1991.

Knight, Elaine E., review of *The Codebreaker Kids, School Library Journal,* September, 1987, p. 183.

Prater, Larry W., review of *Rats in the Attic: And Other Stories to Make Your Skin Crawl, Kliatt,* May, 1995, pp. 18-19.

Roback, Diane, review of *The Codebreaker Kids, Publishers Weekly,* May 8, 1987, p.71.

Roback, Diane, review of *The Italian Spaghetti Mystery, Publishers Weekly,* January 16, 1987, p. 74.

For More Information See

PERIODICALS

Booklist, April 1, 1996, p. 1366.
Kirkus Reviews, July 15, 1999, p. 1139.
Library Journal, April 1, 1987, p. 145.
School Library Journal, June, 1997, p. 101.

*   *   *

STEIG, William H. 1907-

Personal

Born November 14, 1907, in New York, NY; son of Joseph (a housepainter) and Laura (a seamstress; maiden name, Ebel) Steig; married Elizabeth Mead, January 2, 1936 (divorced); married Kari Homestead, 1950 (di-

vorced, 1963); married Stephanie Healey, December 12, 1964 (divorced, December, 1966); married Jeanne Doron, 1969; children: (first marriage) Lucy, Jeremy; (second marriage) Margit Laura. *Education:* Attended City College (now City University of New York), 1923-25; National Academy of Design, New York City, 1925-29.

Addresses

Home—301 Berkeley St., #4, Boston, MA 02116.

Career

Freelance cartoonist contributing mainly to the *New Yorker,* 1930—; author and illustrator of children's books, 1968—. Worked for various advertising agencies. Sculptor. *Exhibitions:* Steig's drawings and sculptures were exhibited at Downtown Gallery, New York City, 1939, Smith College, 1940, and have been included in collections at the Rhode Island Museum, Providence, the Smith College Museum, Northampton, MA, and in the Brooklyn Museum, New York City.

Awards, Honors

Children's Book of the Year nomination, Spring Book Festival picture book honor, National Book Award finalist, and *Boston Globe-Horn Book* honor, all 1969, American Library Association (ALA) Notable Book designation and Caldecott Medal, both 1970, and Lewis Carroll Shelf Award, 1978, all for *Sylvester and the Magic Pebble;* National Book Award finalist, *New York Times* Best Illustrated Children's Book of the Year, *New York Times* Outstanding Book, and ALA Notable Book designation, all 1971, and Children's Book Showcase title, 1972, all for *Amos and Boris;* Christopher Award, 1972, National Book Award finalist, 1973, *Boston Globe-Horn Book* honor, ALA Notable Book designation, and William Allen White Children's Book Award, Kansas State College, all 1975, all for *Dominic; New York Times* Outstanding Book of the Year and ALA Notable Book designation, both 1973, for *The Real Thief;* Children's Book of the Year nomination and ALA Notable Book designation, both 1974, for *Farmer Palmer's Wagon Ride; New York Times* Outstanding Book of the Year, 1976, Newbery Honor Book, Children's Book Showcase title, ALA Notable Book designation, Lewis Carroll Shelf Award, and *Boston Globe-Horn Book* honor, all 1977, for *Abel's Island;* Caldecott Honor Book, Children's Book Showcase title, ALA Notable Book designation, and *Boston Globe-Horn Book* honor, all 1977, and Art Books for Children Award, 1978, all for *The Amazing Bone;* Irma Simonton Black Award for best children's book, *New York Times* Best Illustrated Children's Book, *New York Times* Outstanding Book, all 1980, for *Gorky Rises;* nomination, Hans Christian Andersen Medal, 1982, for illustration; *New York Times* Outstanding Book, 1982, American Book Award, Parents' Choice illustration award, *Boston Globe-Horn Book* honor, and Newbery Honor Book, all 1983, and International Board on Books for Young People Honor Book, 1984, all for *Doctor De Soto;*

Children's Picture Book Award, *Redbook,* 1984, for *Yellow and Pink;* Children's Picture Book Award, *Redbook,* 1985, for *Solomon the Rusty Nail; New York Times* Best Illustrated Book, and Children's Picture Book Award, *Redbook,* all 1986, for *Brave Irene;* Parents' Choice Picture Book Award, 1987, for *The Zabajaba Jungle;* nomination, Hans Christian Andersen Medal, 1988, for writing; Children's Picture Book Award, *Redbook,* 1988, for *Spinky Sulks;* Parents' Choice Picture Book Award, and Reading Magic Award, both 1990, and both for *Shrek!;* New England Book Award, 1993.

Writings

FOR CHILDREN; SELF-ILLUSTRATED, EXCEPT AS NOTED

C D B! (word games), Windmill Books, 1968.
Roland the Minstrel Pig, Windmill Books, 1968.
Sylvester and the Magic Pebble, Windmill Books, 1969.
The Bad Island, Windmill Books, 1969, revised edition published as *Rotten Island,* David Godine, 1984.
An Eye for Elephants (limericks), Windmill Books, 1970.
The Bad Speller (reader), Windmill Books, 1970.
Amos and Boris, Farrar, Straus, 1971.
Dominic, Farrar, Straus, 1972.
The Real Thief, Farrar, Straus, 1973.
Farmer Palmer's Wagon Ride, Farrar, Straus, 1974.
The Amazing Bone, Farrar, Straus, 1976.
Abel's Island, Farrar, Straus, 1976.
Caleb and Kate, Farrar, Straus, 1977.
Tiffky Doofky, Farrar, Straus, 1978.
Gorky Rises, Farrar, Straus, 1980.
Doctor De Soto, Farrar, Straus, 1982.
Yellow and Pink, Farrar, Straus, 1984.
C D C? (word games), Farrar, Straus, 1984.
Solomon the Rusty Nail, Farrar, Straus, 1984.
Brave Irene, Farrar, Straus, 1986.
The Zabajaba Jungle, Farrar, Straus, 1987.
Spinky Sulks, Farrar, Straus, 1988.
Shrek!, Farrar-Straus, 1991.
Doctor De Soto Goes to Africa, HarperCollins, 1992.
Zeke Pippin, HarperCollins, 1994.
Grown-ups Get to Do All the Driving, HarperCollins, 1995.
The Toy Brother, HarperCollins, 1996.
Toby, Where Are You?, illustrated by Teryl Euvremer, HarperCollins, 1997.
Pete's a Pizza, HarperCollins, 1998.
Made for Each Other, HarperCollins, 2000.
Wizzil, illustrated by Quentin Blake, Farrar, Straus, 2000.

ILLUSTRATOR

Will Cuppy, *How to Become Extinct,* Garden City Books, 1941.
Eric Hodgins, *Mr. Blandings Builds His Dream House,* Simon & Schuster, 1947.
Wilhelm Reich, *Listen, Little Man!: A Document from the Archives of the Orgone Institute,* translation by Theodore P. Wolfe, Noonday Press, 1948.
Cuppy, *The Decline and Fall of Practically Everybody,* Holt, 1950.
Phyllis R. Fenner, editor, *Giggle Box: Funny Stories for Boys and Girls,* Knopf, 1950.

Irwin Steig (brother), *Poker for Fun and Profit,* Astor-Honor, 1959.
Jeanne Steig (wife), *Consider the Lemming* (poetry), Farrar, Straus, 1988.
J. Steig, *The Old Testament Made Easy,* Farrar, Straus, 1990.
J. Steig, *Alpha Beta Chowder,* Farrar, Straus, 1992.
J. Steig, *A Handful of Beans: Six Fairy Tales,* HarperCollins, 1998.
Arthur Yorinks, *The Flying Latke,* Simon & Schuster, 1999.

CARTOONS

Man about Town, Long & Smith, 1932.
About People: A Book of Symbolical Drawings, Random House, 1939.
The Lonely Ones, preface by Wolcott Gibbs, Duell, Sloan, 1942.
All Embarrassed, Duell, Sloan, 1944.
Small Fry (*New Yorker* cartoons), Duell, Sloan, 1944.
Persistent Faces, Duell, Sloan, 1945.
Till Death Do Us Part: Some Ballet Notes on Marriage, Duell, Sloan, 1947.
The Agony in the Kindergarten, Duell, Sloan, 1950.
The Rejected Lovers, Knopf, 1951.
The Steig Album: Seven Complete Books, Duell, Sloan, 1953.
Dreams of Glory, and Other Drawings, Knopf, 1953.
Continuous Performances, Duell, Sloan & Pearce, 1963.
Male/Female, Farrar, Straus, 1971.
William Steig: Drawings (*New Yorker* cartoons), Farrar, Straus, 1979.
Ruminations, Farrar, Straus, 1984.
Our Miserable Life, Farrar, Straus, 1990.
Strutters and Fretters, or, The Inescapable Self, HarperCollins, 1992.
Collected Drawings, Moyer Bell, 1994.

Steig has contributed cartoons to periodicals, including *Collier's, Judge, Life,* and *Vanity Fair.* Steig's manuscripts are included in the Kerlan Collection at the University of Minnesota, Minneapolis.

Adaptations

Many of Steig's children's books have been adapted for film, including: *Doctor De Soto,* Weston Woods, 1985; *The Amazing Bone,* Weston Woods, 1985; *Abel's Island,* Lucerne Media, 1988; *Brave Irene,* Weston Woods, 1989. Steig's books have also been adapted as filmstrips: *Amos and Boris* (narrated by Steig), Miller-Brody, 1975; *Farmer Palmer's Wagon Ride,* Miller-Brody, 1976; *Brave Irene,* Weston Woods, 1988. *Doctor De Soto and Other Stories* was adapted for read-along cassette, Caedmon, 1985; *Shrek!* was adapted for audiocassette by Live Oak Media and a computer-animated film.

Sidelights

Called the "King of Cartoons" by *Newsweek,* William Steig has carved out dual careers as both a highly respected and entertaining cartoonist and an award-winning, best-selling author of children's picture books and novels. Illustrating for the *New Yorker* since 1930, Steig has produced more than sixteen-hundred drawings as well as one-hundred-seventeen covers for that publication. His cartooning work is collected in more than a dozen books. Beginning in 1968, at the age when others are contemplating retirement, the then sixty-one-year-old Steig launched a career in children's books, bringing to that medium the same tongue-in-cheek and sometimes gallows humor that has made his adult work so popular. With his third title, *Sylvester and the Magic Pebble,* he captured the prestigious Caldecott Medal. Many critics, including Roger Angell writing an appreciation of his colleague in the *New Yorker,* consider this to be "still his masterpiece." His first venture into children's novels, the 1972 *Dominic,* won for Steig the coveted Christopher Award. Other award winners followed: the Newbery Honor Books *Abel's Island* and *Doctor De Soto,* as well as such popular picture books as *Farmer Palmer's Wagon Ride, The Amazing Bone, Yellow and Pink, Brave Irene,* and *Spinky Sulks.* Steig's book sales worldwide approach two million.

In semi-retirement since the 1990s, the prolific Steig continues to turn out winning titles even in his own tenth decade of life. Picture books such as *Shrek!, Zeke Pippin, Grown-ups Get to Do All the Driving, The Toy Brother,* and *Toby, Where Are You?,* attest to the longevity of Steig's illustrative line and wit. Additionally, he continues to illustrate the work of others, including that of his artist wife, Jean, all of which demonstrate that humor truly is for Steig a fountain of youth. Joshua Hammer described Steig in *People* as "an idiosyncratic innocent in a never-never land of his own making, waging a private war against the craziness of modern life with the pen of a master and the eye of a child." Steig's humane and insightful books are so popular with children simply because kids immediately respond to the author's vision, which is as enthusiastic and wide-eyed as their own.

Steig was born in Brooklyn, New York, on November 14, 1907, and spent his childhood in the Bronx. His father, an Austrian immigrant and a house painter by trade, dabbled in fine arts in his spare time, as did his mother. As a child, Steig was inspired by his creative surroundings with an intense interest in painting and was given his first lessons by his older brother, Irwin, who was also a professional artist. In addition to painting, his childhood imagination was captured by the romance of many other creative works that crossed his path: Grimm's fairy tales, Daniel Defoe's *Robinson Crusoe,* Charlie Chaplin movies, Howard Pyle's *Robin Hood,* the legends of King Arthur and the Knights of the Round Table, Englebert Humperdinck's opera *Hansel and Gretel,* and especially Carlo Collodi's *Pinocchio.*

As a young man, Steig found an outlet for his talent by creating cartoons for the high school newspaper. Throughout his youth he also excelled at athletics, and during college he was a member of the All-American Water Polo Team. After high school graduation, Steig spent two years at City College, three years at the National Academy, and five days at the Yale School of

Fine Arts before dropping out. "If I'd had it my way," Steig tells David Allender in *Publishers Weekly,* "I'd have been a professional athlete, a sailor, a beachcomber, or some other form of hobo, a painter, a gardener, a novelist, a banjo-player, a traveler, anything but a rich man. When I was an adolescent, Tahiti was a paradise. I made up my mind to settle there someday. I was going to be a seaman like Melville, but the Great Depression put me to work as a cartoonist to support the family."

"[My] father went broke during the Depression," Steig recalls to *People's* Hammer. "My older brothers were married and my younger brother was seventeen, so the old man said to me, 'It's up to you.' The only thing I could do was draw. Within a year I was selling cartoons to the *New Yorker* and supporting a family." His father's strong, independent values greatly influenced Steig: "My father was a socialist—an advanced thinker—and he felt that business was degrading, but he didn't want his children to be laborers. We were all encouraged to go into music or art." Steig has passed his father's ethic on to his own children by encouraging them never to take nine-to-five jobs, and they have taken his advice to heart: son Jeremy is a jazz flautist, daughter Lucy a painter, and Maggie an actress.

Before Steig started writing children's books, he was well established as a noted cartoonist in the *New Yorker.* During his early days as a free-lance artist, he supplemented his income with work in advertising, although he intensely disliked it. During the 1940s, Steig's creativity found a more agreeable outlet when he began carving figurines in wood; his sculptures are on display as part of the collection in the historic home of Franklin D. Roosevelt in Hyde Park, New York, and in several museums in New England. Steig also claims responsibility for originating the idea of the "contemporary" greeting card, telling Alison Wyrley Birch in the *Hartford Courant:* "Greeting cards used to be all sweetness and love. I started doing the complete reverse—almost a hate card—and it caught on."

Writing books for children was a career Steig began relatively late in life and it came about by chance rather than intention. In 1967, Bob Kraus, a fellow cartoonist at the *New Yorker,* was in the process of organizing Windmill Books, an imprint for Harper & Row. Kraus suggested that Steig try writing and illustrating a book for a young audience. The result was Steig's letter-puzzle book entitled *C D B,* published in 1968. *Roland the Minstrel Pig,* published the same year, is the story of a pig who sings and plays the lute for the entertainment of a harmonious assortment of other animals. Roland abandons the security of his community: "He dreamed for days of fame and wealth, and he was no longer satisfied with the life he'd been living." The pig embarks on a romantic quest, discovering loneliness and evil along the road to fame and fortune. He encounters Sebastian the Fox who, true to fox-form, plans to feast on the portly pig. Roland is saved by his own resourcefulness; his singing is heard by the King—a lion—who saves him from the hungry fox and appoints the talented pig court minstrel. In *Pipers at the Gates of Dawn: The*

Wisdom of Children's Literature, Jonathan Cott called *Roland the Minstrel Pig* "a charming but hardly major work" and "Steig's testing ground as a children's book creator."

The process of creating children's books proved a short learning curve for the inventive Steig. With his very next title, *Sylvester and the Magic Pebble,* he joined the ranks of the best, winning the Caldecott Medal. The story of a young donkey who collects pebbles for a hobby, *Sylvester and the Magic Pebble* has been interpreted variously as a metaphor for death and for childish helplessness. Sylvester finds a lovely red pebble one day which allows him to make a wish. On his way home to show his parents, he meets a lion and without thinking wishes he were a rock so that the lion can not hurt him. Thereafter he is trapped inside a stone's body, until one day his parents finally come on a picnic, sit on him and find the magic pebble, and return their donkey son to his true form. Anita Moss, writing in the *St. James Guide to Children's Writers,* commented that this picture book "justly deserves its wide recognition as one of the most distinguished works in contemporary American picture books .... Steig addresses children's fears of separation from their parents, as well as their fears and terrors and even wishes for radical transformations."

"Like Isaac Bashevis Singer, E. B. White, and a select company of others, Steig is a writer of children's books whose work reaches beyond the specific confines of a child audience," noted James E. Higgins in *Children's Literature in Education.* "[He] has the unusual childlike capacity to present incidents of wonder and marvel as if they are but everyday occurrences. He writes not out of a remembrance of childhood, but out of the essence of childhood which no adult can afford to give up or to deny." The power of luck, the capacity of nature for transformation and rebirth, the existence of beneficial magic; all are a part of this "childhood essence" and are ever-present in Steig's books. Wishes, even unspoken ones, are granted in the author's vision of how the world should be. In the Caldecott Honor Book, *The Amazing Bone,* the daydreaming Pearl the Pig dawdles on her walk home from school. "She sat on the ground in the forest, ... and spring was so bright and beautiful, the warm air touched her so tenderly, she could almost feel herself changing into a flower. Her light dress felt like petals. 'I love everything,' she heard herself say." She discovers a magic bone, lost by a witch who "ate snails cooked in garlic at every meal and was always complaining about her rheumatism and asking nosy questions." That the bone talks is not surprising to our heroine, or even to her parent, and is accepted as a matter of course by the reader.

Positive themes reoccur throughout Steig's works: the abundant world of nature, the security of home and family, the importance of friendship, the strength that comes from self-reliance. Many of the animal characters inhabiting Steig's sunlit world also possess "heroic" qualities; quests, whether in the form of a search for a loved one or for adventure's sake alone, are frequently undertaken. Higgins wrote, "In his works for children

... [Steig] sets his lens to capture that which is good in life. He shares with children what can happen to humans when we are at our best."

Steig populates his stories with animals because they give him more latitude in telling his tales and because it amuses children to see animals behaving like people they know. "I think using animals emphasizes the fact that the story is symbolical—about human behavior," Steig told Higgins. "And kids get the idea right away that this is not just a story, but that it's saying something about life on earth." Steig avoids interjecting political or social overtones to make his books "mean" anything. Human concerns over existence, self-discovery, and death are dealt with indirectly. "I feel this way: I have a position—a point of view. But I don't have to think about it to express it. I can write about anything and my point of view will come out. So when I am at work my conscious intention is to tell a story to the reader. All this other stuff takes place automatically."

In 1972, Steig published his first children's novel, *Dominic,* the story of a dog hero. Dominic, a latter-day King Arthur, saves victims from the evil Doomsday Gang, and in between battles plays tunes on his piccolo. Moss declared that "*Dominic* is a beautifully crafted, highly lyrical wish fulfillment fantasy." So enchanted was Steig with the Homeric quest he set Dominic on, that he followed it up a year later with another longer story for children, *The Real Thief,* about a goose called Gawain on an exiled journey. Another long tale is the Newbery Honor Book, *Abel's Island,* in which a rich and idle Edwardian mouse, dressed in a smoking jacket, is stranded on an island after a storm. Here, Robinson Crusoe-like, he must learn to survive; in the process he learns to appreciate all of life, including nature and art.

From **Caleb and Kate,** *written and illustrated by* **William H. Steig.**

Finally, one Sunday in June, when the family was lazing around the living room, Zeke whipped out his harmonica and started regaling them with the prelude to *La Traviata.* "Wow!" said his sister. "Bravo, Zekey!" his mother cried.

Even his father crowed, "Isn't that boy a Pippin."

From **Zeke Pippin,** *written and illustrated by Steig.*

Reunited with his wife, he is a changed mouse. In a *Junior Bookshelf* review of the book, M. Hobbs called *Abel's Island* "a remarkable, I would venture to say a great, book, absorbing on any level but beneath it all, a fable of our times."

Another mouse appears in *Doctor De Soto,* this time as a rather inventive dentist who must stand on a ladder and use a winch for his larger clients. One day, going against his own rules, the good doctor agrees to treat an animal that could prove dangerous to him, a fox in need of relief. But the fox, true to form, can think of only one thing during the dental procedure—how good the kindly doctor might taste. Yet De Soto is no fool: he coats the fox's teeth with glue, preventing any such nonsense. Kate M. Flanagan, writing in *Horn Book,* felt that this Newbery Honor story "goes beyond the usual tale of wit versus might: the story achieves comic heights partly through the delightful irony of the situation."

Caleb and Kate was the first of several books where major characters are portrayed in human form. "Caleb the carpenter and Kate the weaver loved each other, but not every single minute," the book begins. It is a story of the separation, loss, search, and joyful reunion of a married couple who love each other deeply despite their human folly. Joy Anderson writes in *Dictionary of Literary Biography:* "Steig is at his best in *Caleb and Kate,* combining what he has learned about prose and

using all his artistic gifts; the tongue-in-cheek humor that is never beyond the child, eloquent language as well as inventive play, both in language and illustration."

"Steig's themes are rendered in elegant, sometimes self-consciously literary language," Moss wrote in *St. James Guide to Children's Writers.* "The presiding voice in these works is urbane and witty, yet never condescending; rather it invites the young reader to participate in this humorous, sophisticated view of the world." Steig will often pepper his writing with "big words," giving his readers a chance to expand their vocabulary while adding to the verbal patterning of his stories. "And there are the noises!" Steven Kroll of the *New York Times Book Review* commented. "Mr. Steig knows children are just beginning to experience language and love weird sounds. 'Yibbam sibibble!' says the bone in *The Amazing Bone.* 'Jibrakken sibibble digray!' In *Farmer Palmer's Wagon Ride,* the thunder 'dramberambe-roomed. It bomBOMBED!' Beyond the noises, there is a rich, wonderfully rhythmic use of language .... How clear that is in his very first illustrated story, *Roland the Minstrel Pig,* as Roland and the fox walk along with 'Roland dreaming and the fox scheming.'"

Steig explained to Higgins the process by which he begins his stories: "First of all I decide it's time to write a story. Then I say: 'What shall I draw this time? A pig or a mouse?' Or, 'I did a pig last time; I'll make it a mouse this time.' Then I start drawing .... [Usually] I just ramble around and discover for myself what will happen next." Sometimes Steig conjures up a visual image that inspires a story, as with the book *Amos and Boris.* "It was one of the book's last illustrations (the picture of two elephants pushing a whale into the sea) that provided the seed from which the story grew." As noted in *Children's Books and Their Creators,* "Steig's illustrations are instantly recognizable, as he uses a consistent style involving a fairly thick sketchy black line with watercolor added loosely, often including stripes, polka dots, and flowered patterns in his characters' clothing and in the backgrounds."

In *Spinky Sulks,* Steig also uses an all too human character, a young boy who goes into the world's longest funk after being hurt by a parent's stinging words. A green monster, however, is at the center of *Shrek!,* who leaves home in search of an equally repugnant bride. A reviewer for *Horn Book* commented that this "satire is written with Steig's unerring sense of style and illustrated with pleasingly horrid pictures of the lumpy, repulsive Shrek." The 1994 *Zeke Pippin* tells the tale of a harmonica-playing pig who leaves home in a snit after his family falls asleep at one of his performances. Slowly the pig begins to discover that his harmonica is magical, having the ability to put listeners to sleep. Magical music comes to the rescue when he is threatened by dogs and a coyote. Beth Tegart, writing in *School Library Journal,* noted that "this is another whimsical journey into family relationships that focuses on the magical objects and the ingenuity of youth." Tegart concluded that *Zeke Pippin* was a "humorous and heartwarming book." Comparing *Zeke Pippin* favorably to such classic Steig titles as *Sylvester and the Magic Pebble* and *The Amazing Bone,* Ann A. Flowers noted in a *Horn Book* review that "Steig's hand has lost none of its cunning; his trademark illustrations are as bold and funny as ever, and the text gives no quarter to the idea of limited vocabulary." Flowers concluded that *Zeke Pippin* was "[a]nother hit by the master."

A crossover title for Steig was the 1995 *Grown-ups Get to Do All the Driving,* which Steig intended for adults but which his publishers packaged for both adults and children. *The Toy Brother,* on the other hand, is clearly kid-oriented. Yorick is a medieval boy who finds his younger brother Charles "a first-rate pain in the pants." When his alchemist parents leave for a trip, Yorick fools around in their laboratory only to turn himself into a miniature boy. Charles loves the role reversal, until Yorick is finally restored to full size. *Booklist's* Susan Dove Lempke remarked that "Steig embellishes his always rich vocabulary with medieval words to delightful effect and decorates his artwork with rich hues and

purple borders." Barbara Kiefer concluded in a *School Library Journal* review of *The Toy Brother* that readers "will delight in Steig's droll expressions, both visual and verbal, but the subtle lesson about brotherly love will not be lost amid the comic goings-on."

Toby, Where Are You? is a 1997 tale of a hiding boy whose parents search throughout the house, pretending not to see him. Illustrated by Teryl Euvremer, the book contains the usual Steig humor in a game of hide-and-seek. *Pete's a Pizza,* a 1998 picture book offering written and illustrated by Steig, presents a sulking soulmate to Spinky, but in this case the depressed youth is cheered up when his father turns him into a pizza. Pete is kneaded and tossed like dough, adorned with checkers instead of tomatoes and thrown into the couch-oven, much to the boy's delight. *Publishers Weekly* remarked that the "amiable quality of Steig's easy pizza recipe will amuse chef and entree alike." Signe Wilkinson declared in the *New York Times Book Review* that "America will

From **The Toy Brother,** *written and illustrated by Steig.*

be a better place if the Steig family pizza party catches on."

America has been, if not a better place, at least a funnier place, for the nearly seventy years of William Steig's cartooning and writing career. As Moss noted, "Steig is quite simply one of America's finest artists. His witty humorous books celebrate the powers of the imagination, art, language, and nature. His comic works are deeply humane and appeal to children and adult critics alike. He has created enduring gifts for the world's children and has reminded all of his readers that laughter helps us to survive."

Steig's recipe? "I enjoyed my childhood," he told Angell in the *New Yorker*. "I think I like kids more than the average man does. I can relax with them, more than I can among adults .... Children are genuine .... I like to think that I've kept a little innocence. Probably I'm too dumb to do anything else."

Works Cited

Allender, David, "William Steig at 80," *Publishers Weekly*, July 24, 1987, pp. 116-18.

Anderson, Joy, "William Steig," *Dictionary of Literary Biography*, Volume 61: *American Writers for Children since 1960: Poets, Illustrators and Nonfiction Authors*, Gale, 1987, pp. 297-305.

From **The Amazing Bone,** *written and illustrated by Steig.*

Angell, Roger, "The Minstrel Steig," *New Yorker*, February 20, 1995, pp. 252-61.

Birch, Alison Wyrley, "Our Foibles in Simple Lines," *Hartford Courant*, September 8, 1974.

Children's Books and Their Creators, edited by Anita Silvey, Houghton, 1995, pp. 626-27.

Cott, Jonathan, "William Steig and His Path," *Pipers at the Gates of Dawn: The Wisdom of Children's Literature*, Random House, 1983, pp. 87-136.

Flanagan, Kate M., review of *Doctor De Soto*, *Horn Book*, March-April, 1983, p. 162.

Flowers, Ann A., review of *Zeke Pippin*, *Horn Book*, January-February, 1995, p. 55.

Hammer, Joshua, "William Steig," *People*, December 3, 1984, pp. 87-98.

Higgins, James E., "William Steig: Champion for Romance," *Children's Literature in Education*, spring, 1978, pp. 3-16.

Hobbs, M., review of *Abel's Island*, *Junior Bookshelf*, February, 1978, pp. 49-50.

Jones, Malcolm, Jr., "The King of Cartoons," *Newsweek*, May 15, 1995, pp. 60-63.

Kiefer, Barbara, review of *The Toy Brother*, *School Library Journal*, February, 1996, p. 90.

Kroll, Steven, "Steig: Nobody Is Grown-Up," *New York Times Book Review*, June 28, 1987, p. 26.

Lempke, Susan Dove, review of *The Toy Brother*, *Booklist*, February 15, 1996, p. 1027.

Moss, Anita, "Steig, William," *St. James Guide to Children's Writers*, edited by Sara Pendergast and Tom Pendergast, St. James Press, 1999, pp. 1004-06.

Review of *Pete's a Pizza*, *Publishers Weekly*, July 6, 1998, p. 58.

Review of *Shrek!*, *Horn Book*, January-February, 1991, p. 60.

Steig, William, *Roland the Minstrel Pig*, Windmill Books, 1968.

Steig, William, *The Amazing Bone*, Farrar, Straus, 1976.

Steig, William, *Caleb and Kate*, Farrar, Straus, 1977.

Steig, William, *The Toy Brother*, HarperCollins, 1996.

Tegart, Beth, review of *Zeke Pippin*, *School Library Journal*, December, 1994, p. 87.

Wilkinson, Signe, "Some Pepperoni on Your Little Boy?," *New York Times Book Review*, November 15, 1998.

For More Information See

BOOKS

Children's Literature Review, Volume 15, Gale, 1988.

de Montreville, Doris, and Donna Hill, *Third Book of Junior Authors*, H. W. Wilson, 1972.

Fisher, Margery, *Who's Who in Children's Books: A Treasury of the Familiar Characters of Childhood*, Holt, 1975.

Kingman, Lee, editor, *Newbery and Caldecott Medal Books: 1966-1975*, Horn Book, 1975.

Lanes, Selma G., *Down the Rabbit Hole: Adventures and Misadventures in the Realm of Children's Literature*, Atheneum, 1971.

Lorenz, Lee, *The World of William Steig*, with an introduction by John Updike, Artisan, 1998.

From **Pete's a Pizza,** *written and illustrated by Steig.*

Townsend, John Rowe, *Written for Children: An Outline of English-Language Children's Literature,* revised edition, Lippincott, 1974.

PERIODICALS

Booklist, November 1, 1994, p. 510; April 1, 1995, p. 1393; December 15, 1996, p. 734; October 1, 1998, p. 323.
Bulletin of the Center for Children's Books, December, 1994, p, 146; May, 1995, p. 323; February, 1996, pp. 205-06.
Horn Book, September-October, 1998, pp. 602-03; January-February, 1999, pp. 76-77.

Kirkus Reviews, November 15, 1994, p. 1544; May 1, 1995, p. 640; January 1, 1997, p. 66; September 15, 1998, p. 1390.
Publishers Weekly, February 20, 1995, p. 204; January 15, 1996, p. 461; December 2, 1996, p. 59.
School Library Journal, May, 1995, p. 96; December, 1998, p. 116; January, 1999, p. 70.*

—Sketch by J. Sydney Jones

STEVENS, Peter
See GEIS, Darlene (Stern)

*   *   *

STEWART, Melissa 1968-

Personal

Born December 9, 1968, in Hartford, CT; daughter of Bruce (a mechanical engineer) and Dorothy (a laboratory supervisor; maiden name, Jayes) Stewart. *Education:* Union College, Schenectady, NY, B.S. (cum laude), 1990; New York University, M.A., 1991; Attended University of Bath, 1998.

Addresses

Home—38 Padanaram Ave., No. A10, Danbury, CT 06811.

Career

Healthmark Medical Education Media, New York City, associate editor, 1991; Foca Co., New York City, project editor, 1992-93, senior editor, 1993-95; Grolier Publishing Co., Danbury, CT, science editor, 1995-97, senior science editor, 1997—; freelance writer, 1991—. *Member:* American Association for the Advancement of Science, Sigma Xi.

Writings

Science in Ancient India, F. Watts (Danbury, CT), 1999.
Life without Light: A Journey to Earth's Dark Ecosystems, F. Watts, 1999.

Contributor to the books *Blueprint for Life, Secrets of the Inner Mind,* Time-Life (Alexandria, VA); *Biology: Visualizing Life,* Holt (New York City); and *Biology,* Addison-Wesley (Reading, MA). Contributor of articles and columns to magazines and newspapers, including *Science World, Family Planning Perspectives, Her New York, New York Doctor, Washington Square News,* and *New York Daily News.*

Work in Progress

Birds, Fishes, Mammals, Insects, Amphibians, Reptiles, completion expected in 2001.

Sidelights

In the "About the Author" section of her first book, Stewart relates a story about walking in the New England woods with her father. Having been asked if she noticed anything different about the trees in that particular part of the woods, Stewart said she noticed that the trees were smaller. Her father told her that there had been a fire approximately twenty-five years earlier, and that all the trees were new growth.

"I was hooked," Stewart stated. "Ever since that moment, I have wanted to know everything about the natural world." Of her career choices, Stewart said, "I chose this path because I didn't want to limit myself. I didn't want to spend my entire life doing research in just one area. Now I get paid to learn everything I can about every area of science."

Works Cited

Stewart, Melissa, *Life without Light,* Franklin Watts, 1999, p. 128.

For More Information See

PERIODICALS
School Library Journal, June, 1999, p. 154.

*   *   *

STROMOSKI, Rick 1958-

Personal

Born December 25, 1958, in New Jersey; son of Charles (a chiropractor) and Patricia (a homemaker; maiden name, Thomas) Stromoski; married Danna Gauntner (a buyer), November 21, 1987; children: Molly. *Education:* Attended high school in Edison, NJ. *Politics:* Independent Democrat. *Religion:* Christian.

Addresses

Home—569 North Main St., Suffield, CT 06078. *Electronic mail*—rstromoski@aol.com.

Career

Freelance humorous illustrator and cartoonist, Suffield, CT, 1983-. *Member:* National Cartoonists Society (member of board of directors, 1997-; first vice-president), Graphic Artists Guild.

Awards, Honors

Four Louie Awards, Greeting Card Association, between 1995 and 1998; Reuben Division Award, National Cartoonists Society, 1996, for greeting cards.

Writings

40 Happens, Trisar, 1994.
50 Happens, Trisar, 1994.
Middle Ager—Crabby, Flabby, Gabby, Trisar, 1994.
The Official Old Geezer Humor Book, Trisar, 1994.
Old Babe, Trisar, 1994.
Old Dude, Trisar, 1994.
Bad Cats: A Collection of Feline Pranks and Practical Jokes, Contemporary Books (Chicago, IL), 1995.
Bad Dogs: A Collection of Canine Pranks and Practical Jokes, Contemporary Books, 1995.
Guidebook to Fishing, Trisar, 1995.
Madame Wrinkleski Predicts, Trisar, 1995.

From **Bad Cats,** *written and illustrated by Rick* **Stromoski.**

ILLUSTRATOR

Kathryn Boesel Dunn and Allison Boesel Dunn, *Trouble with School: A Family Story about Learning Disabilities,* Woodbine House (Rockville, MD), 1993.

Katy Hall, *Really, Really Bad Sports Jones,* Candlewick Press (Cambridge, MA), 1998.

Cynthia Cappetta, *Chairs, Chairs, Chairs!,* Children's Press (Danbury, CT), 1999.

Mildred D. Johnson, *Wait, Skates!,* Children's Press, 1999.

Work in Progress

Illustrating two reading books, *Hands* and *Feet,* by Dana Meachen Rau, publication by Children's Press expected in 2000; and *Get a Clue,* Golden Books.

Sidelights

Rick Stromoski told *SATA:* "Born on Christmas day in 1958, I am the seventh in a family of twelve children. Originally from Edison, New Jersey, I traveled west and lived for ten years in the Los Angeles area. My wife Danna and I moved back east to Connecticut in 1989 and have been New Englanders ever since. We live with our daughter, Molly, our dog, Odin, and our cat, Crusty, in the historic district of Suffield, Connecticut.

"Growing up in such a large family has given me a sense of humor that I have expressed through drawing ever since I could pick up a pencil. I am a self-taught cartoonist and humorous illustrator. My work has appeared in national magazines, children's books, newspapers, licensing and national advertising, and network television. I have illustrated greeting cards for such companies as Recycled Paper Greetings, Paramount

Cards, Renaissance Greetings, Marcel Schurman, and West Graphics."*

* * *

SYMONS, Stuart
See STANLEY, George Edward

* * *

TUSA, Tricia 1960-

Personal

Surname is pronounced "*too*-sa"; born July 19, 1960, in Houston, TX; daughter of Theodore S., Jr., and Francese (Moran) Tusa. *Education:* Attended University of California, Santa Cruz, 1978; studied art in Paris, 1981; University of Texas at Austin, B.F.A., 1982; New York University, M.A., 1989. *Hobbies and other interests:* Horseback riding, oil painting, reading.

Addresses

Home—1357 Santa Rosa, Santa Fe, NM 87501. *Office*—c/o Farrar, Straus & Giroux, Inc., 19 Union Square W., New York, NY 10003.

Career

Author and illustrator of children's books. Art therapist with learning-disabled and emotionally disturbed children, Acquired Immune Deficiency Syndrome (AIDS) patients, and psychiatric-care patients at various institutions, including Mount Sinai Hospital, New York City, 1988, Kingsboro Hospital, Brooklyn, NY, 1988, and Reece School, New York City, 1989. Art instructor at numerous institutions, including Houston Retarded Center, Houston, TX, 1980, Children's Museum, Houston, 1984, and Post Oak Montessori School, Houston, 1989-90. Designer and illustrator for Estee Lauder, 1982, DC Comics, 1983, and Cooper Hewitt Museum. Head chef at soup kitchen in Santa Fe, NM. *Member:* American Art Therapy Association, Southwest Writers.

Awards, Honors

Children's Choice, International Reading Association/ Children's Book Council, 1986, for *Miranda;* Pick of the List, American Booksellers, 1987, for *Maebelle's Suitcase; Miranda, Maebelle's Suitcase,* and *Stay Away from the Junkyard!* were chosen as *Reading Rainbow* selections, 1989.

Writings

AUTHOR AND ILLUSTRATOR

Libby's New Glasses, Holiday House, 1984.
Miranda, Macmillan, 1985.
Chicken, Macmillan, 1986.
Maebelle's Suitcase, Macmillan, 1987.
Stay Away from the Junkyard!, Macmillan, 1988.

Sherman and Pearl, Macmillan, 1989.
Camilla's New Hairdo, Farrar, Straus, 1991.
The Family Reunion, Farrar, Straus, 1993.
Sisters, Crown, 1995.
Bunnies in My Head, afterword by Barbara Bush, University of Texas, 1998.

ILLUSTRATOR

Steven Kroll, *Loose Tooth,* Holiday House, 1984.
Angela Shelf Medaris, *We Eat Dinner in the Bathtub,* State House Press (Austin, TX), 1990.
William H. Hooks, *Lo-Jack and the Pirates,* Bantam, 1991.
Stuart J. Murphy, *Lemonade for Sale,* HarperCollins, 1998.
Susan Bartlett Weber, *Seal Island School,* Viking, 1999.

Contributor of illustrations to children's magazines.

Work in Progress

"Carefully studying my family, friends, and cousins! Their quirks, mannerisms, shoes, hairdos...."

Sidelights

Picture-book author and illustrator Tricia Tusa brings an off-beat, humorous slant to the stories she enlivens with her colorful artwork. In addition to illustrating texts by authors such as Steven Kroll and Stuart J. Murphy, Tusa has also authored several books of her own, which she fills with her unique illustrations. Describing Tusa's watercolor work for her 1995 storybook, *Sisters, School Library Journal* contributor Tana Elias noted of the author/artist that her "sly illustrations perfectly capture small details, such as expressions of shock and annoyance on the faces of the characters," resulting in a book that youngsters would "delight in." Other titles both written and illustrated by Tusa include *The Family Reunion, Bunnies in My Head,* and the award-winning *Miranda.*

Born in 1960, Tusa attended the University of California, continuing her art training in Paris and earning a master's degree in art therapy from New York University in 1989. Her first illustration projects were Stephen Kroll's *Loose Tooth* and her own *Libby's New Glasses,* both published in 1984. *Libby's New Glasses* expresses the discomfort children often feel upon donning their first pair of eyeglasses. While a *Bulletin of the Center for Children's Books* reviewer noted that the text was weak, praise was given to Tusa's artwork as possessing "vigor, humor, and scrabbly details." Responding to the story about a young girl with new glasses who meets a beautiful ostrich, only to discover that the reason his head is buried in the sand is that he, too, sports the hated eyewear, a *Publishers Weekly* contributor called *Libby's New Glasses* "a fanciful tale that will hearten children as much as it amuses them."

Tusa once told *SATA* of how she finds the inspiration for her artwork: "I study people's faces down the aisles at the grocery store, at the laundromat. I eavesdrop at the hardware store. One unusual face or some innocuous comment from a stranger can spark or complete an

From **Maebelle's Suitcase,** *written and illustrated by Tricia Tusa.*

idea." Indeed, several of her books depict very unusual faces, attached to rather eccentric characters. In *Maebelle's Suitcase,* an elderly woman who loves birds makes her own home in a tree so that she can look out on her feathered friends while she plies her trade as a hat-maker. Her creativity helps to solve a problem for her friend Binkle, whose plans to fly south for the winter have been stalled until he can find a way to transport his belongings. Maebelle works Binkle's tiny possessions—small rocks, dirt, some flowers, leaves, and a lovely forked branch—into a hat that is put on permanent display in town over the winter, allowing Binkle to take flight unencumbered, knowing his things will be under lock and key. *Booklist's* Denise M. Wilms praised Tusa's use of charcoal and watercolor, noting that the artwork creates "a feeling of spaciousness that suits the story's mood and concept." And in *School Library Journal,* Helen E. Williams concluded of *Maebelle's Suitcase:* "Text and illustrations are harmonious and wonderfully complementary in this quiet but humorous book."

Eccentric characters are also the focal point of 1993's *The Family Reunion,* as the Beneada family converges on a quiet house in the suburbs, food and drink in hand, only to discover that two of the people assembled are strangers to everyone present. Indeed, the Beneadas try to place Esther and Fester, who arrive on time but seem strangely uncomfortable amid the genial gathering. Finally it is discovered that the Beneadas have met at the wrong house—Esther and Fester are the home's owners, and the party is taking place across the street. "The dazzling visual humor will have young readers rolling on the floor while acknowledging the common problem of not remembering who someone is," maintained *Booklist* contributor Deborah Abbott, while a critic for *Kirkus Reviews* called *The Family Reunion* "pure comedy—especially Tusa's wonderfully pointed cartoon caricatures of family types in full, over ebullient swing."

In contrast to her growing cast of humorous eccentrics, several of Tusa's picture books highlight young people's discovery of their own creativity, whether it be through drawing or some other form. In 1985's *Miranda,* a young pianist has been fed a daily dose of Mozart, Bartok, and Hayden by her supportive parents and piano teacher. But when she hears a street musician playing boogie-woogie music, she realizes that her piano is capable of entirely different sounds. However, she is met with so much resistance by well-meaning adults that she boycotts the piano altogether. Finally, a solution is found: Miranda can play both kinds of music. Tusa has created a "spirited story" through what reviewer Clarissa Erwin characterized in *School Library Journal* as "scratchy comical drawings ... that capture a wild Miranda who just has to cut loose." And in *Bunnies in My Head,* a young artist is struck with an equally powerful muse, filling every part of her life with artwork. In addition to reflecting the exuberance of a creative child, this book has a special significance for Tusa: it is filled with miniature versions of drawings by young patients at Houston's M. D. Anderson Cancer Center where Tusa has worked as an art therapist. Noting that Tusa's framing illustrations successfully enhance the children's art, *School Library Journal* contributor Christine A. Moesch added that "some of the

pictures ... are charming preschool efforts, while others ... are astounding in their maturity and beauty." Former First Lady Barbara Bush contributed an afterword to the book, which was published in 1998.

"I think I do what I do because I am endlessly fascinated by children—how they think and feel, what delights them, what scares them, how they wonder about things," Tusa once told *SATA.* "I often wonder if children aren't here as complex gifts for us to learn from. I admire their uncanny ability to cut to the truth. They can often be the most honest reflection you may have around of yourself.

"I am also aware of and am concerned about children's vulnerability. There are so many outside influences interfering with the child doing what comes so very naturally—discovering and developing into and becoming who they are. Quite unconsciously, my books seem to repeatedly reflect this idea of becoming who you are—and that it's okay to be different. Also, my books are embarrassingly autobiographical. Again, quite unconsciously, they inevitably reflect whatever feelings, issues, struggles I am dealing with at the time. And, strangely enough, they are usually the same issues I wondered about as a child—yet, now with older eyes and ears."

Works Cited

Abbott, Deborah, review of *The Family Reunion, Booklist,* January 15, 1994, p. 941.

Elias, Tana, review of *Sisters, School Library Journal,* January, 1996, p. 97.

Erwin, Clarissa, review of *Miranda, School Library Journal,* September, 1985, p. 127.

Review of *The Family Reunion, Kirkus Reviews,* November 15, 1993, p. 1469.

From **The Family Reunion,** *written and illustrated by Tusa.*

Review of *Libby's New Glasses, Bulletin of the Center for Children's Books,* November, 1984, p. 57.

Review of *Libby's New Glasses, Publishers Weekly,* July 20, 1984, p. 82.

Moesch, Christine A., review of *Bunnies in My Head, School Library Journal,* February, 1999, p. 90.

Williams, Helen E., review of *Maebelle's Suitcase, School Library Journal,* June-July, 1987, p. 91.

Wilms, Denise M., review of *Maebelle's Suitcase, Booklist,* April 1, 1987, pp. 1210-11.

For More Information See

PERIODICALS

Booklist, September 1, 1991, p. 64; March 1, 1998, p. 1142; February 1, 1999, p. 983.

Kirkus Reviews, October 15, 1995, p. 1503.

Publishers Weekly, 25, 1993, p. 61; February 22, 1999, p. 95.

School Library Journal, December, 1991, p. 107; November, 1993, p. 95; May, 1998, p. 122.

V–W

VAN LAWICK-GOODALL, Jane
See GOODALL, Jane

*   *   *

WATTS, Irene N(aemi)

Personal

Immigrated to Canada from the United Kingdom in 1968. *Education:* University College, Cardiff, Wales, B.A. in History (with honors), 1953.

Addresses

Agent—Playwrights Union Canada, Toronto, Ontario, Canada.

Career

Citadel of Wheels and Wings, Citadel Theatre, Edmonton, Alberta, Canada, artistic director, 1969-1975; freelance director and theatre instructor, 1970—, including Stratford Festival, Ontario, Neptune Theatre, Halifax, Nova Scotia, and Carousel Theatre, Vancouver, British Columbia. Her plays for children have been produced across Canada and the United States. *Member:* Writers Union of Canada, Canadian Actors Equity, Playwrights Union of Canada, Canadian Society of Authors, Illustrators, and Performers.

Awards, Honors

Achievement Award for Drama from the Province of Alberta, 1976, for drama; Playwright Award from the Pacific Northwest Writers, 1986, for "A Small Adventure." Shortlist, Ruth Schwartz Children's Book Award, Ontario Arts Council, 1998, for *The Fish Princess;* Geoffrey Bilson Award for Historical Fiction for Young People, 1998, Toronto Jewish Book Award, 1999, and regional winner, Ontario Silver Birch Award, 1999, all for her novel *Good-bye Marianne.*

Writings

PLAYS FOR CHILDREN

A Chain of Words: A Play, Talonbooks, 1978.
A Blizzard Leaves No Footprints: Listen to the Drum: Patches: The Rainstone: Four Children's Plays, Playwrights Co-op, 1978.
Martha's Magic: A Play, Playwrights Canada, 1981.
Tales from Tolstoy; Once Upon a Time; The Taming of the Wild Things: Three Children's Plays, Playwrights Canada, 1982.
Season of the Witch, Playwrights Canada, 1986.
(Adapter with Tom Kerr) *A Christmas Carol,* Playwrights Canada, 1986.
(Adapter) Robert Munsch, *The Paperback Princess and Other Stories,* Playwrights Canada, 1986.
Just a Minute: Ten Short Plays and Activities for Your Classroom: With Rehearsal Strategies to Accompany Multicultural Stories from Around the World, Heinemann, 1990.
Goodbye Marianne, Scirocco Drama and Anchorage Press, 1994.
This Pet's Allowed, one-act musical with Bruch Kellett, Playwrights Canada, 1998.

Also author and director of scripts, including "Martha's Magic," 1982; "The Rainstone," 1983; and "A Small Adventure," 1986.

OTHER; FOR CHILDREN

(Editor) *Tomorrow Will Be Better: The Writings of British Columbia Schoolchildren,* Playwrights Canada, 1982.
(Compiler) *Beyond Belief: A Collage of the Supernatural,* Playwrights Canada, 1983.
The Great Detective Party and Other Theme Games for Children, Pembroke Publishers, 1989.
Great Theme Parties for Children, Sterling Publishing Company, 1991.
Making Stories, Pembroke Publishers, 1992.
The Fish Princess, illustrated by Steve Mennie, Tundra Books, 1996.

Watts's novel tells the story of eleven-year-old Marianne Kohn, who must say good-bye to her mother forever before she is sent to Britain as part of a children's rescue operation. (Cover illustration by Sari Ginsberg.)

Good-bye Marianne: A Story of Growing Up in Nazi Germany (novel), Tundra Books/McClelland and Stewart, 1998.
Remember Me, Tundra Books/McClelland and Stewart, 2000.

Sidelights

After writing and creating children's theater productions for many years, Watts began writing children's stories, tapping into personal experiences and a love of mythology for subject matter. Her first novel for children, *Good-bye Marianne,* describes what it was like to be a Jewish child in Berlin in 1938.

Eleven-year-old Marianne Kohn's life of school and friends quickly comes to an end as the Nazis impose increasingly harsher restrictions on Jews. Marianne's father has gone into hiding, and Marianne and her mother are forced to live more and more in the shadows. When a space becomes available on one of the *Kindertransports* to England, Marianne's mother insists that Marianne go despite her protestations.

Booklist commentator Hazel Rochman maintained that *Good-bye Marianne* successfully portrays "the racist persecution that drove parents to send their children away to safety," concluding: "The mother is idealized, but her heartbreaking letter to Marianne [is] as unforgettable as their anguished parting." *Quill & Quire* reviewer Maureen Garvie declared: "Watts's book sets out to do something important, and it succeeds because it leaves readers wanting urgently to know what happened next." Watts was honored with the Geoffrey Bilson Award for Historical Fiction for Young People in 1998 and a Toronto Jewish Book Award in 1999 for *Good-bye Marianne.*

Watts collaborated with illustrator Steve Mennie to produce her first picture book, *The Fish Princess.* In this "folk tale with Selkie echoes," as described by Jane Doonan in *School Librarian,* an old fisherman rescues an infant from an abandoned rowboat and raises her as his granddaughter. Emotionally attached to both the sea and the old man, the young girl is depicted as a lonely, romantic figure, isolated from superstitious village neighbors, who accuse her of bringing them bad luck. When the old fisherman dies, the girl buries him on the beach, where a giant salmon appears. Earlier, the girl had freed the salmon from the nets of the village fishermen; now, the salmon is killed at its own behest, subsequently turning into a handsome young man who takes the girl back to the sea. "This original folktale," noted *School Library Journal* contributor Susan Hepler, "is well served by the muted and foreboding artwork; misty colors and a lack of greenery focus attention on the vast sea and those who live by its shores." Similarly, *Horn Book Guide* contributor Cyrisse Jaffee declared: "This original folktale is enhanced by muted illustrations and lyrical language." *The Fish Princess* was shortlisted for the Ontario Arts Council's Ruth Schwartz Children's Book Award.

Works Cited

Doonan, Jane, review of *The Fish Princess, School Librarian,* August, 1997, p. 148.
Garvie, Maureen, review of *Good-bye Marianne, Quill & Quire,* April, 1998, p. 34.
Hepler, Susan, review of *The Fish Princess, School Library Journal,* March, 1997, pp. 168-69.
Jaffee, Cyrisse, review of *The Fish Princess, Horn Book Guide,* spring, 1997, p. 53.
Rochman, Hazel, review of *Good-bye Marianne, Booklist,* August, 1998, p. 2009.

For More Information See

BOOKS

Directory of Canadian Plays and Playwrights, edited by Jane Cunningham, Playwrights Canada, 1981.

PERIODICALS

Books in Canada, February, 1997, p. 32.
Bulletin of the Center for Children's Books, July, 1998, p. 416.
Children's Bookwatch, December, 1996, p. 3.

School Library Journal, August, 1998, p. 168.

* * *

WEIR, Diana (R.) Loiewski 1958-

Personal

Born April 15, 1958, in Norwalk, CT; daughter of Frank and Rose Loiewski; married Mark Weir (an engineer), August 23, 1981; children: Lauren, Jacqueline, Catherine. *Education:* Southern Connecticut State University, B.S., 1980, M.Ed., 1999. *Politics:* "No affiliations." *Religion:* Roman Catholic.

Addresses

Home—17 Tubbs Spring Dr., Weston, CT 06883. *Electronic mail*—westonriew@worldnet.att.net.

Career

Schoolteacher. Lecturer on educational and nature topics; guest on television programs, including *Fox's Pet News.* Southern Connecticut Library Council for Lecturers. *Member:* Society of Children's Book Writers and Illustrators.

Awards, Honors

First place awards, Medill School of Journalism, Northwestern University, 1996 and 1998, for a nature column.

Writings

Fish Farming, Creative Education (Mankato, MN), 1999.
Factories, Creative Education, 1999.
Tree Frogs, Creative Education, 1999.

Author of a monthly nature column for a parenting magazine.

Work in Progress

A book that teaches the writing process; a book on the calls that frogs make.

Sidelights

Diana Loiewski Weir told *SATA:* "The writing craft for my column is tied to the seasons, and it answers common questions that people rarely consider. The column typically looks no further than my own back yard for topics, and they are about the experiences that I have shared with my very own children.

"The writing style for my books has been informative and factual. I am currently working on weaving more story and description into nonfiction writing to help it come alive!

"I dive into a topic with my entire soul. I usually begin with the live animal and a significant amount of research

Diana Loiewski Weir

before drafting. My first writing was on frogs in 1980. I wrote a series about a fantasy town that was run by a bumpy-grumbly old toad and a lively young pond frog. As part of my research, I purchased some toads and frogs from a local pet shop to learn more about their behaviors. Since then, my animal collection has grown considerably. I now have a collection of live frogs from all around the world, and I find the calls of amphibians make spring and summer evenings magical.

"My strategies for writing usually begin with original research. This past spring, I was writing about the life cycles of insects, and my kitchen was turned into a caterpillar farm. Only after raising and studying the tent caterpillars did I write about them.

"I love to write; I enjoy the process of gathering ideas and putting my thoughts into prose, which I hope others will find interesting."

* * *

WINFIELD, Julia,
See, ARMSTRONG, Jennifer

Autobiography Feature

Elizabeth Winthrop

1948-

I was born and brought up in Washington, D.C., but I trace my roots back to New England on my father's side and England on my mother's.

My father grew up in Avon, Connecticut. His father was a dairy and shade tobacco farmer. I remember my grandfather had a kind face with a mischievous look about his fierce blue eyes. Once he walked me down to the barn to see his herd of prize Ayrshire cows. "Grandfather, which one gives chocolate milk?" I asked, and he led me solemnly to the end of the row and pointed to a big brown-and-white milker. "This one," he said, and we stood and admired it in reverent silence. That's my only clear memory of my grandfather. He died when I was six.

My father's mother was Theodore Roosevelt's niece. She came from a big noisy family and was brought up in the high society of New York City during the turn of the century. She married my grandfather in 1909 and moved up to his farm, which must have seemed very primitive to her in those days. But Grandmother was an energetic optimist and, like all Roosevelt women, a political activist. Soon she wormed her way into the hearts of the granite-faced New England farmers. They twice voted her into the Connecticut State Legislature, which was a remarkable thing for the time, but as she pointed out to me years later, they much rather would have voted for a woman than a Democrat.

My father was very sickly as a child. He had asthma (which I inherited) and eczema and a nurse named Agnes Guthrie who, according to the other three children in the family, spoiled Daddy terribly. The tale is told that when he was six, he spent most of his time wrapped in Vaseline and gauze and laid out like a mummy on the tin-topped kitchen table. Aggie figured out that both the Vaseline and the company in the kitchen kept him from scratching. Years later, when my father went to England to fight in the Second World War, he wrote to Aggie almost as often as to his parents. In some ways, because Aggie spoiled him so terribly, he didn't really grow up until he went to war.

My father met my mother in England during the war. He was twenty-eight years old, and she was only sixteen. But my father noticed right away that my mother had an efficient, calm way about her and that she seemed years older than her actual age, perhaps because she had already seen a lot of war. She grew up in Gibraltar, and at the age of ten, she watched the opening battle of the Spanish Civil War from the roof of her grandparents' house. Four years later, she and her mother and her brother were evacuated from Gibraltar along with the other English women and children on two troop ships. They were told they were being sent to Southampton because the harbor there had not been mined, but to their horror, the ship in front of theirs blew up. Ever so carefully, the captain of their vessel reversed his engines and backed away. He steered a course for London up along the Cliffs of Dover. My mother remembers hanging over the side watching hundreds of boats crossing their bow. Big boats and little ones, fishing boats and trawlers, sailboats and destroyers. It wasn't until they landed in London that she found out she'd been witnessing the evacuation from Dunkirk.

So by the time my father met her, my mother had already lived through far more war than he had ever known. She was working as a code breaker for the British Admiralty, her only brother had been killed in North Africa at the age of twenty, and she had survived months of air raids in London. No wonder she seemed calm to him. With bombs dropping all around them and the sense that the world might never be the same again, theirs was a romance out of the storybooks.

They married just before he parachuted into France in June of 1944, and by December of that same year, she was crossing the Atlantic Ocean in another troop ship, pregnant with my oldest brother and headed for a new country and a new life.

I was born in Washington, D.C., when my mother was only twenty-three years old. I was the third child and the first—and as it turned out, only—girl. We lived then in a tiny house in Georgetown with one big front bedroom where my two older brothers and I slept in bunk beds. I remember the bay windows of that room and the cries of the children from the street in the summertime because my strict English mother put us to bed long before anyone else in the neighborhood. We moved from that house when I was only six because yet another brother had been born and the only place left to fit his bassinet was in the closet. My first picture book, *Bunk Beds,* came from those first and earliest memories. A child in a Texas school once asked me how I remembered everything I wanted to write about. I told him, you don't have to hold on to your memories. When you are ready to use them, they will come back.

Elizabeth Winthrop

There are many reasons that I turned out to be a writer. First of all, my father was one. He was a journalist. We lived in Washington, D.C., and he reported on the presidents and the Congress. Twice a year, he traveled abroad and reported on political situations around the world.

One afternoon, I came home from school to find John Glenn sitting in my living room. He had just completed his orbit of the earth, and my father was interviewing him for an article for the *Saturday Evening Post*. Daddy told me to come in and shake hands. Mr. Glenn was a polite man: he stood for a thirteen-year-old girl. His handshake was firm, his eyes steady, his voice low. I went to school the next day and offered my hand to various friends as the hand that had touched the hand that had been around the world three times. They were singularly unimpressed. In Washington, D.C., children are hard to impress.

My clearest memory of my father working is the distant pounding of typewriter keys, which was the first sound I heard when I opened the kitchen door after a day at school. My father used an old Underwood typewriter, and he was a "hunt and peck" typist. To the ears of a child, the unevenness of his stroke made what was actually a very sedentary job sound dangerous and indispensable through that closed study door. In my imagination, he was the classic reporter in a film noir movie, always rushing against a deadline, typing with the equivalent of a loaded gun at his temple—and if his words were good enough, they might be able to save the world.

My father and Uncle Joe, his writing partner for twelve years, mixed their entertaining with their interviewing. On party nights, one or another of my five brothers would huddle with me at the top of the stairs and peer through the banister rail as the people came through the front door, touching cheeks and shedding coats and dropping ice into glasses. Often we were called into the living room to shake hands all around, but it wasn't long before the grown-ups turned back to their conversations and we could take up our posts again on the stairs to wait for the procession into the dining room. Like the women's exotic perfume and the ever-present cloud of smoke, words like Oppenheimer, Suez, missile gap, U-2, balance of power, and Bay of Pigs hung in the air. Most of the people who came in and out of our house on a regular basis worked for the government, many of them specifically for the CIA. They were "spooks," although I didn't know that then. Because, in Washington, information represents power, the journalists and diplomats and congressmen were all spies of their own sort as well, always looking for the tip or the insight which would lift them up to the next rung on the ladder. The talk of sources and breaking stories permeated the atmosphere of our lives, and although I was too young to understand the actual facts and details of the historical events, I was drawn to the sense of urgency in the comings and goings and to the rise and fall of voices telling stories. I became a spy myself and learned the subtle art of eavesdropping, so crucial to a writer of fiction.

Our house was dripping in books. We had no television until I was a teenager, and in retrospect I am deeply grateful. Sadly, for so many children these days, imagination has been either sapped or twisted by our national love affair with television and other visual media. Why bother to think up an adventure when you can simply lie on the couch and be fed one electronically?

My father did not allow music to be played in the house because he said it hurt his ears. So we read. Unlike the books in my uncle Joe's house, which were treated as if they were revered and esteemed companions, the books in our house were treated as neglected foster children. Books teetered on bedside tables and were stacked haphazardly in bookshelves. They lurked behind cushions and piled up on the floor by my father's chair. If we knew nothing else about our parents, we experienced them as readers, and it made us want to do the same.

I remember a woman once lamenting to me over tea that her ten-year-old son never read. When I looked around her living room, I saw an enormous television set and a state-of-the-art stereo system, but nothing, absolutely nothing, to read. Not a book or a magazine or even a newspaper. The poor child, if he had wanted to read, was reduced to scanning the back of the cereal box over breakfast. "But you don't read," I said to her. "So why would he?"

My family took reading for granted. We read fiction and history and poetry. If you had a question, you were encouraged to look it up in a book. My father read the Bible, not because he was in any way a religious man but because he said it was the best book of stories he had ever encountered. We read *Macbeth* out loud with my father assigning the parts. If you happened to pass by his bathroom while he was taking a shower, you heard Hamlet's "O that this too too sallied flesh would melt, thaw

"My grandfather, Joseph Wright Alsop, on his farm in Avon, Connecticut."

and resolve itself into a dew" or "Whether 'tis nobler in the mind to suffer the slings and arrows of outrageous fortune...." Shakespeare for my father was a source of solace and amusement and distraction from daily cares.

Words were precious. I remember how furious he was when advertisers produced the line "Winston tastes good like a cigarette should." "AS!" my father would roar, "as a cigarette should." I hate to think what he would do with the ridiculous proliferation of the word "like" today. I used to charge my children a nickel every time they misused the word, and they would groan and roll their eyes at my old-fashioned ways. My father would have told them that our language is a precious natural resource not to be squandered. He was a man in love with words, and you could not spend much time in his presence without falling in love with words yourself.

So a writing father and a reading family certainly gave me the tools of my trade. But a life with five brothers in postwar Washington gave me even more—adventures to write about. My childhood memories revolve around my brothers.

We children in the family had our own hierarchy, and we knew our places. Joe was boss man, above all, the unquestionable. Ian was the second in command; I was the second second, the henchman. I was always looking for opportunities to displace Ian, to move up in rank, and he

was always wary of the attacks from below. Stewart was the much-abused mascot. My younger two brothers, Nick and Andrew, weren't born until much later. Usually Ian and Joe teamed up in any disputes because they were older and they were both boys. Occasionally, Ian sided with me. We were only thirteen months apart and remained the same height through much of our childhood, and sometimes, for a brief moment, the planets seemed to shift and Ian and I would be mysteriously aligned in both our sentiments and our outlook on life. Perhaps we were simply sick of being bossed around by Joe. These moments of partnership rarely lasted long. There was too much at stake, particularly for Ian. He could be accused of siding with a girl; he might even have to give up his place in the line of command. But no matter what happened, we never sided with Stewart. Stewart had a big goofy smile and tightly curled hair in contrast to our dead-straight lank mops. He was a charmer, and grown-ups seemed to go easier on him than on the rest of us. In our exploits, Stewart was merely tolerated.

In the 1950s, my parents bought a weekend house an hour outside of Washington. My father wished us to have some taste of the farm life he had known as a child, and he himself longed for a place to fish and shoot skeet, a place away from the stuffy, provincial politics of the Eisenhower administration. We christened the farm Polecat Park in honor of the family of skunks that lived under the front porch. (In that part of Maryland, a skunk was always known as a polecat.)

Not unlike Washington politics, dynamics in a big family are often a matter of power. Who went first, who knew more, who could order whom around, which one of us had our parents' attention. Many of our power games were played out at Polecat. There is a picture of us stuck in a photo album; the date is 1957 or so. I am nine years old, and I am lying down in the grass on the front lawn with a .22 rifle up to my shoulder. My father looks like a country squire. He is dressed in a tie and jacket, probably because some people are coming for Sunday lunch, but dressed the way he is, he has crouched down next to me to explain the workings of the gun. The paper plate target is white and flaps in the wind. My father has drawn circles on it and numbered each circle. The closer you get to the bull's-eye, the more points you get. Each marksman keeps his own score. In the photo, my brother Ian with his wild blonde hair standing on end is watching me carefully. He has already had his turn because he is older, and we always did things by age—with so many children badgering for turns, it was the simplest way to keep things straight. My brother Stewart looks impatient. He is only six years old and not yet old enough to shoot. He is leaning on one elbow, using my father's broad back as a table. He is too young still to pick up the signals my father gave. "Noli me tangere!" Daddy used to roar in the car going home from the farm. No touching, stop badgering each other, stop fighting in the back seat. But it also applied to him. Don't get too close, don't show me your feelings or probe too deeply for mine. Life, after all, is a matter of facts. My oldest brother, Joe, sets himself apart as usual. He is standing off to one side ostentatiously reading a copy of *Popular Electronics*. He is pretending to be oblivious to what's going on. He already has taken his turn, and he has a look of lofty boredom about him. It was always important for him to establish himself as the oldest, to separate himself from us lowly siblings.

Somebody once said about fiction that God is in the details. I remember details of that funny old farmhouse as vividly today as when we lived there. Since my fiction often springs from the intimate knowledge of a particular setting, it is no surprise that I wrote my first full-length novel, *Walking Away,* about Polecat Park. I remember the cement porch where we would sit in wooden sling-back chairs with our bottoms practically resting on the cement. If you were small, you sank so far down in those chairs that your legs stuck straight out and your feet pointed at the sky. You looked like a *V.* I remember sitting on that porch waiting for the rain to come across the fields, the smell of water hanging in the air, and then the steady thrumming on the red tin roof above our heads. We might have to pull our chairs a little nearer the wall of the house, but we could watch and smell and listen without ever getting wet. The curtain of water surrounding us always made me feel as if we lived behind a waterfall.

My mother took us children to church on Sunday mornings. My father was not a Catholic and did not convert when they married, but he did agree that the children should all be raised Catholic. I remember how jealous I was of him sitting on the porch and reading the newspaper as our car bumped out the road to the small country church with dull priests and wooden pews. When I knelt down, my mouth rested on the rail of the pew ahead of us, and I remember gnawing on it with my front teeth and the satisfying taste of wood varnish in my mouth. I loved the time after church because my mother took us to the local grocery store and allowed us to pick out three different kinds of candy. Then we drove back to the farm and roamed around waiting for the people to arrive from Washington for the usual Sunday lunch party.

The way into the farm was a rutted dirt road, a treacherous affair in any weather, but after a heavy rain, it developed small ponds here and there filled with murky red-brown water. You could watch the cars coming from a long distance across the fields.

"Who's that?" someone would say.

"The Bissells," someone else would answer, and we'd sit and watch as the old beat-up station wagon wended its excruciatingly slow way down the road towards us. On particularly bad days, in an effort to save the axle, the driver, who was usually Mrs. Bissell, would run one wheel up into the fields, and the car would draw inexorably closer looking cockeyed, like a sailboat heeling over in a stiff wind.

After the Bissells would come the others. We were never quite sure who would arrive because my father could never remember exactly whom he had invited for Sunday lunch. Every time another car crested the horizon, we would begin a guessing game as to the number of passengers.

"Blue Buick," my brother would say, "the Evans."

"Yes, I remember now," my father would say. "I must have asked him when we interviewed the secretary of defense last week."

"And the children?" my mother would ask.

"I can't remember."

She would shake her head and go back into the kitchen to scrounge around for the makings of another potato omelet. Grown-ups and children together would tumble out of their cars with a great slamming of doors and "Did you

Parents, Stewart and Patricia Alsop, on their wedding day in London, June 1944.

bring a towel for me?" and "God, Stew, you're going to have to do something with that bloody road" and "Let's swim first."

In the warm weather, people changed into bathing suits in whatever upstairs room they found available and made their way down the path my father had cut through the long grass to the pond. The men and women would come trailing down the hill with drinks and cigarettes, talking loudly to each other about politics or the latest scandal in the government. My father would endure a great deal of teasing about the state of his fly rods or his swimming trunks or the pond. The pond was spring-fed, an oval-shaped body of water dammed up at one end and stocked with bass, which we pulled out of it on a regular basis with a fly rod. My father fought a continual battle with the algae which covered the surface of the water in a blue-green scum that became especially noxious in the late summer. The hotter the summer, the thicker the pestilence, as Daddy liked to call it. He rowed himself around and around in a small leaky boat, dragging one of his old black silk socks which had been filled with a green crystallized chemical that seeped slowly out through the thin material of the sock and broke down the algae in some mysterious way.

The thing you most wanted to avoid when swimming in our pond was touching the bottom. The mud felt cold and slimy, and you could imagine things far worse than the algae sucking you under if you weren't careful. It was the kind of pond that invited images of snapping turtles, black snakes, frogs, and fish; and every one of those creatures had been sighted in it at one time or another and was most certainly lurking somewhere just beneath your toes. My father had fashioned a strange facsimile of a raft from a green painted trellis ripped off the side of the porch. This was attached to a string of canvas-covered rings, the kind that are tossed off ships to drowning people. You walked carefully across this jerry-rigged contraption to a small rickety ladder out at the end. It was important to cross to

Elizabeth in the third grade, 1956. "I am in the back row, second from right."

the ladder when nobody else was coming the other way or else the raft would start to tip back and forth in a precarious manner and you might fall off in the shallow end right into the deepest, ooziest mud in the whole pond. Later in the afternoon when the grown-ups were draped around the lawn finishing off their lunch, the kids would all jump up and down on the raft, trying to knock each other off.

Once you had reached the ladder, you lowered yourself slowly, taking care to avoid splinters and the odd nail here or there that had managed to work itself out of the slimy, water-soaked wood. Then you let go with one hand and collapsed into the dark water. The ladies all shrieked when they pushed off and gave each other reports on the various cold spots and warm spots. "Oh," they'd say with a sigh of relief, "I've found a warm spot. Right here, darling. Isn't it delicious. Don't put your feet down. Oh no, I've floated out of it again."

The teenage boys would rush past and dive off the raft just as the ladies were lowering themselves into the water, and this would make for a great deal of argument and shouts back and forth. If the teenager had done this to a close relative such as his mother or his aunt, he usually stayed underwater and swam like a frog to the far end until his lungs gave out. This way he popped up too far out of reach to be seriously chastised.

With his fly rod balanced across his knees, my father already would have launched himself out into the deepest part of the pond in an old black inner tube; he liked to paddle over and drop his fly in a shady spot under a tall evergreen as far away from the noise and commotion as possible. Those inner tubes entertained us for hours. We threw them out to each other, dove through them, tried to tip a person over when she was innocently floating around in one (but when you were horsing around with an inner tube, you had to be very careful not to scrape any exposed skin on the metal piece used for blowing it up). Whenever one of these black rubber circles sprouted a leak, my father would take it down to the local gas station and get it patched. For some reason, the patches were made of red rubber, and the more a tube got patched, the jauntier it looked.

I do remember one day early on when I did not yet know how to swim. I stood on the grassy shore and watched all those people running off the rickety raft and hurling themselves in the water with such abandon. And I thought that's all swimming is about—courage, a devil-may-care attitude, a daring leap. When nobody was paying any particular attention to me, I walked up to the ladder, let myself down, and simply pushed off for the middle of the pond. And sank. Went down like a stone while the water rushed up into my nose and my toes slid into the slime at

Christmas picture of Elizabeth with her parents and three of her five brothers, 1958.

the bottom and it was quite clear that I was going to drown. I pushed my arms around the way I had seen the swimmers do up on the surface but to no avail. I did not move in any direction. It would have been easier to walk out of the water. And then up above, someone must have said, "Where's Elizabeth?" And everybody began to look frantically, and someone must have remembered me pushing off the ladder, and suddenly a hand brushed against me. Strong fingers closed around my upper arm, and my father pulled me out of the muck with one swift movement the way you pull a plug out of a drain. The Sunday guests slapped me on the back and wrapped me in towels, and the ladies hugged me against their wet bellies that were swathed in flowered, skirted suits. Later, when there were no grown-ups around to hush them, my brothers hooted with laughter at the hopelessness of a sister who thought the only thing you needed to know about swimming was how to get into the water. Starting a new book often feels to me like jumping into the water when you don't know how to swim. No matter how many books I write, each time I start I feel like a beginner again and I wonder if this is the

one that will drown me. As Eudora Welty said, "Each story teaches me how to write it but not how to write the next one."

My father used to say that his life at Polecat was a continual war against the elements. And by elements, he meant animals, insects, and reptiles. There were always wasp nests to be batted off the porch and sprayed, stray cats from next door who got chased away by our beagles, rats who lived under the collapsed chicken coop. And snakes. Black snakes. We got rid of the skunks that lived under the front porch, but we never got rid of the snakes. Everybody told us they were harmless, but they didn't look that way. They would surprise you, those snakes. You'd hear a little rustling, and you'd see the grass bending and the thick black body sliding off to seek refuge in some other place when you hadn't even known one was there. They lay in the sun on the tops of rocks near the pond, and they slunk around in the dark places under the barn.

"Snake," we would scream, and if my father were in earshot, he would come running with his .22 rifle. Once

"My father teaching me how to shoot, with three brothers watching."

Daddy had shot the snake and turned it over with the toe of his boot and declared it dead, the boys and I would fall to arguing over who got to carry the carcass to the dump. "You got to do it last weekend." "I never get a chance." Daddy would choose one of us, break the barrel, empty the ammunition out of the gun, snap it closed again, and hand it over to the designated pallbearer.

If you were the lucky one, you hunched down and slid the gun under the corpse at the midway point, taking care not to clog the barrel with dirt because Daddy was still watching and he noticed the way you treated his possessions, particularly his guns. You bounced the black body up and down a few times to move it closer to you along the steel carrying stick until you judged the leverage to be right. Then you kept your back straight and your knees bent and lifted ever so carefully, and up would come the snake, draped like a black garland over the gun, and you would set off for the dump with the funeral party, brothers and guests and friends, all the children on the place skipping along next to you waiting for the first twitches. Long after they are dead, snakes keep jerking and shuddering as if their bodies are trying to restart themselves. So soon after you led off, the thick black lifeless rope would suddenly begin to twitch, and if you weren't careful or even if you were, that dead snake would manage to shake itself right off the gun. Then you'd have to lean down and start all over again with the kids behind you saying, "Let me try," "I can do it,"

"you're no good at this." The dump was not that far away actually, down a little mown path next to the chicken coop, but if the dead body were particularly active, it could take some time to get the snake there. Then the other kids would drop back because this was the moment you'd been waiting for, the whole reason to be the snake carrier. You twisted your body around ever so slowly to move the gun and its cargo back over your shoulder as if you were a fisherman about to cast a spinner, and you held that position for a split second and you prayed the snake wasn't going to slide right down the barrel and end up draped around your neck, and you felt the silence all around you, in the crowd of kids back out of reach and in the woods beyond the dump and even in the dump itself preparing to receive its own, the way the sea waits for the body of a dead sailor. And then you twisted forward with a snap, and if you'd done it right, if the gun swung around fast enough to hold that snake with centrifugal force and then stopped as if surprised at high noon, the black rope body would sail off over the dump in a long, satisfying arc, and behind you, you would hear the sighs from the crowd and you would know you had accorded that snake a fair and decent burial and you would walk proudly back up to the house at the head of the pack of kids to hand the gun over to your father.

Because I was brought up with boys, I was taught the things a man is supposed to know. I can load and shoot a rifle and a shotgun, gut and clean a fish, drive a stick shift, carry the twisting body of a snake to the dump. These are not skills that are of much use in the life of a modern urban woman, but for some inexplicable reason, because I am competent in these ways, I have been willing to try other things I'm not sure I can do. This has come in handy when I negotiate contracts or stand up to speak in front of a large audience. It doesn't mean everything will turn out well or even the way I want it to. It simply means that I'll step up and try where others might hold back. Writing often requires that sense of assurance—some might call it foolishness—that willingness to travel down paths that seem to have no end or at least no connection at all to the main road.

The year I turned eight, our playroom on the second floor above the living room of our house in Washington was requisitioned by the grown-ups. My parents put in a master bedroom, two dressing rooms, a bathroom for themselves, and two doors to close themselves off from the noise of children and maids in the mornings. It was known as "their wing."

In response, Joe went to my father and negotiated with him for the use of the basement. After all, he argued, we children needed a place to play, to set up projects, hang out. Joe expected to have a battle on his hands, but to our surprise, his request was granted without discussion. When my father was working at home, we children knew we were supposed to keep the noise down, but we needed constant reminders. For a brief time, a sign had appeared on my father's office door which read "DO NOT KNOCK UNLESS YOU'RE BLEEDING." This idea of Joe's provided the perfect solution. All our noise and mess would be relegated to the cellar, a part of the house as far away as possible from my father's office. Except for the laundry, a china closet, and a wine cellar, we were given the full run of the place.

The basement was unfinished and filled with narrow, twisting passageways. It reminded me of pictures I had seen of the catacombs. The floors were lined with rough cobblestones, the furnace pumped away in one corner of the first large room, an old stone sink stood in another. There was a drain in the middle of the floor for hosing the place down, but nobody ever did. The rooms were dusty and low ceilinged, and the air smelled of mildew laced with the scent of newly dried clothes when the dryer had been running. It was the kind of hideout kids dreamed about.

Joe was fair. He awarded me a six-by-eight-foot space between two columns in the large furnace room for my dollhouse and Ian a desk in the middle passageway for his woodcarving activities. Joe took the three back rooms for his work. One section was devoted to chemistry, a second to electronic equipment, and a third for storage.

Unlike my father's office door upstairs, Joe's basement door was never closed, and Ian and I often gravitated around the corner to his three rooms because whatever we were doing, he was sure to be cooking up something more interesting. We were careful to stay out of his way except when he needed something. Then Ian and I would fight over which one of us would bring Joe the piece of wire from the supply room or a screwdriver from the desk. He may not have exactly welcomed our constant presence, but he tolerated it. We became a gang of basement ruffians, and he was our noble leader, the father of our downstairs family.

In those days, children were expected to adjust themselves to the schedules and desires of their parents. Ours were busy people. My mother ran a household bursting with children and volunteered for various causes, and my father was often away traveling or interviewing. In a big family like ours, children often raise themselves. We knew it was useless to appeal to our parents for the resolution of daily squabbles, so we made our own rules. And they were imperfect ones.

Because we considered the whole house our stalking plain, we did not knock on doors, ask permission. These transgressions were committed as easily on one another as they were on the adults. We picked up telephone receivers, read other people's mail, poked around in other peoples' closets. If you didn't want your diary read, you'd better hide it. If you didn't want your clothes borrowed, you'd better wear them. If you didn't want your door opened, get a lock. If you didn't want your food speared off your plate, you'd better keep your elbows up and your eyes open. We violated and eavesdropped and trespassed because nobody ever taught us that violating and eavesdropping and trespassing were against the rules. In fact from what we could glean from grown-up conversations, snooping was not only condoned, it was encouraged. The ends justified the means.

Now, looking back, I can see that I developed my own rules, guidelines for keeping myself protected from other gang members whenever that became necessary. Never let down your guard. Always act as if you do know things even when you don't. (Find out the answers secretly later.) Don't ever show your fear. Jump off the high diving board rather than face the humiliation at the bottom of the ladder. Keep it "together" at all times. Anticipate the different crises that might be waiting around the corner. Be prepared to protect yourself, your friends, your pets, your possessions, your territory, your secrets. Get as much on the others as possible. Information is ammunition, and you never know when you might need it.

Of such stuff are writers made.

In Washington in the 1950s, we children had a special fear of the bomb. After all, we lived a couple of miles from the White House and Capitol Hill. If and when the Soviet Union decided to launch their deadly missiles, the ones we read and heard about daily, we were dead center in their sights. Talk was all of bomb shelters. So it seemed absolutely natural one summer when Joe announced to his little band of basement mercenaries that we were going to dig our own bomb shelter at the top of our hill. He approached my father with this project and was granted permission with a vague wave of the hand. Joe was horrified by my father's cavalier attitude towards the safety of the family. Very well, if our real father wasn't going to make some efforts to protect us then Joe, our downstairs father, would step into the breach.

The project took a number of weeks. Joe designed an elaborate pulley system that ran along a path of trees down our hill to the stream. You filled a bucket with earth, hooked it to the rope, and gave it a shove. The weight of the dirt made the bucket go rocketing down the hill at a great speed until it slammed into a branch and tipped over, spilling the dirt out into a pile. The full bucket going down pulled up an empty one that had been waiting at the bottom of the hill.

Back then, none of the kids in the neighborhood went to camp. They just hung out and rode their bicycles up and down the dead-end lane and waited for someone to think of something to do. The news of the pulley system spread quickly, and soon kids started to troop up our driveway to see what was going on. By the end of the first week, Ian and I were no longer diggers. We were managers who

The pond at Polecat Park with infamous raft and inner tubes.

Senior year at Sarah Lawrence College, 1969.

organized the labor force and took in the nickel per day that Joe had determined each worker must pay in order to be allowed to use the bucket system. As soon as one digger got tired, there was a replacement eager to take his place. The pile of dirt at the bottom of the hill soon grew so big that it threatened to dam up our stream, so Joe sent the workers down to spread the dirt up and down the banks.

My parents went away on one of their annual vacations with the Bissells. The other parents in the neighborhood were probably grateful that their kids weren't hanging around the house complaining of the usual summer boredom. Nobody seemed to notice the activity going on just below the driveway wall. At the end of a month, we had dug a fourteen-foot hole and fashioned out a room that could sleep four, back to back. Somewhere Joe laid his hands on a twelve-foot metal ladder, and we threw down some sleeping bags, comic books, and extra food and began to spend nights down in the hole, which Joe continued to insist we call the shelter. Then my parents came home.

They were horrified, not at all happy about the consideration and care we had taken to protect the family from the coming Armageddon. My father seemed far more concerned about the liability provisions in his insurance policy. He hired a carpenter to build a huge cover that no single child or even a pack of children could move by themselves. We were denied any further access. Gradually over the years, all the leaves that were raked off the place were poured down our hole. They molded and compacted into a rich loam, and soon all that was left of our valiant effort was a shallow depression in the earth.

Joe was furious. He stormed around in the basement office for days, and we stayed at arm's length. From that moment on, in his mind and eventually in ours, the grown-ups became the enemy. If there ever had been any doubt in our minds about whose side we were on, it was utterly dispelled that summer of the bomb shelter. It was us against them. All for one and one for all.

Years later, I published a young adult novel called *A Little Demonstration of Affection* in which I described the entire operation of the hole. I changed the circumstances and the emphasis as fiction writers are wont to do. It was not a book about a war between children and grown-ups so much as it was a story about the kind of sexual tension and confusion that can occur around the time of puberty. In my writing, I have often taken an actual experience from my childhood and woven it into a different kind of story. Luckily, I have never run out of childhood experiences from which to draw.

I have found in my eagerness to tell the reader a good story that I sometimes confuse the actual facts of what happened with the requirements of fiction. Did we actually charge the kids who dug the hole? I think so, although I can't be absolutely sure. But whether it's true or not, it reveals character. If we didn't do it, we certainly could have. This is why I have never been that interested in writing a full-length memoir. With fiction, I can mold the memories to make a better story. As Eudora Welty said, "You need to tell the lies of fiction to get to the truth of human nature." I have always cared more about the truth of human nature than I have about getting each and every fact exactly right.

And sometimes fiction can replace memory. Now when I think about my grandmother's house in Avon, Connecticut, I don't remember the real house so much as the one I described in my novel *In My Mother's House*. I don't think so much of the actual people who lived there as I do about the characters I created and placed in that house so that they could work out the daily troubles of their lives. Writing a novel often means that you mourn the death of what truly was at the same time that you welcome the birth of what might have been.

School is mostly a blur to me. I went to an elementary school not far from home through third grade, but I honestly have almost no memories of the place—probably because for so many years, the adventures at home were simply more memorable. From the fourth through the ninth grade, I attended a local Catholic day school. At Stone Ridge, we prayed before and after every class and attended Mass regularly in a small chapel. I liked the mysterious swish of the nuns' black skirts, the flickering candles, the low hum of a Gregorian chant. For a time in the seventh grade, I set up an altar in my room, prayed regularly, and considered joining a convent, but in the end, I found our basement adventures and the lure of spying far more appealing than the contemplative life.

The late fifties and early sixties were the golden days of covert operations for the CIA. Richard Bissell, the mastermind behind the U-2 spy plane and the man responsible for the Bay of Pigs, was one of my father's best friends. Not surprisingly, his son, Richard, was Joe's sidekick. After the betrayal of the bomb shelter, Joe increasingly turned his attention to our own covert actions. He was the downstairs station chief, and we were his operatives. From his basement office, Joe would draw up plans for various projects and deploy us to carry them out. We understood from the beginning that secrecy was vital to our operations. I remember fantasies of holding out until death itself, no matter what tortures would be perpetrated charge the kids who dug the hole? I think so, although I can't be absolutely sure. But whether it's true or not, it reveals character. If we didn't do it, we certainly could have. This is why I have never been that interested in writing a full-length memoir. With fiction, I can mold the memories to make a better story. As Eudora Welty said, "You need to tell the lies of fiction to get to the truth of human nature." I have always cared more about the truth of human nature than I have about getting each and every fact exactly right.

And sometimes fiction can replace memory. Now when I think about my grandmother's house in Avon, Connecticut, I don't remember the real house so much as the one I described in my novel *In My Mother's House*. I don't think so much of the actual people who lived there as I do about the characters I created and placed in that house so that they could work out the daily troubles of their lives. Writing a novel often means that you mourn the death of what truly was at the same time that you welcome the birth of what might have been.

School is mostly a blur to me. I went to an elementary school not far from home through third grade, but I honestly have almost no memories of the place—probably because for so many years, the adventures at home were simply more memorable. From the fourth through the ninth grade, I attended a local Catholic day school. At Stone Ridge, we prayed before and after every class and attended Mass regularly in a small chapel. I liked the mysterious swish of the nuns' black skirts, the flickering candles, the low hum of a Gregorian chant. For a time in the seventh grade, I set up an altar in my room, prayed regularly, and considered joining a convent, but in the end, I found our basement adventures and the lure of spying far more appealing than the contemplative life.

The late fifties and early sixties were the golden days of covert operations for the CIA. Richard Bissell, the mastermind behind the U-2 spy plane and the man responsible for the Bay of Pigs, was one of my father's best friends. Not surprisingly, his son, Richard, was Joe's sidekick. After the betrayal of the bomb shelter, Joe increasingly turned his attention to our own covert actions. He was the downstairs station chief, and we were his operatives. From his basement office, Joe would draw up plans for various projects and deploy us to carry them out. We understood from the beginning that secrecy was vital to our operations. I remember fantasies of holding out until death itself, no matter what tortures would be perpetrated on my body. In the days when I was as steeped in the convent teachings as I was in the loyalties of the basement gang, I often got muddled over which better cause to die for: the children's underground or Catholic martyrdom. It all appealed to my flair for the dramatic.

First, we manufactured and detonated various bombs. Joe miscalculated the fuse on one in the hay barn at Polecat and had to be carried bleeding to the car. He spent quite a few hours in the local hospital while the weekend resident picked bits of small rocks and wood out of his cheek with a pair of tweezers and stitched together the gaping wound on his chin.

The rambling house served our needs. We conducted a relentless search for good hiding places. I came up with the best one, a little rabbit warren of rooms that you accessed through a small door under the liquor cabinet. During dinner parties, I hid in there and scribbled notes on yellow legal pads, but Joe did not like to rely on the vagaries of human behavior. He got electronic. Shipments of materials arrived from various purveyors of electrical equipment. He and Rich huddled together over large sheets of paper anchored with rocks at every corner. They sketched, argued, dispatched us on errands to cut lengths of wire or to measure things. Another headquarters with a tape recorder was set up in Joe's bedroom.

Every time we reached a new goal, Joe escalated the war. He and Rich dropped a microphone down one of the chimneys in the Bissells' house so that they could listen in on the adult conversations, but they were caught. Mr. Bissell was furious. His house on Newark Street was filled with safes and oddly colored telephones that rang at all hours of the night. It must have horrified him to learn that his own son might constitute a breach of security. The boys were admonished, and no doubt with fingers crossed behind their backs, they solemnly promised to reform.

One spring, Joe decided that we should develop our own private telephone system. It was time we watched our own backs, protected our information from the grown-ups, made sure they couldn't listen in on us. It was an indication of the high esteem in which Joe held all our operations that he thought the deputy director of planning for the CIA or the Washington editor of the *Saturday Evening Post* might be the slightest bit interested in what their children had to say to each other. At the time, however, it seemed a perfectly reasonable assessment of the situation.

This was our most ambitious undertaking to date. We were going to run the wiring through the storm sewers of the city to five different houses. Most of them were located on our dead-end street, but one branch went to the Bissells' house on Newark Street, five blocks away up a steep hill. It was decided that Rich would be responsible for getting us

Winthrop with daughter, Eliza, age two.

"Me and all five brothers on summer vacation," 1978.

in and out of the manholes. Somewhere he had managed to lay his hands on a sizable-looking crowbar. I was selected as the second in command to go with Joe. He had done a test run and discovered that he was too tall to stand straight in the sewers, so he'd built a special wooden platform on wheels that would allow him to scoot along taping the wires to the walls while lying on his back. He needed someone my size to follow with the flashlight, the extra tape, and the roll of wire.

I like to think that it wasn't just my height that made Joe pick me. I had shown a certain reliability in other tight situations. If I felt panicky, I didn't show it. I was not a complainer, nor was I squeamish about dark places, bugs, or rodents, all of which we were likely to encounter.

We lowered ourselves down into the sewers without being seen and made our way slowly up the hill from Porter Street to Ordway. Joe lay on his back on his makeshift dolly and pushed himself along, using first one foot and then the other. He taped the wire on the damp walls of the sewer pipe while I followed along behind carrying the rest of the equipment. We turned right on Newark and maneuvered ourselves into position right under the manhole cover opposite the Bissells' house. Everything went according to plan up till that point. I gave the prescribed signal, three knocks on the manhole cover with the butt of

the flashlight. Then Joe and I crouched at the bottom of the metal steps to wait. And Rich didn't come.

Cars passed overhead. The manhole cover clanked. We could hear the distant noise of a lawn mower, then a fire engine. Minutes went by. They felt like hours. The only noise in the sewer was the constant drip of water off the walls and the scratching and scrabbling of some rat in the distance. Every so often, the light would catch the glimmer of a slug making its slow patient way up the curved wall. Joe began to panic. He knocked again, then ordered me up next to him on the ladder so we could try and move the cover ourselves. It was hopeless. If Rich didn't come to let us out, there was no way we'd make it out of there.

We must have been down there for an extra two hours. It felt like a lifetime. The flashlight went out. The thin shaft of light that came down through the crowbar holes shifted with the waning of the day. We worried about storms, a sudden flood, the rising water. Joe was sure there was a slug going down his shirt. He jumped at the distant sloshing of the water down the dark tunnel. The more panicky he became, the calmer I grew. At the bottom of the narrow metal stepladder, I pressed my body up against his to try and stop him from shaking. Finally we heard the slide of the metal bar above us. Joe was the first one out. I followed him, still carrying the extra equipment. Joe and Rich had a huge argument over what had taken Rich so long. It turned out that in all their calculations, they hadn't counted on the next-door neighbor picking that particular afternoon to mow his rather extensive lawn.

By the next week, the phone system was up and running. The wire entered the Bissells' house through a basement window and then ran right up the corner of their dining room through a hole in Rich's floor to his desk. Joe had an elaborate switchboard set up in his room, and bells would start ringing around three in the afternoon when the kids got home from school.

Thinking back on it later, I realized how far out there we had been, how dangerous a caper it really was. Rich was a strange boy, more committed to the cause than to our safety. If rescuing us had meant divulging our secret plan to the enemy, the adults, he might have left us down in the sewers indefinitely.

Sometime late in the summer, the wire gave way. Joe checked all the aboveground connections and found them to be clean. The break was down below, somewhere in the sewers. The kids clamored for him to fix it, but Joe told them to leave him alone, he was too busy, he had other things to do. I knew what he was really saying, but still I kept my counsel. Brave as I had been during those long damp hours under the manhole cover, I wasn't eager to repeat the exercise.

Nobody, not even Richard Bissell, Mr. CIA himself, ever knew about the private phone system. It was our pièce de résistance, our crowning achievement. But not long after that Joe left to go to boarding school, and the basement gang disbanded. We'd come to the end of our childhood together.

I was sent to a girls' boarding school in the tenth grade and was perfectly happy to be there, surrounded for the first time by the company of women. My roommate and I sat up late into the night talking, and although we were in danger of discovery by the housemother, at least I knew the room had not been bugged by my brother. I didn't mind the order of the days and the arcane rituals, and I loved the smell of the books in the old paneled library. My grandmother lived five miles in one direction and my aunt and uncle five miles in the other, and although you weren't allowed to visit your parents more than once a term, there seemed to be no rules for more distant relatives, so I was sprung almost every weekend. Senior year I took a creative writing course. The teacher who remains a good friend of mine was tough, but encouraging. I remember a short story I wrote in the style of Saki and another one about an unhappy family based on a painting by Picasso in his blue period.

Sarah Lawrence was a natural college for me because they took creative writing seriously and allowed students to major in it, which meant that at least one-third of my courses would focus on writing. The writing department included Grace Paley, E. L. Doctorow, and Jane Cooper, and I took courses from all of them. In fact, I took just about every fiction writing course I could get into. My senior year, I handed in a short story entitled "The Sewers" based on my underground adventure with Joe, and Jane Cooper suggested I try my hand at children's books. I was wounded by her suggestion at the time, because it implied that the stories I'd written for adult readers were not as

successful. She could not have been more right. After all, I was only twenty. I had barely lived. How could I possibly bring to life the troubles of the married banker or the ailing grandmother or the brassy young working woman, all of whom played leading parts in my stories?

I began writing picture books and submitting them to various publishing houses. They were all rejected, but I received encouraging letters from Charlotte Zolotow, a senior editor at Harper and Row (now HarperCollins). I like to think this interest in my work helped me land a job there as an assistant editor six months after I graduated from college. At Harper, I worked under the legendary Ursula Nordstrom. Maurice Sendak, Arnold and Anita Lobel, Shel Silverstein, and other notables in the field drifted in and out of the office all the time. Once when I was covering for Ursula's assistant on her lunch hour, I picked up the phone and heard a man growl, "Hello, this is Andy White. Is Ursula there?" (E. B. White's nickname was Andy.) I had been trained in my parents' living room to treat famous people as everyday occurrences, so I took a message in a cool, efficient voice. Now I wish I had told him how much I loved *Charlotte's Web*. To this day, I find the first sentence of that novel to be one of the most commanding in English literature. You simply have to keep reading to find out where Pa is going with that ax.

If I learned discipline from my father's example, I practiced it at Harper and Row. In those days, people left their publishing jobs promptly at five o'clock. Every evening once the office had emptied out, I pushed my day work aside and wrote for an hour. By the end of a year, I had produced a number of picture books and a novel. It had a beginning, a middle, an end, and some plausible characters, and Charlotte Zolotow was encouraging. After another six months of rewriting from five to six in the evening, Harper published *Walking Away* in 1973. I quit to write full time.

My daughter, Eliza, was born in 1974 and my son, Andrew, in 1978, and my picture books took on a new immediacy and energy, taken as they were from real-life

With son, Andrew, 1978.

"The view down onto the terrace where I could hear every word spoken."

situations. My old eavesdropping habit surfaced once again. When my daughter was four, I heard her talking to her stuffed animals. "Bear," she announced in a firm voice, "I am going out. You will stay with Mrs. Duck." A pause. "Now stop that terrible crying, Bear," she scolded. "You like Mrs. Duck." I went around the corner and wrote down those lines of conversation in my journal. Eventually they found their way into a book called *Bear and Mrs. Duck.* And Bear proved so beguiling to me and my publisher that I wrote two more books about him and his adventures.

The years my children were growing up proved to be years of great productivity for me as I could witness firsthand the daily dilemmas and trials of childhood. I wrote lots of picture books and some chapter books, and as my children aged so did my characters. In those days, I accepted all challenges, some from editors and many of them of my own creation. If my editor thought I should try a novel in first person, I did. Adaptations of various folktales and Bible stories appealed to my love of language, so I tried my hand at them. After fifteen years of publishing children's books, I finally must have decided I was old enough to write about the adults I had abandoned at the age of twenty, and so I wrote a five-hundred-page historical novel, *In My Mother's House,* which covered almost eighty years of history.

And as all writers do, I often ran into a dead end and had to rethink a project. Frustrated by a realistic picture book that felt heavy-handed, I turned the story into a fantasy novel about a boy named William who travels through time to right a wrong he has committed. This was the first novel that I didn't outline ahead of time, so the characters were free to wander down side paths, to make mistakes, to lead me into new adventures. Not surprisingly, *The Castle in the Attic* remains my best-selling book. I'm sure that's because the reader must sense as I did that the characters' lives are truly happening on the page, and none

of us, not the author nor the reader nor the character, knows what's coming next.

So here I am some twenty-six years and more than forty books from my first publication, still practicing my craft, still feeling incredibly fortunate that I can make a living doing what I love. People seem to be fascinated by writers and their lives these days. I never thought about C. S. Lewis and Enid Blyton and Laura Ingalls Wilder when I was reading their stories. I was much more interested in their characters and the world they had created for me to live in. Writers travel and talk to their audiences much more frequently these days. Now when I go around visiting schools and reading in colleges, and people ask me how I got to be a writer, I tell them there is no one answer. So I give them many. I say that you have to live a noticing kind of life, be the kind of person as Henry James said, "on which nothing is lost." I say that you have to be a reader. I say that you have to enjoy your own company and be willing to sit alone in a room for hours on end. I point out that writers never really go on vacation; they take characters and stories with them. I tell them you have to be strong enough to ignore the family critics and the reviewers and the worst scourge of the lot—the contemptuous, perfectionist voice inside your own head.

Inevitably, the student then asks me where I get my ideas. They must ask every writer the same question. Perhaps it's because they believe there is some secret formula to writing fiction, some special key that will open the door which separates simply living your life from living your life *and* using that same life as material for stories. I know I used to believe that. Again, I have no simple answer. With picture books, I used to get my ideas from an ancient memory or an incident I witnessed in the playground or a conversation between my four-year-old daughter and her stuffed bear. Now my picture books are triggered more by language: a funny name *(Dumpy La Rue)* or a well-worn phrase *(I'm Going to Tell on You).* I seem to hear whole picture books when other people hear nothing but a cute story or a snatch of small talk.

More often than not, my novels move forward because I know the setting. Let me give you an example. I am writing this piece in the south of France in a house that was built four hundred years ago. The walls are three feet thick, and they keep the house cool while outside, in the hot afternoon sun, the song of the *cigales* creates a constant background serenade. I am here on vacation, but remember we writers never really go on vacation. I am setting some scenes from my new novel in France in 1944, where a character of mine is fighting with the French resistance. Two nights ago I looked down from a narrow slit window in the bedroom to a terrace four stories below, and because of some trick of acoustics, I could hear every word the people were saying. Every syllable of every word. They didn't know I was listening, and they would never have thought to look for a spy so high above them in such a tiny window. The place was an eavesdropper's dream. What if my character were hiding from the Germans and he could look down from this same window and hear them questioning the family below? With that concrete piece of knowledge, a new scene began to form in my head. It will take my characters in new directions, places they might

Family reunion, Christmas, 1994.

never have gone if I had not been able to stand in my bare feet on that cool stone floor and stare through that narrow window, listening yet again to the rise and fall of voices as people told each other stories.

People have often asked me why I write for so many different ages. It keeps me interested is the simplest reply. Last year I published a novel for adults, *Island Justice,* and soon after that I wrote three picture books. *Island Justice* took me two-and-a-half years from first inkling to final draft. An idea for a picture book may germinate for months or even years, but the actual writing time can be as short as a week, and it feels satisfying after years on one project to be able to finish a book in a matter of days. Each of the audiences I write for presents a different challenge and exercises a different writing muscle. *In My Mother's House,* which spanned three generations of American women, forced me to use all of my plotting and character-ization skills, whereas a picture book for young children will remind me to focus on language.

I used to think, although never consciously, that I had to write BIG in order to be taken seriously as a writer for adults. So I chose to work on large stages, either by covering decades of American history *(In My Mother's House)* or by peopling an entire island *(Island Justice).* Now I would like to take all the skills I learned in writing my fantasy novels *(The Castle in the Attic* and *The Battle*

for the Castle) and bring them to bear on a short novel for adults, one that focuses intensely on two main characters and brings them to life for the reader in a deeper, more layered picture. To put it more simply, I'd like to try using fewer words and making sure that each one counts.

So I continue to challenge myself because as I said before it keeps me interested. What would it be like to write this novel in the first person? I ask myself. Or how would it be to use the voice of an omniscient narrator? Or could this be an epistolary novel? Why not try this picture book in rhyme? And of course, each time I set myself a new task, the excitement propels me along until that inevitable moment when I feel once more like that little girl who jumped into the water and then discovered that she didn't know how to swim. Why did I ever start this? I ask myself. How did I ever think I could make this plot work or that character come to life? But the feeling has become a familiar one, almost an old friend by now. Whenever I sense that I'm out of my depth in the midst of a new novel, then it means the story interests me, and sooner or later, I'll flail my way up through the murky water and back to the surface. I no longer need my father to reach in and pull me out. I've learned how to do it myself.

As the Crow Flies, illustrated by Joan Sandin, Clarion, 1998.
Promises, illustrated by Betsy Lewin, Clarion, in press.
Dumpy La Rue, illustrated by Betsy Lewin, Henry Holt, in press.
Hats, illustrated by Sue Truesdell, Henry Holt, in press.
Squashed in the Middle, Henry Holt, in press.

GOLDEN BOOKS FOR CHILDREN

Shoelace Box, illustrated by Kathy Wibburn, 1984.
The Christmas Pageant, illustrated by Kathy Wibburn, 1984.
Happy Easter, Mother Duck, illlustrated by Diane Dawson Hearn, 1985.
My First Book of the Planets, illustrated by John Nez, 1985.

CHAPTER BOOKS FOR CHILDREN

Belinda's Hurricane, illustrated by Wendy Watson, Dutton, 1984.
Luke's Bully, illustrated by Pat Grant Porter, Viking, 1990.

YOUNG ADULT FICTION

Walking Away, illustrated by Noelle Massena, Harper, 1973.
A Little Demonstration of Affection, Harper, 1975.
Knock, Knock, Who's There?, Holiday House, 1978.
Marathon Miranda, Holiday House, 1979.
Miranda in the Middle, Holiday House, 1980.
The Castle in the Attic, illustrated by Trina Schart Hyman, Holiday House, 1985.
The Battle for the Castle, Holiday House, 1993.

ADULT FICTION

In My Mother's House, Doubleday, 1988.
Island Justice, William Morrow, 1998.

OTHER

Contributor of short stories to periodicals and anthologies. *The Castle in the Attic* and *The Battle for the Castle* were recorded on audiocassette in an unabridged multivoice dramatization (author as narrator) with Listening Library in 1996 and 1997.

WOODS, Geraldine 1948-

Personal

Born September 30, 1948, in New York, NY; daughter of John (a clerk) and Frances (a secretary; maiden name, Derpich) Spicer; married Harold Woods (a teacher and writer), July 15, 1972; children: Thomas Merton. *Education:* College Mount St. Vincent, B.A., 1970. *Religion:* Roman Catholic.

Addresses

Home—308 East 79th St., New York, NY 10021.

Career

Teacher in New York City private schools, 1970—.

Awards, Honors

Children's Books of the Year, Child Study Association of America, 1986, for *The United Nations* and *Equal Justice: A Biography of Sandra Day O'Connor.*

Writings

FOR CHILDREN

Jim Henson: From Puppets to Muppets, Dillon (Minneapolis, MN), 1987.
Spain: A Shining New Democracy, Dillon, 1987, revised as *Spain: Gateway to Europe,* 1998.

Science in Ancient Egypt, F. Watts, 1988, revised edition, 1998.
Affirmative Action, F. Watts, 1989.
The Oprah Winfrey Story: Speaking Her Mind, Dillon, 1991.
Drug Abuse in Society: A Reference Handbook, ABC-CLIO (Santa Barbara, CA), 1993.
Heroin, Enslow, 1994.
Science of the Early Americas, F. Watts, 1999.
Animal Experimentation and Testing: A Pro/Con Issue, Enslow, 1999.

FOR CHILDREN; WITH HUSBAND, HAROLD WOODS

Saudi Arabia, F. Watts, 1978.
Drug Use and Drug Abuse, F. Watts, 1979, revised edition, 1986.
Real Scary Sea Monsters, Shelley Graphics, 1979.
Is There Life on Other Planets?, Shelley Graphics, 1979.
Is James Bond Dead? Great Spy Stories, Shelley Graphics, 1979.
Mazes and Other Puzzles (revised edition of Walter Sheperd's *Picture Puzzles*), Shelley Graphics, 1979.
Braincticklers (revised edition of the book by Charles Booth Jones), Shelly Graphics, 1979.
Mad Mind Benders (revised edition of Jones's *Braincticklers II*), Shelley Graphics, 1979.
Magical Beasts and Unbelievable Monsters, Shelley Graphics, 1980.
The Kids' Book of Pet Care, Waldman, 1980.
Kids' Book of Crossword Puzzles, Waldman, 1980.
The Horn of Africa: Ethiopia, Sudan, Somalia, and Djibouti, F. Watts, 1981.

The Books of the Unknown, illustrated by Joe Mathieu, Random House, 1982.

(Adapters) Edgar Rice Burroughs, _Tarzan of the Apes,_ illustrated by Tim Gaydos, Random House, 1982.

Bill Cosby: Making America Laugh and Learn, Dillon, 1983.

Our Earth, Waldman, 1984.

Amazing Places, Waldman, 1984.

Great Explorers, Waldman, 1984.

Insects, Waldman, 1984.

Dinosaurs, Waldman, 1984.

Sea Animals, Waldman, 1984.

The South Central United States, F. Watts, 1984.

Pollution, F. Watts, 1985.

The United Nations, F. Watts, 1985.

Cocaine, F. Watts, 1985.

Equal Justice: A Biography of Sandra Day O'Connor, Dillon, 1985.

The Right to Bear Arms, F. Watts, 1986.

Co-author, with H. Woods, of curriculum guides for Prentice-Hall. Contributor to magazines, including _Babytalk_ and _Learning Disabilities Guide._

Work in Progress

The Salem Witch Trials, for Enslow.

Sidelights

Together with husband Harold Woods and on her own, Geraldine Woods has provided young readers with a number of works valuable for their ability to impart basic facts in a coherent, organized manner. From geography to biography to the history of scientific discovery, Woods has channeled her own curiosity into the creation of books containing useful glossaries, well-researched facts, and a "clear, easy-to-read text," according to _School Library Journal_ contributor Linda Wadleigh. Among the many books Woods has co-authored with her husband since the beginning of their writing career in the mid-1970s are _The Right to Bear Arms, The Kids' Book of Pet Care,_ and _Is James Bond Dead?,_ an anthology of spy stories compiled by the Woods and published in 1979.

Profiling such notable individuals as Muppets creator Jim Henson, talk-show host Oprah Winfrey, and Supreme Court Justice Sandra Day O'Connor has occupied part of Woods' writing efforts. _Jim Henson: From Puppets to Muppets_ recounts the career of the creator of the popular characters from Public Television's _Sesame Street_ series, in a book that _School Library Journal_ contributor Pamela K. Bomboy characterized as "tightly written ... a biography of substance in spite of its brevity." And in _The Oprah Winfrey Story: Speaking Her Mind,_ Woods draws on an interview with the famous television personality as well as other secondary sources to create an "upbeat" and "engaging look at a prominent figure," in the opinion of Jeanette Lambert in her _School Library Journal_ review.

Woods has also provided young readers with a history and description of notable places. _Spain: A Shining New Democracy,_ first published in 1987 as part of the "Discovering Our Heritage" series, profiles the country's development since the time of the first cave-dwellers. In addition to a glossary, pronunciation guide, and a section on the arts, the book also contains a section describing emigration of some Spaniards to the New World, and their contributions to North-American society since their arrival. While _School Library Journal_ reviewer Dennis C. Tucker noted that the tone is at times too "cutesy" to attract older readers, critics have praised the use of full-color photographs and up-to-date information in _Spain,_ as well as other books in the series. Within the pages of her _Saudi Arabia,_ Woods "does not shirk" from a discussion of the region's unstable political system, and includes background information on the Arab-Israeli war, the Palestine Liberation Organization (PLO), and the Saudi's Islamic faith, according to _School Librarian_ contributor Michael Weller.

Woods explores the origins of modern technology in a pair of books written over ten years apart. The first, 1988's _Science in Ancient Egypt,_ examines several topics of interest to young readers, including the process of mummification. Mathematics, medicine, astronomy, agriculture, and architecture also come under discussion, presented in what David N. Pauli judged to be a "clear and concise manner" in his _School Library Journal_ review. "Woods is careful to point out where our knowledge of Egyptian technology is incomplete," Pauli added, concluding that _Science in Ancient Egypt_ serves as a "good general introduction." In 1999's _Science of the Early Americas,_ Woods drew on the discoveries of archaeologists excavating sites throughout North America to provide readers with information on the advanced knowledge gained by Native Americans in the areas of medicine, agriculture, astronomy, and engineering.

Unfortunately, many of the lessons of the Native Americans were lost on North-American society with its European-based culture, the same culture that has industrialized vast portions of the earth's surface with sometimes drastic results. In _Pollution,_ Woods applies what _Booklist_ contributor Denise M. Wilms called a "brisk, straightforward" treatment to issues such as the use of agricultural chemicals, the buildup of garbage, acid rain, the growing problems involving storage of toxic wastes and nuclear weapon stockpiles, and a discussion of recent environmental disasters. Wilms concluded that while not delving deep into the subject, the book "still suggests the dimension of the problem."

While attempting to present both sides of each of her chosen topics in a balanced manner, Woods sometimes finds herself holding definite opinions about her subject. In books such as _Drug Use and Drug Abuse,_ for instance, she provides young readers with basic information about recreational drug usage, as well as tobacco and alcohol, educating them to the dangers in beginning to use any of the substances under discussion. "Although much attention is given to the dangers of drug use and the potential for abuse and addiction," noted _Booklist_ contributor Marilyn Kaye, "'scare' tactics are not employed, and the basic attitude seems to be an appeal to common sense." Woods's *Drug Abuse in Society: A Reference Handbook* again focuses on mind-altering chemical substances, but in a more in-depth manner than her previous work. Published in 1993, the book traces the historical path of narcotics throughout the world, and provides detailed information on drug-related organizations and the key players on both sides of the modern war on drugs. *Voice of Youth Advocates* contributor Cynthia Beatty Brown praised *Drug Abuse in Society* as "a good reference book with which to begin a study of drug abuse."

Works Cited

Bomboy, Pamela K., review of *Jim Henson: From Puppets to Muppets, School Library Journal,* June-July, 1987, p. 102.

Brown, Cynthia Beatty, review of *Drug Abuse in Society: A Reference Handbook, Voice of Youth Advocates,* June, 1994, p. 122.

Kaye, Marilyn, review of *Drug Use and Drug Abuse, Booklist,* October 15, 1979, p. 359.

Lambert, Jeanette, review of *The Oprah Winfrey Story: Speaking Her Mind, School Library Journal,* March, 1992, p. 255.

Pauli, David N., review of *Science in Ancient Egypt, School Library Journal,* May, 1988, p. 108.

Tucker, Dennis C., review of *Spain: A Shining New Democracy, School Library Journal,* October, 1987, p. 136.

Wadleigh, Linda, review of *Science in Ancient Egypt, School Library Journal,* June, 1998, p. 162.

Weller, Michael, review of *Saudi Arabia, School Librarian,* June, 1979, p. 178.

Wilms, Denise M., review of *Pollution, Booklist,* September 1, 1985, p. 72.

For More Information See

PERIODICALS

Booklist, November 1, 1978, p. 473; April 15, 1986, p. 1228; July, 1986, p. 1610; October 1, 1987, p. 322; May 1, 1988, p. 1516; June 1, 1989, p. 1716; January 1, 1995, p. 812; March 15, 1999, p. 1326.

Bulletin of the Center for Children's Books, February, 1986, p. 120; July-August, 1989, p. 286.

Growing Point, July, 1979, p. 3551.

Kirkus Reviews, October 1, 1979, pp. 1148-49; March 15, 1988, p. 450.

School Library Journal, December, 1978, p. 51; February, 1980, pp. 62-63; August, 1981, p. 62; August, 1982, p. 112; March, 1983, p. 186; November, 1983, p. 76; August, 1984, p. 74; September, 1985, p. 141; October, 1985, pp. 188-89; January, 1986, p. 72; March, 1986, p. 172; May, 1986, pp. 98-99; January, 1987, pp. 70-71; July, 1989, p. 98; July, 1994, p. 127; January, 1995, p. 141.

Voice of Youth Advocates, October, 1985, p. 281; December, 1986, pp. 250-51; October, 1989, p. 242; April, 1995.

Y

Jane Yolen

1939-

All the lives of the great fantasy writers are chock-a-block full of wild and improbable childhoods, adventures in mysterious lands, amazing and fortuitous coincidences, and strange, wasting illnesses. It used to bother me that I had lived such an ordinary life: born in New York City, public school education, an uneventful childhood with no major traumas, college that was smooth but unexciting, marriage (no divorce) to the same man for over thirty-five years, and three children. How could I possibly be a fantasy writer, a *good* fantasy writer, even (my secret hope) a *great* writer of memorable books?

The only things out of the ordinary that ever happened to me have been: losing my fencing foil in Grand Central Station during a date with a college boyfriend; learning to ride on the great white Lipizzaner horses from an instructor who spoke only loud and unintelligible German; taking a ballet class from the famous ballerina Maria Tallchief who, afterwards, hung her practice tutu on my locker; chasing after my father, the International Kite Flying Champion, when his twelve-by-twelve-foot kite had dragged him into Long Island Sound; hiking up Mount Pelion in Greece while my husband drove our van because a recent earthquake had made riding in it uncomfortable for me since I was seven-and-one-half months pregnant; swapping songs with Yemenite pickers as we worked side by side in an orange grove in Israel; falling into the swollen Colorado River after a wave had knocked me off our raft into a serpentine rapids filled with forty-two-degree water; mushing in a dogsled in Alaska in the middle of March; saving my eight-and-a-half-year-old son from a three-and-a-half-foot black-tailed rattler; having my seventy-fifth book published before my forty-sixth birthday; and . . . .

I guess any life has its strange adventures and wild accomplishments. What seems to the one who lives it a very ordinary life might sound fairly improbable, wonderful, even fantastic to somebody else. Have I told you about the Melasian merman I saw in Greenwich, England? I have a photo of it. How about learning to do the twist in a bar filled with New York City's finest garbagemen? Well, at least I haven't yet had a wasting illness.

In Which I Recount Events Before My Birth—and What Followed

Two different kinds of immigrant experience informed my life. My father's family were merchants and storytellers (some called them well-off liars!). My mother's family were intellectuals. I seem to have gotten a bit of both, though not enough of either.

My father's grandfather had been an innkeeper and a teller of tales in the small Ukranian village where he lived. He had gone to a *gymnasium,* a high school to which young Jewish boys were rarely allowed to go. (They mostly went to religious schools.) He had come home with his head stuffed with stories he passed off as his own. "Romeo and Juliet" in Yiddish was a favorite at the inn. His daughter Mina, a vivacious redhead, married Sampson Yolen, after whom I am named. Sampson's family had a bottling company. My father liked to say that his family was "in oil," but it was cooking oil and paraffin, not the kind that comes shooting up from the ground and makes fortunes. Mina and Sampson had eight living children and my father, Will, was the next to the last. There were twenty years between oldest and youngest, a spread that was to leave my father with the feeling that he had been unnoticed and unappreciated. He left home early and, though I knew all my aunts and uncles and tens of cousins and second cousins, I never really had a good sense of what my father's early life had been like. In fact I was thirty-five before I found out that he had not been born in Waterbury, Connecticut, but had come to this country as a four-year-old and was a naturalized citizen.

Jane Yolen in her attic writing room, 1996.

In a sense my father invented himself. He came from a family that had little regard for formal education but a lot for making a living and telling tall tales. He became a newspaperman, a foreign correspondent, then a publicity man for Warner Brothers films, the head of midway publicity for the 1939 World's Fair, and a promotion man for WNEW radio. He owned his own publicity firm for a while and his own film company, and ended up as a vice-president in charge of books and magazine articles for the largest public relations firm in the world. He created the job that he had and, in a large part, created a certain kind of public relations. And he re-created kite flying in America. In the 1950s he declared himself Western Hemisphere Kite Flying Champion and then proceeded to defend his title and publicize the sport to such an extent that he forced a renaissance in kiting that is still going on. He was pictured in *Life* magazine flying kites, is in the *Guinness Book of World Records* for kiting, and was also in *Ripley's Believe It or Not*.

When he was still a newspaperman, my father met a beautiful young social worker in New York, Isabelle Berlin. Third oldest of six children, she was a brilliant Phi Beta Kappa graduate of Randolph Macon College in Virginia. Her parents, Fanny and Daniel Berlin, had owned a clothing store in Newport News, Virginia, and raised their children in a brick house in Hampton Roads, near the Chesapeake Bay. Education was always emphasized in the Berlin family. One of the relatives of the Berlins had been a rabbi instrumental in reestablishing Hebrew as a living language.

The Yolens in America: Jane's grandparents, Mina and Sampson, surrounded by their children and grandchildren. "Only Will, my father, is missing!"

Isabelle's two younger brothers became a doctor and a lawyer; her sisters all were psychiatric social workers. Master's degrees, doctorates, Phi Beta Kappas were the norm in her family; they were all brilliant, handsome, and quirky. My mother, though, had no idea that she was beautiful and she adored my father for choosing her. When they were married—first secretly at city hall and then, months later, in a religious ceremony—she could not believe her luck. Her husband was a blue-eyed, pint-sized charmer, a newspaperman with energy, great dreams, and a future that no one doubted would be wonderful.

For five years they led a busy New York City life. My father moved out of newspaper work into the life of a publicity flack. In fact, when I was born, February 11, 1939, he was doing publicity for the MacAlpine Hotel and they were living in an apartment right in the hotel. My birth was announced in the gossip columns, next to the pictures of bathing beauties.

My mother quit her social work job in order to raise me (and later my brother Steven, born November 4, 1942) and she never had a paying job again. Years later, when we were teens, she did volunteer work, heading a family service organization and reading to the blind. In her free time she wrote, mostly short stories that did not sell, and made up crossword puzzles and double acrostics that did.

I remember practically nothing about my early childhood. Some of it was spent in New York City; about a year and a half was in California when my father was doing publicity for Warner's. We lived in a beautiful ranch house next door to Walter Brennan, the grizzled Western star. I have no memory of it. What I do remember, however, is the two years we lived with my Grandma Fanny and Grandpa Dan when my father was stationed in England during World War II. My father was head of the secret radio broadcasting to Europe, called ABSIE. So mother and Steve (who was only a baby) and I moved into the Hampton Roads house. The two books that came directly from that time were *All Those Secrets of the World* and *Miz Berlin Walks* though somehow I couldn't write them until I was in my fifties! The reason I recall that time so vividly was that my grandfather, whom I adored, died of a sudden and unexpected heart attack while we were there.

One morning I woke up and heard a strange sound. It was my grandmother sobbing and sobbing. She cried for months—at least it seems so in my memory—and I was afraid ever to go back into her bedroom, that place of death, even though it was connected by a long closet to the bedroom I shared with Steve. We had loved to play in that closet, running through it with the fresh-smelling clothes brushing over our heads, hour by hour. After my grandfather died, the house seemed haunted and cold. I began to be afraid to go up the long stairs alone because the first door on the left at the top of the stairs was my grandparents' bedroom. Every night after Grandpa's death I closed the closet door and shoved a chair up under the handle. Years later, when my middle child, Adam, had the same kind of fears because of our house's long, dark halfway, I remembered that time in Virginia. I was never able to write about my grandfather's death though it was a story that haunted me, until an editor I knew asked if I would write a short story based on my childhood. A tale I called "The Long Closet" came hurtling out of me onto the page.

"My parents, Will and Isabelle Yolen," 1935.

My Berlin cousins lived close by and for those two years we were inseparable. My cousin Michael Garrick, about a year older than I, used to lead me into trouble, which is not to say that I was an unwilling participant. We would go down to the Bay and wade in it though we had been warned again and again not to. And we were always found out because the Bay was fouled with fuel oil from the great tankers and destroyers that docked there before crossing the ocean to England to aid in the Allied war effort. Michael's and my legs were always coated with the oil when we had been sneaking around. Once we even dared to swim in the Bay, and were both royally spanked for that trick and forced to soak in my grandmother's big tub for an hour, then spanked again. When I was a teenager and spent a summer vacation in Virginia, I fell in love briefly with my cousin Michael. He was not interested in me but in biology, chemistry, and tennis. I was a failure at all three.

I was a failure as a Southerner, too, because all the other girls on the block had names like "Frances Bird" and "Mary Alice." I was just plain Jane.

Years later I would put our neighbors, Frances Bird, Willard A., and Bubba into a mystery novel called *The Inway Investigators,* but I set the story in the small New England town of Conway—which I called Inway—where we then lived. The grandmother in my picture book *No Bath Tonight* has the same sense of humor and love of life that my Grandmother Fanny had. And the line in *Commander Toad in Space,* about not being brave unless you are first very much afraid, comes from something I used to tell my son Adam, something my mother used to tell me, when confronted with those stairs. So the little bits and pieces of my childhood informed my stories, disguised by both memory and time.

In Which My Early School Days Are Detailed

I was in half a dozen schools by second grade, both public and private, as my mother looked for the best school for me. We lived on Central Park West, which was elegant, but on Ninety-seventh Street, which was not. The public school I was supposed to attend was dark, dirty, and to my mother's mind, totally inappropriate for me, so I was shifted from place to place. One time we even lied about where we lived to get into a better school, but I was too young to remember the pretend address, and so was found out. And kicked out.

But I was also an early reader. When I read our semester's reading book overnight, the teacher had no alternative but to skip me into second grade. I spent the remainder of my elementary school days at PS 93 which is now only a parking lot on Ninety-third Street and Columbus Avenue. I walked to and from school with my best friend Diane Sheffield who lived in the apartment across the hall. She was skinny and blonde, I was plump and dark, but the boys seemed to pull my pigtails as often as hers. We were both tomboys, and we played rough-and-tumble games in the grass and rocks of Central Park.

At PS 93 the teachers encouraged my reading and writing. I won gold stars and gold stars and more gold stars. I was the gold star star. And I was also pretty impossibly full of myself. In first or second grade I wrote the school musical, lyrics *and* music, in which everyone was some kind of vegetable. I played the lead carrot. Our finale was a salad. Another gold star.

The next year I wrote a song, a story, and drew an elaborate map of something called "Candy Cane Island." The lyrics went something like:

> Where is that Candy Cane Island,
> Where in the world can it be?
> Right over dreamland, across the canal,
> Just come and follow me.

When I was in my forties, a boy from that class whom I hadn't seen or heard from in over twenty years wrote to me. He remembered the entire song! All I really remembered from PS 93, besides my first kiss in the school yard, were the names of all the boys and girls, in alphabetical order. I had been class secretary for three years in a row and had to read out the roll call every morning. Even today, as a party trick, I can call them out. "Alan, Arthur, Barry, Bruce, Carl, Claude . . ." the boys begin. "Barbara, Breena, Carol, Diane, Dolores, Ellen, Gail C., Gail S., Jane, Judy, June . . ." the girls.

Gold stars, roll calls, my first (and second) kiss and the slap I dished out for it, are all I really recall. And marching around Fire Island with my friend Susan Hodes, singing songs and passing a hat. Some days we collected enough for several sodas *and* an ice cream. Our harmonies, especially on "Dona Nobis Pacem," were terrific.

In sixth grade I took a test for one of the New York special schools and was accepted by Hunter, an all girls'

Jane with her mother, 1939.

school for "intelligently gifted" students. With my gold stars and my writing ability, I expected to be a superior gift to Hunter. To my surprise—and horror—I was barely in the middle of the class and managed to stay there only by studying extremely hard. Once again, though, I was elected to class secretary, two years in a row. I can still say the names (in alphabetical order of *last* names): "Adele, Berliner, Brenner, Cutney, Damoshek, Deutsch ..." I was to use many of those names—and the names of two men I almost married—in a short story called "Names" that I wrote years later.

Since it was clear that I was not nearly as smart as I had thought, I turned my attention to those gifts I did have. Music became a mainstay in my life. I starred as Hansel in our class rendition of *Humperdinck's Hansel and Gretel,* though I was about a head shorter than the girl who played Gretel. She had a pure lyric soprano voice while I had a low alto. I also played piano, with more vigor than talent, and liked to write little songs. I also was one of the leading dancers in my class at Balanchine's American School of Ballet, again a question more of vigor than ability, plus a genius for remembering the complicated succession of steps. (In my sixtieth year I would call on my old ballet experience to write a picture book about the Firebird ballet.) My writing continued to bring me approval, though Hunter did not give gold stars. I wrote my eighth-grade social studies essay in rhyme. It was all about New York State's manufacturing, with a great rhyme for Otis Elevators which I have, quite thankfully, forgotten. I also wrote my first two books: a nonfiction book on pirates, which I bound with a linen-over-cardboard cover, and a novel. The novel was seventeen pages long and included a trip by covered wagon across the West, death by snake bite, a

plague of locusts, the birth of an infant on the road, a prairie fire, slaughter by Indians, and marriage to a schoolmarm. It was a masterpiece of economy.

This reflected later in my appreciation for the short form. Short stories and poetry have remained my first loves. I have come to writing full-scale novels almost reluctantly, and it is always a struggle for me to make them long enough. Somehow seventeen pages still seems about right! Music, too, has remained an important part of my writing. Many of my books have been inspired by songs: *Dream Weaver* by a bad rock song; *Bird of Time* by a rock song mis-heard; *Greyling* and "The White Seal Maid" by a folk song; the solution of "Princess Heart O' Stone" by an Irish ditty. There are often lyrics in the stories that I write, and I have also written many song books (*The Fireside Song Book of Birds and Beasts, Rounds about Rounds,* and *The Lullaby Songbook*), two musical plays, and half an opera. I write songs and song lyrics for folksingers, rock groups, and composers, some of which have been recorded. A number of my stories have been about musicians: *The Magic Three of Solatia, The Minstrel and the Mountain,* and "The Boy Who Sang for Death" among them. And songs that I composed are in at least three of my books: *Spider Jane, All in the Woodland Early,* and *Sister Light, Sister Dark.*

In Which I Really Get Educated (Sort Of)

My parents sent me off to summer camp two years in a row, when I was twelve and thirteen. It was a wonderful Quaker camp in Vermont called Indianbrook (now Farm and Wilderness), where I learned about pacifism, swimming, storytelling, mucking out horse stalls, planting a garden, and kissing, not necessarily in that order. At the end of the second summer, my Aunt Isabelle and Uncle Harry came to take Steve and me home because our parents had suddenly and without warning bought a house in Westport, Connecticut. We were not even allowed to go back to New York to say good-by. It was quite a blow to me for two reasons. My camp boyfriend—my first and a second cousin once removed—lived in New York. And I had just been accepted into the High School of Music and Art where I was desperate to go.

So I did not get to say farewells or exchange addresses with any of my school or ballet friends and the worst loss was Ann Rosenwasser who was my best friend at both places. Ann, who was much brighter than I and a better dancer, with a great arch (I was flat-footed and cared about such things), had been my partner for over two years in a strange little game of imagination in which we pretended she was the prima ballerina of The Company (the New York City Ballet Company, which was Balanchine's) and I was the top young choreographer. We each included in the game a kind of soap opera schedule of events having to do with boyfriends (mine was supposedly Jacques D'Amboise, the youngest man in the company who was destined in real life to become the *premier danseur* of the company). We spent hours at "The Game," as we called it, playacting the parts and devising intricate plots for both the ballets and our lives. After finishing Hunter High School, Ann actually became a member of the corps de ballet of the New York City Ballet Company. But while I continued to dance in Connecticut, it became increasingly clear that my body type harkened back to the Yolens—short, squat, and while athletic and graceful, not sylphlike and anorexic like a Balanchine dancer. One day I plan to write a novel about "The Game," but meanwhile such characters as Plain Jane in *Sleeping Ugly* and in *The Lady and the Merman* reflect a lot of my ideas about physical beauty. And the attention to plots, both the romance of young love and the romance of storybook ballets which Ann and I worked on, has stayed with me for all of my writing life.

In Westport I started school at Bedford Junior High School, and went on to Staples High School where I was involved with the singing groups, the literary groups, and was captain of the girls' basketball team. (Even though I was the shortest one on the team, I could jump just like a dancer. Training will out!) I took piano lessons, ballet lessons, and horseback riding lessons. I wrote a lot of poetry, including one poem, "Death, You Do Not Frighten Me," which won a Scholastic Writing Award. And when our senior class voted for "The Perfect Senior," it was my voice they chose. That is probably why many of my heroines have lovely, low voices—and can sing.

My first best friend in Westport was Stella Colandrea who was Catholic. I had never really been close to anyone but Jews and Quakers before. But I began going to church—and Christmas Midnight Mass—with Stella who sang in the choir with the loveliest soprano voice I had ever heard. She had a wicked sense of humor, too. We used to do our homework on the roof of her porch, right outside her bedroom window, on warm evenings. We'd also make up naughty limericks about the boys in our class, being terrible flirts the both of us. It was because of Stella's influence that I became enamored of different religions. My own Judaism and camp-discovered Quakerism were the most morally appealing, but the panoply of Catholic rites seem to have taken hold of my imagination and wind in and out of many of the elaborate religious rituals I write about in my fantasy tales. And, since I am an Arthurian buff and a lover of things medieval, knowing a bit about the church helps. In *The Magic Three of Solatia,* the ceremony of Thrittem is a kind of bar mitzvah crossed with a silent Quaker meeting. In *Cards of Grief,* I worked in storytelling, Seders, and the Mass, along with Communion, Confession, and the Viaticum, if you read it with care.

Later on in high school my two closest girlfriends were LeeAnn Walker and Mariette Hartley, the one an artist, the other an actress—the two careers I would have loved if I had not been a writer. Mariette and I especially have kept in touch over the years. I had her in mind to play the part of Sister Agatha in *The Gift of Sarah Barker,* writing the description to fit her. Unfortunately it has not been made into a movie.

I was only marginally popular in high school, running around with two very different crowds: the intellectuals and the fast social crowd. I was a nondrinker and too slow for the latter, too fast and flirty and insubstantial for the former. I developed a wisecracking, cynical patter and an ability to tell funny stories which was, I think, why I was kept around in each. In college I dropped that veneer and let my natural poetic and romantic side show.

The greatest influence on me in high school was neither parents nor friends but my cousin-in-law Honey Knopp. A pacifist, a peace activist, who held hootenannies (music fests) at her home, Honey gave me my first copy of

George Fox's *Journal.* (Fox was the founder of Quakerism and I wrote a biography of him, *Friend: The Story of George Fox and the Quakers.*) This secret, alien, meditative, poetic side I kept well hidden throughout much of high school except from Honey and some of the people I met at her house. This was in the mid-1950s, when to be interested in such things branded one an outsider, a beatnik, a left-winger. I adored Honey and her husband Burt, and their home became my haven. Oh, I still went to basketball games and dances and parties, wisecracking with my friends and being outrageous. But Honey called out another side of me. Her influence can be seen in many of my works: *The Minstrel and the Mountain,* "The Boy Who Sang for Death," *The Transfigured Hart, The Hundredth Dove, The Gift of Sarah Barker* among them. My poetry, much of which I shared only with Honey and my mother, was filled with the imagery of life/death, light/dark, and cadences of the folk songs I learned at the hoots.

From Staples I went on to Smith College, an all-women's college in western Massachusetts, one of the famous Ivy League's Seven Sisters. It was a choice that would, all unknowingly, change my life. It made me aware of friendships possible—and impossible—with women. It created in me a longing for a particular countryside, that of New England. It charged me with a sense of leftsidedness, of an alien or changeling awareness. And it taught me, really, about poetry and literature and the written word.

Smith had not been my first choice. I had wanted to go to Radcliffe (partially because a boyfriend was in Boston) or to Swarthmore, a coed Quaker school. But though I was accepted by Smith, Wellesley, and Oberlin, my two top choices did not want me. I had been high—but not top—of my class, ranked seventh in a class of over two hundred. I

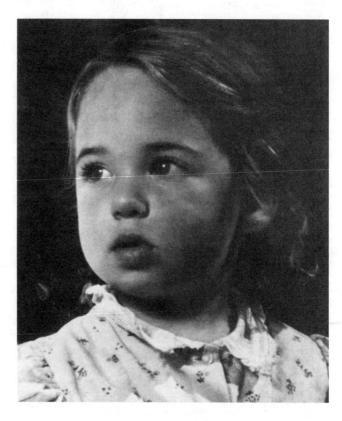

About two years old.

Jane, left, at family summer camp in Bar Harbor, Maine, about 1946.

had had good—but not spectacular—test scores. I had been captain of the basketball team, news editor of the paper, head of the Jewish Youth Group, vice-president of the Spanish, Latin and jazz clubs, in the top singing group, winner of the "I Speak for Democracy" contest, winner of the school's English prize, and contributor to the literary magazine. But still I did not stand out enough. So I chose Smith because Smith emphasized that everyone at Smith sang. I loved singing.

Actually I only sang for a year in the choirs at Smith before turning my attention elsewhere. I didn't find it easy making good friends at Smith. I just didn't like women that much. Except for LeeAnn and Mariette, most of my friends in high school had been boys. In fact I ran around with a gang of boys who lived nearby, one more boy amongst them. So I made some of my earliest friends among the faculty.

The five greatest influences on me while I was at Smith were: a teacher of seventeenth-century poetry, Joel Dorius, who showed me just how beautiful language could be; my first advisor and critic of my poetry, Marie Boroff, who showed me that one might be critical of the writing without tearing down the writer; Dudley Harmon, the head of the Smith News Bureau, who believed in my future with the written word; Edna Williams, a gracious teacher of Chaucer who made me realize that women could be scholars and live the life of the mind without giving up gentleness and beauty; and Bill Van Voris, my senior advisor and an anarchic soul, who gave me the greatest gift—that of self-recognition. He made me believe that being a writer was a wonderful thing to be for itself, not because it was easy and familiar and meant gold stars.

At Smith I wrote vast amounts of poetry and studied English and Russian literature, minored in religion, and took a smattering of history, sociology, and geology. I also discovered I had a flair for both politics and poetry and a minor talent for the musical stage. I ran many of the campus organizations, wrote and performed in the class

musicals, and penned my final exam in American Intellectual History in verse, thereby receiving an A+ for a C-worth of knowledge. But it was poetry—and folksinging, which I did with a boy friend, Mike Lieber, from Trinity College—that became the real constants in my life. My early poetic efforts were published in Smith's *Grecourt Review, Poetry Digest,* and other small magazines. I won all of the poetry prizes given out my senior year. The folk songs I had first begun learning at Honey's and then with Mike (who went on to become an anthropologist and studio musician) became part of both my writing and my later great interest in oral storytelling.

In Which I Join the Work Force

I had earned spending money by babysitting in high school and working one summer as a "page" in the local library. (I was almost fired from the library because I wore a strapless sundress one impossibly hot afternoon, and it was considered "unsuitable.")

My summer between high school and college I went to an American Friends (Quaker) Service Committee work camp in Yellow Springs, Ohio, where I worked harder than I had ever worked before—for no pay. We built an outdoor education center for migrant laborers' children, ran a day-care program for them, and traveled by bus through the South learning about race relations and singing peace songs.

The summer of my freshman/sophomore year, I worked as a cub reporter for the *Bridgeport Sunday Herald.* It was there I wrote my first signed pieces for a newspaper. My very first byline read "by Joan Yolen." I did not take it as a sign. But I quickly learned that I was not a tough reporter when the editor assigned me to write an article on welfare recipients. I came back after the interviews and cried at my desk. I wanted to help those people, not write about them.

The next summer I was a camp counselor. I had wanted to go with the AFSC to Alaska to help move a village of tubercular Eskimo. But my parents would not let me go, so I spent two months being a junior counselor in New Jersey. The following summer I lived in New York City with another Smith student and worked for *Newsweek* magazine as a summer intern. Mostly I delivered mail, went for coffee, sorted photos, and helped in the research and fact-checking departments. It was not glamorous.

My real life work began when I graduated, broke up with my fiance because—as I told him—"I have to find out if I can be a writer," and moved to New York City for good. Or so I thought. I got another summer internship, this time with *This Week* magazine, on the strength of my scrapbook of bylined magazine and newspaper articles from such diverse places as the *Bridgeport Sunday Herald,* the *New Haven Register* (about Smith College activities), and *Popular Mechanics* (about kites). I stayed there until halfway through the fall, in the research department, mail room, and facts-checking department, and then all the editors returned from vacation and there was no room for me. Knowing that would probably happen, I had already lined up another job, with the *Saturday Review.*

At *SR,* I was in the production department, a job which meant I had to help lay out the magazine, as well as choose the cartoons and let the poetry editor know how much room we had for a poem. To my horror, poetry was seen as "filler" material. We would need a three-inch poem, or a seven-inch poem. However, the production manager and I did not get along, and a few days before Christmas I was fired. In fact, I was the seventh person she had fired within two years, and I had already been warned by friends at *This Week* that life for the underlings at *SR* was usually short and not so sweet.

I spent the first few months of 1961 trying to make a living as a free-lance writer. I researched and helped write a book for my father who had been asked to do *The Young Sportsman's Guide to Kite Flying*. Since he loved signing contracts, signing autographs, and countersigning checks, but not writing books, he hired me to put it together. And I loved—and still love—the writing part best of all. It was no hardship, but the pay was very low! With the help of my father's best friend, Will Oursler (author of *The Greatest Story Ever Told*), I also got a number of small free-lance assignments, including writing short, pithy bios for Cleveland Amory's *Celebrity Register*. My best line was about the then-Senator from Connecticut, Thomas Dodd, a silver-toned orator of the old school. I wrote that he "had one of the finest voices to ever vox the populi." That was my first in-print pun. Later such things were to show up regularly in books like *The Witch Who Wasn't,* in short stories like

"The Five Points of Roguery" and "Inn of the Demon Camel," and in my "Commander Toad" series.

But the life of a free-lancer is long on searching and short on payment. I was literally living in a garret, a skylit studio apartment in the attic of a four-story house on Commerce Street in Greenwich Village, next to the Cherry Lane Theater. And I was beginning to write books.

The Commerce Street garret was actually my second venture in living in the city. The first, a ground-floor "shotgun" or "railroad" apartment, where the rooms are laid out all in a row and connected by sliding doors, had not been as successful. I lived there with two roommates, young women I had met that summer when I had been commuting from my parents' home in New Rochelle. One woman was to remain my roommate for another six months, the other (who was a friend of the singing group called The Clancy Brothers and Tommy Makem) lasted only two. The problem was partly the Clancys who used to spend a lot of time at our apartment with their friends and hangers-on (who were legion in those days), and partly the layout of the apartment. But that place was special for a different reason.

Between the three roommates, we knew about half of the young artists, writers, musicians, and radical politicians in the Village the summer of 1960. We invited everyone we could think of to our housewarming party, and the Clancys brought even more. There were so many people coming in the front door of our ground-floor apartment, that one handsome moustached young man decided not to wait any longer and climbed through the window. He saw me standing in the crowd, my long dark braid over one shoulder, and came over, kissed me on the nape of the neck, and introduced himself.

"I'm David Stemple," he said, with a slow smile. "I'm a friend of one of the girls who lives here."

"I'm Jane Yolen," was my icy reply. "And I'm one of those girls. You're not my friend!"

It was not a great beginning.

Two mornings later (it was a wild party!), the landlord threw the three of us out, relenting only when we began to weep simultaneously in a flood tide that threatened to drown him. We lasted in the apartment only two more months.

David Stemple and I were married in 1962, after a slow-starting friendship and a long courtship, in the garden of my parents' New Rochelle house. By that time he had a beard as well. All my cousins showed up at the wedding with fake beards in his honor, and my brother and other folk musicians played such songs as "I Wish I Were Single Again," which I performed with great gusto. My father, who had warned me that David "was not the marrying kind," professed admiration at my choice. We are married to this day. Years after our marriage, while recounting this story to some school children who wanted to know if my "real" life was in my stories, I realized that my fairy tale *The Girl Who Loved the Wind,* which is dedicated to David, is about our meeting. In it a Persian girl is kept in a walled-in palace by her overprotective father until the day the wind leaps over the garden wall and sweeps her away into the wide, everchanging world.

About the time I was being married in New York something else happened that would set the pattern of my life for good. I received a letter from an editor at A. A.

Captain of the Staples High School girls' basketball team, 1956.

Knopf. She wrote that she had been traveling around the colleges asking about recent graduates who might be working on book manuscripts. At Smith she talked to Dudley Harmon at the News Bureau. Now, if she had approached the English department, this story might have a different ending. I was thought of as a poet and a journalist by the department, not a novelist. But Dudley, my journalism mentor, believed in me. She told Judith Jones, the editor, that there was only one recent graduate with talent—me. It wasn't true, of course. There were many better writers who graduated at the same time. But Dudley was faithful to her young protegee, which is why I—and not any other recent Smith grad—received a letter from Ms. Jones. She asked if I had a book-length manuscript she might see.

Well, there is no getting around it. I lied. I wrote to her and said that of course I had several book ideas, what budding young author does not. In fact I had none, only a group of poems in less-than-final stages and my magazine articles. I would have thought little more about it, just filed it away for future reference, except that Ms. Jones wrote back and asked to see me and my books.

Caught in the web of this deceit I, who always prided myself on my honesty, realized there was nothing to do but sit down at my typewriter and get something done quickly. Children's books! I thought. They'd be the easiest and quickest. (I was to discover painfully and thoroughly over the next thirty or so writing years that, in fact, children's books are among the most difficult things to write—well.

Jane at a bridge game at Wesleyan College, 1959.

They have the compression of a poem where every single word must count. As the great stage director Stanislavsky once remarked to a young actor who was going to perform in front of an audience of children for the first time: "Act as you always do—only better." Words for would-be children's books writers as well.) However, I knew very little about children's books; I had been reading adult books since ninth grade (this was before the advent of young adult books, which arrived on the book scene after I was past being a young adult). What I remembered was—pictures. The problem was that I could not draw. Luckily, or so I thought, a high school friend with whom I had shared a boyfriend on and off for eight years had moved to New York; and she was an artist. So Susan Purdy and I put together several quick little picture books without regard to the nature of the beast. One was an alphabet book of names (sounding remarkably like the roll call from elementary school), one was a kite flying book (thanks Dad!), one was about a whale who wanted to be a minnow (which David laconically remarked was awfully autobiographical). I also set down ideas for two longer books. One was to be about kite flying, putting in all the romance and lore I had not been able to shoehorn into *The Young Sportsman's Guide,* and a one-page idea about a book on lady pirates cribbed from the report I had done in eighth grade.

Armed with these "book-length manuscripts" I went to see Judith Jones. I still wonder what she must have thought of me. Though she was ever gracious and spent several hours talking to me, she did not (needless to say) buy anything. However she did introduce me to Virginie Fowler, the children's book editor, who was, I must honestly report, equally appalled at my lack of knowledge and the temerity I showed in bringing such feeble material to their attention.

Of course I was crushed. Rejection, in person or by letter, is never easy to take. But it is one of the constants in the world of publishing and anyone too shaken in confidence by a first refusal (or a second or a twenty-second) will never make it in the writing world. Susan Purdy was crushed as well. But we still had those books to sell, so we gamely began sending them around in the more traditional way, from editor to editor. They all came back. I could paper a wall with those rejection letters if I had them still.

Then my father remarked that he had a friend, who was a vice-president of David McKay Publishing Company, that he would be happy to introduce me to. I hesitated about half a minute, embarrassed to use any influence, until I realized that Judith Jones had been "influence" and it hadn't gotten me published—but it had gotten me a personalized course in writing and literature. "Introduce me," I said at last.

Eleanor Rawson at McKay was as polite and as generous as Judith Jones had been, and she also introduced me to her children's book editor, a muffin-shaped woman named Rose Dobbs. Rose greeted me with the words, "I never buy from unknown writers."

Eleanor Rawson left me in the care of this dragon and I slumped down in my chair, fearful of what would happen next.

She dismissed the alphabet book quickly, and only glanced and grimaced at the whale. She paused a little longer over the kite picture book, and longer still over the

Beside a painting of David at the time of their engagement, 1961.

history of kites, explaining in a matter-of-fact voice, "It doesn't know if it wants to be an adult book or a children's book." Then she studied the one-page synopsis of *Pirates in Petticoats,* and tapped it with her finger.

"This interests me," she said.

I sat up in my chair.

"But I never buy from unknowns."

I slipped back down.

"Still ..."

Up I shot.

"... this interests me. Leave it with me for a few weeks. I want to think about it."

I was dismissed. I couldn't leave her office fast enough.

It wasn't two weeks—it was several months—and I still had to pay rent and eat, so I found a job. I worked as first reader, manuscript clerk, and assistant editor at Gold Medal Books, a paperback house known for its western novels and spy thrillers, what we called in the trade "bang-bang-shoot'em-ups." Eventually I even got to write cut-lines, those one-liners on the covers that explain pithily what a book is about. I was famous for about a moment in publishing as the one who coined "She was all things to two men" for some Gothic novel.

And then, on my birthday, February 11, 1961, the phone rang at work. It was Rose Dobbs, summoning me to her office. She did not say why.

It was snowing lightly as I walked the several blocks to get there at lunchtime. Once more in the dragon's lair, I huddled down in my chair again.

Ms. Dobbs looked up at me. I remember she had a hair net on, with those little colored beads that seemed to be winking and blinking at me.

Preemptively she said, "I never buy from unknowns."

I nodded.

"But ... " and she hesitated, putting one plump finger atop the paper on her desk. I could read upside down. It was my synopsis, slightly wrinkled and coffee-stained.

"But...," I prompted.

"But this interests me and I know you have written magazine articles and worked on your father's book. So you are not *entirely* unknown. Do you think you could write a full-length manuscript?"

I took a deep breath, then didn't trust my voice, and nodded instead.

"Then I shall give you a contract," she said. "And you will deliver a 150-page manuscript to me in one year."

I nodded again.

"But I won't give you any money in advance," she said. "Because you are an unknown and I don't take such chances."

I said in a very small voice, "If you give me a little bit of money, then I couldn't back out of it. I'd *have* to finish." I shut my mouth quickly, amazed at my own boldness.

"Well ... all right," she said, well-placed pauses apparently the coin of her trade. "All right. But remember, you must not tell anyone about this. It would get around. And I would be flooded with unknowns."

We shook hands and I escaped once more from the dragon and ran out into the street. There was suddenly a different kind of light in the air. Dazed, I walked the two blocks to the Overseas Press Club where my father usually had lunch. He was secretary of the club, and later would become president. Sure enough, he was sitting at the bar with a variety of cronies.

"Dad!" I shouted as I ran in, "I've sold a book!"

Everyone's head turned. This, after all, was a club dedicated to writing.

"My daughter's first book," said my father, gesturing expansively. "Drinks are on me."

The bar was suddenly mobbed, but my father looked meaningfully first at me and then at the bartender. "And a Coke for my little girl."

Not every author's story of a first book goes like that. It is rare, indeed, that an editor buys a synopsis from an unknown. But Rose Dobbs took a chance that *Pirates in Petticoats* would turn into a solid book. And though the book is out of print now and Rose may be dead, it was her willingness to sit down with a young writer a year later and go over the completed manuscript, word by word by word, that started me on the path of publication.

Rose bought a second book from me, a picture book called *See This Little Line,* but I hated the orange and purple illustrations and the sans serif type she chose for it. We didn't see eye-to-eye on the visual look of the book, and she never bought anything more from me. She never bought anything from my friend, Susan Purdy, either. And though Susan is now a well-known illustrator (and author, too), she and I have never worked together on a published book. We went our separate ways professionally, but at the beginning we were there helping one another.

In Which I Keep Writing, Writing, Writing— and Working

My desk at Gold Medal Books became a repository for soon-to-be-famous derrieres. Since my office was right next to the editor-in-chief's, young authors waiting to talk to him often sat on the edge of my desk and chatted till they were summoned. Kurt Vonnegut and Harlan Ellison were the ones I remember best, Vonnegut because he was nervous and Ellison because he could barely sit still. I came to understand that as talented as a writer might be (and they are certainly two of the best), publishing is a buyer's market. The writer trying to sell his or her work is in the inferior or beggar's position. And even today, with more than two hundred published books, I often feel this way.

Working at Gold Medal was always fun—and funny— but as I had sold two children's books I wanted to find out more about my newly-chosen field. (It had chosen me, not I it.) So I changed jobs and became an associate editor with Rutledge Press, a small packaging house.

Rutledge (and the adult division, Ridge Press) created books, hiring writers and illustrators and then selling the entire "package" to a larger publishing company for distribution. Since a number of the books were created "in house," that is to say, the editors wrote the stuff, I actually authored a number of published books that do not carry my name. There was a counting rhyme book for Doubleday with pictures by Gail Haley (who later won the Caldecott medal for *A Story, a Story*) called *One, Two, Buckle My Shoe*. Any nontraditional rhymes in the book, I wrote. I also created games, puzzles, and activities for a variety of Activity Books that Rutledge put together, my ability to write instant verse (harkening back to the days of Candy Cane Island, Otis Elevators, and my final exam) serving me well.

While I was at Rutledge, my first two books were finally published, making me a very minor minor sort of celebrity. But under the terms of my contract with Rutledge, I had to submit all my new book ideas to the company first. That was a major annoyance, though they never actually bought anything from me. I learned a lot working there, mostly about book production and how art and text have to mesh. I also learned how to do a book index. But I learned a lot of bad habits, too, especially a facileness which I have worked hard to lose over the years. And I have been left with a kind of sneering attitude towards book packagers.

One of the Rutledge Press editors was a charming, multitalented, slightly scatty woman named Frances Keene. When she left Rutledge to become editor-in-chief of the children's book department at Macmillan, she called me up and asked to see a story I had submitted to Rutledge, *The Witch Who Wasn't*. It was the beginning of an editorial relationship that I *really* count as the start of my writing career. Keene (as she preferred to be called) was a great teacher as well as a fine editor. She taught me to trust my storytelling ability and to work against being too quick. She once said, in her gentle, chiding manner, always delivered with a kind of wise-woman smile, "Don't let your facility betray you." She was right. She also pushed me into delving deeply into folklore while at the same time recognizing my comedic talents. Eventually at Macmillan—and later on at Funk and Wagnalls—she published five of my books. If she had remained in publishing, instead of becoming a college professor, we would have worked together a great deal more.

Through Keene's influence, I was beginning to prefer a more literary approach to children's books, and if there was one thing Rutledge Press was not, it was literary. So I

Jane and David, just before their wedding, September 2, 1961.

looked around for a new job and found one, surprisingly, with Virginie Fowler, the editor at Knopf who had so kindly but permanently turned down my feeble stories three years earlier. She remembered me with affection, evidently, and offered me the job at once. I became her assistant editor and spent almost three years working happily and learning about the literature of childhood. Along the way I got to meet some of the finest authors and illustrators in the business: Roger Duvoisin (courtly and generous), Beni Montresor (elegant and aloof), Roald Dahl (very tall, mysterious, imperious, funny) among them. I also got to write jacket copy for Knopf books, my two most famous being for Dahl's *Charlie and the Chocolate Factory* and Ian Fleming's *Chitty-Chitty-Bang-Bang*.

And of course I was writing, writing, writing. At this point I had practically stopped writing serious poetry, but my poetic instinct was finding its way into my stories in other ways—as chants, as euphonious names, as songs.

David and I were living on the third floor of a renovated East Village brownstone. He was working at IBM, doing mysterious things with computers, none of which I understood. I had started a weekly writer's workshop with several other aspiring young writers and editors of children's books. Included were Jean Van Leeuwen, Alice Bach, Jim Giblin, Richard Curtis, Anne Huston. We took turns meeting at one another's apartments to read our work aloud and critique it. It was my first such group, but over the years I have been involved in many continuing workshops and find them indispensable. They make me want to have something to read, if not every week, at least several times a month. They also help sharpen the critical faculties. (And there are other benefits.

Anne Huston and I wrote a book together, *Trust a City Kid,* which Jim Giblin edited for his company. Publishing children's books is a very inbred business.) I also found I have a good eye and ear for criticism. Over the years I have run many ongoing groups and taught at seminars and conferences on writing children's books across the country. Many of my students have become published authors, and I love to help them fine-tune their work and find an interested publisher. I truly believe that no one gets to the top without a leg up along the way. I certainly did not. I think it is imperative, therefore, to turn around and help others. As I wrote in my book *Touch Magic,* "one must touch magic—and pass it on."

In Which We Live Off the Land etc. for Nine Months

After five years in New York David and I were getting restless. He had been working on an early Fortran compiler at IBM as well as being a free-lance photographer. I was working as an editor and writing at the office by getting there an hour earlier than everyone, staying an hour later, and rarely going out for lunch. I wrote on weekends, I wrote in the evenings, and I loved the writing. But we were both ready for some radical change. So we decided to save my entire salary and live on his for the year, buy a VW camper bus in Europe, and travel until our money ran out.

A year and almost $10,000 later, we were ready.

We gave my mother power of attorney over our checking account, sold most of our furniture, stored the rest with friends, put a down payment on a blue van which we planned to pick up in Cologne, Germany, and quit our jobs.

Then in August 1965 we set sail.

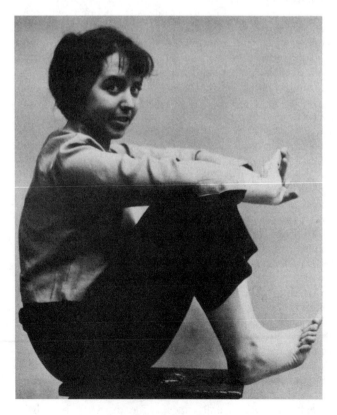

Jane Yolen, 1962.

I have to explain that in most ways David is more adventurous than I. One of four sons of two West Virginia teachers (his father was also superintendent of schools for a number of years), David was born and grew up in the small mountain town of Webster Springs. He lived one life in their brick two-story home on the main street where his mother also taught piano, and another life in the woods, hunting, fishing, and trapping. So he developed a kind of *other* sight for things in nature, a peripheral vision that I, a city girl transplanted to the suburbs for my adolescence, had never known. He has taught me some of this over the years. At the very least he has made me aware of birds (he was an avid birder and became a working ornithologist when he retired from computer science), trees, flowers, weeds, the subtle interlacing of the seasons and the world of growing things. He was also the perfect partner for a yearlong camping trip. Slow to anger, with a wicked sense of the absurd, a fine memory for history, and the ability to speak German and workaday French, he charted our course through the cities, towns, and forests with ease. Only the London roundabouts gave him any trouble. I, on the other hand, am a quick igniter with only a passable sense of direction. The only language I had studied in school was Spanish. I could read Garcia Lorca and Cervantes in the original but I could not order lunch.

And so we set sail on the *Castel Felice,* a small ocean liner filled with what seemed to be an overflow from Greenwich Village. It was, without a doubt, the hippest ship afloat. A strange, sweet smell hung in the air. And the passengers were always engaged in singing, putting on plays, poetry readings, etc. (We had a madrigal group formed aboard ship and led by Joel Cohen, now director of the Boston Camerata but then a student going to Paris to study with the famous Nadia Boulanger.) I had my typewriter with me and tried to sit on deck and write something every day.

David and I really only had two things planned for the trip. He had a commission to mount a photographic show for his alma mater, West Virginia University, with the pictures he would take in Greece. And we wanted to see the International Sheepdog Trials in Cardiff, Wales—because it sounded like fun. Other than that, we had no firm plans. We planned only to drift through the countryside of Europe and the mid-East for as long as our money lasted.

We spent nine glorious months that way. We camped in the Paris park, the Bois de Boulogne; traveled down the Rhine; stayed in a bed-and-breakfast hotel in Mumbles, Wales; wandered around museums in Spain, France, Italy, and England; picked wildflowers atop mountains and swam in the Mediterranean Sea. The month in Italy I seemed to be sick a lot. We thought it was bronchitis picked up in England, possibly a slight flu.

Actually I was pregnant.

We found that out in Rome, in between visits to the Colosseum and a museum, from a doctor who—luckily— spoke English. My Italian sounded a lot like Spanish and David's Italian sounded a lot like French, and neither of us would have made total sense of the news the doctor gave us if he had told us in Italian.

We were delighted because we wanted a family, but we decided not to cut our camping trip short. We would continue traveling until the very end of my pregnancy and then come home. I really wanted to have the baby in

Jane and David, Naples, Italy.

America, not in a strange country where I knew no one. It turned out to be a wonderful decision. After a month of only slight indisposition, I felt terrific. We sailed from Italy to Israel where we spent three months. For five weeks we worked at a small kibbutz, Kivutzat Shiller. I picked oranges and swapped songs with the Yemenite hired help. David worked in the chicken farm and also out in the fields picking bananas. We went snorkeling in the Red Sea, collected pottery shards at archeological digs, and lived for awhile on the beach at Eilat. At last we sailed for Greece so that David could spend a month taking pictures for his show.

About twice a week I sent a journal/letter home to my mother. She saved all the letters and so we have a complete account of our months on the road. But even if I never use that material directly in a detailed book of our travels, bits and pieces of our wanderings have already found their way into my stories. In Greece, for example, we spent one night in an olive grove, which became the setting for *The Girl Who Cried Flowers*. We stayed another night in a different Greek forest, the backdrop for "The Sleep of Trees." In Thessaly, the tableland inspired the opening of *The Boy Who Had Wings*. The mountains sheering off into the sea in Wales were the background for *Greyling*. The feel of the countryside thirty years later fed itself into my Young Heroes series of novels. And so it went: places and people

we met were stored away in my memory and months, even years, later were transformed into the magical landscapes of my tales.

In Which I Become a Country Gal

We returned home in May aboard a large ocean liner. As the boat sailed through the tail end of a great storm, everyone on board seemed to be sick, except for the five obviously pregnant ladies who carried with them their own ballast. We were the only ones who ate and enjoyed ourselves throughout the trip.

David and I moved in with my parents who were now living in a lovely apartment in New York. Or at least I moved in with them. David spent much of his time out interviewing for jobs. We wanted to be in an academic area in either Pennsylvania or Massachusetts/Connecticut. The best offer came from the University of Massachusetts Computer Center in Amherst. David took the job, we bought a seven-room house in Conway, Massachusetts, in mid-June, and began trying to fill it with furniture from auctions. On July 1, two weeks earlier than expected, I gave birth to a baby girl we named Heidi Elisabet.

Heidi was not my only production, however. Before leaving for Europe I had gotten an agent, the best in the business, a tall, elegant, dark-haired, mothering woman named Marilyn Marlow. But the entire time we had been in Europe, Marilyn had been unable to sell anything for me. She was distraught about it, conferring often with my mother. Knowing I was about to return, she put on an extra push, and nudged a few editors into early decisions. So it was that two days after I returned, I got a phone call at my parents' house. Marilyn wanted me to come to her office. When I arrived, Marilyn was smiling her wonderful sly I've-got-something-special smile. She had just sold three books for me—on the same day!

One of the books—*It All Depends,* which I had written at the kibbutz—was sold to my old editor, Frances Keene, now at Funk and Wagnalls. The other two books were the ones that Keene had purchased for Macmillan before she left and the new editor had turned back to me, on my birthday in 1965, with the admonition "You do not know how to write. Perhaps if you have a child, when it is six months old, you will begin to understand how to write for children." Those two books, *The Minstrel and the Mountain* and *The Emperor and the Kite,* were sold to an editor who would become another seminal influence in my writing life: Ann K. Beneduce of World Publishing Company. I met her that first week I was home, waddling into her office, eight months pregnant. Ann—an elegant, quiet, persuasive woman with an ageless face and an artist's eye for detail—became my friend from that first meeting. She *loved* fairy tales and, for the next fifteen years or so, she was to be my major editor, publishing my first fairy tale collections and pushing me to try my wings in other genres as well. She announced to the world that I was the "American Hans Christian Andersen," and while I have always felt that claim quite a bit wide of the mark, she produced book after book in the handsomest way possible, including *The Girl Who Cried Flowers, The Hundredth Dove, Dream Weaver, Neptune Rising, The Girl Who Loved the Wind, The Seeing Stick* . . . the list goes on and on. We worked on almost thirty books together.

And so I became a born-again New Englander with a small child, a true free-lance writer, with several publishers vying for my stories and an agent who was always looking out for my best interests. With only small variations, it was to be my life from then on.

By living in western Massachusetts in the Connecticut River (or Pioneer) Valley, we were near five great colleges—Smith, Amherst, Mt. Holyoke, Hampshire, and the University of Massachusetts. That meant we were close to a wide assortment of cultural activities, yet surrounded by trees. Every day there were lectures, symphonies, art exhibits. In the nearby towns were artists, artisans, academics, writers. At the same time, we were right where birds sang cheerily in the mornings, our neighbors grew mammoth tomatoes, and maple sugar buckets hung on our own trees. It was certainly a wonderful setting for an author.

I also found that having a new baby stimulated my imagination. This was true with Heidi, and later on, with each of my sons. A new baby meant that I was often sitting quietly for long periods of time nursing the child in the quiet darkness. There was nothing else to do but think—and dream. And what I thought and dreamt were stories. They just flowed out of me.

Of course having an infant also meant that I had to readjust my time and make every little bit of freedom work for me. One cannot type out a story if a baby is crying, or needs feeding, or changing. So another pattern began to emerge, a way of using those little patch pieces of time and quilting them together to make a larger story.

And then there was David. With a fine critical eye and an appreciative nature, he had always been my greatest supporter, the first one who read everything I wrote. He took more than a father's usual share of time with Heidi. Long before the concept of being a *house husband,* or *augmented fathering,* became popular, he was putting it into action. He would cart Heidi off for long rides or walks in the woods, partly so that I could have time to write, partly so he could have more time with his daughter.

When Heidi was three months old, we noticed something wrong with her legs. The bones below the knees were bent at a strange angle, like a cowboy's bowed legs. The specialist put her in casts for four months, then into a contraption called a "Denny Brown splint." "Don't be surprised," he warned us, "if she has trouble walking." Never daunted, she began *running* at ten and a half months and ended up as a medal-winning gymnast and captain of the high school cheerleading squad which won trophies in every tournament in Massachusetts. She has grown into a headstrong, determined, thoughtful, caring woman, who is articulate, individual, empathic. Married now to an easy-going disc jockey, Brandon Piatt, they have two children—one an adopted teenager, Lexi Callan, and one their own birth child, Maddison Jane, named after her grandmother and an avenue, as I like to say. They live in South Carolina. Heidi studied social work and criminal justice in college, worked for a while as a probation officer and a private detective, and now is a stay-at-home mom and a writer. She has had books, poems, short stories published, some written with me—like *Meet the Monsters* and the series Unsolved Mysteries from History—and some stories and poems on her own.

Heidi is the prototype for Sarah Barker in *The Gift of Sarah Barker* and, except for the red hair, looks like Sarah

as well. She is also Akki in the Pit Dragon books (*Dragon's Blood, Heart's Blood, A Sending of Dragons*) and Jennifer in my Tartan Magic series. Most famously, she is the little girl in *Owl Moon.* She posed for a number of book jackets drawn by a local artist, so the picture of Melissa on the jacket of *The Stone Silenus* is really Heidi. Some of the lines are hers, too.

A year after Heidi's birth I had an early miscarriage, then got pregnant again and gave birth in 1968 to a lusty eight-pounder, Adam Douglas. Towheaded, an early walker, early talker, a reader at age two and a half, left-handed Adam was always a handful. He used to rock himself to sleep at night in his crib and was always drumming on chairs and stairs. He is extremely musical, plays piano and guitar (and used to play cello), formed his own rock band, and at fifteen did the musical arrangements for *The Lullaby Songbook,* which I edited. He is Commander Toad, and he is also Jakkin in the Pit Dragon books as well as the accident-prone part of the little boy Jeremy in *No Bath Tonight.*

Adam has become a rock-and-roll musician, most recently in two bands in Minneapolis, the cult favorite Boiled in Lead which was reviewed on NPR as "the most consistently innovative world beat band in America," and a local Irish pub band called the Tim Malloys. We have done eight music books together, and he and his wife Betsy Pucci Stemple own a record company, Fabulous Records, so he is a music producer as well as a musician and composer. Brilliant, quirky, amazingly funny, with one of those steel-trap minds that forgets nothing he's ever heard, he is also a writer, having had several published short stories and poems in anthologies. We have done eight books together, he the music and me the words. They

Parents, Isabelle and Will Yolen, 1967.

include among others: *The Lap Time Song and Play Book, Milk and Honey, Sing Noel, Hark, The Mother Goose Song Book.* However his most wonderful production to date has been his daughter, Alison Isabelle who (with her cousin Maddison Jane) was the impetus for my picture book *Off We Go.*

We moved to the Boston area for two years while David and some of his friends began a computer company, and the house we had there was one of those wonderful four-chimney Georgian brick houses. It was so elegant and we were so—*not* elegant—that I always felt that the house was slumming to have us living there. Our third child, Jason Frederic, was born while we lived in Bolton. Another big baby, he was almost nine pounds. Jason had a placid disposition and a ready smile. He rarely cried. From the beginning he was interested in animals, animals, animals— and trucks. Now as an adult, he is interested in those same things. He studied art in college, as well as business. He lives in the mountains of Colorado where he is a professional photographer of wildlife and outdoor sports. We have done five books together—his photographs, my words. They include *Water Music, Once Upon Ice, House/ House, A Letter from Phoenix Farm,* and *Snow, Snow.*

Like many third children, Jason is easygoing, sweet-tempered, and shy. He is also the dirty part of Jeremy in *No Bath Tonight,* the male counterpart of the little sister in *The Stone Silenus,* and the boy in *The Boy Who Spoke Chimp.*

Just nine days after Jason was born, my mother died. A smoker, she had developed lung cancer that traveled quickly into the lymph glands. The doctor told us she had six months to live. She lived eight. She died never having seen Jason, only a photograph of him I had sent special delivery from the hospital. Her death affected me in ways I am still discovering.

For years I have mourned her in my tales. *The Bird of Time* was begun the day I heard she had cancer, my way of wanting to slow time down or stop time altogether. I dedicated that story to her memory. "The Boy Who Sang for Death" carries in it a line that I realized only later was meant for her. The boy Karl says "Any gift I have I would give to get my mother back." In *Cards of Grief* I invented a culture in which grieving is the highest art, and the story comes straight from my heart.

In Which We Slide Back into the Valley Again

There is a joke in western Massachusetts that the Connecticut River Valley is greased. There's no escaping it. You may try to leave, but you always come sliding back down into it again. And so, when Jason was about a year

With her children, Heidi, Jason (foreground), and Adam, 1975.

Jane Yolen, Hatfield, Massachusetts, 1981.

old, we left the Boston area, and returned to the Valley. David went back to work at the computer center at the University and we found a fourteen-room farmhouse in the small Polish farm community of Hatfield, population 3,000.

Of course we were (and still are) a bit of an anomaly in the town. The bulk of our neighbors are older, Catholic, Polish, farmers and blue-collar workers. At first we were thought of as hippies, then we began to put down roots. I planted a garden and in one of the large barns on the property we started a crafts center. Over seven years we gave space to craftspersons of all sorts—potters, leather workers, silversmiths, and the like. Because of the barn, stories came. "The Pot Child" was one that came directly, "Man of Rock, Man of Stone" indirectly.

In the early 1970s I became very involved with the newly-formed Society of Children's Book Writers (SCBW, later SCBWI—for Illustrators as well) and took a position on its Board of Directors. I have held that position ever since. By being involved in all the SCBW activities, I began to feel that I was giving back—or rather paying forward—to all those folks who had helped me along the way.

For ten years I single-handedly ran an SCBW New England conference, before handing it over to the University of Massachusetts School of Education who are running it still. For twenty-five years I held a monthly children's book

writers/illustrators group that met in the basement of the Hatfield Public Library. Though I am no longer part of that, it continues on. I helped start an Illustrators Group—The Western Mass. Illustrators Guild, and I am the only non-artist member. I was president of the Science Fiction and Fantasy Writers of America for two years, and am currently on the board of a number of journals in the field of literature, children's books, and fairy tales.

I am also part of a long-term weekly workshop which I started back in the early 70s. Many different writers have come and gone in that group, but it now consists of Patricia MacLachlan, Corinne Demas Bliss, Anna Kirwan, Barbara Diamond Goldin, Leslea Newman, and me. All women. All published children's book writers. We read aloud and critique one another's work, and give much-needed support through the many twists and turns of the publishing world.

My writing begins at 6:30 in the morning, with a quick scan of email and a cup of tea up in my attic writing room. I call the place the Aerie, or the McDowell Colony. It is a wonderful sanctuary for me. Except for food and potty breaks, and time to answer the phone and get the mail, the rest of my day—often until 5 in the evening—is taken up with writing. As William Faulkner said: "I only write when I am inspired. Fortunately I am inspired at nine o' clock every morning." For me writing is both work and pleasure and I am very focused, especially now that only my husband and I live in this big old house.

In the fall and winter months, we stay in Massachusetts. Or rather—in between my husband's birding trips to South America and my speaking and teaching engagements—we are there. In late spring and all the long summer—as much as four or five months of the year—we live in a beautiful turn of the century stone house in St. Andrews, Scotland, called Wayside. I still work there, in a lovely room that overlooks our garden. I set my novels *The Wild Hunt, Queen's Own Fool,* and the Tartan Magic Books there. I wrote the Young Merlin trilogy there, as well as the looking-back-at-America picture book *All Those Secrets of the World.* I gathered material for my collection *The Fairies' Ring* from books found in the old bookshops and in the St. Andrews University library. But I also take long walks into the Scottish countryside, have tea with friends by a fifteenth-century sea wall, visit castles, spy on badger setts. In other words, I use our Scottish sojourn—as I call it—to re-invigorate myself.

For most of my writing life I wrote books for young readers, but as my own children grew and their interests changed, mine did, too. I took more and more lecturing and teaching jobs, which meant that I be came involved in the history of children's literature as well. For about five years I stopped writing for younger children and concentrated on older boys and girls and fiction for adults. Only in 1984 did I turn again to picture books.

I think one of the reasons I went through this change was my children—and the other my father. In 1982, extremely ill with Parkinson's disease, my father moved in with us. After one death-defying hospital stay (the doctors had given him up but he did not die), we brought him home to be taken care of by nurses. For over three years my house always had at least one RN in residence at all times. Such a change, of course, found its way into my stories. *The Stone Silenus* is very much about my father and me, and *Cards of Grief* is a death-centered fantasy novel. "Old

Herald," a rather brutal science fiction story, is about tending an old, ill, and crotchety artist. Some of the power in those stories has been fed intravenously with my father's blood.

It was in the 1980s that I was discovered! Adults as well as children were suddenly reading my tales. Or perhaps it was just that the boys and girls who had loved my stories were growing up and remembering them. My stories started appearing regularly in adult magazines like *Fantasy and Science Fiction* and *Isaac Asimov's SF Magazine.* I became a much-anthologized short story writer, in such collections as *The Year's Best Fantasy Stories, The Hundred Greatest Fantasy Short Shorts* (in which I had *three* tales), *Heroic Visions, Hecate's Cauldron,* and many, many textbooks. Storytellers had begun a renaissance in America and they were coming upon my work. I now receive about one letter a month from storytellers requesting permission to tell one or more of my stories. And there is no guessing what things they will tell. One told "Dawn Strider" at a wedding, another told "The Pot Child" at nursing homes, another told "The White Seal Maid" at feminist gatherings.

One teller even told a shortened hand-signed/spoken version of my novel *The Mermaid's Three Wisdoms,* which is about a hearing-impaired child. However the two books which really broke me out of the pack were *Owl Moon,* published in 1987, and *The Devil's Arithmetic,* in 1988.

Owl Moon is a family story, about my husband taking Heidi out owling. No—it didn't happen exactly that way. The story is a combination of many trips with all our children. When the book won the 1988 Caldecott Medal for the tremendously moving watercolor paintings by John Schoenherr, the book took on a life of its own. I get an enormous amount of mail from readers still—young and old.

The Devil's Arithmetic struck a different kind of chord with readers. A novel about the Holocaust, it was the first book to take a child inside an actual death camp. The reviews were stunning, the response overwhelming. As I explain to the many young readers who write to me: "I had thought about doing a book on the Holocaust for a long time, but quite frankly the idea overwhelmed me. Finally one of my editors, who was a rabbi's wife, persuaded me the time had come to confront the task. Writers and storytellers are the memory of a civilization, and we who are alive now really must not forget what happened in that awful time or else we may be doomed to repeat it." The research and writing of *The Devil's Arithmetic* took me several years. When I was done, I swore to myself I would never write another book on the Holocaust because it was such an emotionally difficult task.

However, I did!

The idea for an adult novel on the subject came to me when I was watching the documentary *Shoah* in which the concentration camp Chelmno was described—a camp inside a castle. Castle, barbed wire, and the gassing of innocent folk. It suggested the fairy tale "Sleeping Beauty" in a horrible way. Yet I did not want to get into the awful world once again. It took another editor to persuade me that *Briar Rose* was a book that needed to be written.

Recently there was a TV movie based on *The Devil's Arithmetic* starring Kirsten Dunst that was shown on Showtime and then went on sale at Blockbuster Video. It got me interested in attempting to write movie scripts. So I think that may be my next great writing adventure.

Many of my books have won prizes. Besides the Caldecott for *Owl Moon,* there was a Caldecott Honor for *The Emperor and the Kite,* the Jewish book award for *The Devil's Arithmetic,* the Golden Kite Award for *The Girl Who Cried Flowers,* the World Fantasy Award for *Favorite Folktales from Around the World,* three Mythopoeic Society Awards for *Young Merlin Trilogy, Cards of Grief,* and *Briar Rose,* and five bodies of work awards: the Kerlan, the Regina Medal, the Boston Literary Lights Award, the Keene State Award, the Anna V. Zarrow Award. Two of my stories—"Sister Emily's Lightship" and "Lost Girls"—have won Nebula Awards. My poem "Will" about my father, won the Rhysling poetry award, while another poem, "Angels Fear," won the Asimov's Reader's poll. I have run out of shelves for the awards.

And my books and stories have been translated into sixteen different languages.

So my life, like anyone else's, is a patchwork of past and present. By writing this long autobiographical essay, I see that clearly for the first time. And I also can see a pattern that might tell me my future—as long as I remain consistent.

Weary travelers in the southernmost part of England, 1988.

The family gathered at Jane and David's house for brother Steve's wedding: front row, Jane, her father Will, newlyweds Maria and Steve; second row, Jason, Steve's son Greg, and Adam; standing, Heidi and David.

I consider myself a poet and a storyteller. Being "America's Hans Christian Andersen" means trying to walk in much-too-large seven-league boots. I just want to go on writing and discovering my stories for the rest of my life because I know that in my tales I make public what is private, transforming my own joy and sadness into tales for the people. The folk.

But the wonderful thing about stories is that other folk can turn them around and make private what is public; that is, they take into themselves the story they read or hear and make it their own. Stories do not exist on the page or in the mouth, they exist *between*. Between writer and reader, between teller and listener. I wrote *The Girl Who Loved the Wind* for myself, out of my own history. But once I received a letter from a nurse who told me that she had read the story to a dying child, and the story had eased the little girl through her final pain. *The story* did that—not me. But if I can continue to write with as much honesty and love as I can muster, I will truly have touched magic—and passed it on.

Writings

FICTION; FOR CHILDREN

The Witch Who Wasn't, illustrated by Arnold Roth, Macmillan, 1964.

Gwinellen, the Princess Who Could Not Sleep, illustrated by Ed Renfro, Macmillan, 1965.

The Emperor and the Kite, illustrated by Ed Young, World Publishing, 1967.

The Minstrel and the Mountain: A Tale of Peace, illustrated by Anne Rockwell, World Publishing, 1967.

Isabel's Noel, illustrated by Arnold Roth, Funk, 1967.

Greyling: A Picture Story from the Islands of Shetland, illustrated by William Stobbs, World Publishing, 1968, second printing illustrated by David Ray, Philomel, 1991.

The Longest Name on the Block, illustrated by Peter Madden, Funk, 1968.

The Wizard of Washington Square, illustrated by Ray Cruz, World Publishing, 1969.

The Inway Investigators; or, The Mystery at McCracken's Place, illustrated by Allan Eitzen, Seabury, 1969.

Hobo Toad and the Motorcycle Gang, illustrated by Emily McCully, World Publishing, 1970.

The Seventh Mandarin, illustrated by Young, Seabury, 1970.

The Girl Who Loved the Wind, illustrated by Young, Crowell, 1972.

The Boy Who Had Wings, illustrated by Helga Aichinger, Crowell, 1974.

The Adventures of Eeka Mouse, illustrated by Myra McKee, Xerox Education Publications, 1974.

The Rainbow Rider, illustrated by Michael Foreman, Crowell, 1974.

The Little Spotted Fish, illustrated by Friso Henstra, Seabury, 1975.

The Transfigured Hart, illustrated by Donna Diamond, Crowell, 1975.

Milkweed Days, photographs by Gabriel A. Cooney, Crowell, 1976.

The Seeing Stick, illustrated by Remy Charlip and Demetra Maraslis, Crowell, 1977.

The Sultan's Perfect Tree, illustrated by Barbara Garrison, Parents Magazine Press, 1977.

The Giants' Farm, illustrated by Tomie de Paola, Seabury, 1977.

Hannah Dreaming, photographs by Alan R. Epstein, Museum of Fine Art (Springfield, MA), 1977.

The Lady and the Merman, illustrated by Barry Moser, Pennyroyal, 1977.

Spider Jane, illustrated by Stefan Bernath, Coward, 1978.

The Simple Prince, illustrated by Jack Kent, Parents Magazine Press, 1978.

No Bath Tonight, illustrated by Nancy W. Parker, Crowell, 1978.

The Mermaid's Three Wisdoms, illustrated by Laura Rader, Collins, 1978.

The Giants Go Camping, illustrated by de Paola, Seabury, 1979.

Commander Toad in Space, illustrated by Bruce Degen, Coward, 1980.

Spider Jane on the Move, illustrated by Bernath, Coward, 1980.

Mice on Ice, illustrated by Lawrence DiFiori, Dutton, 1980.

The Robot and Rebecca: The Mystery of the Code-Carrying Kids, illustrated by Jurg Obrist, Knopf, 1980.

Shirlick Holmes and the Case of the Wandering Wardrobe, illustrated by Anthony Rao, Coward, 1981.

The Robot and Rebecca and the Missing Owser, illustrated by Lady McCrady, Knopf, 1981.

The Acorn Quest, illustrated by Susanna Natti, Harper, 1981.

Brothers of the Wind, illustrated by Barbara Berger, Philomel, 1981.

Sleeping Ugly, illustrated by Diane Stanley, Coward, 1981.

The Boy Who Spoke Chimp, illustrated by David Wiesner, Knopf, 1981.

Uncle Lemon's Spring, illustrated by Glen Rounds, Dutton, 1981.

Commander Toad and the Planet of the Grapes, illustrated by Bruce Degen, Coward, 1982.

Commander Toad and the Big Black Hole, illustrated by Bruce Degen, Coward, 1983.

Commander Toad and the Dis-Asteroid, illustrated by Bruce Degen, Coward, 1985.

Commander Toad and the Intergalactic Spy, illustrated by Bruce Degen, Coward, 1986.

Owl Moon, illustrated by John Schoenherr, Philomel, 1987.

Commander Toad and the Space Pirates, illustrated by Bruce Degen, Putnam, 1987.

Piggins, illustrated by Jane Dyer, Harcourt, 1987.

(Reteller) *The Sleeping Beauty,* illustrated by Ruth Sanderson, Ariel/Knopf, 1987.

Picnic with Piggins, illustrated by Jane Dyer, Harcourt, 1988.

Piggins and the Royal Wedding, illustrated by Jane Dyer, Harcourt, 1989.

Dove Isabeau, illustrated by Dennis Nolan, Harcourt, 1989.

Baby Bear's Bedtime Book, illustrated by Jane Dyer, Harcourt, 1990.

Sky Dogs, illustrated by Barry Moser, Harcourt, 1990.

Tam Lin, illustrated by Charles Mikolaycak, Harcourt, 1990.

Elfabet: An ABC of Elves, illustrated by Lauren Mills, Little, Brown, 1989.

Letting Swift River Go, illustrated by Barbara Cooney, Little, Brown, 1990.

Wizard's Hall, Harcourt, 1991.

Eeny, Meeny, Miney Mole, illustrated by Katheryn Brown, Harcourt, 1992.

Encounter, illustrated by David Shannon, Harcourt, 1992.

Hands, illustrated by Chi Chung, Sundance Publishing, 1993.

Welcome to the Green House, illustrated by Laura Regan, Putnam, 1993.

All Those Secrets of the World, illustrated by Leslie Baker, Little, Brown, 1993.

Beneath the Ghost Moon, illustrated by Laurel Molk, Little, Brown, 1993.

Grandad Bill's Song, illustrated by Melissa B. Mathis, Putnam, 1993.

Mouse's Birthday, illustrated by Bruce Degen, Putnam, 1993.

The three beautiful granddaughters together, winter of 1998.

Honkers, illustrated by Leslie Baker, Little, Brown, 1993.

(Compiler) *Weather Report,* illustrated by Annie Gusman, Boyds Mills Press, 1993.

And Twelve Chinese Acrobats, illustrated by Jean Gralley, Putnam, 1994.

Good Griselle, illustrated by David Christiana, Harcourt, 1994.

The Girl in the Golden Bower, illustrated by Jane Dyer, Little, Brown, 1994.

King Long Shanks, illustrated by Victoria Chess, Harcourt, 1994.

Old Dame Counterpane, illustrated by Ruth Tietjen Councell, Putnam, 1994.

Little Mouse and Elephant: A Tale from Turkey, illustrated by John Segal, HarperCollins, 1994.

The Musicians of Bremen: A Tale from Germany, illustrated by John Segal, HarperCollins, 1994.

The Ballad of the Pirate Queens, illustrated by David Shannon, Harcourt, 1995.

Before the Storm, illustrated by Georgia Pugh, Boyds Mills Press, 1995.

A Sip of Aesop, illustrated by Karen Barbour, Scholastic, 1995.

The Wild Hunt, illustrated by Francisco Mora, Harcourt, 1995.

Too Old for Naps, Harcourt, 1995.

Child of Faerie, illustrated by Jane Dyer, Little, Brown, 1996.

(With Heidi E.Y. Stemple) *Meet the Monsters,* illustrated by Patricia Ludlow, Walker & Co., 1996.

Nocturne, illustrated by Anne Hunter, Harcourt, 1996

Wings, illustrated by Dennis Nolan, Harcourt, 1997.

Commander Toad and the Voyage Home, illustrated by Bruce Degen, Putnam, 1997.

Miz Berlin Walks, illustrated by Floyd Cooper, Philomel, 1997.

The Sea Man, illustrated by Christopher Denise, Putnam, 1997.

(Reteller) *Once Upon A Bedtime Story: Classic Tales,* illustrated by Ruth Tietjen Councell, Boyds Mills, 1997.

Pegasus, the Flying Horse, illustrated by Li Mei, Dutton, 1998.

Prince of Egypt (with illustrations from the movie), Dutton, 1998.

Raising Yoder's Barn, illustrated by Bernie Fuchs, Little, Brown, 1998.

Moonball, illustrated by Greg Couch, Simon & Schuster, 1999.

Off We Go!, illustrated by Laurel Molk Little, Brown, 2000.

"Wayside, the place of our Scottish sojourn," 1998.

Where Have The Unicorns Gone?, illustrated by Ruth Sanderson, Simon & Schuster, 2000.

Eeny Up Above, illustrated by Kathryn Brown, Harcourt, forthcoming.

Harvest Home, illustrated by Greg Shed, Harcourt, forthcoming.

Baba Yaga, illustrated by V. Vagarin, Harper, forthcoming.

Dinosaur Goodnight, Scholastic, forthcoming.

Elsie's Bird, Scholastic, forthcoming.

Fairy Holiday Book, illustrated by David Christiana, Scholastic, forthcoming.

Firebird, HarperCollins, forthcoming.

Grandma's Hurrying Child, Harcourt, forthcoming.

Little Angel's Birthday, Scholastic, forthcoming.

Travelers Rose, Scholastic, forthcoming.

Welcome to the River of Grass, illustrated by Laura Regan, Putnam, forthcoming.

Odysseus, Boy Wanderer (Young Heroes Series), forthcoming.

Hippolyta, Amazon Princess (Young Heroes Series), forthcoming.

Stretching the Truth (story collection), Scholastic, forthcoming.

FOR CHILDREN; NONFICTION

Pirates in Petticoats, illustrated by Leonard Vosburgh, McKay, 1963.

World on a String: The Story of Kites, World Publishing, 1968.

Friend: The Story of George Fox and the Quakers, Seabury, 1972.

The Fireside Song Book of Birds and Beasts, musical arrangements by Barbara Green, illustrated by Peter Parnall, Simon & Schuster, 1972.

The Wizard Islands, illustrated by Robert Quackenbush, Crowell, 1973.

Ring Out! A Book of Bells, illustrated by Richard Cuffari, Seabury, 1974.

Simple Gifts: The Story of the Shakers, illustrated by Betty Fraser, Viking, 1976.

(Compiler) *Rounds about Rounds,* musical arrangements by Barbara Green, illustrated by Gail Gibbons, F. Watts, 1977.

Lullaby Song Book, musical arrangements by Adam Stemple, illustrated by Charles Mikolaycak, Harcourt, 1984.

The Lullaby Songbook, musical arrangements by Adam Stemple, illustrated by Charles Mikolaycak, Harcourt, 1986.

The Lap-Time Song and Play Book, musical arrangements by Stemple, illustrated by Margot Tomes, Harcourt, 1989.

Hark! A Christmas Sampler, musical arrangements by Adam Stemple, illustrated by Tomie dePaola. Putnam, 1991.

A Letter from Phoenix Farm, illustrated with photographs by Jason Stemple, Richard C. Owen, 1992.

Jane Yolen's Mother Goose Song Book, musical arrangements by Adam Stemple, illustrated by Rosekrans Hoffman, Boyds Mills Press, 1992.

Jane Yolen's Songs of Summer, musical arrangements by Adam Stemple, illustrated by Cyd Moore, Boyds Mills Press, 1993.

Jane Yolen's Old MacDonald Songbook, musical arrangements by Adam Stemple, illustrated by Rosekrans Hoffman, Boyds Mills Press, 1994.

Sing Noel, musical arrangements by Adam Stemple, illustrated by Nancy Carpenter, Boyds Mills Press, 1996.

Welcome to the Sea of Sand, illustrated by Laura Regan, Putnam, 1996.

Milk & Honey: A Year of Jewish Holidays, musical arrangements by Adam Stemple, illustrated by Louise August, Putnam, 1996.

Tea with an Old Dragon: A Story of Sophia Smith, Founder of Smith College, illustrated by Monica Vachula, Boyds Mill, 1998.

House/House, photographs by Jason Stemple, Cavendish, 1998.

Welcome to the Ice House, illustrated by Laura Regan, Putnam, 1998.

(With Heidi E.Y. Stemple) *An Unsolved Mystery from History: Mary Celeste,* illustrated by Roger Roth, Simon & Schuster, 1999.

(With Heidi E.Y. Stemple) *An Unsolved Mystery from History: The Wolf Girls,* Simon & Schuster, 2001.

An Unsolved Mystery from History: Roanoke Colony, Simon and Schuster, forthcoming.

FOR CHILDREN; POETRY

See This Little Line?, illustrated by Kathleen Elgin, McKay, 1963.

It All Depends, illustrated by Don Bolognese, Funk, 1970.

An Invitation to the Butterfly Ball: A Counting Rhyme, illustrated by Jane B. Zalben, Parents Magazine Press, 1976.

All in the Woodland Early: An ABC Book, illustrated by Zalben, Collins, 1979.

How Beastly!: A Menagerie of Nonsense Poems, illustrated by James Marshall, Philomel, 1980.

Dragon Night and Other Lullabies, illustrated by Demi, Methuen, 1980.

Ring of Earth: A Child's Book of Seasons, illustrated by John Wallner, Harcourt, 1986.

The Three Bears Rhyme Book, illustrated by Jane Dyer, Harcourt, 1987.

Best Witches: Poems for Halloween, illustrated by Elise Primavera, Putnam, 1989.

Bird Watch, illustrated by Ted Lewin, Philomel, 1990.

Dinosaur Dances, illustrated by Bruce Degen, Putnam, 1990.

(Compiler) *Street Rhymes Around the World,* illustrated by multiple artists, Boyds Mills Press, 1992.

Raining Cats and Dogs, illustrated by Janet Street, Harcourt, 1993.

What Rhymes with Moon?, illustrated by Ruth Tietjen Councell, Philomel, 1993.

Alphabestiary: Animal Poems from A to Z, illustrated by Allan Eitzen, Boyds Mills Press, 1994.

Sacred Places, illustrated by David Shannon, Harcourt, 1994.

Animal Fare: Zoological Nonsense Poems, illustrated by Janet Street, Harcourt, 1994.

Three Bears Holiday Rhyme Book, illustrated by Jane Dyer, Harcourt, 1995.

The author and husband with their three granddaughters, baby Alison, teen Lexi, and Maddison.

Water Music: Poems for Children, photographs by Jason Stemple, Boyds Mills Press, 1995.

Merlin and the Dragons, illustrated by Ming Li, Dutton, 1995.

(Compiler) *Mother Earth Father Sky, Poems of Our Planet,* illustrated by Jennifer Hewitson, Boyds Mills Press, 1996.

Oh, Jerusalem, illustrated by John Thompson, Scholastic, 1996.

The Originals, illustrated by Ted Lewin, Putnam, 1996.

Sea Watch: A Book of Poetry, illustrated by Ted Lewin, Putnam, 1996.

(Compiler) *Sky Scrape: City Scape Poems of City Life,* illustrated by Ken Condon, Boyds Mills Press, 1996.

(Compiler) *Once Upon Ice and Other Frozen Poems,* photographs by Jason Stemple, Boyds Mill, 1997.

Snow, Snow, photography by Jason Stemple, Boyds Mill, 1998.

Dear Mother, Dear Daughter (poetry collection), Boyds Mill, forthcoming.

STORY COLLECTIONS

The Girl Who Cried Flowers and Other Tales, illustrated by David Palladini, Crowell, 1974.

The Moon Ribbon and Other Tales, illustrated by Palladini, Crowell, 1976.

The Hundredth Dove and Other Tales, illustrated by Palladini, Crowell, 1977.

Dream Weaver and Other Tales, illustrated by Michael Hague, Collins, 1979, second edition, Philomel, 1989.

YOUNG ADULT FICTION

(With Anne Huston) *Trust a City Kid,* Seabury, 1966.

The Magic Three of Solatia, illustrated by Julia Noonan, Crowell, 1974.

The Mermaid's Three Wisdoms, illustrated by Laura Rader, Philomel, 1978.

The Gift of Sarah Barker, Viking, 1981.

Neptune Rising: Songs and Tales of the Undersea Folk (story collection), illustrated by David Wiesner, Philomel, 1982.

The Stone Silenus, Philomel, 1984.

Children of the Wolf, Viking, 1986.

(Compiler) *Spaceships and Spells,* Harper, 1987.

The Devil's Arithmetic, Viking, 1988.

The Faery Flag: Stories and Poems of Fantasy and the Supernatural, Orchard Books, 1989.

The Dragon's Boy, Harper, 1990.

Here There Be Dragons, illustrated by David Wilgus, Harcourt, 1993.

Here There Be Unicorns, illustrated by David Wilgus, Harcourt, 1994.

Here There Be Witches, illustrated by David Wilgus, Harcourt, 1995.

Here There Be Angels, illustrated by David Wilgus, Harcourt, 1996.

Twelve Impossible Things before Breakfast: Stories, Harcourt, 1997.

(With Bruce Coville) *Armageddon Summer,* Harcourt Brace, 1998.

Here There Be Ghosts, illustrated by David Wilgus, Harcourt Brace, 1998.

The Wizard's Map (Tartan Magic Book One), Harcourt, 1999.

The Pictish Child (Tartan Magic Book Two), Harcourt, 1999.

(With Robert J. Harris) *Queen's Own Fool,* Philomel, 2000.

The Fairies' Ring: A Book of Fairy Stories and Poems, illustrated by Stephen MacKey, Dutton, 1999

Queen's Own Fool, Philomel, 2000.

"PIT DRAGON" TRILOGY

Dragon's Blood: A Fantasy, Delacorte, 1982.

Heart's Blood, Delacorte, 1984.

A Sending of Dragons, Delacorte, 1987.

"YOUNG MERLIN" TRILOGY

Passager (Book 1 in Young Merlin Trilogy), Harcourt, 1996.

Hobby (Book 2 in Young Merlin Trilogy), Harcourt, 1996.

Merlin (Book 3 in Young Merlin Trilogy), Harcourt, 1997.

ADULT FICTION

Tales of Wonder (story collection), Schocken, 1983.

Cards of Grief (science fiction), Ace Books, 1984.

Merlin's Booke (story collection), Ace Date/Steel Dragon Press, 1984.

Dragonfield and Other Stories (story collection), Ace Books, 1985.

Sister Light, Sister Dark (novel), Tor Books, 1988.

White Jenna (novel), Tor Books, 1989.

Briar Rose (novel), Tor Books, 1992.

Storyteller (story collection), New England Science Fiction Association, 1992.

The Book of Great Alta (compilation of *Sister Light, Sister Dark* and *White Jenna*), Tor Books, 1997.

The One-Armed Queen (novel), Tor Books, 1998.

Sister Emily's Lightship, forthcoming, 2000.

ADULT NONFICTION

Writing Books for Children, The Writer, 1973, revised edition, 1983.

Touch Magic: Fantasy, Faerie, and Folklore in the Literature of Childhood, Philomel, 1981.

Guide to Writing for Children, Writer, 1989.

POETRY COLLECTION

Among Angels, Harcourt Brace, 1995.

EDITOR

Zoo 2000: Twelve Stories of Science Fiction and Fantasy Beasts, Seabury, 1973.

Shape Shifters: Fantasy and Science Fiction Tales about Humans Who Can Change Their Shape, Seabury, 1978.

(With Martin Greenberg and Charles Waugh) *Dragons and Dreams: A Collection of New Fantasy and Science Fiction Stories,* Harper, 1986.

Favorite Folktales from Around the World, Pantheon, 1988.

(With Martin H. Greenberg) *Werewolves: A Collection of Original Stories,* Harper, 1988.

(With Martin H. Greenberg) *Things That Go Bump in the Night,* Harper, 1989.

2041 AD (science fiction anthology), Delacorte, 1990.

(With Martin H. Greenberg) *Vampires,* illustrated by Greenberg, Harper, 1991.

Sleep Rhymes Around the World, illustrated by various artists, Boyds Mills Press, 1993.

(With Martin H. Greenberg) *Xanadu,* Tor Books, 1993.

(With Martin H. Greenberg) *Xanadu Two,* Tor Books, 1994.

(With Martin H. Greenberg) *Xanadu Three,* Tor Books, 1995.

Camelot: A Collection of Original Arthurian Tales, illustrated by Winslow Pels, Putnam, 1995.

(With Martin H. Greenberg) *The Haunted House: A Collection of Original Stories,* illustrated by Doron Ben-Ami, HarperCollins, 1995.

Gray Heroes, Viking, 1998.

Sherwood, Philomel, 2000.

(And commentator, with Heidi E.Y. Stemple) *Mirror, Mirror: 40 Tales From around the World and What One Mother and Daughter Found There,* Viking, 2000.

(Reteller) *Not One Damsel in Distress,* Harcourt Brace, 2000.

Also author of *The Whitethorn Wood,* a chapbook. Contributor to books, including *Dragons of Light,* 1981; *Elsewhere,* Volume 1, 1981, Volume 2, 1982; *Hecate's Cauldron,* 1982; *Heroic Visions,* 1983; *Faery!,* 1985; *Liavek,* 1985; *Moonsinger's Friends,* 1985; *Imaginary Lands,* 1985; *Don't Bet on the Prince: Contemporary Feminist Fairy Tales in North America and England,* 1986; *Liavek: Players of Luck,* 1986; *Liavek: Wizard's Row,* 1987; *Visions,* 1987; *Liavek: Spells of Binding,* 1988; *Invitation to Camelot,* 1988; *The Unicorn Treasury,* 1988, and dozens more. Some of Yolen's manuscripts are held in the Kerlan Collection at the University of Minnesota.

MOVIES AND MUSICALS

(With Barbara Green) *Robin Hood* (musical), first produced in Boston, MA, 1967.

Merlin & The Dragons (movie), Lightyear, 1990.

Author of column "Children's Bookfare" for *Daily Hampshire Gazette* during the 1970s. Contributor of articles, reviews, poems, and short stories to periodicals, including *Writer, Parabola, New York Times, Washington Post Book World, Los Angeles Times, Parents' Choice, New Advocate, Horn Book, Wilson Library Bulletin, Magazine of Fantasy and Science Fiction, Isaac Asimov's Science Fiction Magazine,* and *Language Arts.* Member of editorial boards of *Advocate* (now *New Advocate*) and *National Storytelling Journal* until 1989. Some of Yolen's books have been published in England, France, Spain, Brazil, Germany, Austria, Sweden, South Africa, Australia, Japan, and Denmark.

ADAPTATIONS

The Seventh Mandarin was filmed by Xerox Films, 1973; *The Emperor and the Kite* is available as a filmstrip with cassette, Listening Library, 1976; *The Bird of Time* was produced as a play in Northampton, MA, 1982; *The Girl Who Cried Flowers and Other Tales* was taped by Weston Woods, 1983; *Dragon's Blood* was made into an animated television movie, *CBS Storybreak,* 1985; *Commander Toad in Space* was taped by Listening Library, 1986; *Touch Magic ... Pass It On* (a group of Yolen's stories retold by Milbre Burch) was taped by Weston Woods, 1987; *Owl Moon* is available as a filmstrip with cassette, Weston Woods, 1988; *Piggins* and *Picnic with Piggins* were taped by Caedmon, 1988; *Merlin and the Dragons* was made into a movie by Lightyear about 1990; *Devil's Arithmetic,* starring Kirsten Dunst and Mimi Rogers was produced for Showtime Television by Punch Productions, introduction by Dustin Hoffman, 1999.

Cumulative Indexes

Illustrations Index

(In the following index, the number of the *volume* in which an illustrator's work appears is given *before* the colon, and the *page number* on which it appears is given *after* the colon. For example, a drawing by Adams, Adrienne appears in Volume 2 on page 6, another drawing by her appears in Volume 3 on page 80, another drawing in Volume 8 on page 1, and so on and so on....)

YABC

Index references to *YABC* refer to listings appearing in the two-volume *Yesterday's Authors of Books for Children,* also published by The Gale Group. *YABC* covers prominent authors and illustrators who died prior to 1960.

T

Y

Yakovetic, Joe *59:* 202; *75:* 85
Yalowitz, Paul *93:* 33
Yamaguchi, Marianne *85:* 118
Yang, Jay *1:* 8; *12:* 239
Yap, Weda *6:* 176
Yaroslava *See* Mills, Yaroslava Surmach
Yashima, Taro *14:* 84
Yates, John *74:* 249, 250
Ylla *See* Koffler, Camilla
Yohn, F. C. *23:* 128; *YABC 1:* 269
Yorke, David *80:* 178
Yoshida, Toshi *77:* 231
Youll, Paul *91:* 218
Youll, Stephen *92:* 227
Young, Ed *7:* 205; *10:* 206; *40:* 124; *63:*
   142; *74:* 250, 251, 252, 253; *75:* 227;
   81: 159; *83:* 98; *94:* 154; *YABC 2:* 242
Young, Mary O'Keefe *77:* 95; *80:* 247
Young, Noela *8:* 221; *89:* 231; *97:* 195
Yun, Cheng Mung *60:* 143

Z

Zacharow, Christopher *88:* 98
Zacks, Lewis *10:* 161
Zadig *50:* 58
Zaffo, George *42:* 208
Zaid, Barry *50:* 127; *51:* 201
Zaidenberg, Arthur *34:* 218, 219, 220
Zalben, Jane Breskin *7:* 211; *79:* 230, 231,
   233
Zallinger, Jean *4:* 192; *8:* 8, 129; *14:* 273;
   68: 36; *80:* 254
Zallinger, Rudolph F. *3:* 245
Zebot, George *83:* 214
Zeck, Gerry *40:* 232
Zeiring, Bob *42:* 130
Zeldich, Arieh *49:* 124; *62:* 120
Zeldis, Malcah *86:* 239; *94:* 198
Zelinsky, Paul O. *14:* 269; *43:* 56; *49:* 218,
   219, 220, 221, 222-223; *53:* 111; *68:*
   195; *102:* 219, 220, 221, 222
Zelvin, Diana *72:* 190; *76:* 101; *93:* 207

Zemach, Margot *3:* 270; *8:* 201; *21:* 210-
   211; *27:* 204, 205, 210; *28:* 185; *49:* 22,
   183, 224; *53:*151; *56:* 146; *70:* 245, 246;
   92: 74
Zemsky, Jessica *10:* 62
Zepelinsky, Paul *35:* 93
Zhang, Ange *101:* 190
Ziegler, Jack *84:* 134
Zimic, Tricia *72:* 95
Zimmer, Dirk *38:* 195; *49:* 71; *56:* 151;
   *65:*214; *84:* 159; *89:* 26
Zimmermann, H. Werner *101:* 223
Zimnik, Reiner *36:* 224
Zinkeisen, Anna *13:* 106
Zinn, David *97:* 97
Zoellick, Scott *33:* 231
Zonia, Dhimitri *20:* 234-235
Zudeck, Darryl *58:* 129; *63:* 98; *80:* 52
Zug, Mark *88:* 131
Zuma *99:* 36
Zvorykin, Boris *61:* 155
Zweifel, Francis *14:* 274; *28:* 187
Zwerger, Lisbeth *54:* 176, 178; *66:* 246,
   247, 248
Zwinger, Herman H. *46:* 227
Zwolak, Paul *67:* 69, 71, 73, 74

Author Index

The following index gives the number of the volume in which an author's biographical sketch, Autobiography Feature, Brief Entry, or Obituary appears.

This index includes references to all entries in the following series, which are also published by The Gale Group.

YABC—*Yesterday's Authors of Books for Children: Facts and Pictures about Authors and Illustrators of Books for Young People from Early Times to 1960*
CLR—*Children's Literature Review: Excerpts from Reviews, Criticism, and Commentary on Books for Children*
SAAS—*Something about the Author Autobiography Series*

Author Index

